C000062138

Jeff Stokley

3/20

TSR2

Britain's Lost Cold War Strike Aircraft

Tim McLelland

www.crecy.co.uk

Crécy Publishing Ltd

Published by Crécy Publishing Ltd 2017

First published 2010
Reprinted 2011

Copyright © 2010 Tim McLelland

All rights reserved. No part of this book may be reproduced or transmitted in any form or by any means electronic or mechanical, including photocopying, recording or by any information storage without permission from the Publisher in writing. All enquiries should be directed to the Publisher.

A CIP record for this book is available from the British Library

ISBN 978 1 91080 913 6

Printed In Malta by Melita Press

Crécy Publishing Limited
1a Ringway Trading Estate, Shadowmoss Road, Manchester M22 5LH

www.crecy.co.uk

Front flap top:
Interesting aerial view of XR219 being prepared for a test flight at Boscombe Down. *BAC*

Front flap bottom:
An unusual view of XR219 parked on its designated test area at Boscombe Down's shortest runway. Visible is the hinged cowling which houses the brake parachute, positioned between the jet pipes. *BAC*

Rear cover clockwise from top:
A beautiful colour picture of XR219 in a gentle descent at high altitude, with the four air brake doors fully opened. *BAC*

Lifting smartly into the air, XR219 gets airborne from a snowy Boscombe Down during 1965. *BAC*

XR222 stands tall on her undercarriage, looking almost like a huge bird of prey. Some commentators suggested the aircraft should have been named "Eagle". *BAE Heritage*

XR219 venturing into the darkness for a night-time photo shoot at Boscombe Down, with the shapes of a Beverley transport and Valiant bomber just visible in the background. *BAC*

Returning from a test flight, XR219 is pictured with her huge brake parachute deployed. *BAC*

Table of Contents

The Author

Tim McLelland was an established aviation writer and photographer with an interest in all aspects of aerospace, but specialising primarily in post-war military subjects. He authored a wide range of books on a variety of subjects.

He also produced numerous features for many aerospace magazines and journals and had been a contributor to Aircraft Illustrated, Air Extra, Armed Forces, Air Forces Monthly, Flypast, Aviation News and other magazines. Tim McLelland also edited Air Forces International magazine, and Scale Models magazine, in addition to the house magazine of the International Plastic Modellers Society (UK). As part of his photography and writing work, Tim counted himself fortunate to have been afforded a great deal of direct access to military units around the world. He had talked to serving air crew and staff officers on all aspects of operational and training activities. He had also been given many opportunities to fly as a passenger in a wide range of combat aircraft, enabling him to see first-hand what military flying was all about.

His 'log book' included types such as the Jaguar, Lightning, Harrier, Tornado fighter and bomber, Hawk, Hunter, F-4 Phantom (both in US and British service), Buccaneer, Nimrod, Canberra, Hercules, VC10, Chinook, and many others, as well as historical types such as the Lancaster and Shackleton and a number of flights with the world-famous Red Arrows, and the US Navy's Blue Angels team. Away from the world of military operations, Tim McLelland also worked with Channel 4 Television as a stills photographer.

His published works included Buccaneer, Vulcan – A Complete History, The RAF Manual, Fighter Pilot, Tiger Meet, Flying Tankers, Hunter – A Complete History, Avro Vulcan, Fight's On, C-130 Hercules and for Classic Publications in 2009 the acclaimed English Electric Lightning – Britain's First and Last Supersonic Interceptor. In all Tim McLelland, who was formerly known as Tim Laming, produced over 40 different book titles covering many different subjects. He died on 6 November 2015.

Acknowledgements

Creating a book of this nature relies upon the support of many individuals who freely gave their time and support to it. The author would like to express his thanks to everyone who so enthusiastically provided information, photographs, drawings, advice, viewpoints, and other support, all of which has hopefully resulted in an interesting and thorough examination of a truly fascinating aircraft. In particular, the author would like to specifically thank the following individuals:

Lord Healey, Albert Kitchenside, John Pulford and John Forbat (Brooklands Museum), Ken Hillman and David Ward (BAE Heritage, Warton), Darryl Burge (Hornby), Brian Pallett, Robert Swanson, Cyril Parrish, Jan Hajicek (CMK), David Jordan, Gerard Drummy, Pavla Smyrova, Clint Gurry, and Anthony Thornborough.

Introduction

BRITAIN's military aviation industry is justifiably credited with many great achievements. Although often overshadowed by the modern dominance of America's strength, it was Britain which led the way through many years of innovative design and development, much of which was driven by the expediency of the long, dark years of World War Two and the subsequent Cold War. Britain's seemingly voracious appetite for military warplane design was remarkable but entirely understandable, given the nation's status as major power with a huge range of commitments both at home and throughout Europe, and far beyond. But for many decades, Britain was a country which was – to use a well-worn boxing cliché – punching above her weight. In the years following World War Two, the country was faced with severe austerity and a financial situation which often approached bankruptcy, and yet the country's military commitments remained diverse and astonishingly numerous. Clearly, it was a situation which could not be sustained forever.

XR219 taxying onto the apron in front of English Electric's famous flight sheds, upon arrival at Warton and what was expected to be the beginning of a long and thorough flight test programme. Sadly, XR219's active life at Warton was woefully short and months later the aircraft left by road for the P&EE at Shoeburyness. *BAC*

While Britain's citizens endured grim years of post-war food rationing, the country's aviation industry soldiered on into the uncertain and perilous years of the Cold War, addressing the demands of successive Governments which were obliged to divert huge sums of taxpayers' money into the development of increasingly complex and expensive weapons of war, many of which never progressed beyond the proverbial drawing board. The perceived threat of Soviet power was sufficient to convince Britain's politicians that defence expenditure was one of the country's unavoidable priorities which had to be sustained almost regardless of the cost, and Britain's aviation industry was – thankfully – more than capable of meeting the challenges with which it was presented. But while Britain possessed the will to maintain a strong defensive posture, it often did not have the resources that it needed to achieve this aim, and a great deal of support came directly from America, without whom it is fair to say that Britain could not have adequately defended herself through the years of the Cold War. Maintaining a credible defence against a whole range of perceived threats was considered to be a vital national commitment, but as the 'swinging sixties' dawned, it was equally clear that Britain could no longer enjoy the luxury of defending herself at any price.

It was against this background that TSR2 was born. The Royal Air Force, delighted with its new jet-powered Canberra bomber, was already looking towards the future and the question of what aircraft would replace the Canberra by the mid-1960s. Having become entrenched in the belief that no military aircraft was likely to remain viable for more than a decade, the need to replace the Canberra had been identified almost from the moment that the aircraft had entered RAF service. Continual advances in Soviet tec hnology and military might (which, it has to be said, were probably not as great as Britain and her allies imagined) effectively demanded that the design and creation of new fighter and bomber aircraft was a fast-moving, progressive procedure of almost breath-taking proportions which spawned new projects almost on a monthly basis. Naturally, many of these designs did not progress very far, but it is true to say that the aviation industry was firmly fixed into a mindset whereby larger, better, faster or more capable aircraft were always in demand, and as soon as a new aircraft settled into RAF service, something even more complex was already being considered with which to replace it. TSR2 was undoubtedly the classic example of how this process reached its inevitable conclusion.

Designed as a 'Canberra Replacement', the TSR2 programme represented the culmination of the RAF's belief in the necessity for the ultimate performance capabilities attainable, the aviation industry's belief in its ability to create whatever was demanded of it, regardless of its cost, and the Government's belief that Britain would (or should) maintain a strong and significant military presence across the globe. It was a situation which was completely at odds with the realities which faced the country in the early 1960s. From the very beginning of TSR2's long and lamentable history, it was already becoming increasingly clear that the Air Staff, Government and aviation industry were not entirely certain of their aims. The Government seemed confident that it would require a strike aircraft which would enable Britain to maintain its military commitments in the Middle East and Far East (the 'East of Suez' role) even though the country was increasingly committed to NATO and the defence of the European mainland against Soviet aggression, which was undoubtedly a more dangerous and immediate threat to the security of the United Kingdom. The Royal Air Force saw no reason to question the Government's position, and demanded an aircraft which would be capable of undertaking all of the nuclear and tactical strike commitments which the Government's 'global' position would imply. The aviation industry, entrenched in its complacent belief that even the most ambitious plans could be translated into hardware with little consideration of the time and cost which would be incurred, simply supported the Air Staff's demands and had no inclination to question whether the RAF's demands were entirely realistic, or indeed whether the Government's view of Britain's defence needs was entirely plausible. Together, without any firm and unambiguous sense of direction, they embarked upon what became Britain's most expensive, complex and ambitious military aircraft programme which was, by its very nature, doomed to failure almost from the moment that it began.

Over the following pages, I have attempted to trace the fascinating history of the TSR2 programme, from its origins through to its eventual demise in 1965. This is not the first book about TSR2 nor will it be the last, and a great deal has been written about TSR2 in the decades which have followed the project's cancellation. But despite the quantity of material which has already been published, surprisingly little has been said about the TSR2 programme. In effect, the same limited amount of information has been regurgitated time and time again without any attempt to make an incisive and honest appraisal of the whole project. In some ways this is perhaps understandable, as only a limited amount of information has been available from which to construct an account. Documentation is scarce, as a great deal was simply destroyed at the time of the project's cancellation. Most of what did survive remained buried in archives under secrecy laws until being finally released over recent years. The people who were directly involved in the project were often reluctant to discuss freely their experiences, sometimes because of professional ties with either the RAF, Government or manufacturer, but often because of a deeply-held sense of bitterness towards the whole sorry saga which left the Air Staff stranded in a difficult and embarrassing decade of uncertainty; it ultimately deposited many talented and able individuals from the aviation industry into new lives overseas, or into the Unemployment line. Even Government ministers have often been reluctant to comment on a story which – either rightly or wrongly – has often portrayed them as fools, vandals or a combination of both. But fifty years on, the true nature of the TSR2 programme is now clear, and it can be examined from the comfortable distance of a new millennium where we now fully understand that even the seemingly impossible can sometimes be achieved – but only at a cost. We now know that everything has a price and we also accept that Britain is not the world power which she once was – or thought she was. Inevitably TSR2 has become a story of great controversy which – like all good fiction – becomes more fascinating as more and more supposition, fantasy, gossip and scandal is apportioned to it. The further we progress from the 1960s, the further we drift from the realities of the TSR2 programme, it becomes increasingly difficult to steer the story back to the true facts of the events which unfolded, and the rather less-salacious reality of the project's history which contrasts quite starkly with the lurid tale of scandal which so many writers have shamelessly attempted to perpetuate. There never was any scandal. TSR2 is a story of over-ambition, political indecisiveness and industrial complacency which graphically illustrates the outstanding potential of Britain's technical and industrial expertise, and the paucity of political wisdom and financial strength with which to exploit it. Through the following chapters, I have endeavoured to trace the story of TSR2 as thoroughly and accurately as possible, avoiding the distractions of what might have been in order to concentrate on the true nature of this fascinating project.

Introduction to the second edition

The original edition of Tim McLelland's book describing the full history of TSR2 was published by Ian Allan. By the time the publishing rights had been acquired by Crécy Publishing Tim had died, so when Jeremy M Pratt of Crécy asked me to write a new section for this new edition covering Britain's attempt to acquire the American General Dynamics F-111 strike aircraft as a TSR2 replacement, I was both flattered but nervous, the latter because I could only guess how Tim might have approached the task. I never met Tim, but I think we must have had pretty similar interests. In the end I decided to research as much as I could at the British National Archives at Kew and just present what I found which, because the British F-111K version never became airborne, is at times rather a political affair. The files accessed all came from Groups Air 2, Air 19 and Air 20; Air 19 containing private papers for the Secretary of State for Air while the other two hold Air Ministry papers including aircraft development. The main TSR2 section and text of this book remains exactly as it was written by Tim McLelland, save for a number of tiny errors and corrections.

Tony Buttler, March 2018

One of the most creative photographs ever taken of XR219, this picture (taken from Dell's Lightning chase aircraft) shows the aircraft's upper surfaces to good advantage, including the very pronounced joint between the (flexible) main wing unit and the fuselage. The stark contrast of the aircraft's white structure would have only applied to early pre-production aircraft. For operational use the aircraft would have been painted with standard RAF Dark Grey/Dark Green camouflage and the white undersides would have been replaced with silver (and ultimately Light Aircraft Grey) colours. *BAC*

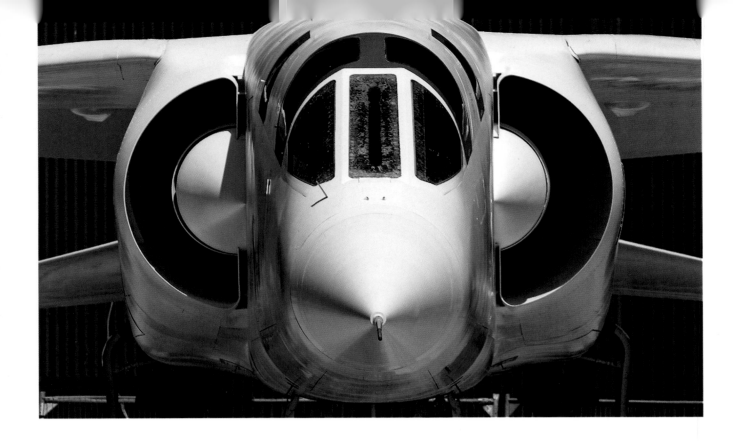

CHAPTER ONE

'Supersonic Canberra'

IT is impossible to pinpoint a precise date on which the long and complicated story of the TSR2 truly first began but history records that the aircraft's roots are buried somewhere within 1956. During the summer of that year, a seemingly innocent letter was delivered to the Headquarters of The English Electric Company in London. Written by a schoolboy in the West Indies who wished to congratulate English Electric on the creation of their magnificent Canberra bomber and Lightning interceptor aircraft, the author ventured to ask what plans were being made to produce a successor to the Canberra, his letter thoughtfully including a series of carefully-prepared sketches which illustrated what he imagined an all-new 'Supersonic Canberra' might look like. Rather than merely sending a polite 'thank-you' to the schoolboy and consigning his letter to the waste bin, his comments and drawings were forwarded to the Chief Engineer at English Electric's Warton factory in Lancashire, where they were subsequently passed around the Project Office. The design staff were both amused and genuinely interested in the ideas which the letter contained, and the enthusiasm with which the sketches were received illustrates that the concept of a Canberra replacement was already a topic which was the subject of some discussion and serious thought, even if no practical efforts had yet been made

to address the issue. Indeed, the only vaguely serious tentative steps towards such a goal had been the creation of a Draft Requirement for a new light bomber which was issued by the Air Ministry in March 1952, but this was generally accepted to be little more than a discussion paper, providing the basis for further future research, rather than a serious proposition, however the prospect of replacing the Canberra had certainly been considered, and even as the aircraft was still entering service back in 1952, informal discussions on this very subject were first conducted between the RAF and Air Ministry, largely based upon the Draft Requirement, but at this stage there was certainly no decision to embark upon any sort of replacement project. Despite the fact that the Canberra was an outstanding aircraft with a performance which marked a huge improvement over the lumbering piston-engine types (such as the Avro

Nose-on view of XR222 at Duxford. The ravages of time have damaged the laminated layers of the windscreen glazed panels, but the clean lines of the airframe are still evident. This view illustrates that the intake fairings do not sit flush with the fuselage, and small gaps around the variable-position intake cones can also be seen. The precise nature of XR222's construction is unclear, as it is believed that components from a variety of airframes may have been used to create a complete structure, when the aircraft was first donated to the Cranfield Institute of technology. Consequently, XR222 is something of a representation of the aircraft rather than a complete "authentic" airframe. *BAE Heritage*

Lincoln) equipping Bomber Command at the time, it is also true that the new bomber was never regarded as anything other than an 'interim' aircraft which would inevitably make way for even more capable and sophisticated designs, and in many respects the Canberra was regarded as a 'lead-in' to the more sophisticated V-Bombers which were coming into service. It is also worth bearing in mind that although modern combat aircraft can be expected to remain in operational use for decades, back in the 1950s the Air Staff's outlook (which was heavily influenced by increasing East-West tensions) was rather more immediate and the relatively rapid advances in technology which were prevalent at the time (both in the East and West) encouraged a much faster rate of weapons development, which effectively meant that as any new aircraft entered operational service the question of designing and creating its successor would immediately become a subject for consideration. It had to be this way if the RAF was to stand any chance of keeping pace with progress, thereby maintaining a credible effectiveness. So, even with the remarkable advances represented by the introduction of the new Canberra, there was still a consensus of opinion within the Air Ministry that a new aircraft which would in effect be the 'real Canberra' had yet to be developed. Consequently, English Electric's Head of Aerodynamics (Ray Creasey) had already given the idea of developing a follow-on design some serious thought and by the end of that summer in 1956 he had approached both the Air Ministry and Ministry of Supply to seek some tentative support for the basic concept of a replacement design. Following his discussions with Handel Davies (Scientific Advisor to the Air Ministry), on 29 October 1956 he instructed Ollie Heath (Chief Project Engineer) to produce a series of conceptual design drawings based on his feedback from the Air Ministry, and a week later he gathered his design team to examine the results which Heath had carefully prepared on sheets of foolscap paper. These designs bore little resemblance to what eventually

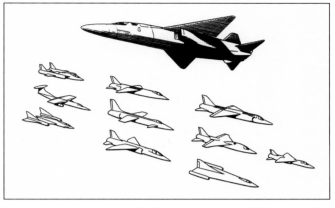

Fascinating drawing made by Ollie Heath, showing some of the many and varied designs which English Electric considered for GOR.339. All of these designs were given due consideration but none could fully meet the demands of GOR.339. *Courtesy BAE Heritage*

became the TSR2 but at this stage this was hardly surprising, not least because there was no clear indication as to precisely what sort of aircraft would actually be required. The notion of a 'Supersonic Canberra' was now alive but nobody was entirely sure what this creation should really be and – more importantly – precisely what functions it would be required to perform. Initially, the Ministry officials had vaguely indicated that a 'multi-role strike fighter' would be an appropriate aspiration (this term being sufficiently vague as to cover a whole range of possibilities), creating an aircraft with a Mach 1.3 performance (this being estimated as necessary to counter advances in Surface-to-Air Missile technology) and a nominal range of 350 nautical miles. This potentially versatile aircraft would undertake a variety of roles including the tactical strike and reconnaissance tasks undertaken by the Canberra, and at Warton it was briefly envisaged that in view of the aircraft's anticipated high-speed performance, the English Electric P.1

General arrangement drawing of English Electric's P.17A (dated January 1958) in its final configuration. *Courtesy BAE Heritage*

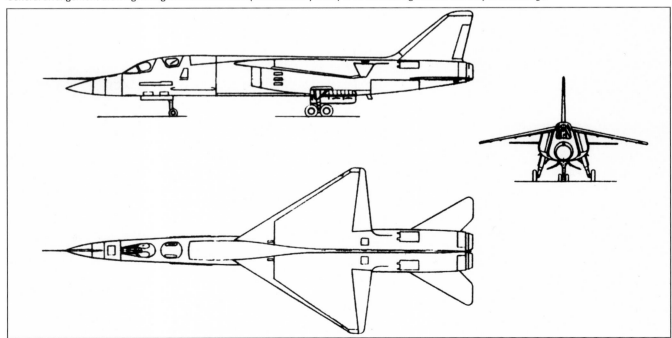

(which became the Lightning) could possibly be used as the basis of this new design. However, as the realities of the new aircraft's diverse requirements began to fall into place (and the Air Ministry began to establish in more detail what it actually wanted from the aircraft) it quickly became clear that a completely new (and significantly larger) design would have to be created from scratch, especially when the aircraft's projected capabilities began to look increasingly ambitious and far beyond anything which could be achieved by simply developing an existing interceptor project. In a matter of weeks the Ministry's thoughts had gravitated towards a more specific tactical strike/attack aircraft which would have a nuclear and conventional capability, together with sophisticated reconnaissance abilities. The top speed requirement was now (inexplicably) set at an even higher figure of Mach 1.5 with a projected range of an equally ambitious 1,000 nautical miles, pushed still further to 2,000nm for ferry flights in order to ensure that the aircraft would have sufficiently 'long legs' to meet the RAF's commitments in the Middle and Far East. This firmer set of figures would also be combined with a high-speed 'dash' capability for operations over a battle area, the aim being to produce an aircraft which would be capable of destroying vital military targets within a defined area of conflict using either conventional or nuclear weapons – a supremely effective Tactical Strike aircraft. With this impressive top speed the aircraft would be able to evade the attention of defensive ground forces (particularly Surface-to-Air Missiles in the European Theatre) and be more than capable of avoiding interception by marauding enemy fighters (prevalent outside Europe) which were expected to become more and more sophisticated. But it was accepted that speed in isolation would no longer be sufficient to render the aircraft invulnerable, and would need more than a pair of powerful engines to ensure survival. Contrary to conventional wisdom, the increasing sophistication of Soviet defences was gradually convincing the Air Staff that flying at high altitude was in fact no longer a guarantee of safety and in contrast to the usual practice of conventional bomber design, which adhered to the notion that altitude guaranteed survivability, the new aircraft would need to be specifically designed for low-level operations and be able to perform flawlessly with both speed and agility at heights of less than 1,000ft where it would remain largely hidden from enemy radar, be less susceptible to guided missiles, and be able to press home an attack with pinpoint accuracy. In response to this emerging (and surprisingly bold) requirement, English Electric swiftly drew-up a completely new shoulder-winged design combined with a high-mounted tail plane and a long, slender fuselage which accommodated a weapons bay in which a variety of tactical bombs and other munitions could be carried. The substantial size of the aircraft would inevitably require two engines and these were to be housed in pods fixed to the undersides of the wing in order to avoid additional density within the fuselage (a lesson learned from the Lightning programme) although attaching them to the exterior of the rear fuselage was also investigated in detail before the idea was eventually dropped. The resulting slim, yet capacious, fuselage would accommodate a crew of two seated in tandem configuration. This initial design (designated as the P.17)

showed great promise and the initial drawings led to the construction of a test model which underwent low-speed wind tunnel testing at Warton from December 1956 as part of the design team's aerodynamic investigations.

Some weeks later, English Electric produced a report entitled 'Possibilities of a Canberra Replacement P.17' which defined the fundamental aspects of the proposed design, as had been discussed with the Air Ministry's advisors. The aircraft's Radius of Action would be 600nm at sea level and a top speed of Mach 0.9, compared with 1,000nm and 1.5M at altitude (plus a ferry range of 2,000nm). The most suitable engine available would be the Rolls Royce Conway and the aircraft's AUW (All Up Weight) was expected to be around 80,000lb. The estimated take-off and landing distance was expected to be around 900yds and the possibility of providing the aircraft with a STOL (Short Take Off and Landing) capability was given a great deal of consideration, largely at the insistence of the Air Ministry. Airfield performance was an issue which would later have a significant effect on the overall design of the aircraft and it was an important consideration from the very beginning of the TSR2's story. Flexibility was to be the key to the aircraft's success and reliance upon long concrete runways was no longer expected to be a viable proposition, should the aircraft become involved in a conflict where recognised airfields would undoubtedly be priority targets for enemy attack. Fixed runways would inevitably be destroyed or disabled as soon as any conflict began, therefore it seemed likely that the new aircraft would have to operate successfully from small semi-prepared strips (which might be little more than flat fields cleared of obstacles) either because no better site was available once the primary airfields had been destroyed, or as a means of dispersing aircraft in order to render them less likely to attack (on the basis that scattered air assets are difficult and time-consuming to locate and destroy). In this respect the aircraft would build upon the dispersal techniques which were successfully adopted by the V-Force, but while the RAF's mighty strategic bombers would require support facilities and an adequate paved runway of at least 6,000ft no matter where they went, it was agreed that the new tactical aircraft would be expected to comfortably operate as a self-sustained system within a site that was no larger or better than that required to operate a C-47 (Dakota) which in essence meant a simple grass strip of approximately 3,000ft – quite a feat for a large, heavy nuclear bomber. Other less important potential performance aspirations were also included in the report, and it even explored the possibility of eventually developing the design for use as an interceptor, taking advantage of the aircraft's projected range and endurance capabilities. This idea was never seriously considered beyond the basic concept stage and attention remained firmly on the aircraft's strike and reconnaissance capabilities. This report enabled the Air Staff to develop its thoughts still further and its considerations finally came together on a formal basis in Air Staff General Operational Requirement No.GOR.339 (later referred to more simply as 'OR.339') which was established and written in March 1957 and subsequently circulated to manufacturers on 29 October of the same year. Although it was clearly stated that the contents of GOR.339 provided only the

'...broad, though tentative outlines of the project' (and was never intended to become the actual basis of an operational aircraft) it did at least give a fairly clear official indication of what kind of aircraft would be required and as intended, it was sufficient to generate a number of potentially viable proposals from Britain's aircraft manufacturers. GOR.339 specified the performance of this new tactical strike/ reconnaissance aircraft, scheduled to be in service by 1964 or 'as soon thereafter as possible' as a direct replacement for the Canberra bomber. It would incorporate an all-weather capability with a self-contained bombing system, minimum take-off and landing requirements, and would operate mainly at low level at heights of 1,000ft or less. With a radius of action of 1,000nm it would be capable of delivering its weapons by loft manoeuvre from low level, or by dive toss attack from medium level – effectively throwing bombs at the target. Although there was no clear preference for the type of weapons to be carried at this stage, it was already accepted that in order to successfully destroy heavily-defended tactical targets, a significant degree of delivery accuracy would be vital, and the prospect of developing reliable and capable targeting systems for a low-level and high-speed bomber looked like a formidable task. Likewise, the idea of exposing what would surely be a very complex and expensive aircraft to such a hostile environment seemed unnecessarily risky, therefore it was self-evident from the outset that the aircraft would primarily rely upon a nuclear capability. The destructive power of a nuclear weapon would not require extremely precise delivery, nor would it necessarily require the aircraft to be exposed to the most hostile defensive environments for prolonged periods, and the destructive power of a nuclear weapon would effectively ensure that whatever target was assigned to the aircraft, it would inevitably be destroyed. Consequently, from the very beginning of the project, the primary weapon for the new aircraft was nuclear, and was initially expected to be a weapon called Red Beard, a bulky and often temperamental tactical atomic bomb (with a nominal 15 Kiloton yield) which eventually entered service in 1962 (carried by both RAF and FAA strike aircraft). This was the weapon which the new aircraft would effectively be built around, with the weapons bay dimensions, aerodynamic performance and therefore the overall size and layout of the aircraft being directly based on the ability to successfully deliver the Red Beard bomb. The GOR.339 specifications clearly indicated that the new aircraft would be designed to operate primarily in a relatively short-range tactical role, however in contrast, the introductory text which accompanied the issue of GOR.339 also took into account that despite being a tactical design, a high-speed, low flying nuclear bomber obviously had unexplored potential, and the accompanying specification notes mentioned that with the aid of in-flight refuelling, the new aircraft could 'pose a low-level threat to Russia and thus augment the primary deterrent'. This comment was possibly intended merely as an enthusiastic indication of the new aircraft's versatility, but linking the aircraft with a possible strategic capability was both an asset and a liability, and one which would eventually contribute (albeit indirectly) to the abandonment of the whole programme.

Interesting nose-on image of XR219 at Boscombe Down, illustrating the straight-edged conical shape of the radar fairing. The aircraft's futuristic shape contrasts with the adjacent wartime-era refuelling bowser. For operational missions, the aircraft's inertial navigation system would be aligned using a surveyed fixed site, such as the position from where XR219 operated for test flying (as illustrated). Once aligned, the aircraft could not be moved again without having to re-align the INS. Although the system could be updated in flight (providing that a fixed navigational point could be found with which to input the data), maintaining INS accuracy in field conditions would undoubtedly have been a difficult task. *BAC*

Having established the basics of GOR.339 which was now in the hands of Britain's industrial base, the UK's aircraft manufacturers immediately embarked upon the creation of their own individual design projects, each of which would (at least in theory) produce a suitable aircraft with which to meet the Air Ministry's specifications. A wide variety of potential solutions emerged, some of which were clearly the result of meticulous and lengthy investigations, while others seem to have been offered more as gestures than serious proposals. For example, the mighty Avro company (which was by now part of the Hawker Siddeley group) proposed its Type 739 design (and prepared a very significant brochure with which to support the submission), whereas in stark contrast, its traditional competitors at Handley Page offered only the results of a detailed study project, and stated that the company did not propose to tender for a contract. The main reason behind this move was that Handley Page (and indeed other manufacturers)

Lifting smartly into the air, XR219 gets airborne from a snowy Boscombe Down during 1965. All of XR219's initial test flights were conducted from Boscombe Down, and all the flights commenced and ended at the base. No diversions to any other airfields were ever made. The second phase of the test programme was conducted from Warton, with all subsequent flights being made from and to that base. XR219 (as the only flying example of the type) never visited any other airfields. Had the test programme continued, it is likely that some aircraft would have gone to the Vickers airfield at Wisley (in association with systems development) whilst others would have been re-assigned to the A&AEE at Boscombe Down. However most of the test programme would have been conducted from Warton. *BAC*

had already learned of the Ministry of Supply's insistence that any production contract would only be offered to a company with 'very large resources' although in effect this actually meant that the contract would go to an amalgamated team comprising of two or more companies. With no appetite for amalgamation (or at least no serious prospect of doing so), Handley Page in particular saw little reason to pursue the Operational Requirement with any vigour. Other submissions made in response to GOR.339 included Bristol Aircraft's Type 204, Hawker's P.1129, plus proposals from Fairey, Boulton Paul, Folland and Vickers-Armstrong who offered two versions of its Type 571 design which had been created by its Supermarine division, in addition to a separate proposal which came directly from its Weybridge headquarters based on Barnes Wallis' variable-geometry ('swing wing') Swallow project, which caused a great deal of interest but was ultimately discounted on the basis that variable geometry was (at that time) a new and unknown concept which would inevitably require many years of development work. Blackburn aircraft submitted a thorough proposal for a development of its NA.39 strike aircraft which was already being designed for the Royal Navy, and although it was received with relatively little enthusiasm, it was this design which was destined to become a familiar part of the seemingly endless political drama which surrounded and dogged much of the TSR2 programme. But while the various companies prepared their submissions, work had also continued with great

enthusiasm at Warton where the English Electric team devoted considerable time and resources to its embryonic P.17 concept, confident that it supersonic experience would given it a distinct advantage, and that the contract for the Canberra's replacement was likely to be given to the company that had created the Canberra so successfully. It seemed like a logical assumption. Some of the design staff worked eighty-hour weeks over the Christmas period into 1957 in order to create a complete and extremely detailed proposal document with which to dazzle the Air Ministry. As the design process progressed, English Electric's initial straight-wing layout with a high-set tail plane had slowly developed into a delta-wing configuration combined with a low-set tail plane (which was occasionally referred-to by the design team as a '...Lightning with the wing notch filled-in') although in contrast to the Lighting, the engines were still mounted in pods under the wings and the crew remained positioned in a tandem seating arrangement – a configuration which had actually been proposed for some Lightning variants too, but was never adopted. As more aerodynamics data became available, the design progressed still further with the engines eventually being shifted from the wings into a more conventional side-by-side arrangement, buried inside the fuselage structure. By now the design had progressed so far from the original drawings that it had in effect become a completely different aircraft and in recognition of this fact, the project was re-designated accordingly as the P.17A.

CHAPTER TWO

Paper Planes

ONE of the most significant factors which influenced the very beginnings of the TSR2 programme was the now infamous 1957 Defence White Paper, presented to the House of Commons by Defence Minister Duncan Sandys just two weeks after GOR.339 had first been issued. It was the first serious, radical and far-reaching reappraisal of Britain's defence posture to have taken place since the end of the Second World War. To some extent (but probably not as much as many commentators

Pictured in a very impressive climb, XR219 heads skyward, Jimmy Dell keeping pace in BAC's chase Lightning. XR219 performed effortlessly even with the de-rated development engines which were fitted to the aircraft. With full production-standard engines, the aircraft would undoubtedly have been capable of sustained flight at speeds of Mach 2.2 or more. Whether there was any serious need for such phenomenal performance is, however, questionable. *BAC*

have suggested) Sandys' review of Britain's military spending was influenced fundamentally by his belief that missile technology was the key to future defence policy, and that manned aircraft were likely to become unnecessary as missile technology improved. More importantly, he firmly believed that the foundations of Britain's security would ultimately rest upon nuclear deterrence. Driven by the Government's growing budgetary pressures, his policy document set out a whole range of drastic cuts and project cancellations, partly in an attempt to meet the Treasury's desperate attempts to bring the country's flagging economy under control, but also to allow more funding to be available for the hugely expensive nuclear arsenal which Sandys (and the rest of the Government) believed essential. Many very promising aircraft programmes were terminated,

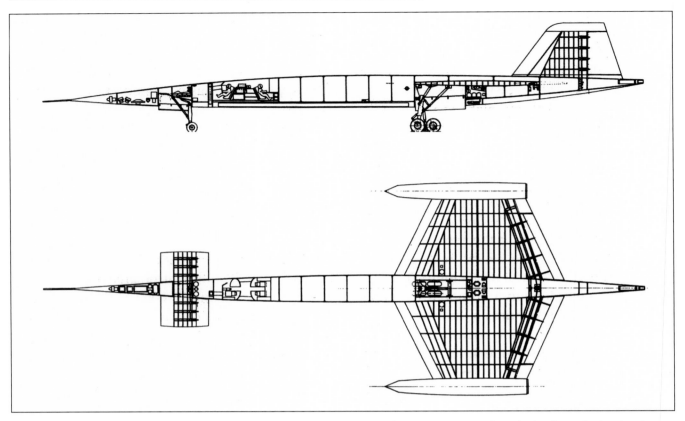

Manufacturer's drawing of the mighty Avro 730 supersonic bomber, cancelled shortly before construction was due to begin. The production aircraft varied from this drawing slightly in that the engine fairings were moved slightly inboard along the wing structure. The 730 would have been a truly awesome machine, but ultimately it was not one which the RAF needed. Designed exclusively for high speed flight at high level, the RAF actually needed a low-level bomber, and the decision to cancel the project (effectively concentrating attention on TSR2) was undoubtedly a wise move, even though it was portrayed as political vandalism at the time. *Courtesy BAE Heritage*

much to the horror of defence and industry chiefs, but Britain's financial situation demanded that serious decisions had to be made and in many respects Sandys simply did what was necessary, taking the controversial but vital steps which challenged the very structure of Britain's defence strategy. Certainly it is true that in retrospect some of the cancelled projects can be seen to have had great potential, and some have been portrayed (particularly by commentators with their own agendas) as hugely significant, their summary cancellation being nothing short of a national scandal. However a more honest appraisal creates a slightly different conclusion. For example, one of the most controversial cancellations was Avro's Type 730, a stainless steel high-altitude supersonic bomber for which a prototype airframe was already being constructed. Originally destined to replace the V-Force's Vulcans, Victors and Valiants, the 730's phenomenal high-altitude and high-speed performance showed great promise, but by the time of the Defence White Paper's emergence, the Air Staff was already seriously doubting whether it really was the right design to pursue. Convinced that enemy defences would soon make high-altitude attack difficult if not impossible, the Mach 3 bomber was being created to operate in an environment where even its impressive top speed would probably be insufficient to ensure invulnerability, and no matter how impressive the 730's performance might have been, it would be of little use if it could not provide the RAF with a viable successor to the existing V-Force. Low-level attack was

undoubtedly the only sure way forward, and although the loss of the 730 was portrayed as a major blow to both the aircraft industry and the RAF, its cancellation was probably a wise decision, given that the RAF might well have been saddled with a sophisticated and capable aircraft, designed for entirely the wrong role. Indeed, it can be argued that all of the aircraft programmes cancelled by Sandys were ambitious, exciting and full of potential, but ultimately they might well have been the wrong choices for Britain's requirements. But regardless of the relative merits of each systematically cancelled programme, the Government certainly did not have the option of doing nothing. Whilst it might well be true that Britain's defence posture and the country's aviation industry were never quite the same after the 1957 Review, it would be wrong to conclude that the Defence Review was anything other than necessary. Sandys simply did what had to be done.

Clearly, Britain's defence strategy was confused, over-complicated and unrealistic, and Sandys set out a more practical and affordable policy, stating that: "If the weapons and equipment of the armed forces are to be kept up to date, an adequate effort on research and development must be continuously maintained. However, in view of the shortage of scientists and technicians in civil industry, it is important to restrict the military programme to those projects which are absolutely essential." He also made a clear reference to a funda-mental aspect of the UK's defence policy which would have a

XR219 captured during a long approach back to Boscombe Down, the familiar Wiltshire countryside rolling by below as Beamont sets the aircraft up for landing. *BAC*

direct effect upon TSR2 when he stated that: "It must be frankly recognized that there is at present no means of providing adequate protection for the people of this country against the consequences of an attack with nuclear weapons. Though, in the event of war, the fighter aircraft of the Royal Air Force would unquestionably be able to take a heavy toll of enemy bombers, a proportion would inevitably get through. Even if it were only a dozen, they could with megaton bombs inflict widespread devastation. This makes it more than ever clear that the overriding consideration in all military planning must be to prevent war rather than to prepare for it. While comprehensive disarmament remains among the foremost objectives of British foreign policy, it is unhappily true that, pending international agreement, the only existing safeguard against major aggression is the power to threaten retaliation with nuclear weapons." This theme was developed further and in 1958 an Air Ministry note on GOR.339 progress remarked that the development of hydrogen bombs had '…enormously strengthened the power of the deterrent' and that any immediate threat of 'deliberate global war' had receded. However the note also accepted that there was an increased risk that the Soviet Union might seek to pursue their political agenda '…by resort to cold and limited war by proxy.' If such conflicts were allowed to develop uncontained, there was a grave risk that they could develop into an all-out nuclear war, almost by accident. Forces would therefore be necessary which could employ 'conventional and if necessary nuclear weapons' against localised aggression both as a means of containment and defeat. The note added that a new tactical aircraft (GOR.339) would be required by 1965 for 'situations of this kind' for which no other planned aircraft would be suitable. Significantly, the note also added that the new aircraft would enable the RAF to '…maintain an effective contribution to Saceur's (Supreme Allied Commander Europe) forces on the Continent' and (as mentioned previously) to 'augment the main deterrent by posing

a low-level threat to Russia itself.' In effect, this meant that although the new design would be deployed primarily as a tactical strike aircraft with worldwide commitments, it would have a very important role within Europe, and clearly would also be capable of reaching into the heart of the Soviet Union. It would therefore, also be a strategic asset and it was identified as such from the very beginning of the project.

The Defence Paper had also addressed the very nature of Britain's aviation industry and had concluded that it was over-complicated, over-sized and uncompetitive. Rationalisation became a key word and although the tentative steps towards creating an aircraft to fulfil GOR.339 had successfully survived Sandys' drastic review (despite his assertion that Britain would not require any new manned fighters, which implied that manned bombers would be no less obsolete), it soon became clear that the project would still become hopelessly politicised. On 16 September 1957 a meeting was arranged for representatives of the eight aircraft manufacturers (including the new Hawker Siddeley group) and Sir Cyril Musgrave, Permanent Secretary at the Ministry of Supply. Musgrave explained that fundamental changes to the industry were vital and that its very survival was at risk. However he believed that a contract would still be placed for a design to meet GOR.339 and that this would obviously be a huge undertaking – and possibly be the basis of the last all-British combat aircraft ever to be developed (of course his prediction was not strictly accurate, with both Harrier and Hawk being developed subsequently). The Ministry had decided that the ensuing contract would not be placed with a single manufacturer but that it would be issued to a designated group or alternatively, a single company working in co-operation with two (or more) other manufacturers. Musgrave added that the Ministry would prefer the industry to take the lead on this initiative but as a last resort it would nominate the groups itself. In effect this was nothing short of a rather clumsy 'shotgun wedding' arrangement which simply forced the aircraft industry to amalgamate in order to even be considered, and GOR.339 was to be the catalyst with which to put the Government's industrial policy into effect. It seemed that at this stage, the Government's primary concern was not the precise nature of GOR.339's design and manufacture, but the industrial arrangement through which it was to be created – a bizarre basis on which to embark upon such a significant programme. As if to add to the aircraft industry's misgivings, Musgrave also specified that in order to qualify for the GOR.339 contract, the companies would be expected to have sufficient work to maintain their production facilities without any initial financial support from the Government (in other words, they would be expected to pursue the project at their own expense during the initial stages) and that full inter-company amalgamation should be achieved by January 1958. Although GOR.339 was undoubtedly recognised as a major programme worth competing for, it became obvious to all parties concerned that it was to be a difficult one, which was being used shamelessly by the Government as a means of forcing the aircraft industry to rationalise itself, almost by means of bribery. Few could have imagined just how difficult the programme would eventually become.

As work on the P.17A continued in Lancashire, many miles to the south another project was being created in pursuance of the GOR.339 contract by Supermarine at its South Marston offices. Supermarine (designers of the immortal Spitfire) had become part of the Vickers-Armstrong empire many years previously although the company name had still been applied to successive designs, the most recent of which was the Scimitar which was now in service with the Fleet Air Arm. A variety of concept designs (ultimately more than 40 in all) were explored by the Supermarine team, and whilst all of these designs offered potential solutions to the GOR.339 requirements, just two were eventually selected with which to tender for the contract, these being identified as the most practical. Both were similar, the main differences being their overall size and corresponding performance, with one being a larger, heavier twin-engine derivative of the other, which was a smaller, lighter and more agile aircraft, powered by just one engine. Compared to English Electric's P.17A, the Supermarine Type 571 was a substantially different design (particularly the single-engine derivative which was much smaller and lighter), incorporating a small, straight swept wing positioned just aft of mid-fuselage, combined with conventional tail surfaces. Jettisonable fuel tanks were attached to the wing tips and the fuselage 'cheek' intakes were of a straight-edged design with inward-facing leading edges. English Electric had also considered some very similar intake designs for its own project but eventually opted for variable cones within circular shrouds (similar to the Lockheed F-104), as at the time there was insufficient aerodynamic research data to indicate any significant advantage of one layout over the other, and the final choice was as much a symptom of preference and instinct rather than research-based knowledge. The Supermarine team had quickly concluded that in order to undertake the roles specified by GOR.339, the aircraft would have to rely upon a large and complex avionics system and that the necessary range and speed would result in a fairly large aircraft. Although this was an achievable aim (and therefore presented in Supermarine's

submission as the larger of the two designs) the team's firm belief in small, compact and relatively inexpensive aircraft (as exemplified, of course, by the magnificent Spitfire) convinced them that the smaller design – effectively half the weight of the projected GOR.339 – would still be a better solution, especially if miniaturised system components could be developed. Sadly, although such systems (particularly digital technology) were attainable, they were still some years away; however the concept of developing interchangeable packs to equip the aircraft for different roles was something which could be achieved, and would enable the aircraft to handle a variety of tasks with a minimum of support. Supermarine was also keen to explore the design's potential as a naval aircraft (the company had in fact been encouraged to do so by the Ministry of Supply) and the smaller aircraft was naturally more suitable for this purpose. Powered by a single RB.142 engine (the Conway 11R/3C being identified as an alternative), the larger design would use the same engine but incorporate two of these power plants, and both designs would utilise the engine's power to provide additional lift over the full-span trailing edge flaps, this 'wing blowing' system having first been successfully developed for use on the Scimitar design. It was anticipated that the system would reduce landing speed by almost 20mph – vital for deck landings but equally useful for the projected GOR.339 requirement for short-field operations. Both versions of the Type 571 had an estimated top speed of Mach 2.3 above 36,000ft, and both would have a maximum range of 1,000nm, although the single-engine aircraft would require external fuel tanks in order to achieve this. Although both designs were eventually submitted, the Supermarine design team clearly believed that the marginally better performance of the larger aircraft was outweighed by its greater cost, and with possible naval applications still in mind, they undoubtedly preferred the smaller single-engine option. This was reflected in the proportion of information and detail given for each aircraft in its submission. Significantly, the completed Vickers-Supermarine design was considered to be a very thoroughly researched proposal, second only to English Electric's in terms of overall detail, although when compared to English Electric's impressive three-volume submission, it is difficult to understand how the Vickers-Supermarine one-volume submission could have been received so enthusiastically. Indeed, Vickers subsequently admitted that little more than a month's work had been put into the design, but the combination of the company's aerodynamic expertise and the experience of the Vickers Guided Weapons Department enabled the teams to create a comprehensive 'weapons system' proposal which represented a very considered design – much more than just the basics of a flying machine. Additionally, Vickers had already gained considerable knowledge of TFR (Terrain Following Radar) which would be vital for low-level tactical operations, and had already placed a development contract with Cornell University in the United States to explore the concept further – much to the indifference of Britain's Royal Radar Establishment which was still unconvinced of the system's potential. When Vickers and English Electric both finally submitted their completed proposals, it quickly became clear that they were the two leading designs which had evidently showed the greatest promise of success, the P.17A's excellent aerodynamic performance being

XR219 thunders into the air to begin test flight No.5 on 14 January 1965. TSR2 was a brutally noisy aircraft and some consideration was given to the disturbance that the aircraft might cause when it entered RAF service. Noise nuisance was a factor which eventually discounted Wyton as a potential base for TSR2 reconnaissance aircraft, and Coningsby's long acceptance of noisy Vulcan bombers was one of the reasons why the base was selected as the projected home of the TSR2's Operational Development Squadron and Operational Conversion Unit – both of which would have been collectively referred-to as the Tactical Strike Establishment. *BAC*

matched by the more sophisticated nature of the Type 571's 'weapons system' approach. However, the choice of either of these designs was not an easy one to make, not least because there was a third proposal which, although inferior in terms of overall performance, was one which already had significant support from within Government circles because it could, at least in theory, provide the RAF with the aircraft it needed, even if it was not necessarily the aircraft that it wanted.

Back in 1953 the Admiralty had identified the need for a new strike aircraft which could counter the Soviets' new Sverdlov class cruisers. Issued as Naval requirement NR/A.39, this resulted in a series of proposals from various manufacturers, the successful design being produced by Blackburn as the NA.39, later named Buccaneer. Equipped with a tactical atomic bomb (built around Green Cheese – a weapon which was subsequently abandoned, to be replaced by Red Beard) the Buccaneer was designed to operate from the Fleet's carriers and would attack from low level so as to evade radar and enemy defences – effectively employing the same tactics as those which GOR.339 would embrace for overland operations. Of course the Buccaneer was created as a maritime aircraft with a shorter range and systems which were never intended to be as sophisticated as those employed by the GOR.339 aircraft. But the similarities between the two aircraft were obvious, particularly so to politicians who were unable (or sometimes

unwilling) to accept the proposition that GOR.339's specified role was materially different to that which was being undertaken by the Buccaneer. Not surprisingly, Blackburn produced a proposal (the B.103A) for a development of the Buccaneer which incorporated increased fuel capacity and more powerful de Havilland Gyron engines, with which to meet the GOR.339 specifications more precisely. With a respectable range of 850nm and a speed of Mach 0.85 it showed some potential, but clearly it was not as ambitious as the English Electric or Vickers proposals. A more sophisticated derivative of the Buccaneer (the B.108) was also proposed but its maximum speed was still expected to be subsonic. Blackburn's view was that supersonic performance was not as vitally important for the role as had been suggested by the Air Ministry and that the aircraft's delivery date was much more relevant. The company also believed that the development of an existing aircraft would enable it to be brought into service much more rapidly, whilst a longer term supersonic development could (if still necessary) be produced as a follow-on project. The concept certainly had some merit, but the Air Ministry was less than enthusiastic for a number of reasons. Firstly, the Blackburn designs would not entirely meet the GOR.339 specifications as they stood, especially as the required performance figures were still creeping upwards. Secondly, whilst the concept of developing an existing design was plausible, it effectively meant producing what would be only an 'interim' aircraft, and design of the definitive aircraft would be just as expensive (and time consuming) as producing an ideal aircraft from scratch (although this obviously failed to address the benefits of bringing an aircraft into service more rapidly). But perhaps most importantly (at least in the Air Ministry's view), the Buccaneer was unashamedly designed for naval operations and the RAF had no interest in adopting what was regarded (at least by the RAF) as an inferior aircraft designed for the Navy. Indeed, the RAF had already poured scorn on the very concept of the NA.39 and had even attempted to prevent the Navy from obtaining the aircraft, producing a study report which suggested that a modified Scimitar would have been a less expensive and entirely suitable aircraft for the Fleet Air Arm's requirements. Naturally, having made the Navy fight hard for the Buccaneer, there was little appetite for subsequently accepting the same aircraft for itself.

But despite the RAF's reservations, there was an obvious and credible case for adopting the Buccaneer as a suitable aircraft with which to meet the requirements of GOR.339. In February 1958 the Secretary of State for Air (George Ward) suggested that on the basis of his information, it seemed unlikely that the GOR.339 aircraft would be ready for operational service until 1968 at the very earliest and that the more logical solution to providing a more immediate replacement for the Canberra would be to adopt an existing design such as the NA.39, or at least an RAF version of it, in the shape of the B.103. In response to this assertion, Deputy Chief of the Air Staff (AVM Tuttle) replied rather tersely that the B.103 offered no significant improvement over the Canberra, other that "its superior speed". DCAS continued on this theme at a subsequent meeting of the Air Council where the question of whether an all-new aircraft was necessary became the subject of heated debate. He emphasised what he believed would the key requirements of GOR.339; it would have to be supersonic, and it would have to operate from runways no longer than 1,000yds. It would have to incorporate a blind bombing and navigation system and would also need considerable range. He pointed out, however, that in reality the Buccaneer could never be supersonic, that it would need a runway of up to 3,000yds (in tropical conditions) and that the bombing system and range performance would be inadequate. In order to address the advantage of bringing an aircraft into service sooner, DCAS also stated that there was now no urgent need to replace the Canberra fleet because fatigue life estimates for the Canberra had become rather more encouraging, and because Valiant bombers might be made available to meet the requirements of Saceur (NATO Supreme Allied Commander, Europe). Ironically, he also added that because of dwindling work for the aviation industry "…immense resources could be deployed on any new project", although he failed to express any considerations of the ways in which the use of all these resources might simply lead to huge cost increases and almost inevitable delays. However he believed that even if the RAF was not to get GOR.339 in its ideal form, there was little point in getting the Buccaneer. Parliamentary Under Secretary Sir Maurice Dean commented that he felt it would be "disastrous" if the Air Staff was not permitted to proceed with GOR.339 which it might well not get at all if the NA.39 project was given serious consideration, and George Ward added that his main concern was

the perceived gap in capability which might have to be filled by an interim aircraft. Their conclusion was that the Minister of Defence should be advised that the Council could not yet forecast the projected life of the Canberra nor the in-service date of GOR.339, but that their studies were sufficiently advanced to confirm that the aircraft would certainly be needed and that the NA.39 would not be suitable as an alternative. It was clear that every effort was being made by the Air Staff to keep the Buccaneer out of the picture, but the aircraft had already become a major subject of debate. It had already been mentioned in the 1958 'Report on Defence' in which the aircraft was described as being prepared to make its first flight later in the year and that adoption by the RAF was "being considered" (which it was, but only in terms of how it might be avoided). VCAS Air Marshal Sir Edmund Hudleston reported that the Admiralty would soon be compelled to place an order for the NA.39 Buccaneer but that it would be "unlikely to be able to do so" unless the RAF also ordered it too, which it was patently "not prepared to do." Consequently, he believed that the matter would be referred to the Defence Committee and "…inevitably go to the Minister of Defence" which indeed it did a few weeks later. George Ward put the Air Ministry's case to Duncan Sandys on 16 April, explaining that a replacement for the Canberra was clearly an essential requirement: if it was to perform effectively over a useful lifespan it would need a "greatly improved performance" over the Canberra and that the NA.39 would not be able to achieve this aim. By this stage his initial interest in the Buccaneer had been diminished (largely through the actions of the Air Staff) to such an extent that he was prepared to dismiss the NA.39 whenever challenged. Although he believed that it was still in the interests of both the Air Ministry and Admiralty "…to make common cause in the field of future aircraft whenever possible" he considered the Buccaneer to be far short of the RAF's requirements to such an extent that he believed "it would be quite wrong" for him to advocate it's adoption by the RAF. His advice to the Minister of Defence was that GOR.339 was a "realistic specification" which the aircraft industry appeared more than capable of meeting without resorting to less capable alternatives. Ward stated that the only practical way in which the Air Ministry could assist the Admiralty with its order would be to take delivery of Buccaneers as interim aircraft until GOR.339 was completed, but now that the Canberra appeared capable of remaining operational for some time, the "considerable cost" of such a proposal was not justified. George Ward's recommendation to Duncan Sandys was that the RAF should adopt GOR.339 as its Canberra replacement and accompanied his notes with various documents to support the concept, including performance comparisons between the various aircraft. The following day a contradictory view was submitted to Sandys by the First Lord of the Admiralty (the Earl of Selkirk). He stated that NA.39 would be in service by 1961 whilst GOR.339 would not enter service "until at least four years and probably five or six years later." He accepted that NA.39 did not represent a direct substitute but would be "a great step towards" what was required by the RAF. He stated that the Buccaneer clearly out-performed the Canberra in all respects and was "remarkably close" to GOR.339's requirements in all respects; the "marked superiority over the Canberra" should be sufficient to prompt the Secretary of State to "…look once again at the Blackburn project." He added that the Admiralty would "…be delighted to form a joint RN/RAF Development Unit" using aircraft from the Buccaneer pre-production fleet. Not surprisingly, George Ward dismissed the Admiralty's position, claiming that GOR.339 would, in fact, be in service during 1965 if an order to proceed was given immediately, and refuted the notion that the Buccaneer was clearly superior to the Canberra. He pointed out that the Buccaneer's radius of action would be 25 per cent shorter and that airfield performance was also inferior under tropical conditions (this was of course a less than full and honest appraisal of the Buccaneer's true capabilities). Whilst he appreciated the offer to form a joint RAF/RN Buccaneer unit, he stated that his decision to opt for GOR.339 "was inevitable" and he did not feel justified in recommending NA.39 as an interim aircraft. In response, the First Lord commented (with a prophetic ring of irony, given the events which unfolded a decade later) that he regretted this decision and that "the considerable effort" given to NA.39's development "…would have made a useful contribution to the strength of the RAF as well as that of the Navy."

Pictured during part of XR219's all-too brief experience of high-altitude flight, the Olympus engine contrails are captured by BAC's photographer as they flow over the Lightning chase aircraft during the transit from Boscombe Down to Warton. *BAC*

CHAPTER THREE

Marriage of Inconvenience

WHILE the increasing acrimony between the Navy and RAF continued, consideration of the various GOR.339 submissions was being made. By the summer of 1958 interest had gravitated towards only the most promising proposals. One of the more significant was the Hawker Siddeley Strike Aircraft (the project never actually received a numbered designation) which brought together an Avro and Hawker proposal (both companies now being part of the Hawker Siddeley Group). Although the project offered a good solution to the requirements of GOR.339, the designs being offered by Vickers and English Electric were equally impressive, and there was little evidence to indicate which of these designs was likely to achieve the best results. The decision to opt for the Vickers and English Electric proposals was undoubtedly influenced by the greater amount of

work that had clearly been put into both projects, with a significant quantity of preliminary study data having been submitted by Vickers, and a wealth of experience in supersonic design already being available to English Electric, thanks to the success of the P.1B Lightning. Futhermore English Electric had been pursuing the concept of a Canberra replacement (at varying depths of interest) for much longer than anyone else. In comparison, the Hawker Siddeley project was behind schedule in terms of research and development by at least nine months and it seemed likely that if it was adopted for production, the

An early development trials model, attached to a Mayfly II launching rocket prior to a test. As can be seen, this model still features the saw-tooth leading edge which was subsequently abandoned, although the design has progressed as far as down-turned wing tips. *BAC*

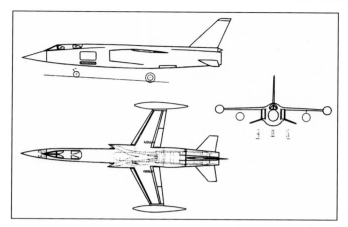

A manufacturer's drawing of the basic Type 571 layout when first devised. This was the smaller single-engine derivative of the design which Supermarine favoured, although it was accepted that its small size would rely upon the use of miniaturised systems technology (particularly digital systems) which were still realistically some years away. But with Ministry encouragement, Supermarine believed that the smaller design had useful potential as a carrier-borne strike aircraft. *Courtesy Brooklands Museum*

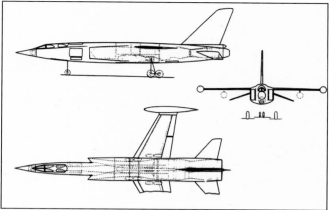

The manufacturer's drawing for the twin-engine Supermarine Type 571. As can be seen the general layout of this second design was quite similar to the firm's single-engine study and it used the same Rolls-Royce RB.142R engine as the primary choice for the powerplant. The predicted performance was also quite similar, but this project was about 30% bigger and around double the weight. *Courtesy Brooklands Museum*

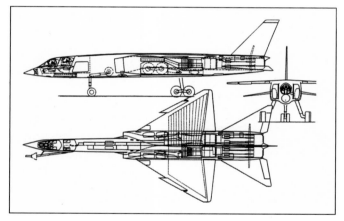

Vickers-Supermarine drawing of the Type 571 at a later stage in the design process (July 1959), by which stage a great deal of English Electric's P.17A design had been incorporated into it. At this stage the wing still featured a "dog-tooth" leading edge which was subsequently found to be unnecessary. By this stage the general features of the original Supermarine design had been dropped in favour of English Electric's more practical proposal. *Courtesy Brooklands Museum*

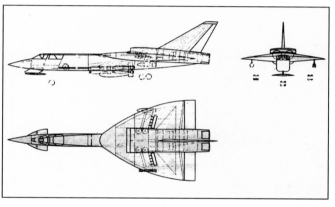

Manufacturer's drawing of the very unorthodox Bristol Type 204, proposed in response to GOR.339, featuring their unique "Gothic Wing" design which had been proved to be more stable than a conventional narrow delta shape, creating less induced drag than a simple delta design. As with English Electric's design, the possibility of developing the design into an interceptor was also considered. *Courtesy Brooklands Museum*

in-service date of the completed aircraft would probably slip by at least a year. At this stage the in-service date was perceived as being particularly important, not only in anticipation of an increasingly capable Soviet threat, but also from a political viewpoint, in that a speedy entry into RAF service would emphasise the Air Ministry's lack of requirement for an interim aircraft – in the shape of the Buccaneer. After some consideration of the possibility of allowing all three projects to proceed further (this was one potentially expensive mistake that was thankfully identified and avoided) it was finally agreed that the best solution would be to combine the English Electric and Vickers designs, merge the two companies, and create a single project with which to meet the demands of GOR.339. This would enable advantage to be taken of the two most promising designs, whilst also accommodating the Government's fervent desire for company amalgamation. The Air Ministry sought the

approval of the DRPC (Defence Research Policy Committee) and during a meeting in June it agreed that GOR.339 should be entered into the Government's Research and Development programme and that some £150,000 should be sought from the Treasury to cover an initial six months of work, subject to successful negotiations with English Electric and Vickers. It is worth noting however that even at this early stage the project's long term future was the subject of some doubt. The Chairman of the DRPC (Sir Frederick Brundrett) expressed concern that although GOR.339 would be able to meet the RAF's requirements (in fact he referred specifically to the Army support role which would be provided by the RAF), he believed that NA.39 could perform the same task maybe five years earlier and that two aircraft were effectively being created to do the same job. Unusually, Brundrett wrote to the Minister of Defence to express his reservations and in a copy of his note forwarded

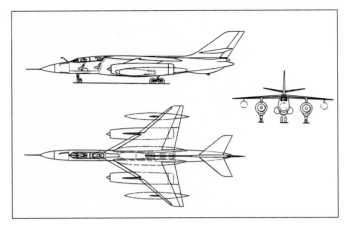

General arrangement drawing of de Havilland's unspecified submission for the GOR.339 contract. In order to address the requirement for short-field STOL operations, de Havilland proposed that their design should feature a variable-incidence wing which could be raised at the leading edge to achieve greater lift and lower speeds – a concept which had been proved by Chance-Vought in their Crusader fighter. It was also believed that this system would enable the design to be used as the basis for a ship-borne attack or fighter aircraft. *Courtesy Brooklands Museum*

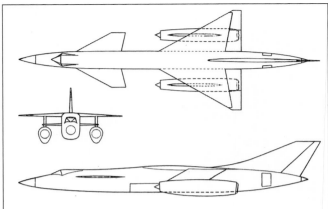

General arrangement drawing of Fairey's unspecified submission for GOR.339 which featured some of the design configurations which English Electric had also briefly considered. The design was based squarely on the company's successful Fairey Delta 2 research aircraft, employing the same wing layout, with no additional lift devices. Although falling short of some of GOR339's requirements, Fairey believed that the aircraft would provide the RAF with a reliable and uncomplicated aircraft. *Courtesy Brooklands Museum*

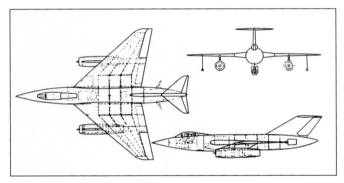

Gloster produced a report which stated that a development of their "thin wing" Javelin derivative (illustrated) could be developed to meet GOR.339. However the company did not make a formal submission. In order to meet the Air Staff's requirements, the existing Javelin design was developed further, the engines being moved out of the fuselage (on to pods) in order to provide more space for fuel, but even with the benefit of considerable re-design, it still fell short of the required top speed of more than Mach 2. *Courtesy Brooklands Museum*

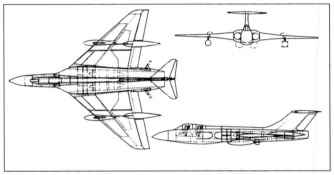

General arrangement drawing of Gloster's P.386, a development of their "thin wing" Javelin design which was created to meet the requirements of GOR.339 – but never formally submitted. In its original unmodified form the design was undoubtedly inadequate and would probably have been capable of achieving a top speed of little more than Mach 1.0. Likewise, the aircraft would have lacked the necessary range which had been stipulated. *Courtesy Brooklands Museum*

to Chief of the Air Staff he even added that he would be "…very glad if you ensured that no quotation is ever made from it nor that its existence is ever known." In his letter to the Minister, he stated that he was "by no means happy" that the proposed aircraft to meet GOR.339 was "necessarily the aircraft we ought to have"; whilst he accepted that a Canberra replacement was clearly necessary, he had doubts over the thinking behind it. Most significantly, he understood that the RAF would be obliged to undertake operations in various theatres across the world as part of various existing treaties but given the proposed in-service date of 1965, he wondered what bases and responsibilities the UK might actually have by then, and therefore, whether the Air Staff were "planning on a realistic basis." He believed that if it was not, then much of GOR.339's specification was obviously unnecessary and if only an "Army Support" aircraft was required it could be much less sophisticated and thus much less expensive. As with the earlier comments from the Admiralty,

there was a distinct hint of prophecy in Brundrett's comments but nobody within the Government seemed ready to accept the notion that Britain might somehow withdraw from its worldwide commitments, thereby rendering the supremely capable GOR.339 design unnecessary. However, the DRPC's endorsement was accepted and while a decision was awaited from the Minister of Defence on whether to proceed, the Air Ministry refined GOR.339 into a final draft (now officially termed as OR.339) which was circulated to everyone involved with the project. It was at this stage that a major crisis in the Middle East intervened which involved the deployment of British forces into Jordan and the Minister of Defence naturally became pre-occupied with this operation. The Parliamentary Under Secretary at the Ministry of Defence (Sir Richard Powell) reported that the Minister was "…considering urgently whether he should authorise the production of the NA.39 and the development of OR.339". In order to help him reach a decision

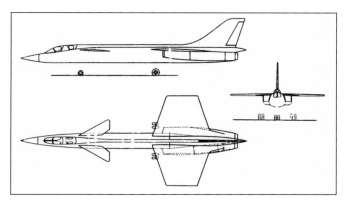

Interesting illustration of an early P.17 design which was tested in English Electric's wind tunnel facilities from December 1956 until February 1957. *Courtesy BAE Heritage*

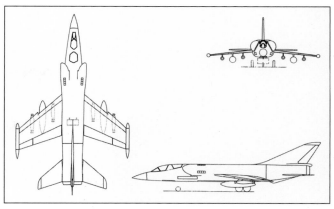

General arrangement sketch of a joint Hawker Siddeley project designed in response to GOR.339 (dated November 1958). Had the Vickers and English Electric designs not been pursued, this design was the most favoured alternative which looked capable of achieving all of the requirements laid down by GOR.339. *Courtesy Brooklands Museum*

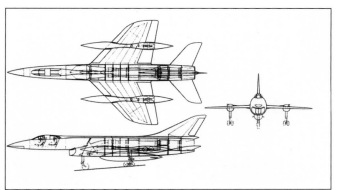

The Hawker P.1123 Mach two tactical bomber (drawing dated January 1957) was a development of the earlier P.1121 proposal, which had suffered from an unresolved design problem – the flaps could not have been lowered when the undercarriage was extended. The revised design featured four-wheeled landing gear units housed in "Kuchemann" pod fairings. *Courtesy Brooklands Museum*

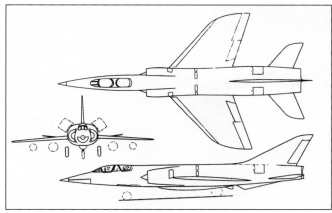

General arrangement drawing of the Hawker P.1125 air superiority strike fighter – another of the varied designs produced by Hawker in response to GOR.339 (drawing dated March 1957). *Courtesy Brooklands Museum*

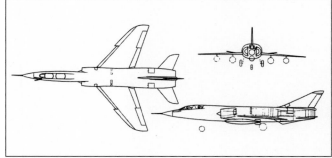

Outline sketch of Hawker's P.1129, dated January 1958. Hawker claimed that a prototype for this design could have been flying by the end of 1960. *Courtesy Brooklands Museum*

Sir Frederick Page, who ultimately became Chief Engineer for the TSR2 project. Having joined English Electric in 1945 as part of WEW Petter's team, he was influential in the design of both the Canberra and (even more so) the Lightning, before becoming involved with the huge TSR2 programme. He subsequently contributed significantly to the Concorde, Jaguar and Tornado programmes and was the driving force behind Warton's post-TSR2 emergence as a leading centre for military aircraft production. *BAE Heritage*

Left: The test model specimen, pictured at the point of launch, attached to a rocket. These high-speed trials provided BAC with a great deal of useful research data which was incorporated into the preliminary design of the airframe. *BAC*

Below: Extensive trials of TSR2's parachute braking system were conducted by the RAE at Farnborough, using their Shackleton aircraft WR972, the tail glazing having been removed and replaced by a mounting structure for the parachute pack assembly.

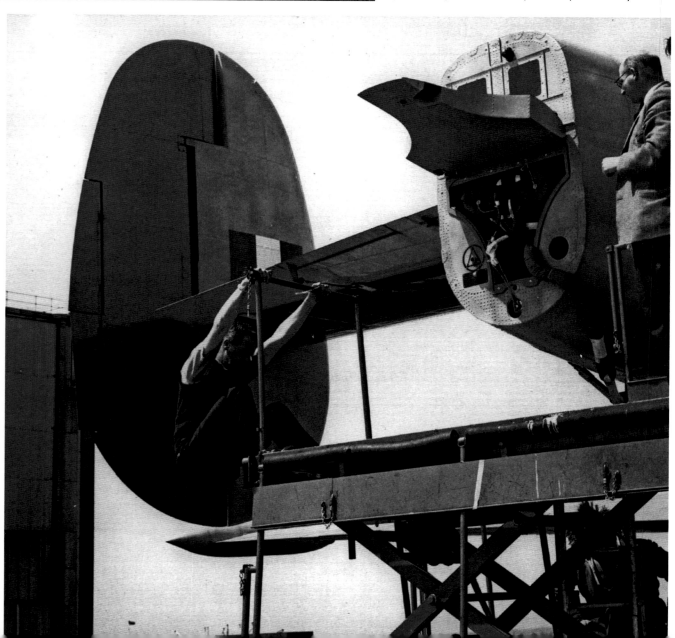

(whilst preoccupied with the Middle East situation), some questions needed to be answered by the Air Ministry, Admiralty and War Office. The Minister wanted to know what the operational tasks for both aircraft were intended to be (i.e.: for operations in cooperation with police action, limited war or global war), what requirements for reconnaissance in support of the Army were required for each aircraft in these situations, and which (if any) of all these tasks could not be performed by the Canberra, V-Bombers or other existing aircraft. Powell also sought clarification as to those tasks that would be performed by OR.339 which could not be undertaken by NA.39 or a modified (for RAF requirements) version of it, and whether a modified version of NA.39 could enter service sooner than OR.339. In essence, Powell (on behalf of Sandys) was clearly still pursuing the question of whether the Buccaneer could successfully take on OR.339's tasks, but not necessarily as an 'either/or' choice. It was hardly surprising that the various responses to the questions repeated the same entrenched positions which the Admiralty and RAF had assumed, and the various hypotheses, projected scenarios and procurement options which were postulated simply served to complicate the decision-making process still further. But some clarification emerged on 10 September when the Minister of Defence finally authorised a production order for NA.39 Buccaneers for the Royal Navy, having satisfied himself that a strong case for the aircraft had been made. The Air Staff immediately interpreted this move as a determination to bring the Buccaneer into RAF service too and further pressure was put upon Sandys to make a firm decision on OR.339. By this stage however, Sandys had again shifted his attention to other issues and had arranged to visit the US for inter-governmental talks which would cover "interdependence, development and so on." He would make a final decision "in the light of these discussions" as soon as he returned. It was not until 11 November that Sandys met with the Secretary of State and the Chief of the Air Staff to discuss OR.339 in detail, and two days later he informed the Secretary of State that "…after very full consideration I am now satisfied that you have made out the case for replacing, in due course, the Canberra with an aircraft which would comply with the general specification defined in OR.339. The way is therefore clear for you to ask the Ministry of Supply to approach the Treasury for authority to place a development contract for this aircraft."

With more than a touch of irony, Sandys had seemingly contradicted his conclusion (on which much of his Defence White paper had been based) that Britain would require "no more manned combat aircraft." On 15 December the Treasury gave approval for a design contract at an estimated £150,000 whilst requesting that it be informed and – when possible – "…consulted on measures to control the progress of the programme, to check on the estimates and the costs of the firms engaged on it and to limit the introduction of improvements and modifications."

As 1958 drew to a close the progress of OR.339 looked encouraging. The debate over the necessity of an aircraft more sophisticated than the Buccaneer appeared to have been settled in the RAF's favour, a suitable design with which to meet the requirement had been chosen, and Government funding for the project was now available. But despite this apparently bright picture, the Treasury's rather guarded authorisation indicated that even from the outset, the question of costs and project control was an important issue which it would not overlook, even if other departments did. Just a few months later, the Treasury's initial funding of £150,000 was reluctantly increased to £600,000.

The Government having finally made the decision to select the English Electric and Vickers-Supermarine submissions, the two companies immediately turned their attention to the informal amalgamation of the two proposals in order to produce a combined design which incorporated the recognised advantages of each approach. Likewise, there was still a wider official pressure for the Government's desire for industry rationalisation to be brought into effect as quickly as possible and by the end of 1958, both companies were in no doubt that unless they successfully combined their talents and amalgamated on a formal basis as swiftly as possible, they risked losing the entire contract to the Hawker Siddeley Group. But while plans to formally merge the management structure of the Vickers and English Electric companies continued, a joint project team was first established in December and detailed design work began the following month, resulting in a joint specification being produced in just six months. This became the basis for an abandonment of the original OR.339 specifications (which had been constantly revised) and their replacement by a completely new specification under OR.343 which was effectively written around the new combined design, taking into account what was now required by the Air Staff and what could realistically be achieved by the designers. Issued by the Air Staff on 8 May 1959, OR.343 outlined the requirements for a 'Tactical Strike and Reconnaissance Weapons System'. Significantly, the original OR.339 document which had covered just 48 paragraphs had now expanded to some 114 paragraphs which outlined in great detail the basis for a large, twin-engine design with a radius of action of at least 1,000nm without in-flight refuelling, an ability to conduct reconnaissance for tactical purposes by day and night in all weather conditions, to deliver tactical nuclear weapons from low altitude, or high-explosive conventional weapons as an alternative. It would be able to operate in any part of the world and would be flown by a two-man crew (pilot and navigator). Speed at 40,000ft was now firmly set at Mach 2.0 (instead of Mach 1.7) and low altitude flight was to be set at just 200ft (instead of 1,000ft), whilst the standard conventional weapons load was to be six 1,000lb HE bombs. Ferry range would be 2,500nm, ECM (Electronic Counter Measures) would be incorporated, and the aircraft would have to be capable of landing on a grass surface instead of concrete (although this latter requirement had been implicit all along). Precisely why the aircraft's specifications became even more ambitious at this stage is open to question, but there is little doubt that the Air Staff was increasingly eager to exploit the aircraft's full potential in comparison to the Buccaneer which was still perceived as being a threat to the RAF's ambitions.

Rather than giving serious consideration to just how capable the aircraft would realistically need to be (in relation to the costs and delays which would inevitably result from increasing complexity), the driving motivation seems to have been to ensure that the aircraft had to be clearly portrayed as being far more capable than the Buccaneer. It was also almost inevitable that in response to the Air Staff's aspirations (which were already arguably over-ambitious), the manufacturers (particularly those within the Vickers team) were keen to promise more than was strictly necessary simply to ensure that they retained the Air Ministry's confidence and support. In contrast however, the English Electric team was very careful to avoid this temptation and its practical (and therefore often less ambitious) approach was sometimes not what the Air Staff wanted to hear. Sir Michael Beetham (who had been responsible for the origins of the first GOR.339 draft) later defended the Air Staff's approach by stating that the Operational Requirements Staff was always obliged to look as far ahead as possible and was reluctant to underestimate potential enemy defences. Furthermore, the Intelligence community was always keen to be seen to have not been left behind in its appraisal of potential threats. Consequently, it was always necessary to strive for the best performance possible. But when the Air Staff's ambitions were combined with the aircraft manufacturer's natural eagerness to accommodate all of the Air Staff's requirements whenever possible, often without question, there was clearly an ever-present danger of 'over-egging' OR.343's capabilities. Beetham believed that the quest for very high speed combined with both a low-level and high-altitude capability made perfect sense though: "…if the enemy had solved the problems of defence at low level," he opined, "the aircraft might have been driven to operate at higher levels." Therefore the Air Staff was right to build in as good a performance as could be achieved – presumably with no regard to the cost of doing so. But despite the increasingly ambitious nature of OR.343, the two manufacturers were still supremely confident of joint success, even though there seems to have been little consideration of how this would inevitably affect the overall cost of the programme and the projected service entry date. As Sir Frederick Page, English Electric Aviation's Director and Chief Executive, explained in subsequent years, the combined assets of the two companies formed the necessary strength and experience to produce the aircraft more cheaply and more quickly – but separately they both had significant weaknesses. Vickers had a business which was integrated "…under the control of an able and forceful character, Sir George Edwards, and had got the Valiant into service quickly", but Vickers also lacked "…any experience of, and facilities for, the design and testing of supersonic aircraft". The latter was preoccupied with "some difficult and unprofitable civil aircraft". Freddie Page also believed that Vickers "…lacked adequate definition of the relationship between project management and specialist departments, particularly finance."

By comparison, he stated that English Electric had the experience of its Canberra programme and "proven expertise and facilities for the design, development and flight testing of supersonic aircraft, plus a clearly defined project management system." Its weakness was that it had no properly integrated control of manufacture which had to be sub-contracted to the main English Electric parent company, and that it was also heavily committed to production of the Lightning interceptor. Page also claimed that because some of the company's exchanges with the Air Ministry "challenged the increasingly severe requirements in OR.339, English Electric was sometimes possibly seen as being uncooperative." The company's geographical distance from Whitehall "was also a handicap in the intense lobbying." English Electric was undoubtedly both surprised and disappointed when the Air Ministry finally outlined the terms of the initial contract. Having been made aware of the Air Ministry's preference for the English Electric and Vickers designs during the summer of 1958, it had also become evident to the company that the P.17A was clearly the most favoured design. With this fact in mind and the company's supersonic experience and successful production of the Lightning under way, it was assumed that the OR.339 design would be a project shared equally between the two companies but with English Electric naturally taking the lead role. What emerged was a complete reversal of this assumption and although work-share was indeed to be settled on a 50/50 basis, the overall control of the project was to be given to Vickers, with Sir George Edwards heading the programme. In effect, English Electric would be a sub-contractor and all subsequent project contracts connected with OR.343 would be awarded to Vickers, even after the companies had merged. This meant that all of the programme's definitive decision-making processes would ultimately be controlled by Vickers. Freddie Page later recalled that "…the Project Director, Chief Project Engineer and all leaders of specialist design, manufacturing, finance and procurement activities were all Vickers men"; indeed only the flight-test crew was led by English Electric, simply because Vickers had no personnel with substantial supersonic test experience.

No plausible reason was ever offered for the way in which the overall control of the project was handed to Vickers. Handel Davies (who had in effect been responsible for the decision) later commented that his main motivation had been to exploit the capabilities of Sir George Edwards, who was both an engineer and Chairman of the huge Vickers company, and he therefore had the ideal leadership qualities with which to lead the TSR2 project. However he also accepted that with hindsight, the decision "might not have been ideal" as Edwards was clearly pre-occupied with the various civil aircraft projects which Vickers was working on, notably the VC10 and BAC-111. Some commentators believed that giving the contract to Vickers was merely a symptom of the Government's traditional and historic preferences, with Vickers being an important, established and influential player in the corridors of power when compared to the less familiar faces from English Electric's base from far away in Lancashire. It is certainly true that English Electric's distinctly northern tendency towards plain speaking was often unwelcome, and even after the project got under way, this attitude still prevailed as Freddie Page subsequently recalled: "The Vickers project management team accepted all the increased demands spread out over many meetings with officials. At one (meeting) when the design speeds and temperatures were again increased I said 'Gentlemen, I hope you realise that what you have done will cost the Earth', but this comment was dismissed as coming from a disgruntled sub-contractor."

However despite this delicate situation, on 1 January 1959 a press release was issued by the Minister of Supply (Aubrey Jones) stating that subject to satisfactory negotiations, a "new aircraft would be undertaken" jointly by Vickers-Armstrong and English Electric, the work being shared on an equal basis with a joint project team being drawn from both companies to be based at the Vickers works at Weybridge. It was also stated that, subject to negotiations, "…the development of the engine for the new aircraft will be undertaken by Bristol-Siddeley Engines, the new company formed out of Bristol Engines and Armstrong-Siddeley Motors." Jones' statement continued: "The TSR2 is a tactical support and reconnaissance aircraft. The specification was originally based on General Operational Requirement No.339. In the course of study it has been found technically possible to incorporate in the final operational requirement, modifications which will greatly increase the usefulness of the aircraft in limited operations and for close support of the Army."

Jones added that "…while the TSR2 will be capable of performing the roles of all the various marks of Canberra, it will by reason of its greater flexibility and higher general performance be far more versatile and more in the nature of a general-purpose tactical aircraft."

This statement was the first occasion on which the term 'TSR2' was used in public. It had first been applied by Jones' own Ministry of Supply rather than the Air Ministry, where it had been expected that a standard bomber designation (similar to the B.35/46 designation given to the V-Bombers) would be given to the aircraft. Jones incorrectly attributed part of his chosen acronym to denote 'support' rather than 'strike' (the latter term implying nuclear delivery) and had therefore (either unintentionally or otherwise) down-played the aircraft's potential capabilities. However, having introduced the 'TSR2' acronym to the world, there has always been some doubt as to where the use of the term '2' came from, and various Ministry and industry officials have shared different views on this. It seems possible that it was a reflection of the aircraft's projected Mach 2 performance, but that it might also have been an indication that the Canberra was somehow regarded by the Ministry of Supply as the 'TSR1' although there is no evidence to support either notion, nor is there any surviving documentation to clarify this minor mystery. Regardless of its origins, after the circulation of Jones' press release, the aircraft was subsequently and inevitably always referred to as 'TSR2'.

Artist's drawing of the bizarre design proposed by Shorts, which could have provided TSR2 with a vertical take-off and landing capability. The delta-winged lifting body would have enabled the aircraft to be launched and recovered in flight, although the complexity of the system (and the necessity for an additional pilot to operate the system) made the concept far too complicated to seriously contemplate.

CHAPTER FOUR

Bombs and Bureaucracy

IT was not until June 1960 that complete company amalgamation took place (although a public announcement was made in January), but after a year of complicated inter-company negotiations, the British Aircraft Corporation was finally formed under the chairmanship of Lord Portal, with Sir George Edwards as Managing Director. The new 'super company' comprised Vickers (including Supermarine which had already been absorbed by this company), English Electric, and the Bristol Aeroplane Company (plus Hunting, which was also merged with BAC at a later date). Having finally satisfied the Government's demands for rationalisation (and having successfully been working together on the very detailed aircraft specification for some time), it seemed reasonable to assume that the project could now make swift progress and that a

production contract would quickly emerge. But much to the surprise of BAC and its 60-strong joint design team, the Government's eagerness now appeared to be waning, almost as if its pre-occupation had been the merger of the various companies rather than the actual production of a viable weapons system. Work on OR.343 had continued on an almost hand-to-mouth basis under a series of smaller design contracts which gave BAC little confidence and caused endless problems

A look inside the Weybridge assembly hall, with three forward fuselage sections nearing completion, and further aircraft in earlier stages of assembly in the background. Although TSR2 never received an official name, the first three completed airframes did at least earn themselves unofficial nicknames, used by the workers at Weybridge. XR219 was referred-to as "Jim", XR220 as "Joe" and XR221 as "Jasper". *BAC* in securing the co-operation of sub-contractors and suppliers who were naturally reluctant to invest support in a project which had not been fully endorsed by its customer. It was summer 1959 when Edwards finally managed to secure a holding contract which covered expenditure for a few weeks, but by September it had lapsed again and BAC was left to finance the project from its own resources. When BAC was formally established, the aim had been to produce a prototype which would be ready for a first flight in March 1963, but Edwards subsequently warned the Air Ministry and Ministry of Supply that they had effectively delayed the project by at least three months already through their own lack of urgency. Yet even this warning was insufficient to expedite the allocation of proper finance and instead of addressing the issue, the Government's interest drifted away towards the setting up of unwieldy project control committees which wasted yet more time and ultimately created the basis for even greater delays in the future. More months passed by until – at long last – a contract for nine pre-production aircraft (and two structural test airframes) was placed in October 1960. However it came as no surprise that any further orders seemed to be a very distant prospect, and Edwards worked hard to maintain his team's confidence in the project when both BAC and the many sub-contractors were often convinced that the Government was being curiously reluctant to offer more than the most grudging support for what was, of course, its own project. It took a staggering two years to secure a second contract (issued in June 1963) for a batch of 11 aircraft, together with permission (given ten months later) to order stocks for the eventual production of an initial production batch of 30 aircraft – effectively a proper production order even if it had not been described as such. Throughout this period BAC had forged ahead while in stark contrast, its customer (the Government) had slipped into a state of almost passive contemplation and indecision, combined with a seemingly obsessive interest in the project's management structure which (contrary to its belief) did nothing to improve the project and actually did a great deal to delay (and ultimately destroy) it. Instead of concentrating on the speedy production of a viable weapons system, the Air Staff diverted valuable time to almost peripheral considerations surrounding the possibilities of future potential weapons fits, projected operational use and political issues which were secondary to the main task of actually getting the TSR2 into operational service. Already, the project was proceeding without a proper sense of direction and without any effective means of control.

Although frustrated by the slow pace of official support, Edwards was undoubtedly delighted to have been handed overall control of the project. He had consistently believed that no matter how the division of design and production work was finally fixed, a single contractor (and preferably the one which he controlled) should retain overall responsibility for the programme, and the Ministry of Supply readily accepted this viewpoint; indeed Aubrey Jones insisted that the American 'Weapons System' procedure be adopted whereby a 'prime contractor' would agree an overall price and then sub-contract work as necessary to other firms, whilst remaining directly responsible to the MoS for the whole contract. The concept made good sense and had it been fully adopted without further

elaboration, it would have undoubtedly ensured that the project progressed without delay and without unnecessary cost increases. But simplicity was never a word which could be equated comfortably with TSR2. Vickers (as part of BAC) was never able to establish direct relationships with its suppliers and sub-contractors, of which there were eventually more than a thousand. In most cases it had to begin negotiations after the MoS had already discussed terms and cost estimates with it first, and these terms were inevitably based on the Ministry's narrow views as to whether any given work or equipment was deemed to be justified. Fundamentally, the MoS was not qualified to make any such judgements as to what work or equipment was strictly necessary or appropriate, this being the responsibility of another department (and communication between the two was often poor); therefore this was patently a hopelessly inefficient way to conduct an extremely complex design and manufacturing programme. But when Edwards highlighted the absurdity of the arrangement, the MoS could only justify its position by stating that its judgements were based on cost estimates of the type and amount of work involved and no more. This was of course self-evident and Edwards was all too aware of this, but he was unable to convince the MoS that Vickers should be given the freedom to conduct unfettered negotiations with its preferred contractors. The situation was never properly resolved and instead of communicating directly with BAC, many of the contractors continually invited Ministry estimators to 'second guess' its arrangements with BAC, which inevitably wasted even more time – and wasted much more money.

Perhaps the most damaging example of this process was the choice of engine for the aircraft – a decision which obviously should have been made by Vickers (on the basis that only the designer and manufacturer can make an informed decision as to which engine is most appropriate). However although Vickers were given the opportunity to make a recommendation, it did not have the power to insist upon it. Had the situation been different, it is possible that Vickers (based on its own preference and also due to English Electric's traditional employment of Rolls-Royce power plants) would have opted for the Rolls-Royce Medway turbofan engine, but the choice was finally made by Government officials who were still clearly obsessed by their quest for industry amalgamation.

Bristol Aero Engines had already merged with Armstrong-Siddeley Motors and they were subsequently joined by de Havilland and Blackburn to create what became Bristol-Siddeley Engines. With this merger completed, the choice of engine seemed obvious – at least to the MoS. Bristol-Siddeley Engines and its all-new Olympus 22R turbojet would be adopted for TSR2 and this was a decision which subsequently had a major, almost pivotal effect on the project's cancellation. It was also another illustration of the fact that despite the terms of the contract, Vickers did not actually have overall control of the TSR2 project which was actually being steered by the Government. After a great deal of heated discussion, the MoS eventually attempted to address the issue and laid down a procurement process which embraced three clear types of equipment and the methods through which they would be obtained:

Category One covered equipment which would be purchased from 'associate contractors' by the Ministry to its own specification. This included key components such as the engines, inertial platform and forward-looking radar together with the reconnaissance system.

Category Two consisted of equipment specified and purchased by BAC, although these purchases would still be subject to Ministry approval even though BAC would be responsible for development. Included in this category was the automatic flight control system, sideways-looking radar and the central digital computing system.

Category Three encompassed other equipment which could be sourced and purchased by BAC providing that such items met requirements laid down by the Ministry in supplementary specifications (including cost limits). Included were items such as fuel pumps, wheels, tyres and hydraulic actuators.

This arrangement's absurd complexity was matched – if not surpassed – by the way in which the Ministry maintained an almost suffocating influence on the direction of the whole project through the introduction of a hierarchy of committees, led by the TSR2 Steering Committee with the Ministry of Aviation's Permanent Secretary as chairman, the Controller of Aircraft, the Managing Director of Bristol-Siddeley and the Managing Director of BAC. Beneath them sat the Management Committee chaired by the Director-General of Military Aircraft, together with a whole host of sub-committees: the Production Panel, Systems Integration Panel, Development Progress Committee and Cockpit Steering Committee, together with four smaller sub-systems panels each of which comprised at least 12 members. The Development Progress Committee had more than 60 members and met quarterly, producing a written report on each occasion. As if this staggering line-up was not enough, two more committees were created to handle the financial aspects of the project.

It was evident that the Government wanted the entire TSR2 programme to be designed, manufactured and procured by committee and although this in itself should not have represented a major hurdle to TSR2's ultimate success (indeed one of the aims of this vast management structure was, ironically, to expedite progress), it was the way in which the committees functioned and communicated (or failed to communicate) with each other which caused so many difficulties. There is no doubt that many of the Ministry and RAF officials who sat on these panels did not have the appropriate qualifications for the tasks at hand and generally lacked the technical expertise which ought to have been present. There was no proper structure through which each committee could operate and liaise with its counterparts and, most importantly, there was no firm and decisive overall management, not even from Edwards who inevitably found that whenever he attempted to exercise control, it was taken away from him. Fundamentally (and for very valid reasons), it would seem that Edwards believed that he should have exercised far greater control of the project than the Ministry ever intended him to, but the Ministry consistently failed to make its position

clear, opting instead to muddle through with no clear direction. But despite this seemingly insurmountable management structure, the project did proceed and some surprisingly advanced production techniques were introduced which formed the basis of modern design and production procedures which are still used today. Amongst these was the concept of Value Engineering and PERT (Programme Evaluation and Review Technique). The first of these is a method of examination and evaluation which is performed by a team of trained engineers when component parts are first fixed at the design stage, in order to improve efficiency and improve cost effectiveness. It was understood that enthusiastic, often young, designers shared a tendency to over-engineer and the imposition of Value Engineering did a great deal to keep costs down.

PERT was a system imposed by the MoS, and was first employed by the American designers of the Polaris missile programme. In essence, it is a computer-generated system of production planning which ensures maximum efficiency and speed. It was extremely beneficial to the TSR2 project although with more than a little irony, the PERT programme did readily forecast many of the project's production slippages and cost over-runs. Although these synthetic warnings of trouble often enabled BAC to identify and avoid potential problems, delays and costs before they arose, the wider implications of these sometimes worrying forecasts seem to have had little influence on the steering committees, or any effect on the overall programme which, in the absence of a rigid management structure, continued to drift without any ultimate control.

As described previously, it took more than three years to proceed from the release of the basic OR.343 requirement to the stage where the Government effectively gave approval to build TSR2. This long period, during which BAC was obliged to continue design and development with little support, was dogged elsewhere by endless debate over the project's aims and likely costs.

When the Operational Requirement had first been changed to OR.343, the Treasury was immediately suspicious that the requirement had somehow changed to "…the extent of demanding a whole new weapon system", although the main aim of the new OR was to simply build a more precise requirement around the aircraft now that both the RAF and the manufacturer were entirely certain of what the new weapons system would be expected to do. The original OR.339 by comparison was more of an exploratory document which was designed partially to establish what could be achieved, rather than what would actually be required. But OR.343 was undoubtedly a far more ambitious proposition and by the end of 1959 it had aroused a great deal of concern over its likely cost. Chief of the Air Staff (MRAF Sir Dermot Boyle) was advised that development costs were likely to reach £80 million which was roughly twice the estimate which had been made back in 1958. By the beginning of 1960 the Ministries of Transport, Civil Aviation and Supply had been replaced by the Ministry of Aviation which drew up a submission for the Research and Development Board, asking for acceptance of the TSR2's development programme at an estimated cost of £62 million up to CA Release (the point at which the aircraft would be officially approved for use). The R&D Board approved a request which would be made to the Treasury, the estimated cost being subject to an additional amount which might be as much as £25 million. The Treasury was naturally alarmed by the request and immediately asked the Ministry of Defence (on 16 December) to reconsider the entire project, including (once again) the much discussed possibility of buying the NA.39 (Buccaneer). In the meantime only limited support would be given to enable the project to continue.

The MoD did indeed reconsider, and it informed the Treasury that the case for excluding NA.39 had already been made as clearly as possible but accepted that the effort required to develop TSR2's weapon system had been "far greater than was originally expected", adding that the already delayed programme would require a "very concentrated" effort if it was to enter RAF service by the end of 1965.

In response, the Treasury expressed great concern at the "enormous increase" in developmental costs, adding that if the latest estimates had been presented to Ministers a year before, it would seem "…not impossible that the question of meeting the RAF requirement with a version of the NA.39 would have been more strongly pressed." This was probably something of an understatement, since had the potential cost of TSR2 been known from the outset, it seems inevitable that the Buccaneer would have been chosen, despite the Air Ministry's objections. When the Minister of Defence (now Harold Watkinson) attended an Air Staff presentation on TSR2 in March 1960, he informed the Chiefs of Staff that he was not yet convinced of the need for further development of TSR2 because of its projected cost. Not surprisingly the Treasury used this lack of commitment in support of its reluctance to release further

funding, advising the MoA that it was difficult to give unqualified approval for a "contract of this size" when the MoD was not willing to go forward with it. The Chiefs of Staff duly re-examined the whole project in order to give the Minister of Defence a clear appraisal of the situation and submitted a report in May 1960 entitled 'Aircraft Requirements for Tactical Strike, Reconnaissance and Offensive Army Support.'

The Minister of Defence announced that he would give the paper the "earliest possible consideration" but only after he had returned from a trip to the USA where he hoped to secure American interest in the aircraft (the resulting US interest never translated into any serious prospect of an export order and probably only served to encourage the production of the Americans' own design in the shape of the F-111). But at the same time Watkinson complicated matters still further by sending a minute to the Chief of the Defence Staff in which he commented that he was "attracted to the idea" of giving TSR2 "an increased strategic capacity by fitting it with some kind of missile" in order that "a very high cost aircraft like this" could be given "all the capacity that we can."

Watkinson's motives were probably based on a perceived 'value for money' approach, and providing TSR2 with an even greater capability probably seemed like a sensible idea. But of course the notion of developing what had been created as a purely tactical aircraft into a strategic bomber would inevitably incur yet more research, more development, more delays and of course yet more expense – and would also serve to create even more confusion within the Government (and beyond) as to what the TSR2's true purpose actually was.

Excellent colour image of XR219 nearing completion at Weybridge, pictured in undercoat primer yellow, prior to being painted-up in her familiar glossy white scheme. The main landing gear is positioned in a semi-retracted position in order to maintain the aircraft's lower access height. The rear portions of XR219's fuselage, plus the tail and wings were supplied by English Electric in an unpainted condition. Subsequent components for pre-production and production machines were delivered fully painted. *BAC*

Other developments during 1960 ensured that Watkinson's seemingly spontaneous remarks became part of a wider picture. Early in the year the Government had finally decided to abandon Britain's ambitious and hugely expensive Blue Streak ICBM (Inter Continental Ballistic Missile) programme after having concluded that it showed every sign of becoming obsolete before it had even been completed. The concept of relying on fixed launch sites for missiles which required 15 minutes of refuelling prior to launch (when only a four-minute warning of enemy attack might be given) suggested that Blue Streak's value as a credible deterrent was debatable, and when combined with an ever-increasing cost, the Government finally accepted that the project was unsustainable. As an alternative, interest shifted to the USA where the Douglas Skybolt Air-Launched Ballistic Missile (ALBM) was being developed for use by the USAF. Prime Minister Macmillan secured President Eisenhower's approval for a British purchase of the missile system, minus warheads, which would be of British design. When successfully developed, the system was to be adopted for the RAF's Vulcan-equipped strategic bomber fleet, two missiles to be carried by each aircraft, operating from dispersed sites around the country. This would provide Britain which a much more flexible (and therefore more credible) deterrent, at a much lower cost. In view of Defence Minister Watkinson's comments regarding TSR2's potential as a strategic bomber, it is not surprising that the possibility of arming TSR2 with Skybolt was also immediately considered. However, by 1960 the basic design of the TSR2's airframe had been firmly established, and it quickly became clear during preliminary studies that neither it, nor a development of the Blue Steel missile (designed by Avro for the Vulcan and Victor) could be successfully carried by TSR2, chiefly because of the missile's size which would have required major modifications to TSR2's airframe structure and layout.

By the middle of 1960 the Air Ministry had accepted that "neither Skybolt nor Blue Steel could be made compatible with this aircraft." Eventually, a surprisingly wide variety of other weapons studies were considered for the TSR2, some ambitious, some more practical, but with costs of the core TSR2 programme already drifting inexorably upwards, there was little appetite to embark upon an additional programme which would create its own costs and complexities.

All of the proposals were ultimately dismissed in favour of a relatively simple 450 kiloton free-fall bomb (in effect, simply a more powerful version of the Red Beard tactical bomb which the aircraft had first been designed to carry), but the events of 1960 illustrated that while the Government was carefully (almost painstakingly) considering the perceived value of TSR2 as a future tactical strike aircraft, plans were also clearly being made to operate TSR2 as a strategic bomber too.

Sadly, the Skybolt programme eventually followed Blue Streak into oblivion. Development of the missile in the US had not proceeded smoothly and with the arrival of the submarine-launched Polaris system, the US Government was increasingly inclined towards cancellation of the project, not least because the successful Polaris system provided the US with an almost undetectable worldwide missile launch system which could remain on station for weeks. This compared to the air-launched Skybolt which could operate only for a matter of hours, attached to aircraft which would always be vulnerable to attack. A combination of development problems and the very obvious flexibility of Polaris was enough to convince the Department of Defense that Skybolt was unnecessary. When Defense Secretary Robert McNamara finally informed the British Government of his intention to abandon Skybolt, it was suddenly faced with a very difficult situation. Having effectively pinned the nation's hopes on Skybolt, there was now no credible nuclear deterrent with which to arm the UK through the mid-1960s and beyond and a major political furore immediately ensued, Liberal Leader Jo Grimond exclaiming: "Does not this mark the absolute failure of the policy of the Independent Deterrent? Is it not the case that everybody else in the world knew this, except the Conservative Party in this country?"

Indeed, the Conservatives were saddled with a seemingly desperate situation and Macmillan immediately arranged to have an emergency meeting with President Kennedy in order to find some sort of solution to this urgent and deeply serious problem. Meeting at Nassau in the Bahamas on 18 December 1962, little progress was made on the subject of Skybolt until late in the evening when Macmillan and Kennedy had face-to-face talks away from their team of advisors. Although Kennedy fully understood Britain's position, he was also aware of McNamara's opposition to Britain's nuclear independence. McNamara had been clear about this, commenting that "… limited nuclear capabilities, operating independently, are dangerous, expensive, prone to obsolescence and lacking in credibility as a deterrent" and that "…relatively weak national nuclear forces with enemy cities as their targets are not likely to perform even the function of deterrence."

Venerable statesman Dean Acheson was even more direct, stating, "Great Britain has lost an empire and has not yet found a role. The attempt to play a separate power role – that is, a role apart from Europe, a role based on a 'special relationship' with the United States is about played out."

Not surprisingly, Macmillan's view was very different. Convinced of the need for an independent nuclear deterrent, Britain would be left naked without a credible weapons system; but with party politics also in mind, he clearly needed to find a route out of the embarrassing corner into which the Conservative Government had manoeuvred itself, and Kennedy undoubtedly sympathised with Macmillan's predicament. After emphasising that Britain had no intention of ever abandoning its nuclear independence, Kennedy offered to transfer the now-defunct Skybolt project to Britain, where it could be completed in cooperation with Douglas, the system's manufacturer. The idea was certainly practical, but as an unproved system (although ironically, it was later demonstrated to be successful) it was a risk which the Government did not wish to take. The only other obvious option was for Kennedy to offer Britain Polaris, and this was undoubtedly the best outcome which Britain could have hoped for. Polaris would represent the most viable and cost-effective means of maintaining the effectiveness of Britain's independent deterrent into the 1970s and it would be more effective (i.e. more credible) than either Blue Streak or Skybolt. The flaw in the proposal was that it would take some years to manufacture the launch submarines, develop and deliver

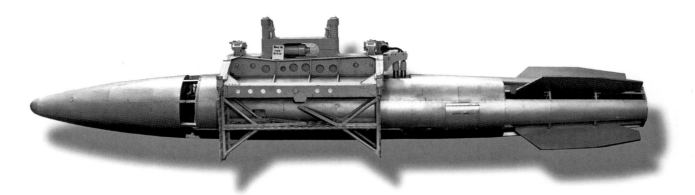

Above: Like the British WE.177B seen here, the American Mk.43 bomb was too large for two weapons to be accommodated internally in tandem, and the weapon was to have been carried on wing hard points, with just a single weapon being carried internally if required. Ultimately, the bomb might not have been accepted as a regular part of TSR2's arsenal, as American restrictions on its use would have prevented the weapon being available for dispersed operations – which were expected to be a key part of TSR2 strategy. *BAC*

Top: The American Mk.43 tactical "lay-down" nuclear bomb. This weapon was planned to have been supplied for TSR2 operations and because of its size (too big for dual carriage in the weapons bay), it would have been attached to the aircraft's inner wing pylons, although one weapon could also be carried internally. Under American control, the weapon would not have been suitable for the RAF's proposed dispersal operations, therefore it seems likely that the weapon would have only been assigned to part of the RAF's envisaged fleet, or possibly relinquished completely. *BAC*

Middle right: The American Mk.43 nuclear bomb shown attached to the inner wing pylon on a mock-up airframe at Weybridge. In addition to this weapon and the WE.177, conventional free-fall bombs would also have been compatible with the aircraft, together with other weapons as they emerged. The American Bullpup ASM and the French AS.30 were both considered, the latter missile eventually being preferred (having been adopted for use by the Canberra). However by May 1963 the Air Staff opted to drop AS.30 in favour of a new ASM being developed in co-operation with France. This became Martel and it is this ASM which would have been purchased for TSR2 had the project continued. *BAC*

Right: Trial installation of a dummy Mk.43 bomb in the TSR2 mock-up bomb bay at Weybridge.

Mock-up installation of the twin WE.177B weapons in TSR2's bay. As can be seen, the bombs were an extremely tight fit, necessitating the modification of the weapons bay doors.

Trial installation of two WE.177A bombs in the TSR2 weapons bay mock-up at Weybridge. The aircraft's inner wing pylons could also carry the same weapon, giving the aircraft the capability to carry four of these bombs in total. *BAC*

the missiles and produce new British warheads, before bringing the system into service. Until that date, Britain's deterrent would be increasingly vulnerable, relying on high-altitude bombers armed with free-fall bombs and a relatively small number of unreliable stand-off missiles.

Despite having secured what was undoubtedly a 'good deal' with America, Whitehall still buzzed with discontent which almost verged on panic at times and in order to create weapons which could serve as a credible nuclear deterrent until Polaris came into service, two options were pursued. The first was to switch the V-Force to low-level operations in order to render the aircraft less vulnerable to Soviet defences, and the switch from conventional high-level delivery techniques began to be introduced on Vulcan and Victor squadrons just a few weeks after the Nassau conference.

The second option would be to embrace the TSR2 weapons system as a stopgap. As the concept of using TSR2 in a strategic role had already been raised as a possibility, it had spawned a variety of weapons fit proposals, all of which had emerged around 1960, demonstrating that the aircraft could successfully undertake this role. Amongst these weapons proposals was one submitted by Avro to create a scaled-down version of the V-Force's Blue Steel missile, and an equally-promising system called Blue Water, a BAC (Vickers) development of an existing Surface-to-Air missile (SAM) system which showed great potential. These (plus many others) had never proceeded beyond the concept stage as there had been insufficient Ministry support for what would have effectively been little more than an 'insurance policy' against the possible failure of Skybolt. But now that Skybolt had been abandoned, the possibilities of developing TSR2's capabilities still further became a serious and urgent issue. As had happened three years previously, a number of ambitious proposals emerged, including a re-submission of the Blue Water missile. In March 1963 the Royal Aircraft Establishment (RAE) issued a report which examined all of the possible weapons proposals, entitled 'Stop-Gap Deterrent Weapons.' After addressing the options for the Vulcan and Victor (which mostly concerned the Yellow Sun free-fall bomb and the Blue Steel missile), the report turned to TSR2 and despite acknowledging the value of the various proposed missile systems (particularly Blue Water), the cheapest and fastest solution to the requirement was identified as being a free fall bomb which TSR2 could deliver at high speed and low level.

If TSR2 was operated from dispersed sites (in line with existing V-Force policy) it was believed that the aircraft actually posed a more credible strategic deterrent than the main Vulcan and Victor fleet, as it had the ability to penetrate enemy defences more successfully than the slower, larger, heavier (and less agile) V-Bombers. Significantly, a bomb was already under development as a long-term replacement for the unreliable and complex Red Beard weapon around which TSR2 had originally been designed. This joint Naval/Air Staff project was described under Operational requirement No.1177 for 'An Improved Kiloton Bomb':

'Since the Joint Staff requirement for Red Beard was drawn up in 1953, technical advances have made possible the development of a bomb which will far more closely meet the requirements of the Air Staff for a tactical nuclear weapon.

Movie image capturing a WE.177 test specimen during drop trials. The parachute retardation system would have been vital for the proposed lay-down delivery technique for which the weapon was devised, enabling the crew to escape the target area to a safe distance before detonation. However, a variety of delivery techniques would have been available to the crew, many of which employed the LABS (Low Altitude Bombing System) technique which effectively threw the bomb towards the target, requiring precise and reliable navigation and release information from the aircraft's computer system. *A&AEE*

Warhead design improvements now permit the use of a far smaller and lighter warhead in packaged form which will give yields of the order required for the destruction of hard targets (such as bridges, passes, defiles, etc.) In addition this warhead will be much safer, more robust and have fewer climatic restrictions than existing designs. To take advantage of these improvements in warhead design it is necessary to develop a new carcase in which to fit it. This carcase must also match the advances in aircraft performances and the developments in unorthodox delivery techniques that have taken place. This requirement supersedes that stated in draft OR.1127 for a Mk.2 version of Red Beard, which can now be regarded as cancelled.'

Using this as the basis for a new 'stopgap' weapon, the OR was re-drafted: 'Because of envisaged enemy counter-measures and the need to change aircraft approach and delivery tactics, the existing British nuclear bombs Yellow Sun, Blue Steel and Red Beard will be unsuitable as primary weapons beyond 1975. Moreover, with the cancellation of Skybolt as the planned replacement for Yellow Sun and the introduction of Polaris unlikely to become fully effective before 1970, an urgent need exists for a new bomb to maintain the United Kingdom independent deterrent during the interim period and as supplementary capability thereafter. By 1966 the manned bomber may survive enemy defences in the European theatre and deliver a successful strike only by flying at high speed at very low level. Yellow Sun and Blue Steel are designed for release at medium/high altitude where the delivery aircraft and/or bomb is vulnerable to interception, whilst Red Beard cannot stand the low-level flight environment, is limited in method of fusing and delivery, and possesses some undesirable safety restrictions when held at readiness in an operational state. Early replacement is essential. The replacement bomb must be multi-purpose by design. It must satisfy joint Naval and Air Staff requirements for carriage and delivery in current medium bomber aircraft and planned high-performance aircraft, to exploit fully their low-level strike capability against strategic and tactical, hard and soft targets… with corresponding different warhead yields. Research and development studies show clearly that such a bomb can be produced fully within the timescale. However, to maintain an effective United Kingdom nuclear deterrent during development of the Polaris weapon system, priority is to be given to production of the high-yield version for the RAF medium bomber force.'

This draft of the Operational Requirement effectively outlined what would have been TSR2's primary weapon load had the programme survived. The high-yield free fall bomb designed to OR.1177 translated into the WE.177B which was contracted to Hunting Engineering for development and production, while the (thermonuclear) warhead was developed by the Atomic Weapons Research Establishment (AWRE) at Aldermaston. It was stipulated that the Type B version should be ready for service entry in June 1966 and ultimately the weapon's destructive power was set at 450 kilotons – somewhat modest when compared to Yellow Snow, but sufficient to give TSR2 an ability to strike hard at strategic targets. Bearing in mind that the American atomic weapons dropped on Japan produced yields of between 15 and 20 kilotons, the TSR2 armed with WE.177B would, by any standards, be a serious deterrent. The Government's priority was now to develop and deploy WE.177B as rapidly as possible, so that it could be used to supplement the Vulcan's and Victor's free fall bombs and stand-off weapons, and to give TSR2 sufficient strike power to represent a credible nuclear deterrent until Polaris entered service. This meant that the original plan to create a smaller tactical bomb (to replace Red Beard) would have to be put on hold even though this was effectively the key weapon that TSR2 had first been created to deliver. Development of this weapon (WE.177A) continued at a slower pace however, and it was envisaged that it would eventually be supplied with different yield options (50kt, 100kt, 200kt and 300kt) which would enable the RAF to deliver a bomb appropriate to the size of the anticipated tactical target. Eventually, WE.177A did enter RAF service, equipping Vulcan, Jaguar, Buccaneer and Tornado squadrons during the 1970s, with the final operational examples being withdrawn in 1998. For TSR2 however, WE.177B created yet more difficulties which delayed the aircraft's progress during the design process still further.

Having designed the basic structure of TSR2 around the established size of Red Beard, it was anticipated that any subsequent weapon developments would be no larger. Both WE.177A and WE.177B could easily be accommodated in the TSR2's weapons bay, as Red Beard's 28-inch diameter was significantly greater than the estimated 16.5ins of the new bomb. However, during 1962, a Government decision was made to limit the size of all types of British tactical weapons to a yield of no more than 10kt. The reasons behind this policy decision remain unclear (much of the supporting documentation is still classified as secret), but the immediate result of this development was that the RAF was no longer able to confidently assure destruction of all the types of tactical targets which might be encountered by TSR2.

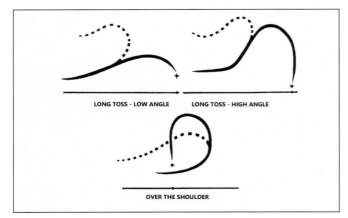

LONG TOSS - LOW ANGLE   LONG TOSS - HIGH ANGLE

OVER THE SHOULDER

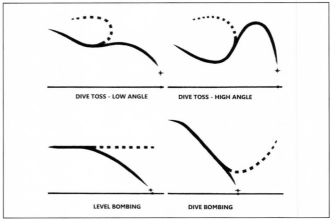

DIVE TOSS - LOW ANGLE   DIVE TOSS - HIGH ANGLE

LEVEL BOMBING   DIVE BOMBING

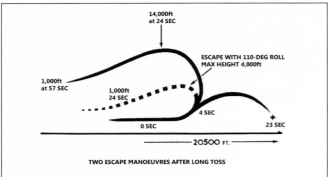

14,000ft
at 24 SEC

ESCAPE WITH 110-DEG ROLL
MAX HEIGHT 4,000ft

1,000ft
at 57 SEC

1,000ft
24 SEC

4 SEC

0 SEC   23 SEC

20500 FT.

TWO ESCAPE MANOEUVRES AFTER LONG TOSS

Fundamental to TSR2's role was the capacity to deliver nuclear weapons. Key to this role was the need to avoid undue exposure to enemy defences over the target, combined with an ability to successfully escape from the detonation area as swiftly as possible. Trajectory information for the aircraft's bombs and targets would be held in the CCS (Central Computing System) and a variety of delivery modes could be employed, as illustrated here. The LABS (Low Altitude Bombing System) means of "toss bombing" (ie- throwing the bomb towards the target) generally required a 4g pull-up, with the weapon being automatically released at the required point, based on the computer's data. High and low angle releases could be employed, one of the most accurate delivery techniques being a "button hook" manoeuvre whereby the aircraft flew past the target (using it as a final accurate fix point), before turning back to release the bomb. The most accurate delivery technique of all was to release the bomb "over the shoulder" although the aircraft would be particularly vulnerable to enemy defences as a result. Alternatively, a simple lay-down delivery could be employed, flying over the target at low level, relying on parachute retardation and/or delayed detonation to allow the aircraft to escape the area.

In order to overcome this limitation at least partially, it was proposed that two WE.177As could be carried in tandem and this arrangement was subsequently incorporated into the aircraft design process. But having established that two bombs could be carried, it seemed logical that TSR2's strategic strike capability could also be enhanced by the carriage of two WE.177Bs. Unfortunately, the 'B' model, being of thermonuclear design, was substantially longer than the tactical 'A' model, and a tandem arrangement proved impossible. Without major structural changes to TSR2's design, a far simpler solution presented itself to the BAC design team, and by modifying the design of the weapons bay doors, recesses could be incorporated into the door's inner faces which would enable two WE.177Bs to be carried abreast, their tail fins fitting neatly into the door recesses. As an additional bonus, the remaining space to the rear of the weapons bay could accommodate a fuel tank which would provide TSR2 with additional fuel to extend its strategic capabilities still further.

However, in order to retain a flexible tactical strike ability, the Air Staff investigated ways in which the 10kt limitation could be overcome, and eventually it was proposed that in addition to the carriage of two WE.177As in the weapons bay, another weapon could also be carried under each wing, giving TSR2 an equivalent combined destructive power of 40kt if the bombs could all be delivered simultaneously.

Naturally, it was accepted that repeated bombing of the same target would be an impractical and probably suicidal proposition for the TSR2's crew, but it was also understood that a simultaneous drop of four weapons would adversely affect the detonation mechanisms of the nuclear devices in each bomb, therefore the most suitable method of release would be to enable all four weapons to be dropped in delayed

succession as a 'stick' which would create the same effect as a single 40kt bomb. This procedure was eventually accepted as the preferred solution. The WE.177A/B became an integral part of the TSR2's design process long before the aircraft reached the test-flight phase and had the aircraft entered RAF service, it would have been TSR2's primary in-service weapon.

Although TSR2 had been created around the carriage of a completely different bomb (albeit one which had been created to fulfil the same role), the subsequent creation of a more powerful and sophisticated bomb had only a minor effect on the final configuration of TSR2's design structure, thanks largely to the smaller dimensions of the later weapon. However WE.177 did have a more profound effect on the TSR2 programme in that it enabled the aircraft to be developed along two very different paths. Accordingly, while ingenious delivery methods conspired to enable TSR2 to retain an impressive tactical capability with low-yield atomic bombs, the aircraft was concurrently developed as a strategic bomber armed with two high-yield thermonuclear weapons. After years of confusion, cancellations and policy changes, the immediate future of Britain's nuclear posture appeared to finally be settled, and TSR2 would be at the centre of it. Created as a tactical strike aircraft to replace the Canberra, the aircraft had now become a pseudo-strategic bomber which would ultimately replace the Vulcan. But just around the political corner waited a new Government which would regard TSR2 as having little or no value as a nuclear bomber at all.

CHAPTER FIVE

Antipodean Antipathy

DESPITE the obvious opposition of both the British Government and (eventually) the Air Staff, the TSR2 programme might well have survived had an export order been secured for the aircraft. One of the key reasons why TSR2 became an unsustainably expensive aircraft was because the relative cost (per airframe) could not be spread through a large production order in the way that most modern military aircraft

Pictured in a gentle climb, TSR2 was not only phenomenally fast, it was also surprisingly agile. The Canberra had astonished observers with its outstanding speed and manoeuvrability and TSR2 – the Canberra's replacement – took this leap in capability still further, combining high level sustained supersonic speed with ultra low-level automatic terrain following, and extremely short take-off and landing performance, all from a heavy nuclear strike aircraft with strategic capabilities. Beamont even rolled the aircraft on at least one occasion and the test pilots reported that the aircraft handled like a heavy Lightning. *BAC*

programmes inevitably are. Indeed, it has been suggested that even when the aircraft was first proposed, the projected orders for the RAF were set at an artificially high figure not in response to the Air Staff's actual needs, but in order to spread the cost of production as much as possible, thereby lowering the cost. Given that TSR2 was an all-British aircraft primarily suited to purchase by only its country of origin, the aircraft was doomed to suffer from a disproportionately high cost right from the start. There was however some confidence (or at least a fervent hope) within Government and industry circles that the aircraft might be exported to other countries and in pursuit of this possibility, BAC did offer the aircraft to a surprisingly long list of potential customers as the project slowly developed, issuing brochures to a number of countries for their consideration. But it seems fair

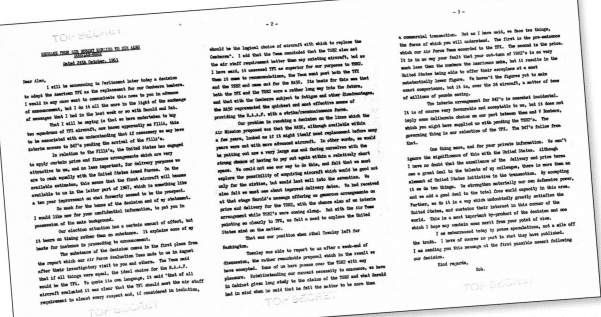

Copy of the letter sent from Australia's Prime Minister, Sir Robert Menzies to his British counterpart, explaining his decision to purchase F-111 in preference to TSR2.
Courtesy Ken Billingham

Australian Prime Minister Sir Robert Menzies meets with US Secretary of Defense Robert McNamara at the Pentagon in June 1964.

to assume that most of these sales attempts were either less than serious or naively optimistic; TSR2 was of course a very complex and capable aircraft, designed for a specific role which was vital to Britain's defence policy, but rather less vital to most other countries aside than the USA where, of course, efforts were being made to produce their own aircraft in the shape of TFX (which became the F-111).

Ultimately, if it can be argued that TSR2 was over-specified and over-priced for Britain, it was unquestionably so for almost any other country, and eventually only one export order was seriously pursued, this being to Australia, where – uniquely – TSR2 promised to be an ideal purchase for that country's requirements. Like the RAF, the Royal Australian Air Force was an operator of the Canberra and as Australia approached the 1960s it became clear that the relatively slow and unsophisticated Canberra would not be suitable for the RAAF's needs for very long. In any case, by the 1970s, if not sooner, the aircraft would be worn out. With South East Asia and Indonesia firmly in mind, Australia required a new, non-nuclear strategic deterrent, and by 1960 the Australian Government already had TSR2 firmly in its sights.

BAC first presented the project to Australia in 1959, continuing to provide additional technical representations to the country as the project progressed. Australia was certainly enthusiastic, although the country's ability to allocate huge funds to defence spending was even more limited than Britain's. Having already embarked upon a major re-equipment programme with new French-built Mirage fighters, the prospect of funding another very expensive weapons system was a major issue. When further orders of Mirages were proposed in 1963, the RAAF Chief of the Air Staff (Sir Valston Hancock) actively opposed the idea, not because he did not see any requirement for more Mirages, but on the grounds that this would preclude the possibility of finding enough money to replace the Canberra.

Despite his position, more Mirages were eventually ordered and this was undoubtedly a reflection of the Government's desire for defensive rather than offensive strength, given that its primary concern at the time was the threat of air attack from Indonesia. When Opposition Leader, Arthur Calwell, claimed (presumably with his tongue firmly in his cheek) that Indonesia could effectively destroy any Australian city almost at will even if it provided 24 hours' notice, it was clear that the Australian Government was in an embarrassing situation. The Mirage order was a partial solution, but accusations of inadequate defences continued, led by the influential Sydney Morning Herald newspaper, which pursued the notion that not only was Australia's defensive posture inadequate, but that the country suffered from a very obvious lack of offensive power too. The combination of Government Opposition, and media pressure, was sufficient to persuade the Australian Cabinet to send an RAAF evaluation team overseas during 1963 to look at potential candidates for its emerging 'Air Staff Requirement 36' for a new all-weather strike and reconnaissance aircraft. TSR2 was undoubtedly at the top of the shopping list, although the team also investigated the F-4C Phantom, Mirage IV, the RA-5C Vigilante and, of course, the emerging TFX project. Unfortunately, Australia's appraisal of TSR2 provoked more questions than answers. The aircraft was technically ideal for the RAAF's requirement, but there was initially some surprise when it was discovered that enthusiasm for the project came mostly from the manufacturer rather than the customer. Official support for TSR2 seemed to be lukewarm at best, when the Chief of the Defence Staff, Air Chief Marshal Scherger, met with Lord Mountbatten (Britain's Chief of the Defence Staff) in London. At the meeting (also with Chief Scientist Solly Zuckerman) Scherger was presented with what had become Mountbatten's almost traditional anti-TSR2 monologue, which mischievously implied that the aircraft would be ultimately abandoned and that the RAF would buy Buccaneers – something that Mountbatten fervently believed, but more in hope rather than expectation. Returning home from the meeting, Scherger commented that he found himself "…sceptical that the British chiefs of staff fully supported the project." Of course his conclusion was correct, and Mountbatten in particular had been keen to emphasise TSR2's huge cost (which was still increasing), and the advantages of a submarine-launched deterrent (i.e. Polaris) over an air-launched system. The precise nature and contents of this meeting were never recorded in full, but Mountbatten's biographer subsequently stated that Mountbatten "…pushed his campaign against the TSR2 to the limit of the scrupulous, some would say beyond it."

In retrospect, it is clear that Mountbatten's forceful views had a major influence on the RAAF's interest in TSR2 – probably far more than they should have done – but when Australia sent its RAAF team to the UK in order to evaluate the TSR2 programme, the British Government also failed to offer any overt support for TSR2, offering little more than a half convincing belief that the programme would go ahead. When Air Marshal Hancock (Chief of the Air Staff) met with BAC officials, George Edwards, in typically forthright matter, asked what, if anything, BAC could do to make TSR2 more attractive to the RAAF. Hancock immediately replied: "Get a production order for the RAF, because there's no way that the RAAF are likely to support this as the sole purchaser."

But by the time that the British Government placed the first tentative order for production aircraft in September 1963 (many weeks after the RAAF visit), it was too late to influence the RAAF any further although, somewhat ironically, this 'order' (which was ostensibly for materials rather than a straightforward order for the aircraft) embraced 30 aircraft, eight of which would actually have been for part of an anticipated Australian order. Had the Government ordered TSR2 for the RAF sooner, it seems likely that the RAAF's confidence in TSR2 would have been sufficient to recommend a purchase. However, in the absence of a firm commitment for the RAF's adoption of TSR2, it was Mountbatten's hostile views which prevailed and they ultimately soured the RAAF's interest in TSR2 to such an extent that its final report was shamelessly biased towards TFX and

misrepresented TSR2's projected performance and cost figures quite significantly in order to portray TFX as a preferable solution. An even more surprising outcome of the report was that although TFX had emerged as the preferable aircraft, purchase of the RA-5C Vigilante was actually recommended. Hancock subsequently explained that this decision had been made on the basis that the Vigilante already existed and could be brought into RAAF service more swiftly. Carefully avoiding any suggestion that the Vigilante would be merely an interim solution, he had recommended it in the belief that unless this aircraft was purchased and brought into service as soon as possible, the RAAF might ultimately be left without any strike aircraft at all. Concerned that Australia's political climate would conspire to preclude the purchase of any strike aircraft, and convinced that the RAF would ultimately fail to receive TSR2, the Vigilante seemed like the best option for the RAAF at the time. However, with the RAAF's recommendation in mind (but by no means the deciding factor) the Australian Government continued to debate the matter for some time, and TSR2 remained viable as a potential candidate even though the RAAF had clearly put its support behind TFX (regardless of its attempts to obtain Vigilante as an interim purchase).

But the Government's final choice was clearly an issue which went far beyond the specific requirements and preferences set out by the RAAF. The wider political situation was undoubtedly the main motivation behind the eventual purchase of TFX, even though it was dressed up by politicians as a decision based on cost. Australia's Minister of Defence, Athol Townley, enjoyed a close working relationship with his American counterpart, Robert McNamara, and as negotiations between the two progressed, TSR2 was slowly becoming a victim of international politics. While Britain was confidently expecting TSR2 to be purchased by Australia almost as a 'done deal', the Australian Government was developing a wider view which took into account the realities of the country's future.

Australia was aware of Britain's emerging inability to maintain a significant presence East of Suez, and despite being

The rear fuselage cowling, illustrating the hinged upper section in which the tail parachute was housed. Also visible is the structural facility for an arrestor hook attachment, although no plans for the introduction of such a system had been established by the time of the project's cancellation.

TSR2 was designed to be both tough and durable, much of this strength coming from the incorporation of milling techniques, as illustrated. Fashioning components from solid blocks of alloy ensured that the aircraft's structure was extremely robust, a similar technique having been employed on the Buccaneer which was being developed almost simultaneously by Blackburn. The aircraft's rugged construction should have ensured that the aircraft remained operational with RAF squadrons possibly into the new millennium. *BAC*

Busy scene at Weybridge, with the port forward fuselage sections of XR221 (foreground) and XR222 being assembled. *BAC*

a loyal member of the Commonwealth, it was becoming clear that Australia could not rely confidently upon Britain to maintain an influence in parts of the world that were of direct concern only to Australia. Although both countries maintained historical ties with each other, the practicalities of foreign policy issues and – even more importantly – defence and economic issues, meant that Australia would have to foster a much closer relationship with America rather than Britain. The eventual choice of TFX was clearly based on the political need to create closer ties with the US rather than any perceived technical merits of TSR2, as clearly illustrated by a note written by John Bunting, the Departmental Head of the Prime Minister's Office, which was given to Prime Minister Menzies, stating that the offer of the TFX "… seems to achieve what was the unexpressed core of the Cabinet's decision to send Mr. Townley to the United States, i.e., almost to get the Americans to tell us what we should have and thus link them to our defence."

This seemingly innocent statement says much more about the whole issue than any of the theories which have been postulated by commentators in subsequent years, most of which have accused the US of shamelessly 'pushing' TFX onto Australia almost at any cost, on the mistaken assumption that Defense Secretary McNamara was somehow determined to ensure that both Britain and Australia purchased TFX, thereby abandoning TSR2 as a direct result. In fact, McNamara strenuously denies any such accusations. The Australian Government however, did believe that McNamara wanted to kill off TSR2 if he could, and a paper prepared for Bunting's PM Department by Allan Griffith states that (at least in Griffith's view) McNamara did not support the notion of Britain maintaining an independent deterrent outside of NATO control and that (therefore) an Australian purchase of TSR2 would have "…perpetuated production of the TSR2 and made it more difficult for Britain to resist the temptation to relinquish

her national deterrent." The paper also mentioned that, based on this same theory, curtailment of the TSR2 programme would also discourage France from maintaining its own 'Force de Frappe'. Anyone with a good grasp of France's history would immediately see the naivety of Griffith's supposition, and it is fair to say that Australia's position was undoubtedly somewhat out of touch with the realities of the prevailing relationship between the US and Britain in much the same way that Britain's grasp of Australia's relationship with the USA was also rather out of date.

McNamara's stated position on the Australian purchase was that he held no hostility towards TSR2 at all, nor indeed the concept of Britain retaining nuclear independence (despite his previous statements which suggested an entirely contrary view), pointing out that Britain had been offered Polaris and even offered the opportunity to continue development of Skybolt when it was cancelled. Likewise, he insisted that his only motivation for facilitating the sale of TFX to Australia with such vigour was to redress what he perceived to be Australia's lack of credible defence against Indonesia. But regardless of McNamara's true motives, Australia was offered a deal which it could hardly refuse, being assured by the US Treasury and Defense Departments that the F-111 would be supplied to Australia under "whatever financial conditions she wanted". Given that Australia was already disposed towards almost any arrangement which enabled the country to ally itself with the US more closely, it is not surprising that Australia's interest in TSR2 evaporated.

The British Government, troubled by TSR2's increasing cost and with an almost grudging support of it, had been freely expressed on the assumption that Australia would inevitably buy TSR2 almost from the very start. After BAC first informed Australia of the project in 1959 it had been expected that in the absence of anything better, TSR2 would be the Australians'

The intake section of XR223 is pictured during assembly at Weybridge. Worthy of note are the apertures for the auxiliary intake doors which have yet to be fitted. These doors opened automatically to increase air flow into the engine when required at low speed. *BAC*

Below: Unusual rear view of an unidentified aircraft, showing the open parachute housing and the internal structure of the rear fuselage. BAC's confident assertions of the aircraft's suitability for short/unprepared field operations were at odds with the realities of the development and test programme. The extremely limited amount of internal space for the engines ensured that changing the power plants would have been a difficult and time-consuming process. The RAF wanted the aircraft to be capable of achieving an engine change (in field conditions) in three hours. The best that BAC could achieve (inside a fully equipped hangar) was 68 hours. This figure would no doubt have been reduced in time, but it was clear that the engine installation was wholly incompatible with the whole concept of field operations. *BAC*

An RAAF F-111C with its wings unswept, photographed whilst in the US in 2006 on a joint military excercise. *U.S. Air Force*

obvious choice, and when TFX first emerged it was not seen as a viable export competitor. Australia would surely stick with Britain, and given that TSR2 was already under development, a new 'paper design' was unlikely to be of any interest to anyone. But Britain clearly misunderstood the wider issues of Australia's international position until it was too late. No longer tied to Britain, unsure of Britain's future influence, and unconvinced that she could be guaranteed to come to Australia's defence if needed, Australia naturally looked towards the US. Adopting an American weapons system under terms which would effectively be dictated by the US, would ensure that Australia was seen to be aligning herself with the US as closely as possible. When the British Government eventually realised what was happening, it did finally increase its efforts to actually 'sell' TSR2, and some fairly intense political lobbying began. Most importantly, Australia's concerns over TSR2's projected delivery schedule were addressed, and BAC gave assurances that a full squadron of aircraft would be in service with the RAAF by the end of 1968, with the second squadron to follow a year later (a total of 24 aircraft in all). Until this date, BAC had proposed that Britain should base a fleet of Valiant bombers in Australia to act as stopgap strike aircraft until TSR2 came into service and the idea had some merit; the RAAF would immediately have a significant strike capability and Britain would have a British presence which would (at least in a moral sense) tie Australia to a purchase of TSR2.

Inexplicably, when BAC proposed the idea to the Ministry of Aviation it was informed that a request for V-Bombers would have to come directly from a formal request from Australia. Not surprisingly, no such request was ever made. The Ministry also refused BAC's proposal that some of TSR2's flight-testing (particularly terrain following and weapons evaluation) could be performed in Australia, believing that French Saharan ranges would be a cheaper alternative (and thereby ignoring the obvious advantage of securing closer relations with Australia). It took some six months to accept that setting up a trials unit at Woomera was in fact a preferable concept, and it was not until October 1963 that Secretary of State for Air Hugh Fraser and Air Minister Julian Amery visited Australia to formally discuss the concept of conducting trials there, as well as to fully discuss the short-term use of Valiants. But despite their efforts, they could not give the Australians the assurances that they required. The future of TSR2 was no more certain (and in many respects less certain) than it had been earlier in the year, and the question of operating Valiants in Australia was hopelessly fudged by the British Government's failure to enable the RAAF to operate the Valiants themselves; simply basing RAF assets in Australia was, as Prime Minister Menzies commented, significantly different to the concept of providing aircraft for the RAAF to operate itself. Finally, Macmillan offered to waive all development costs in order to bring down TSR2's purchase price, but it was too little and far too late. The seeds of doubt had been planted by Mountbatten, the atmosphere of indifference from the Government simply enforced this perception, and finally the US Government had offered

Australia a deal which represented far more than merely the purchase of a fleet of suitable aircraft. As discussions between Australia and the US took place in Washington, Minister of Defence Peter Thorneycroft offered to send a team to Australia to negotiate a final deal on TSR2 but the offer was never accepted. It was clear that the prospect of matching or even bettering the American terms was no longer of interest to Australia, and this very fact serves to illustrate that the sale of the F-111 to Australia could never be described as a simple example of American salesmanship triumphing over Britain. The truth of the story is that Australia wanted to buy American, almost to the exclusion of any other option, and although it is clear that the British Government could have done much more to secure an Australian order for TSR2 much sooner (and done considerably less to actively dissuade the RAAF in particular), by the time that Australia was ready to make a purchase there was no longer any real choice to be made. The RAAF did finally receive its fleet of F-111s in 1973, some six years later than planned, at a cost of $A344 million – almost twice the original estimate but still significantly less than the cost of an equivalent TSR2 purchase.

The Australian Government triumphantly portrayed the F-111 purchase as a 'good deal' which, despite cost increases and delays, it probably still was. But for Britain the purchase was an almost fatal blow for the TSR2 programme. In reality, it seems unlikely that Australia would have finally purchased the aircraft even if the Government had made a more credible effort to sell it. Australia would have only bought TSR2 if it had placed an order much earlier, before the availability and attractiveness of the TFX became obvious to them, and any such order would only have been likely had a similar order already been placed on behalf of the RAF. The fact that no such order had been made, along with Mountbatten's poisonous opposition to the aircraft, was enough to weaken Australia's interest until the point in time that its attention shifted elsewhere. With the loss of an Australian purchase, the slim prospects of selling TSR2 anywhere else beyond Britain's shores were even less likely than they had been at the outset of the project – and it was now clear that the entire burden of TSR2's development and production would have to be borne by the British taxpayer alone.

XR219 engaged in a noisy and smoky engine ground run at Boscombe Down. The aircraft's sooty exhausts became a familiar sight at the airfield's eastern boundary during 1964. Just visible are the opened auxiliary intake doors on the aircraft's port intake fairing. The small sensor attached to the forward fuselage was part of the aircraft's test flight equipment package (fitted in what would have been the aircraft's port camera bay) and would not have been incorporated into production aircraft. *BAC*

CHAPTER SIX

Airborne at Last

A S with so many aspects of the TSR2 programme, initial plans for the flight-testing phase were subject to significant debate, much of which was influenced by the unspoken 'political' climate which still affected relations between BAC's Preston and Weybridge divisions. When the first 'prototype' (not actually a prototype as such, but the first in a series of pre-production aircraft), XR219, neared completion at Weybridge, attention had turned towards the setting-up of the initial flight test programme, including, of course, the very first flight of the aircraft.

Although Vickers would have undoubtedly preferred that one of its own test pilots should fly the TSR2 (Brian Trubshaw was keen to take on the task), none of its team had any significant supersonic flight experience and so the only logical choice was

English Electric's hugely experienced Chief Test Pilot, Roland Beamont, who duly accepted the undertaking. The English Electric airfield at Warton was home to what was arguably the most advanced and comprehensively equipped flight-test centre in the country and the resident team had already investigated the necessary Ministry-approved test requirements for the TSR2's accelerate-stop performance. Warton (from where the Lightning had been operated without any difficulties) was therefore identified as the ideal location from where the TSR2 testing could take place. But Vickers remained set firmly against the notion of allowing a Surrey-borne prototype to be whisked northwards to Lancashire as soon as it had been completed.

Roly Beamont pictured climbing into the cockpit of XR219 at Boscombe Down, shortly before the aircraft's first flight.

A rare and historic colour image of XR219 at the very moment of lift-off on her maiden flight, in front of Boscombe Down's massive weighbridge hangar. The first flight was made almost as a political gesture, BAC being desperately keen to get the aircraft into the air as swiftly as possible, to show the Government, media and public that a functional warplane had finally been created from the long, expensive and controversial programme. But XR219's flight was undoubtedly premature, and with dangerously limited engines, malfunctioning undercarriage, and other unsatisfactory systems, the first flight was very much a "one-off" event. *BAC*

No firm decision was made until it became clear that there would soon be insufficient time in which to set up a flight development and support team without affecting the aircraft's projected first flight schedule. It was at this stage that Weybridge claimed that its airfield at nearby Wisley would be selected as the flight-test base, having been used for many other Vickers projects including the Valiant and VC10. When Beamont heard of this proposal, he immediately met with George Edwards in order to argue against the use of Wisley, where only a relatively modest 2,200-yard runway was available.

Much to Beamont's disappointment, Edwards confirmed that as the prototype had been built at Weybridge, it followed that Vickers should also be responsible for flight-testing even though Beamont would lead the team. But even more surprising was Edwards' view that as it would require considerable effort (and expense) to tow XR219 over to Wisley, the first flight should be made directly from Weybridge, from the adjacent airfield at Brooklands, where the runway was roughly half the length of Wisley's.

Edwards had evidently made this decision on the basis that Jock Bryce had successfully flown the prototype VC10 airliner out of Brooklands recently, and he had concluded that as the TSR2 was much smaller and designed with a short take-off capability, it could also get airborne safely from the small runway there. However, Beamont pointed out that with no passengers and a light fuel load, the VC10 had enjoyed roughly half the wing loading of the TSR2, and XR219 would only be fitted with development-standard de-rated engines. Likewise, the Ministry requirements for a test flight would include the question of brake failure or tail parachute malfunction and the necessary 'V-Stop' distance needed (V-Stop being the speed at which, should an engine fail, the pilot can elect to either take off or stop the aircraft on the runway).

In the case of the VC10 flight there had been effectively no V-Stop speed (Bryce was committed to take-off almost from the moment of brake release) and English Electric at Warton had calculated that if the TSR2's tail parachute failed (and the wheel brakes overheated), it would easily over-run at Wisley and cross the Portsmouth road which passes the airfield perimeter. Edwards took note of Beaumont's position and replied that the only solution would be to transport XR219 to Boscombe Down where a huge runway was available, but that this would incur yet more delays and costs. Beamont naturally pressed his argument that the aircraft should go to Warton, not only because of the very adequate runway and test facilities (and his own familiarity with the base) but also because it was becoming increasingly clear that Warton would ultimately have to take on the later stages of flight-testing in any case. Edwards remained unmoved and refused to argue the point any longer: XR219 would go to Boscombe Down.

During the spring of 1964 the first aircraft was duly completed at Weybridge, partially dismantled, and transported on flatbed trucks to Boscombe Down in April, where it was re-assembled over the following three months in a hangar which was handed over to BAC for the duration of the initial test programme. A few months previously however, the whole programme had suffered a worrying setback which threatened to jeopardise progress. Development of the TSR2's engines had been progressing steadily, and flight-testing of the engine had begun in 1962 when Vulcan B1 XA894 embarked on a series of 35 flights with a development Olympus 22R housed in a streamlined pod slung under the aircraft's bomb bay. Much of the test-flying progressed smoothly and the engine performed satisfactorily, the Vulcan often flying with its four Olympus 101s throttled back to idle (in order to power the electrics and hydraulics), while the 22R effectively powered the aircraft. Such was Bristol's confidence in the engine that the Vulcan even appeared at the 1962 SBAC show and performed a spirited display over Farnborough on each day of the event. Eventually the reheat system was tested through its first two stages, and finally the third stage reheat was introduced, with Beamont flying in the Vulcan on one sortie to assess the engine's characteristics and throttle handling. But on 3 February 1964 the engine programme came to a sudden and alarming halt. XA894 was positioned on a water-cooled engine detuner at Filton for a ground run and when the third stage reheat was selected on the 22R, a sudden, shattering bang saw the Vulcan rock forwards with a discernable shudder and the aircraft was instantly engulfed in flames. The crew swiftly abandoned the aircraft (in less than a minute) and the Vulcan was rapidly consumed by a huge fire which ultimately destroyed the entire aircraft apart from a small portion of the port wing. Investigations quickly revealed that the engine's low-pressure drive shaft had failed, and the associated turbine had spun free, breaking away from the engine casing like a huge (and deadly) circular saw. Shooting upwards into the Vulcan's bomb bay, the turbine disk then ricocheted downwards, bounced off the concrete floor and careered straight through the aircraft's port wing leading edge, before bouncing away across the hard standing and coming to rest just a few feet from Bristol's gleaming 188 prototype research aircraft.

The cause of the catastrophic failure remained a mystery for some time. A replacement test-bed aircraft was quickly identified so that flight-testing could resume, but it was decided that as conversion of another Vulcan would take at least another two years, the TSR2 would have to be flying by this stage. Therefore the time and cost involved dictated that further testing would be better confined to bench runs in the new 'environmental chamber' at the National Gas Turbine Establishment. Having quoted some £20 million for the engine's research programme (almost twice the figure estimated by the Ministry of Supply), Bristol-Siddeley were obliged to make a thorough reappraisal of both the engine and the development schedule. Although the reasons for the low-pressure shaft's failure remained unclear, the shaft's thickness was doubled (by shrinking a metal sleeve over it) and this was assumed to have cured the problem. But early in 1964 another engine (being tested at Bristol's Patchway base) suffered an almost identical failure, although on this occasion the turbine was held within the engine casing and it was the high-pressure disk which broke free and caused a huge amount of damage within the engine test cell.

A third failure then occurred followed by a fourth in July, just a few weeks before the prototype TSR2, XR219, was due to make its first flight. Resonance was thought to be the fundamental cause of the failures as well as weaknesses in the reheat system and the engine-to-jet-pipe joints. The prospect of an engine failure taking place within the TSR2 airframe was almost too unpleasant to contemplate: not only would the crew be placed in great peril (although they would have their 'zero-zero' ejection seats with which to execute a swift escape), the aircraft would be destroyed (the turbine disks would cut straight through the aircraft's fuselage fuel tanks) and the whole TSR2 programme would almost certainly be cancelled as a consequence.

Beamont's gloomy mood was illustrated by a note he submitted to the TSR2 management Committee on 29 July: 'Last week's event at Patchway, namely the latest catastrophic failure, brings into sharp focus the question of whether an engine standard has yet been achieved which can honestly be regarded as fit for flight. The time has come when it is no longer profitable to go along with the idea that a standard of engine suitable for dependence on in the critical exploratory flying is just around the corner and likely to be reached after a few more days of successful bench testing.' In fact the true cause of the engine problems was identified just a few days later, but by this stage the engines installed in XR219 could not be modified without causing a significant delay to the anticipated first flight date. Resonance was, indeed, the root cause of the shaft fracture and modifications to the cooling airflow over the shaft bearings would provide a solution. But XR219 would have to fly with unmodified engines if it was to fly soon, and with a growing political storm surrounding the aircraft, BAC had no appetite for delaying the first flight unless it was absolutely necessary. XR219 needed to fly – and fly soon – if it was to demonstrate that the long and monstrously expensive TSR2 programme had actually produced a tangible result.

Finally, a meeting was held at Boscombe Down between Beamont; the Controller of Aircraft, Morien Morgan; Dr. Hooker, Bristol-Siddeley's Technical Director, and various Air Marshals from the respective ministries. The engine's failure record was examined, the proposed modifications discussed, and the condition of XR219's engines explored. It was estimated that they both had around 25 hours of cleared flight time available, but there could be no guarantee that failure would not occur if they were used at full power. Hooker believed that even with these early de-rated engines, the aircraft would have a more than adequate reserve of power and if they were restricted to 97% rpm the risk of failure would be greatly reduced.

However this posed a risk for Beamont as XR219 had not yet been cleared to fly with the landing gear retracted, and a safe climb-away speed in the event of a single engine failure was vital. BAC's team calculated that with the gear down, 100% reheated power would be required from brakes-off to 1,000ft in order to ensure a safe climb should one engine fail during this period, and so Beamont was presented with a difficult situation which he had actually foreseen before the meeting had even started. The meeting had effectively concluded that no further progress could be made until the engine difficulties had been resolved, but with a surprising display of pragmatism, Morien Morgan asked "What does the pilot think?"

Beamont's response was to reiterate that although most aspects of the aircraft's status were now acceptable, it was clearly only the engine difficulties that were effectively preventing XR219 from flying. Modified engines were not yet available and in order to expedite progress, he would accept the risks associated with operating the engines at 100% power for approximately two minutes as a one-off effort to take XR219 into the air as soon as possible, and review the situation again after the first flight.

Beautiful image of XR219 at the very moment of the aircraft's very first take-off from Boscombe Down. Taken with a wide angle lens close to the runway (hence the oddly-shaped outline of the buildings in the background)) the aircraft's proportions are slightly distorted, but graphically illustrate the clean, flowing lines of the fuselage (designed for sustained supersonic flight) combined with the bulky and ungainly undercarriage, designed for STOL operations. *BAC*

It was agreed therefore that one flight would be performed but that no further flying would take place until the engines had been modified or replaced. With a planned first flight firmly fixed, ground runs of the engines and aircraft systems were completed and a series of taxi trials was initiated on 2 September. At this stage the engines had still not been given full flight clearance and with a limit on their thrust output to avoid the risk of further shaft resonance, the total thrust available to XR219 was little more than half that which would be available to production-standard aircraft. But with two extremely powerful engines such as the Olympus 22R, even these development-standard models (the Olympus 22X) would deliver more than enough thrust for the purposes of test-flying, and so the programme proceeded towards a one-off flight.

A brilliant colour photograph of XR219, captured just seconds after lift-off on her maiden flight from Boscombe Down. Not visible in this picture are the other aircraft which were airborne at the same time – English Electric's Lightning T4 chase aircraft (flown by Jimmy Dell), their chase/photographic platform Canberra B2, and the A&AEE's Search and Rescue Whirlwind, all of which took part in the all-important first flight event. *BAC*

The aim of the taxi trials was to establish confidence in the steering and braking controls, to gain some feel for the pitch and rudder effectiveness, and to prove the reliability of the brake parachute. Experience with the Lightning suggested that ten runs would be sufficient to prove these systems and on 2 September XR219 moved independently for the first time, with Beamont as pilot and Don Bowen as observer. Some defects were immediately found, particularly the function of the wheel braking which was designed to provide steering through differential use of port and starboard wheels, but when Beamont applied braking power to either pedal, the aircraft simply came to a halt. The nose wheel steering proved to be more friendly up to a speed of 40 knots at which stage a slight phase-lag oscillation began to take effect. Engagement of engine reheat was successful, but disengagement of the throttle gates was difficult to achieve and resulted in an unintentional stop-cocking of both engines, followed by a complete loss of electrical power and a freezing spray of frost being deposited onto both Beamont and Bowen as liquid oxygen pumped through to their oxygen masks at high pressure.

Naturally, the risk of a major fire was immediately evident and the crew quickly disconnected their Personal Equipment Connection (PEC) links in order to curtail the potentially lethal flow. On the second taxi run another attempt at differential braking was attempted, but only short stabs on the brakes achieved any useful result and this was clearly still unacceptable even for the test flight stage. Cockpit temperatures were also excessively high, and a hydraulic leak was then spotted by the flight control van which accompanied XR219 along the runway, and at this stage the test was curtailed.

The third taxi test (on 3 September) proved to be more encouraging and with a lighter touch on the brakes, acceptable steering was achieved, and two reheat engagements and accelerations were made along the runway, the first up to 90 knots to check progressive wheel braking and brake temperatures, and the second to 100 knots at which stage the brake parachute was successfully streamed. Brake temperatures rose to 550/450 degrees C (as applicable to each wheel) at standstill and dropped to 450/440 after one minute, which indicated that the wheel's fan cooling system was functioning correctly. Satisfied with the results of this test, the fourth run was made later in the day and this time 20 degrees wing flap was selected and a run to 120 knots was performed before deselecting reheat, but because the engine throttle levels were still unsatisfactory, cancellation took some time and the aircraft actually reached 140 knots before power was cut to idle. At this stage Beamont pulled back on the control

The heroic sight of XR219 at 7,000 ft accompanied by her chase aircraft, after completing the first full airfield circuit at Boscombe Down. As can be seen, the aircraft's engines were surprisingly dirty, producing long plumes of sooty smoke which would be entirely unacceptable by modern standards. However, the engines fitted to XR219 were de-rated test examples which were far from representative of the production-standard power plants which would have been manufactured for production machines. *BAC*

Below: Pictured just seconds before touch-down, XR219 poses in front of the assembled BAC flight test team who can be seen awaiting the aircraft's return at the end of Boscombe's third runway. The landing threshold on runway 28 was designated as the operating base from where XR219 conducted all of her engine runs, taxi trials and subsequent test flights and the aircraft became a familiar sight for those who were fortunate to travel along Boscombe Down's eastern perimeter road during the 1964-5 period when the aircraft was active. *BAC*

Magnificent low-angle view of XR219 during low-speed handling trials, gear and flap extended, and the aircraft's unique twin wing tip vortices clearly visible. The main wheels illustrate that white "creep" markings were applied during the test programme.

column slowly and progressively to establish nose wheel lift, after which he dropped XR219's nose back onto the runway and streamed the brake parachute.

Taxi Run No.5 was performed on 6 September and was designed to explore the effects of maximum braking followed by deployment of the brake chute at 130 knots. In order to pull the parachute handle, Beamont's hand left the throttles temporarily free and the aircraft's rapid deceleration overcame the friction damping incorporated into the engine throttle box, inertial pressure pushing the throttles forward, increasing thrust again. Clearly, this defect would not be acceptable for an operational aircraft, but for the purposes of test-flying Beamont simply resolved to ensure that once the parachute handle was pulled, he would remember to quickly grab the throttle levers again.

The sixth run (performed the next day) explored nose wheel lift at the proposed first flight weight of 74,000lb and a rotation speed of 125 knots. Reheat selection was made and XR219 quickly accelerated to 120 knots at which stage the throttles were closed and at 145 knots the brake chute was deployed. No retardation was felt so Beamont began to apply braking at 140 knots. The parachute appeared to have failed and so he pulled the release handle again but when he reached back to the throttles, he found that the heavy brake deceleration had again shifted them forward. His eagerness to close them again as swiftly as possible resulted in another shut-down and resultant loss of electrical power, and after making an emergency transmission to Boscombe's control tower, Beamont and Bowen disconnected their PECs. With the end of the runway coming perilously close, maximum braking was applied and the brake temperatures were seen to rise to 870/810 degrees. With no electrical power there was no fan system to cool the brakes, and Beamont recognised that the brakes were in danger of welding themselves to their disks, so he carefully released brake pressure just before the aircraft came to a standstill, avoiding what could have been another time-consuming repair and replacement task.

XR219 pictured shortly after completing her first flight, with BAC's photographic/chase Canberra aircraft WD937 making a low fly-by in the background. *BAC*

Although the incident marred what had otherwise been a very successful series of trials, it did have one very positive outcome; it had graphically confirmed the very impressive effectiveness of the TSR2's brakes. Another positive outcome of the incident, at least for Beamont, was that his reluctance to fly from Wisley was now vindicated; had it occurred at Wisley, the aircraft would have cleared the airfield boundary, crossed the adjacent road and deposited itself in a field. Other events at Boscombe were rather less positive. During one September evening a visit had been arranged for the Government's Chief Scientist, Solly Zuckerman. After completing a series of taxy trials, XR219 was carefully parked-up at its usual position on a turning circle at the eastern end of Boscombe's shortest (third) runway. With the day's flying activity completed and most of the A&AEE personnel having gone home, only the BAC team remained on the silent airfield, with the glistening all-white TSR2 perched proudly on the concrete, silhouetted against the setting sun. It was a stirring sight by any standards and a nostalgic one for many of the BAC team, as they were standing in the same place that they had stood ten years previously when the English Electric P.1A had been undertaking similar ground running trials. As Beamont later commented, "Time seemed to have stood still for ten years."

Zuckerman duly arrived by car and after making what seemed to be a surprisingly cursory inspection of XR219 he turned to Beamont who outlined the status of the programme and the progress that was being made. With what Beamont described as a look of "distaste", Zuckerman replied that he felt it was a pity that people should be spending time on such a scandalous waste of public money. He then added that he was late for another engagement and promptly ducked back into his car and left.

A repeat of the previous taxi run was attempted on 9 September, but once again the brake parachute 'candled' (deployed but failed to open) at 145 knots. With modified throttles, Beamont successfully cut power to idle without stop-cocking the engines and with another application of maximum wheel braking, XR219 came to a halt with nearly 2,000ft of runway still available. Bowen reported that he could see burning (molten) material dropping from the starboard brakes and at standstill the brake temperatures had risen to 1,150/1,000 degrees, but as the electric fans brought temperatures down to 750/750 degrees, the flight-test van crew reported that one of the main wheel tyres had blown a core-plug and had deflated, and so the aircraft was shut down on the runway.

A period of intensive rectification work in Boscombe's hangar resulted in XR219 re-emerging on 20 September, ready to perform Taxi Run No.8. This time the brake parachute opened successfully at 120 knots and no other defects were reported, other than the recurrent high temperature in the cockpit, and the still slow throttle retardation. Taxi Run No.9 took place the next day and once again the parachute functioned perfectly. A stopwatch measurement of the throttle disengagement revealed that the best achievable time from maximum reheat to idle was 2.2 seconds and although this would have to be halved in order to meet specified performance figures, it was acceptable for test-flying purposes.

On Saturday, 26 September, Beamont made two final high-speed runs in order to establish nose wheel lift-off ('unstick') speeds relative to tailplane effectiveness. With these complete, just one more (the tenth) parachute test-run would be made on the Sunday morning and this was completed successfully the next day leaving the afternoon free for the all-important first flight. With no difficulties to address from the morning's high-speed run, the flight was set for 1500hrs. Beamont and Bowen (who would be the observer and navigator for the early flights) went to discuss the flight plan over sandwiches, during which Beamont made a series of telephone calls to everyone who needed to be notified of the planned flight.

The first flight date had been fixed provisionally for some time and by now a growing number of people were already aware of the day's planned events. As a variety of VIPs, media representatives and other hugely interested parties drove up to Boscombe Down by road, others arrived by air, including, of course, George Edwards and Freddie Page. Public spectators also began to appear and by the early afternoon the perimeter of the airfield was littered with excited onlookers. After going through a final briefing, Beamont and Bowen collected their flying clothing and helmets, completed their paperwork, checked the meteorological brief and drove out across Boscombe's familiar apron and down across the airfield and main runway to the south-eastern perimeter where XR219 was parked in its usual position on the threshold of Boscombe's shortest runway.

Bowen exchanged a few words with the ground crew and quickly climbed into the rear cockpit to begin his pre-start checks, while Beamont performed a careful examination of the aircraft's exterior, making a last check that every panel was secure and every cover removed before he too climbed into the aircraft, accompanied by a variety of 'good luck' wishes from the assembled ground crew and observers. Once settled into the cockpit a member of the ground crew climbed up to assist Beamont with the routing and securing of the seat harness and parachute connections, but he disappeared only to be replaced on the access ladder by someone who could not have been more qualified to assist – none other than Sir James Martin, Managing Director of Martin Baker Aircraft, the manufacturers of the TSR2's ejection seats. Martin had come to ensure that his Mk.5 ejection seats were entirely in order for this historic occasion and after checking Beamont's seat connections he leaned over and commented: "If you don't need this today you will soon – and it will get you down alright!" He then clambered over to Bowen's cockpit and following a cheery wave, rejoined the onlookers nearby. The long pre-start check lists were the next priority but after numerous taxi trials, the start-up procedure had become familiar to the whole team and in less than half an hour XR219's engines were running smoothly and Beamont declared that they were ready to go, radioing, "All checks complete, ready to taxi, flight test switching over to runway van." With brakes released and a nudge of power the aircraft rolled forward and turned right to head along the secondary runway accompanied by the runway van which would follow XR219 along the short journey to the main runway threshold before driving over to the control tower. Meanwhile on the main runway itself, the Sunday afternoon's silence was broken by the roar of Lightning T4 XM968, one of

Warton's test fleet which was being flown by Jimmy Dell as chase aircraft for the test flight. This was swiftly followed by Canberra WD937 piloted by John Carrodus. As they both climbed away to position in Boscombe's airfield circuit, an A&AEE Whirlwind rescue helicopter chugged into position close to the control tower and as 1500hrs finally approached, Beamont radioed, "Twenty degrees flap set – we'll check fuel on the runway. Flap blow checked. Tarnish One to Boscombe, line up please," to which Boscombe ATC replied, "Boscombe to Tarnish One you are clear to line up." With another rumble of power XR219 rolled forward and turned left onto the 10,000ft main runway. A brief moment of radio transmission difficulty was resolved by switching aerials and then Bowen radioed: "Nearly thirteen thousand pounds." Beamont radioed: "Tarnish One take-off please" and ATC replied, "Boscombe to

Tarnish One, you are clear runway two four, wind two-eighty degrees at ten knots." It was, at long last, time to go.

Inside the cockpit the atmosphere was surprisingly calm even though an air of great excitement was evident amongst the many spectators who were now on their feet and waiting with eager anticipation. Beamont radioed: "Final check, straps tight, parking brake off, twenty degrees flap and blow checked, trims set, power up to max dry ninety-eight point five, ninety-seven point five. Ready to go. Tarnish One flight test van, counting down, five, four, three two, one… now… reheat okay."

The airfield was blanketed by a buffeting roar as the two Olympus engines spooled up to full power and staged into full reheat, spewing two long tongues of shock diamond-studded flame, trailed by a long plume of thick, black, sooty, smoke rising up from the runway threshold. Raising slightly off its

XR219 venturing into the darkness for a night-time photo shoot at Boscombe Down, with the shapes of a Beverley transport and Valiant bomber just visible in the background. Blanking plates are fitted over the Olympus engine exhausts. Had the TSR2 programme continued, many of the initial pre-production batch aircraft would have been assigned to the A&AEE at Boscombe Down for varying periods, enabling the A&AEE crews to evaluate different aspects of the aircraft's performance, and the effectiveness (or otherwise) of the aircraft's systems. *BAC*

nose wheel as the brakes released, XR219 surged forward, and in just a few ear-shattering seconds, the aircraft had reached a speed of 140 knots, having travelled little more than 2,000ft along the runway. Beamont gently lifted the nose wheel off the concrete and held the aircraft in this slightly tail-down attitude for a few more seconds until 170 knots was attained at which point XR219 lifted almost imperceptibly into the air, Beamont checking-back the initial climbing attitude as they passed 185 knots little more than half-way along the runway. The thunderous roar continued to pound the spectators as the aircraft laid a long, smoky trail into the brilliant late summer sky and soared effortlessly away over the western runway threshold, Beamont commenting, "No trouble was it? Just a little buffet, probably from the flaps. Look at this climb!" There was indeed more than a little looking going on. The assembled audience was awestruck by XR219's captivating combination of undeniable aesthetic beauty combined with almost numbing noise from the engines' power and a very impressive aerodynamic performance which seemed almost out of character for an aircraft of such size. The journey to this all-important moment in the project had been a long and troublesome one, but on the basis of these few unforgettable minutes, everyone at Boscombe Down was already convinced that the journey had clearly been worthwhile.

At 220 knots the TSR2 was established in a comfortable climb and as the aircraft passed through 2,000ft Beamont gently eased off the throttles to 97% thrust, safely emerging from the perilous shaft resonance range. A brief check of tailplane effectiveness confirmed that lateral control was good and once 7,000ft was attained, Beamont levelled-out and radioed, "Tarnish One to Boscombe – making first port turn, all systems go."

Roll and pitch control was immediately found to be very good and no trim adjustments were necessary and so Beamont eased XR219 into a gentle left-hand turn to the south before bringing the aircraft back onto a reciprocal heading in line with Boscombe's runway. He had anticipated flying a long downwind leg so that tests could be performed whilst keeping the aircraft within easy reach of Boscombe Down, but with Don Bowen monitoring the fuel system and the cg (centre of gravity) system from the rear cockpit, it was established that with 10,400lb of fuel, a second circuit could be flown, rather than positioning for a straight-in landing. With the Lightning chase aircraft in close formation (and the Canberra chase/photo ship nearby), the combined formation returned to Boscombe much to the delight of the spectators who were assembled below, sweeping majestically overhead before disappearing into the sunlight off to the west. Further tests were performed including a brief check of Dutch roll stability, flap handling at 35 degrees deflection, and handling at the planned landing speed, together with an ASI (Air Speed Indicator) 'position error' check confirmed with Jimmy Dell in the accompanying Lightning.

Once complete on the second downwind leg, Beamont brought XR219's speed down to 190 knots and entered a lazy turn over Thruxton Airfield at 1,500ft, in just the same way he had practised on numerous occasions in Dell's Lightning. Rolling out on the approach path some five miles from Boscombe's runway, everything was proceeding smoothly, Beamont commenting, "Okay Don, we've got it made", as the spectators back at Boscombe looked out to the east to see XR219 settled onto a steady approach, landing lights glistening ahead of the now-familiar trail of smoke. Streaming swiftly over the airfield boundary, Beamont gently eased-up the aircraft's nose and cut the engine power as XR219 rushed over the runway threshold, the main wheel bogies gently kissing the runway surface five hundred yards along the runway as had been planned. The almost imperceptible touchdown was more than satisfactory, but once the aircraft's weight began to load onto the undercarriage, the soft landing was rapidly replaced by a jarring and startling vibration which rattled through the aircraft and caused Beamont to briefly lose focus on the view ahead. Thankfully, the alarming shudder quickly passed and with XR219's nose still held high, Beamont slowly eased the control column forward, allowing the nose gear to sink onto the runway before pulling the brake parachute handle. The parachute deployed and opened faultlessly and the aircraft rolled to a halt with virtually no brake pressure being required – brake temperature being less that 80 degrees at standstill. Popping the canopies open to allow fresh air into the warm cockpit, the first flight was over. It had been a great success, as described in Beamont's written report:

TSR2 XR219 Flight No.1

Take Off

The aircraft was lined up on runway 24 with all systems serviceable.

Wind: 290 degrees/11 knots

Ground level ambient temperature: 18.2 degrees C.

Altimeter: 1,013.2 mbs.

Afterburning off and balancing, fuel was adjusted to 13,300lb, differential 8,000/5,300lb for take-off.

Brake temperatures: 50/50 degrees C.

Maximum dry intermediate: 98.5%/690 degrees C, 97.5%/698 degrees C.

Flaps 35 degrees, blow in mid 35 degree segment.

Reset to 20 degrees, blow in mid 20 degree segment.

Nose wheel steering: "Fine" gear.

Reheat lights to 3rd gutter, satisfactory.

Runway acceleration normal.

Initial rotation at 125 knots and nose wheel checked at 1-2 feet.

Rotation continued at 170kt with lift-off occurring with buffet vibration at approximately 180kt.

In slight crosswind conditions a small lateral correction was required and achieved.

Acceleration in the initial climb-out was slow, and attitude was corrected at about 500ft in order to establish 200kt before resuming the climb incidence necessary to hold 200kt at maximum reheat.

From 1,000ft speed was increased gradually to 240kt and reheat cancelled at approximately 3,000ft with unevenness through the gutters.

Buffet was present throughout this phase, of moderate amplitude and predominantly 4-5 cycles lateral at the cockpit.

On climb: 5,000ft, 200kt, 97.7/97.2%, 696/698 degrees C.

During the initial climb-out phase, the attitude developed was such that forward vision was lost, and the seat was raised to establish forward view. The seat raising switch was conveniently placed and easy to use in this situation.

Normal Flight

Level flight was established at 6,500ft and a rate half port turn set up beginning at 93/93% and increasing to 96/96% to sustain.

On levelling out, 35 degree flap was selected and produced a nose-down trim change of 3-4lb stick force. As the incidence changed with flap, the buffet level was reduced but not eliminated.

Response in roll and pitch was assessed at 220kt in this configuration and pitch damping was dead beat; roll damping was low and subject to the effects of inertia. It was established that control in pitch and yaw was adequate for gentle manoeuvres.

Control inputs in yaw and co-ordinated control movements resulted in relatively low response rates but otherwise normal response, with some adverse yaw from the roll inputs, and speed was reduced as scheduled to 180kt in the landing configuration (35 degree flap).

Buffet continued down to 180kt where it increased in amplitude slightly, and the chase Lightning reported 172kt. This was accepted as possible adverse position error, and adjustments were made to the minimum speeds selected for the remainder of the sortie.

180kt was sustained in level flight in the landing configuration at 35 degree flap (and blow) at 7,000ft with 94/94%.

Up to this point re-trimming had not been required on any axis.

A gentle descent was set up at 80/80% achieving 250kt passing 5,000ft, and the buffet amplitude remained as before. It was confirmed that the predominant characteristic was a 4-5 cycle lateral mode with some higher frequency background.

At the planned pointing the first circuit, review of the state of fuel and general systems serviceability confirmed that the second scheduled circuit was practical, and this intention was confirmed by radio.

The base leg turn was completed at 3,000ft, 210kt, and it was a simple matter to line up and establish the approach path, although a slight tendency to chase the glide slope was noticed due to low pitch response rate and light feel force.

Overshoot was initiated from 1,700ft at maximum dry intermediate, and an adequate though small climb rate established before retracting flap to 20 degrees.

On levelling out for the downwind leg, a left rudder stick-free Dutch roll was carried out at 240kt, flaps 20 degree, developing approximately 45 degrees port bank with damping to half amplitude in approximately 2 cycles and 2 seconds.

Landing

The aircraft was turned on to base leg at Thruxton as planned (5.5 miles from runway 24 threshold) and lined up easily at 1,500ft/190kt; the centre line and glide slope were maintained relatively easily, though with inertia affecting positive precision in roll and a very slight tendency to over-controlling in pitch, again due to low response rate and light feel force.

Final adjustments to landing attitude at short finals including a check in flare response were satisfactory. The threshold was crossed at 190kt/100ft and power reduced very slightly during positive flare initiiation at approximately 180kt. Control of dry engine power was adequate for approach speed adjustment in the prevailing favourable conditions.

As predicted the change in attitude was positive but the effect on the glide slope small, though sufficient to reduce the rate of descent at contact to a low value.

The rear main wheels were felt to touch smoothly at 500-600 yards from the threshold as planned, wings level and without detectable drift; and immediately after contact 2-3 cycles of heavy amplitude undercarriage/structural vibration was felt (wind 290 degrees/15kt). Power was reduced to idle/idle, and the undercarriage vibration was eliminated apparently as the forward main wheels touched; and the nose was allowed to descend gently into contact with the runway with little forward movement of the stick.

At nose wheel contact the speed was down to approximately 155kt, and the tail parachute handle operated. After a relatively lengthy pause development was felt, and subsequent de-reefing produced a powerful, smooth deceleration.

The landing was made with nose wheel steer engaged and no sharp steering effects were noted. It should however be practical to delay nose wheel steer to low speeds in future.

As landing roll conditions were entirely smooth and satisfactory, use of wheel braking was delayed to approximately 100kt, and this resulted in brake temperatures registering only 80/80 degrees C at standstill.

Accumulator pressures 4,000/4,000 pounds per square inch (psi).

The tail parachute was jettisoned normally at approximately 20kt.

Fuel 5,100/2,900lb. Wind 280 degrees/13-15kt.

The navigator reported that the starboard undercarriage bogie rotation may not have been fully complete at the touchdown point, which could have led to the vibration condition experienced.

Cockpit temperatures high throughout the sortie with Auto Full Cold selected, After taxiing back, shut-down checks:

58.5%/314 degrees C 57%/294 degrees C.

Brake temperatures : 180/300 degrees C.

Brake accumulators: 4,100/4,200 psi.

Summary

Due to virtually complete serviceability this first sortie was carried out in full accordance with Flight Test Schedule No. 1.

Stability and response to controls was found to be adequate and safe for flight under the conditions tested, and to conform closely to predicted and simulated values. Noticeably high induced drag was experienced after take-off, due possibly to adverse position error resulting in too early lift-off.

Moderate amplitude buffet was experienced at all speeds tested and this was found to vary in amplitude with incidence.

Control of the approach and landing was especially excellent having regard to the current absence of autostabilisation.

Engine control and behaviour was adequate at all points in the flight, except in disengagement of reheat during the climb-out where the usual difficulty was experienced in throttle-box disengagement of minimum heat.

Engine speed adjustment of the approach was not faulted, but it should be noted that the prevailing weather conditions on the approach were non-turbulent. All supporting systems functioned perfectly with the exception of the temperature and flow control of cabin conditioning, which tended to pulse throughout the sortie and was too warm.

The warning system functioned satisfactorily, and no spurious warnings occurred.

Fuel balancing was not required during flight and fuel system performance was not faulted.

Cockpit layout was satisfactory with some detail exceptions described (separately).

The forward windscreen and instrument shroud layout were particularly excellent and virtually no significant reflections were seen in the glasses in spite of the intense sun-glare during approach and landing.

The canopy transparencies were of very low vision quality as reported previously.

In general the performance, stability and response to controls conformed closely to the briefed values and especially to the simulator studies.

Virtually all scheduled test points were achieved on this flight and this, coupled with the high standard of systems serviceability and the adequate level of on-auto-stabilised control and stability in this high drag, low-speed configuration, reflects a very high standard of design, preparation and inspection. In this first flight configuration and under the conditions tested, this aircraft could be flown safely by any moderately experienced pilot qualified on Lightning or similar aircraft and the flight development programme can therefore be said to be off to a good start, With present engine ratings the aircraft is, however, clearly critically short of thrust, and this situation is likely to dictate the rate of flight development.

Defects

1. Cabin conditioning temperature and flow control unstable.
2: Canopy jettison handle safety pin on floor of navigator's cockpit (in console).
3. Upper UHF aerial unserviceable.
4. 2" bank error on pilot's HDD Attitude Indicator.

R. P. BEAMONT
Manager: Flight operations

CHAPTER SEVEN

Testing Times

THE first flight of XR219 was undoubtedly a technical success, but in many respects it had been more of a political gesture than a practical part of the test programme. Basic stability and control had been demonstrated and aerodynamically, the aircraft had performed even better than anticipated. The only major concern was the unexpected

XR219 emerges into the night for a photo call at Boscombe Down. TSR2 would have been a familiar sight and sound during the hours of darkness, the aircraft being designed for all-weather day and night operations. With an impressive blind bombing capability, TSR2 would have been able to deliver a weapon to its target using a combination of forward-looking radar, sideways-looking radar, Doppler, inertial navigation and computer calculation. Even so, delivery accuracy was expected to be in the order of hundreds of yards, which effectively meant that tactical nuclear weapons (ie- WE.177A) would almost certainly have been the weapon of choice for most strike missions. *BAC*

vibration problems which had occurred when the aircraft touched down, but as this was clearly a fault connected to the undercarriage, it was not regarded as a serious difficulty. The real hurdle which was preventing progress was the aircraft's engines and although other post-flight faults could be rectified relatively easily, the two Olympus engines were transported to Bristol for further modification while undercarriage retraction tests continued back at Weybridge in order to clear the aircraft for a 'clean' gear-up flight. The flight development team listed its minimum requirements for Flight No.2 as follows:

1. Engines to low pressure shaft modification standard and restored to 100% take-off thrust with full clearance.

2. Undercarriage cleared for retraction.

3. Cockpit temperature control system corrected.

4. Replacement for leaking reheat fuel pump.

5. Throttle box modified to further improve reheat cancellation.

6. Review engine relighting drill relative to auxiliary intake door status.

7. Clear functioning and acceptability of cockpit and external night lighting.

Additionally, a list of less important modifications needed to be addressed which had been temporarily approved for a 'one flight only' test, and as had already been accepted, XR219 would have to be laid-up for a lengthy period. Beamont announced that the flight test crew would take a much deserved break but Weybridge claimed that this would have to be of short duration as the second flight would be scheduled to take place in October. Nobody on the flight team took this estimate seriously and it was almost 1965 before the aircraft was fit to fly again. Work on the engines in Bristol continued with great urgency and by the end of November they were re-installed in XR219 and ready for ground running. Another problem then immediately manifested itself: more vibrations which initially defied explanation.

Despite investigation no obvious cause could be found and Beamont was invited to assess the problem. He concluded that there was a very obvious resonance particularly on the starboard engine but he thought that it might improve under flight conditions. Therefore the only option would be to make a second flight to establish just how bad the problem was. But undercarriage retraction clearance had still not been secured and a great deal of work took place at Weybridge on the undercarriage test rig in order to achieve the required ten consecutive successful retraction sequences, which would be followed by five more on XR219, on jacks, in the hangar at Boscombe Down.

It was not until the last week of December that these sequences were finally completed but once clearance had been given, XR219 re-emerged to fly again on New Years' Eve. The autumnal sunshine had gone and Boscombe was shrouded in cloud with a base of around 2,000ft. It was cold and snow seemed likely. The enthusiasm and excitement surrounding the first flight had also gone, and the thrill of getting XR219 into the air had been replaced by a mood of determination, now that the serious business of flight-testing was about to begin for real. The undercarriage delays appeared to have been resolved and so attention was concentrated on the troublesome engines which were now modified, but still proving to be unreliable. Beamont's superiors had decided that in order to avoid unnecessary risks with the engine resonance problems, a set of warning lights would be attached to the pilot's instrument panel shroud. These would illuminate if resonance was detected and immediately alert Beamont to the problem so that he could reduce power and thereby avoid any risk of a catastrophic failure. The idea made sense, but Beamont was concerned that the single-channel detection system would be unreliable and was more than likely to present him with false warnings which might then oblige him to reduce engine power at a critical point on take-off and create the very situation which the warning system had been designed

to avoid. By way of a response, Beamont was told that this outcome would be "highly unlikely", but he remained unconvinced and embarked upon the second flight in the full knowledge that should the warning lights illuminate, it would be his responsibility to judge whether they were for real or not. Warning lights aside, the main purpose of Flight No.2 would be to get the landing gear retracted and take the aircraft up to 400 knots, testing control response and stability at 50-knot incremental stages. Bowen (as observer) would monitor the gear retraction sequence via a periscope, while the familiar Lightning T4 would be along side as chase plane, to observe the sequence externally. Back on the familiar engine-run area to the south of the main runway, XR219 came to life again and with checks complete. Beamont released the brakes and taxied out for take-off. It was immediately apparent that the engine vibration was still present, but as planned, it was accepted and as some late sunshine emerged from the gloom the aircraft was lined up on Boscombe's runway, the engines brought up to pull power and reheat selected, Boscombe's tower calling: "You are clear to take-off and climb at your discretion."

Once again the airfield was immersed in a crescendo of noise as XR219 thundered forward, and as Beamont raised the nose wheels off the runway he was distracted not by any illuminated warnings, but the blinding glare from the low winter sun which created an annoying mottled lighting effect across the windscreen and prevented forward vision. This would obviously require an incidence gauge for the pilot so that an accurate take-off attitude could be adopted even if forward vision was lost, but Beamont elected to proceed, maintaining a slight delay so that wheels unstick was finally achieved at 200 knots, half-way along the runway. As soon as the aircraft lifted into the air there was a sudden onset of high-frequency vibration which suggested to Beamont that the engine resonance problem had returned, so thrust was reduced to just below 97%, but the vibration persisted and with no warning lights shining, the cause was assumed to be the less serious (but mysterious) vibration which had manifested itself during the ground runs. Beamont reduced power on the suspect No.1 engine to around 87% but the vibration worsened making his vision so blurred that he could hardly see. Unwilling to tolerate this dangerous situation, he opened the throttle again and once back above 97% his vision improved.

Some experimentation with the throttle setting soon confirmed Beamont's suspicion that the vibration was matching the natural resonance frequency of his eyeballs and although the phenomenon was not presented by similar throttle settings on No.2 engine, it was clearly not a safe or useful condition in which to continue flying. He thus radioed Boscombe to inform them that he was calling off the test flight. After burning off fuel to bring the aircraft down to landing weight, he headed back to Boscombe using asymmetric engine settings in order to reduce the vision problem, and the short leg back to base as an opportunity to conduct a few more low speed handling checks. Back onto approach to Boscombe he then encountered the same windscreen glare as he had found during take-off and forward vision was again lost, but the approach lights and VASI (Visual Approach Slope Indicator) lights could be seen and so he pressed on to execute another gentle landing.

As with the first flight, once the wheels made firm contact with the runway the same jarring lateral oscillation shuddered through the airframe and Beamont was briefly disorientated until the shaking died down. It was with some relief that he popped the brake parachute with XR219's nose still held high.

The nose wheels then gently sank onto the ground before moderate braking was applied, bringing the aircraft to a halt half-way along the runway. Beamont's post-flight report outlined the results of this disappointing, and distinctly uncomfortable second flight:

TSR2 XR219 Flight No.2

Taxi

As with Taxi No. 12. the vibration level with No. 1 engine in the Nh range 87-95% was greater than during the initial taxiing series, but was not regarded as unacceptable.

Operation of the nozzle override shifted the datum of the critical Nh range of the vibration downwards by 2%.

Nozzle override checks on Nos. 1 and 2 engines satisfactory with Aj gauges indicating SHUT on Override selection (90/90%).

Flap blow checks at 90/90%: 20 degree flap blow at mid 20 degree segment 35 degree flap blow at mid 35 degree segment Reheat lighting checks: Double datum switches at Normal (100%).

No. 1 max. dry 99.0%/720 degrees C.

reheat at 1st gutter satisfactory

No. 2 max. dry 98.0%/702 degrees C.

reheat at 1st gutter satisfactory Fuel : F. 9,600lb. Bulb.

During engine checks it was confirmed that with No.1 engine set above 95% or below 87%, the engine vibration level reduced considerably though not to the low level of the first engine installation (1st flight programme).

In the late afternoon light with the sun low on the horizon close to the end of the runway, lighting conditions in the cockpit were poor and it was impossible to achieve sufficient instrument lighting brilliance to offset the prevailing contrast conditions.

The only instruments which were readily readable under these conditions were the trim gauges on the port side and the Aj and T5 gauges on the starboard panel. CSI reference was particularly difficult in this deep shade under the shroud, and under these circumstances its night illumination could not be seen.

Use of the white floodlighting was also ineffective as the floods illuminated the rear of the pilot's elbows and cast shadows of these across the instrument panels. This inadequate lighting was a limiting feature in the flight.

When lined up on Runway 24 the sun glare at an acute angle to the windscreen resulted in an excessive mottling effect on the centre windscreen which made forward vision difficult. This resulted subsequently in visual reference being lost during the rotation for take-off and in visual difficulties during the landing approach.

Take-off

Runway 24.

Wind/velocity 250 degrees/12kt.

Reheat lights satisfactory and nose wheel initial lift at 120kt checked and resumed on passing 170kt.

Due to loss of visual reference in rotation, take-off incidence was not achieved at the scheduled speed, and unstick occurred at approximately 200kt. This emphasised the need for incidence reference as a take-off monitor.

Double datum switches to intermediate at 220kt moved back to disengage reheat on passing 2,000ft. Due to slowness in disengagement of the reheat stops No.1 engine remained in reheat at the first gutter for a short period until this was identified and power reduced to max. dry intermediate.

Heavy vibration was apparent during the initial climb and this was at first thought to be airframe buffet but on reducing power to level at 3,000ft when the vibration amplitude increased, it was found that this was associated with rpm reduction into the 94-90% range.

No. 1 engine was increased to above all, and this reduced the level to that previously noted for the climb phase. Return to below 96% and in the range 96-87% on No. 1 engine increased the vibration amplitude to a level in which vision was obscured by apparent eyeball resonance. This was intolerable and dictated the pattern of the remainder of the flight Level flight was established in asymmetric power at 95.5/90%, 612/560 degrees C, and a port turn initiated after announcing the decision not to retract the undercarriage.

The vibration level even in these conditions was such as to make It immediately desirable to land, and this intention was declared.

However the aircraft was not positioned at this time for a satisfactory approach, and it was also necessary to burn off some fuel to achieve a suitable landing weight.

Landing

The approach was continued with reference to the approach lighting only, and on passing this the flare and landing were carried out by feel, namely by flaring from 190kt at an altitude judged through the quarter panel to be approximately 50ft. This resulted in a smooth touchdown of the rear wheels followed within one second by a very violent lateral oscillation at the cockpit which persisted for approximately 4 seconds and during which positive control of the situation was momentarily lost. The oscillation was estimated at the time to have been at approximately 4-5 cycles per second (cps) and at least plus or minus lg (Instrumentation confirmed plus or minus 1g at 5 cps. Lateral and some longitudinal). When the oscillation damped out sufficiently to allow the recovery of full control it was found that the nose wheel was still high although the stick had been inadvertently allowed to move forward from the scheduled position for aerodynamic drag. At this time and while still under some degree of disorientation the tail parachute was streamed without recovering reference to ASI, and this resulted in beak door operation at 161kt (Instrumentation), namely 6kt above the scheduled speed. Tail parachute development was felt to be normal with a relatively long pause before smooth development of de-reefing. The nose wheel had been lowered to the runway before operating the tail parachute handle. Upon development of full parachute drag, wheel braking was applied gently at first and then at maximum pedal pressure for approximately 2 seconds passing 120kt. Control of the landing roll-out was smooth and uneventful, and the parachute was jettisoned at approximately 20kt.

At standstill the brake temperatures read 200/700 degrees C with the starboard brake temperature gauge erratic and apparently unreliable.

Fuel: F.7,000/A.4,200lb.

During the latter five minutes of the flight the pilot's cabin temperature became uncomfortably warm at Half Auto Cold, and the controller was adjusted to Full Auto Cold just prior to the approach. This maintained warm but reasonable conditions until taxiing in when the temperature again rose to an uncomfortable level. Through most of the sortie the navigator quoted 'cool' conditions in his cockpit.

Engines at shut down: 58/57%, 300/290 degrees C.

With the exception of No.1 engine and the undercarriage, all systems were serviceable at shut down.

Summary

No. 1 engine vibration level became excessive in flight resulting in blurred vision due to eyeball resonance. This dictated an immediate landing. On touchdown in a normal low rate-of-descent landing (Instrumentation 4ft/sec) the undercarriage lateral oscillation encountered on Flight No.1 recurred with greater amplitude. This was such as to disrupt control and cause disorientation for 3-4 seconds at a critical point in the landing.

In a one-hour sortie the temperature at the pilot's cockpit rose too high for comfort at Full Cold setting.

In this configuration stability and response to controls was excellent, and allowed full attention to be given to the necessary engine-condition investigation. These control qualities also minimised embarrassment from the unfavourable visual conditions prevailing on the approach and landing coupled with the inadequate level of instrument lighting.

R. P. Beamont
Manager: Flight Operations.

As the bleak winter conditions at Boscombe Down continued, XR219 was soon ready for Flight No.3 and on 2 January with snow on the ground and more forecast, it looked as if weather conditions would now become another delaying factor. But with a 3,000ft cloud base and good visibility, conditions were good enough to perform a repeat of the abortive flight test which would hopefully last rather longer than the meagre eight minutes of the previous sortie. After start-up, the engine vibration was found to be still present but the flight went ahead and XR219 was soon airborne after a brisk acceleration on this icy cold morning. The main wheels lifted off the runway at 180kt and almost immediately both LP shaft warning lights flickered into life. Beamont was unashamedly dismissive of the warning lights and assumed that they were both the result of a spurious electrical fault but, instinctively, he closed the port engine's throttle to 80% and reduced the starboard engine's to 96% which still provided him with enough thrust to continue climbing away without risking a single engine failure disaster. The red lights remained illuminated but both engines appeared to be functioning normally and so it appeared as if the "highly unlikely" false warnings had actually appeared on both engines simultaneously.

However Beamont's troubles were not over and the debilitating eyeball resonance problem soon recurred, requiring him to shift the throttles into asymmetric settings in order to maintain his vision. Continuing a steady climb the engine lights defiantly continued to glow and so he elected to return to Boscombe again, free of the low sun glare (this being a morning flight), but prepared for the usual rattling oscillations as XR219 touched down after a flight of just 20 minutes. In his post-flight report, Beamont stated that the illumination of both engine warning lights presented a "… potentially dangerous situation" and also added that the engine vibration levels were still excessive and "cannot be regarded

as acceptable for further flying". Likewise, he turned his attention to the landing gear problems and commented that "… the amplitude of the oscillation (measured at +1.8g at 5 cycles per second at the pilot's station) destroys the pilot's control (of the situation) for the duration of maximum amplitude. This is not acceptable". But despite Beamont's dissatisfaction with these recurrent problems he remained upbeat when describing the aircraft's aerodynamic qualities, stating that: "In these flights involving some distracting or emergency (technical) conditions the handling qualities have been showed to be excellent… the ease of approach and landing including crosswinds of 13-15kt is high by any standards and this aircraft is one of the easiest to land of any high performance aircraft in the writer's experience."

After further detailed examination, the cause of No.1 engine's vibration was finally traced to a reheat fuel pump which was out-of-tolerance, and once this was replaced the problem appeared to have been finally solved, ground runs confirming that both engines were now performing satisfactorily. As for the warning lights, the cause of their malfunction was quickly traced to an electrical socket which had simply worked loose. Rather than repair the system it was agreed that the lights should be removed as the resonance problem appeared to have been resolved thanks to the shaft modifications, and the warning lights were simply creating another possible source of distraction and danger. It looked as if some good progress would now be possible, but as work on the troublesome undercarriage continued, it was decided that some time should be devoted to a more concentrated examination of low-speed handling, airbrake and flap operation.

Flight No.4 was fixed for 8 January and as XR219 again roared into the sky at a weight of 77,073lb (including 18,330lb of fuel) it was readily apparent that the vibrations had indeed gone and Beamont was able to enjoy clear vision, free of any

View from Dell's Lightning as XR219's troublesome port main landing gear hangs precariously in a semi-rotated position during flight No.5. The use of the Lightning as a chase aircraft proved invaluable for unforeseen events such as this, enabling Dell to move around XR219 and obtain a clear view of the landing gear's position, which he reported back to Beamont in XR219's cockpit, and the test crew on the ground at Boscombe Down. *BAC*

Photographed from the cockpit of Dell's Lightning, the starboard main gear is seen in the partially-retracted configuration, as described by Beamont, as he tried (without success) to persuade the landing gear to function correctly on flight No.7. Although the retraction difficulties were finally solved before the next flight, the severe vibration encountered on landing remained as a persistent problem, up until the project's cancellation. *BAC*

resonance problems. The flight proceeded without any further unwanted surprises and a great deal of valuable handling data was gathered, culminating in a revised landing technique which involved maintaining engine power as the aircraft flared, and cutting power only as the wheels touched down, this giving a much softer 2ft/sec descent speed which would hopefully avoid the usual vibrations which shook through the aircraft at this point. The resulting landing was indeed much lighter and although the vibrations were less severe, they were still present and clearly would require an engineering solution rather than any further modification to the way in which the aircraft was handled. Beamont's report commented that "...this satisfactory sortie confirmed that the basic low speed handling qualities are excellent and do not require any further development... this encouraging standard indicates that the breakthrough into normal flight development progress may well have been reached." His remarks reflected his confidence in the aircraft's impressive handling qualities and with the engine problems having been largely solved, it was understandable that Beamont should have adopted such a positive outlook. But the continual problem of severe landing vibration was something which had still to be rectified and although it would not hinder progress with low-speed flight-testing, ultimately it would have to be fixed. Beamont could not have imagined that the landing gear held even more difficulties in store.

Flight No.5 was scheduled for 14 January. After further undercarriage modification work had been performed, it was agreed that on this flight the landing gear would finally be retracted, enabling a more ambitious test sortie to be flown, taking the aircraft beyond the top speed of 270kt which had so far been attained, and up to 450kt – a more representative figure of the kind of speeds at which the operational TSR2 would fly.

With an all-up weight of 79,000lb, XR219 roared skywards at 1528 hrs on a dull, cloud-covered and cold afternoon, with Beamont quickly noticing that the improved cockpit lighting system was much more satisfactory. Jimmy Dell again got airborne in the chase Lightning and together the aircraft climbed up through 3,000ft and settled at 230kt with 88/88% thrust on the engines. With Dell's Lightning tucked in for a close look

(filmed on a cine camera), Beamont selected the undercarriage switches for the first time. A series of muffled clunks ensued as Beamont watched the gear's indicator lights flash on and off intermittently before settling with the port main light illuminated and the others out. From the back seat, Bowen confirmed that through his periscope he could see that the nose and starboard gear had retracted but that the port assembly had not. Worse still, the main bogie appeared to have rotated to a vertical position and stopped. Radio communication with the flight-test team resulted in agreement that the gear should be selected down again and at 5,500ft Beamont duly operated the gear's extension switch. Much to everyone's relief the assemblies all slowly extended and 'three greens' came up on Beamont's indicator panel. But from Dell's Lightning it was clear that things were not quite as the indicator lights were suggesting, and Bowen reported that although the main gears had come down, the bogie assemblies had only partially extended and were now hanging at a vertical angle. More discussion between Beamont and the flight-test crew was conducted and after some debate it was agreed that trying another complete cycle of the retraction and extension sequence might not necessarily be a good idea, as this might result in only one of the two legs extending which would make landing impossible. Rather than risk having to abandon the aircraft, technically it would be possible to land the aircraft onto the unlocked wheel bogies, allowing the forward wheels to make first contact in the hope that they would then rotate and lock into position. It was a risky proposal but far preferable to baling out and abandoning XR219 with the probability of losing the whole TSR2 programme as a consequence. Beamont saw no reason to risk Don Bowen's life and when Bowen asked "What are you going to do Bee?", Beamont replied that he thought a landing was possible and worth a try, but that Bowen should consider ejecting from the aircraft rather than accepting an unnecessary risk of his own life. Bowen's reply was succinct: "You're not going to get rid of me that easily!"

Landing gear still hanging at a bizarre angle, flight No.5 culminated in Beamont bringing the aircraft back to Boscombe Down for a low pass in front of the control tower, enabling the BAC flight test team to see the landing gear problem for themselves. He then positioned the aircraft for a precisely-controlled "tiptoe" landing which was made successfully, thanks to his excellent pilot skills which resulted in a rate of descent which was almost zero at the point of touchdown. Thankfully, the gear shifted into its proper locked position once weight was applied onto it. *BAC*

So with both crew still on board, XR219 settled back onto a steady approach towards Boscombe Down. As the aircraft came into view through the darkening skies, it appeared to be making what had become a routine approach. But shortly before reaching the approach lights Beamont applied power and levelled off just above the runway to perform a low fly-by in front of the control tower so that the flight test crew could see the problem for themselves. As the aircraft passed by and turned back into the airfield circuit, the two main bogies could clearly be seen hanging absurdly at an almost vertical angle. Landing XR219 would require a fast and extremely precise approach and some incredibly careful handling. But even if Beamont could bring the aircraft onto the runway with the lightest of touches, nobody could be sure what would happen.

It was possible that the bogies would rotate into their proper positions and lock, but equally they might rotate to a reversed position and it was impossible to predict what the outcome of such a landing would be. As the aircraft turned over Thruxton, Beamont remained confident both of his skills and the excellent handling qualities of the aircraft which were being compromised so badly by the ever-troublesome undercarriage.

Another steady approach was completed and at 170kt the aircraft swept over the runway threshold at 50ft, Beamont checking the rate of descent until a barely discernable sink allowed the main wheels to lightly kiss the runway surface. Holding the aircraft with rigid precision, Beamont felt a gentle rumble shift through the airframe which he hoped was the

sensation caused by the bogies rotating into their designed positions. A second rumble indicated that the aircraft was now settled onto the main gears and as he and everyone had hoped, the bogies had successfully repositioned themselves, Beamont being almost relieved to feel the now familiar lateral oscillation as the aircraft assumed its more usual landing characteristics. Beamont's landing had been commendably light and precise with a rate of descent recorded at just 0.5 feet per second. With the tail parachute deployed and normal braking applied, the excitement and worry of the previous fifteen minutes was thankfully over.

The flight test team at Boscombe Down were disheartened and frustrated. They now knew that in overall terms the TSR2 was performing well and, as a flying machine, it was surpassing even their most optimistic predictions. But the engine problems had caused many delays and setbacks, and after having solved these difficulties they had been replaced by even more frustrations now that the undercarriage was refusing to function properly. The landing vibrations had been a recurrent problem but one which could be solved almost at leisure, as it had no direct effect upon flight testing. But landing gear which resolutely refused to retract or extend properly was another matter and until it was fixed, the flight test programme could make no further progress. It was also having an effect on both public and official opinion as the media had lost no opportunity to point out that in a period of five months the much-maligned machine had made just five flights, and could not even raise its landing gear.

The situation was not a happy one. Work on the landing gear continued and in the meantime it was decided that the next flight would be an opportunity for Jimmy Dell to exchange his Lightning T4 for the TSR2 and to convert onto the type. With Bowen taking the back seat, he made a 24-minute flight on 15 January during which he familiarised himself with the aircraft's controls and handling qualities, whilst gathering more low-speed data as part of the flight-test programme. After landing he reported that "…impressions gained during take-off, in flight and landing were extremely favourable" and that "…tail plane power during take-off and approach was noted particularly, together with the high degree of speed control in the approach configuration."

Another change of crew took place on the next flight which occurred on 22 January, when Beamont was joined by Peter Moneypenny, Warton's chief navigator, who acted as observer. This flight returned to the undercarriage problems and after having negotiated Boscombe's slippery and slushy taxiways, XR219 took to the air with an all-up weight of 70,573lb, levelling-off under a 2,000ft snow-laden cloud base. Ploughing through intermittent snow showers, the landing gear was selected 'up' and once again, much to everyone's disappointment, the retraction sequence failed and only the port and nose gear assemblies tucked away, leaving the starboard leg extended with a partly rotated bogie. Beamont selected gear down and both the nose and port legs duly re-appeared and locked into place, as did the partly extended starboard leg. With no other option available, the rest of the flight was devoted to more low speed handling and the best that Beamont could do was to report yet again that "…speed stability in the approach and control of the flare and touchdown are a most satisfying experience."

Jimmy Dell then took over for flight No.8 on 23 January although no attempt was made to raise the undercarriage and the sortie was devoted to more low speed handling investigation. Likewise, on 27 January, Beamont flew test No.9 and performed a series of manoeuvres with the aircraft's flaps extended to fifty degrees. He was delighted to report that the aircraft handled magnificently. It was not until 6 February that the next flight was made, and after more investigations and modification work at Weybridge and Boscombe Down, the design team was confident that the landing gear was now in a satisfactory state. Various modifications had been attempted at Weybridge and with increased hydraulic forces now concentrated on the main wheel bogies, everyone was confident that they would rotate as intended when subjected to the pressures of significant airflow in flight. The weather conditions were less than favourable at Boscombe and the snow-covered landscape lay under a thick cloud base which was down to 1,000ft in places. The aircraft had not been cleared to fly in IMC (Instrument Met Conditions) nor could it fly through icing conditions, which meant that Beamont (with Bowen again in the back seat) would have to keep the test-flight low in order to keep clear of any potential icing and to maintain visual contact with the ground.

XR219 duly powered its way back into the air accompanied by Dell in the Lightning, and once settled under the thick cloud cover, Dell moved in to observe the gear retraction sequence. Beamont selected the 'up' switch and the gear assemblies began to shift and rumble. This time, after a few gentle jolts, the legs closed fully into their bays and the doors slammed shut. Finally, after ten flights, the TSR2 was flying 'clean'. Dell confirmed that XR219 was now in a proper flight configuration and in order to establish that the retraction system was functioning properly, Beamont selected the 'down' switch to re-cycle the whole sequence. With great relief and delight on the part of Beamont, the gear slowly extended and locked into place, before being retracted successfully back into the aircraft fuselage. Greatly encouraged, Beamont was now able finally to take the aircraft out of the low speed envelope and explore the its abilities at more representative air speeds.

Flaps were retracted to zero at 240kt, the auxiliary air intakes closed, and without any additional power, XR219 slowly began to accelerate, a slight airframe buffeting disappearing as the aircraft passed through 270kt. At 300kt the controls were checked and Dutch roll handling explored, and as the aircraft headed south, Beamont repeated the process at 50kt increments; 350kt, 400kt, 450kt and finally at 500kt, the aircraft's predicted wing and tail flutter limit which would be subject to later testing. The aircraft handled perfectly and with deteriorating weather, Dell had a difficult task keeping formation on XR219 which intermittently disappeared into patches of low cloud and heavy snow showers. Still at 500kt, Beamont carefully executed a gentle 2g turn low over Dorset, bringing XR219 through 180 degrees back onto a return leg to Boscombe Down, noting that the aircraft was handling magnificently and with a rock-steady smooth ride, in contrast to conditions in the Lightning where Dell was complaining of turbulence. Back at Boscombe a landing was made at 160kt and the aircraft was brought to a comfortable halt in less than 3,000ft. Post flight, Beamont wrote "General flight conditions at 500kt IAS in low cloud/moderate turbulence at low level were extremely satisfactory… particularly at very low altitude where well-matched damping and responsiveness… added up to just the degree of precision essential for low-level combat."

Freed of further undercarriage retraction problems, the flight-test programme now proceeded with speed and the aircraft's flight envelope was gradually expanded over the following five weeks during which XR219 flew another 13 times. The only slight disruption to the schedule was on Flight No.12 on 10 February, when Don Knight made his first conversion flight onto the type. After completing a successful "shake-down" sortie he returned to Boscombe and unintentionally executed a landing which was within the aircraft's rate-of-descent limits but significantly heavier than anything which had occurred previously. XR219 slammed down onto the runway, lurched back into the air and continued to 'pogo' along the concrete, the ungainly landing gear structure visibly flexing. Designed to withstand extremely heavy landings, the undercarriage handled the rather unorthodox arrival successfully, but the port gear's forestay jack was fractured and subsequent inspections and replacements caused a slight delay in the test programme. But in all other respects the test schedule proceeded smoothly and on 16 February Jimmy Dell flew the aircraft to 30,000ft and Mach 0.9, establishing engine and airframe handling conditions which would be necessary for a long overland flight which would now be necessary.

An early morning winter's scene at Boscombe Down, with XR219 being prepared for a test flight while Jimmy Dell's chase Lightning XM968 awaits attention in the background. Most of the short flight test programme was conducted in less-than ideal weather conditions through the winter and early spring of 1965. *BAC*

After having operated from Boscombe Down for so long, it was time to shift XR219's test programme to Warton where BAC's facilities and personnel would be on hand to support the main test programme. Moving to Warton would be a significant step, not only for the programme's progress, but also for the BAC team there who were eager to have what they understandably regarded as their 'baby' brought home to the place where the original P.17 had been drawn up. Beamont and his colleagues were naturally eager to 'go home' too, and although other BAC flight-test personnel would remain at Boscombe Down to handle the second TSR2 XR220 (which was being re-assembled at Boscombe in the hangar assigned to BAC), 22 February would be an important milestone. If everything went to plan, the day would also be significant for one other reason too – it would be the day on which the TSR2 would go supersonic.

With Peter Moneypenny taking the back seat, Beamont said his goodbyes to the flight test team and lined up on Boscombe's runway at 1313 hrs, accompanied by Jimmy Dell in the Lightning. Although they expected to be back soon in order to fly the second aircraft, XR220, it was in fact the last day on which any TSR2 would ever fly out of Boscombe Down. As XR219 climbed away through the murky conditions, the TSR2 was soon out of view.

The Met forecast predicted significant icing conditions in the cloud cover which extended over the whole route from 1,500ft up to 7,000ft. With development engines that had no anti-icing systems, Beamont judged that with careful planning a safe climb and descent could be made in the prevailing conditions and after departing from Boscombe Down he entered into a steady climb up to 28,000ft, settling at a cruising speed of Mach 0.9. The long leg northwards took XR219 and its crew out towards the Welsh coast, using Wallasey's TACAN beacon for navigation, and once clear of the coastline,

Beamont made a further shallow climb to 30,000ft and turned northwards across the Irish Sea into the familiar supersonic flight corridor that he had flown on many previous occasions during the Lightning's test programme.

Having obtained clearance to proceed, he applied maximum unreheated power to both engines, and whilst preparing to light the reheat on No.1 engine at altitude for the first time, he observed that the Machmeter had already crept up to 0.99 and without any buffet or vibration it nudged forward to 1.01. XR219 was supersonic. Reheat on No.1 engine was then selected and at Mach 1.12 a series of response and Dutch roll tests were quickly performed before reheat was cancelled, much to the delight of Jimmy Dell who was having a hard time maintaining a trail formation.

Still supersonic, Beamont turned the aircraft to port with a gentle application of 2g and with a very slight tremor the air speed fell back below Mach One. With fuel now rapidly dwindling it was time to complete the test flight and a long descent towards Warton was initiated, using Warton's TACAN beacon for navigation. Entering cloud at 10,000ft, XR219 emerged under the gloom just above 1,000ft and the familiar shape of Warton Airfield and its surroundings soon came into view, enabling Beamont to make a visual recovery to the airfield, completed by a fast and low (200ft) flypast for the benefit of the assembled spectators who had emerged from the BAC factory to see their magnificent creation for the first time. Once settled into the airfield circuit, a final approach was made from the east and after a gentle landing, the TSR2 was finally on the ground at Warton, trailing the familiar orange brake parachute. Minutes later XR219 rumbled onto Warton's apron and parked squarely in front of the famous English Electric Sheds, while what seemed to be the entire BAC work force looked on with wonder and admiration:

TSR2 XR219 Flight No. 14

Take-off

The aircraft was stopped on the run-up point and power increased to 70/70% and then to 90/90% for nozzle over-ride and flap checks, after transferring to bring the fuel back into 2,500lb balance differential and the cg gauge to 39.2.

Nozzle over-ride checks: SHUT/SHUT.

Flap blow checks : Flaps 20 degree blow in mid 20 degree segment

Flaps 35 degree blow in mid 35 degree segment

Flaps 50 degree blow in mid 50 degree segment

cg checked after reducing to 70/70%: G.39.2 F.39.3

After discussion with the Flight Test Van it was decided to accept this out-of-balance case as probably transitory.

Heading checks 168/168 degrees Max. Dry Normal: 96.4/97.7%:

726/706 degrees C Reheat lights and staging to and gutter satisfactory and take-off normal with lift-off at approximately 190kt.

Runway 06 wind 060 degrees/4kt.

Double Datum Intermediate selected immediately after take-off and followed by undercarriage UP selection at approximately 210kt. The climb angle was maintained to hold speed below 220kt during the undercarriage cycle which was normal, and cloud was entered at 1,700ft before completion of the reheat light sequence.

Reheat was cancelled passing 4,000ft and the cloud layer cleared at 96.2/96.0% (Max. dry intermediate). Flaps 20 degrees selected to zero at 260kt after nearly forgetting them.

Speed was slowly increased on the climb heading (351) to 350kt/0.8 Indicated Mach Number (IMN) at 17,000ft where a small amount of left rudder trim was required to centre the slip ball and correct a light asymmetric lateral stick force. Use of the rudder trimmer was more coarse than the pitch and roll trim circuits, and tended to result in over-correction.

On the northerly climb heading reception with Southern Radar and with Boscombe Radar was soon reduced to Strength 2 (lower aerial), and Warton Radar was received 5/5 from 20,000ft at approximately 150 nm.

Boscombe TACAN was held on back bearing as far as Wallasey where Middleton was selected with Warton Offset and lock-on achieved.

25,000ft/0.86 IMN, 95/95% 666/640 C.

All systems serviceable and flight conditions comfortable except for the cabin conditioning. This had been set at Normal for take-off and after ten minutes had resulted in cold conditions at the pilot's cockpit and uncomfortably cold at the navigator's. Auto Full Warm was selected for the next ten minutes. but this failed to change the temperature which remained uncomfortably cold.

In an attempt to prove the sense action of the selector, it was moved back to one-third from Full Cold and after five minutes no temperature change was noted, so it was re-set at Normal for the rest of the flight; the temperature at the pilot's cockpit becoming a little warmer during the subsequent descent but that at the navigator's station remaining uncomfortably cold throughout.

Speed was increased to 0.9 IMN and level flight established at 0.92/28,000ft power reduced to 82/82% initially.

At 0.9 IMN, the chase Lightning recorded 0.89/344kt.

During the climb, pitch control and damping were excellent as was the directional case, and above 20,000ft the lateral control became noticeably lighter but still adequately damped. In the level cruise condition the effects of inertia in the roll axis were noticeable with sharp inputs, but not with normally smooth stick movements.

Heading holding was of a high standard, and in this first experience constant attention was not given to steering accuracy due to preoccupation with other observations. In spite of this whenever the Heading Indicator was referred to, it was found to be within a degree or so of the originally selected heading throughout the 20-minute cruise. This same effect was apparent subsequently when setting up recovery headings for instrument descent, when heading holding accuracy was of a high order and required little concentration.

Altimeter checks on the Boscombe QFE (1,013mbs): Standby 29,000ft Main 29,100ft 0.92 IMN 86/86%

While preoccupied with taking observations height holding was not as easy as at lower altitudes, and a steady drift up was permitted.

In one speed excursion IMN was allowed to reach 0.935 when mild buffet vibration was felt. For the rest of the cruise approximately 0.92 was maintained at 84/85%,450/488 C. It was noted that the small power corrections necessary to stabilise speed were difficult to set up with this throttle control in the 85% range. Engine control was more precise above 90%.

At Wallasey it was decided to use the Test Run 'A' supersonic run under Warton control monitored by Ulster with position monitored by Middleton TACAN with Warton offset.

Power was increased to Max dry intermediate giving 95/95% and as IMN increased mild buffet vibration began at 0.93/30,000ft and reduced on passing 0.98 until no vibration was present at 1.0.

No perceptible trim changes had occurred in this acceleration, and lateral damping had increased until the sensation of lightness/inertia in the lateral control had disappeared.

P3 indication on the port engine was virtually off the bottom end of the scale at approximately 50-60 psi. This was outside the scheduled limits for reheat light. The condition was discussed with Warton Flight Test who confirmed that this should be a gauge error, and suggested a cautious investigation of reheat ignition within the prescribed Inciting height/speed channel.

While this discussion was in progress some unsteadiness was noted in ASI and Altimeter, and at 1.0/400kt the jump-up occurred to 1.01/405kt with Main Altimeter jump-up amount not recorded accurately.

This condition occurred In a slight descent from 30,500ft and the aircraft was levelled out again at 30,000ft with jump-up/jump-down indications continuing spasmodically. There were no associated trim changes or vibrations.

With No. 2 engine maintaining Max dry intermediate, No.1 reheat was lit satisfactorily and appeared to shunt between 1 and 2 gutters. The throttle was moved forward progressively to 3rd gutter which stabilised and acceleration continued in this condition.

Speed increased quite quickly with a clear jump-up on the Altimeter, but less than 5kt on the ASI, and was continued to 1.12/440kt/29,500ft.

Use of No.1 reheat at 3rd gutter only, resulted in a slight starboard directional trim change (half slip ball), and this was corrected with a small port rudder trim input.

Flight conditions supersonic remained smooth and trim change-free, and damping and response to small inputs on all three axes was smooth and precise.

Any tendency to the feeling of the effects of inertia in the lateral sense disappearing above 1.00 (Mach).

With No.1 reheat only, fuel asymmetry developed normally and this was contained satisfactorily with use of the transfer system.

Fuel : F.7,600/A.5,000lb.

The chase aircraft confirmed passing the jump-up condition but had fallen behind during transition and was not able to give a steady state speed check.

No. 1 reheat was cancelled, and a port turn initiated maintaining height and allowing speed to reduce in the turn at approximately 2g. The jump-down occurred with no trim change and without buffet onset until slight vibration reappeared at approximately 0.98 IMN. This disappeared again at 1.5 g/0 .9 IMN approx.

With extensive cloud cover and a 5,000ft thick cloud sheet below 6,500ft a practical instrument descent condition was established during the initial recovery pattern for a radar controlled cloud break to Warton monitored by Offset TACAN.

Reducing IMN from 0.9 to 0.8 and subsequently to 370-350kt, with half airbrake from 15,000ft and power to trim a 3,500 fpm descent resulted in practical and pleasant instrument conditions.

Cloud penetration was made at fixed power (approximately 80/80%) in view of possible icing, and instrument flight In cloud from 6,000-1,700ft was steady and conducive to confidence. Scan of the main Head-Down Display was not satisfactory due to the wide separation of the VSI from the other main references, and it was once again easier to fly on the Standby group alone as this contains the VSI well within normal scan. The circuit was joined with 1.5 miles visibility in smoke haze, and a low level run was carried out from east to west across Warton at 150ft/460kt. As before control conditions in this configuration were smooth and precise, and no disturbance was felt from turbulence. Fuel: F.6,800/A.4,200lb.

A gentle climbing turn was Initiated while reducing power, and at approximately 450kt/2.0-2 .5g about two seconds of high frequency vibration was felt. This was of low amplitude and approximately 35-40 cycles per second (cps) and disappeared on reducing g, but this may have been coincidental.

Speed was further reduced and the aircraft lined up at 320kt for a second run, and during the turn the buffet boundary encountered clearly at 2g. Fuel: F.6,300/A.3,800lb.

Speed was reduced to 210kt and undercarriage DOWN selected.

The cycle appeared normal but left the Starboard RED on (flickering) for 2-3 minutes. This went out leaving no lights on the starboard leg, and the landing was continued on the basis of visual confirmation of the ankle-lock by periscope and the chase aircraft. Fuel F.6,200/A.3,700lb.

On final approach to 08 runway (approach lights at 2 nm) wind/velocity 055 degrees/7kt, dry surface) judgement of flare point over the undershoot caravan site was not too easy, but the touchdown occurred at 4.2ft/sec and was accompanied by undercarriage/airframe lateral oscillation for approximately two seconds ±1.5g/5cps approx.

Tail parachute normal. Wheel braking increased to maximum at 100kt.

Fuel:F.5,700/A.3,200lb.

The turn to back-track was carried out at the confluence with the eastern perimeter track, and the practical turning radius did not seem suitable for a normal 180 turn within the runway width itself under all operating conditions.

Shut-down checks recorded by Navigator.

Summary

In cruise conditions at 30,000ft the cabin conditioning system temperature control was unsatisfactory, and the cockpits became uncomfortably cold.

Stability and control (un-auto-stabilised) over the currently explored flight envelope from 160kt-520kt at low level, and to 1.1 IMN/30,000ft is of a high quality and requires no design action.

Speed stability and control of the cruise condition at 0.9/30,000ft is similar to other aircraft In this category; but the transition characteristics, which lack buffet or trim change, are superior to those of any other aircraft flown by the writer.

The transition jump-up was reached unexpectedly at Max dry Intermediate in a slight descent at 30,000ft (Met.Temperature 52 C).

The first reheat light-up at altitude was satisfactory.

In the first full instrument recovery on this aircraft, Instrument platform characteristics proved favourable as predicted. Some unsatisfactory features were confirmed in the Head-Down Display layout.

R. P. BEAMONT
Manager: Flight Operations

Once settled in at Warton, XR219's test programme continued and the aircraft was back in the air just three days after having arrived. The troublesome undercarriage was still a concern as the landing vibrations were still present, but now that the gear's retraction sequence had been fixed to a satisfactory standard, the other problems did not have any direct effect on the flight schedule. But as the programme continued, a great deal of effort was devoted to ways in which a solution could be found to the vibration phenomenon, and some of the test flights from Warton ended with a landing onto a bed of foam laid down on the runway by the company's fire crew. This was intended to reduce friction and explore the effects of reduced wheel spin-up drag and although it did not provide a solution, the foam landings did contribute some valuable data and also provided quite a spectacle for any observers who were lucky to witness one of these attention-grabbing arrivals.

Eventually, it was decided that the solution to the vibration problem could be achieved by attaching a simple fixed strut which linked the main leg and the rear of the bogie beam and this had a major effect on the gear's damping qualities. On flight Nos. 21 and 22 (both on 26 March) Jimmy Dell flew XR219 with a temporarily modified undercarriage (locked in the extended position) which incorporated the new strut and after flying a long series of touch-and-go landings, it was confirmed that the persistent vibration problem had finally been cured. At long last the TSR2's landing run was smooth, vibration-free and under complete control. While the undercarriage fixes had been preoccupying many people, other significant flight-testing had still been taking place. On 7 March Dell flew the aircraft up to 600kt and performed a variety of handling tests which indicated that the TSR2 performed faultlessly over a very wide envelope. On 26 February XR219 was given a first taste of what would be the TSR2's main operational environment, with Beamont taking the aircraft east from Warton and down over the Pennine hills where he successfully settled the aircraft into a very low-level run at just 200ft AGL in high-speed cruise conditions. As ever, the aircraft handled perfectly and maintained an impressive rock-steady stability. Beamont was delighted that the aircraft handled very well in the very conditions where it would be expected to operate in RAF service, and after recovering to 5,000ft he performed a series of partial roll tests, finally opting to execute a number of very spirited 360-degree rolls, much to the surprise of Jimmy Dell who accompanied the flight in the Lightning. While Beamont recovered from the difficult task of trailing the aircraft through the Pennine hills, where XR219 had thundered through the gloom with precision and relative comfort, by comparison Dell had to cope with almost intolerable turbulence. Having climbed to medium altitude, he now looked on with amazement as the huge white-painted bomber effortlessly rolled left and right with an agility which seemed to be no different to that of his own Lightning.

Significant problems during this phase of the test programme were few, the most troublesome being various fuel leaks (within the 'fueldraulic' system) which were recurrent and caused the curtailment of Flight No.18 when fuel balancing problems made further test-flying impossible. But progress was steady and on 31 March, Dell flew XR219 on Flight No.24 which included more general handling tests, and investigation of roll/yaw gearing. With this flight complete it had been agreed that the aircraft would be temporarily laid up so that fully modified landing gear could be fitted properly, and further fixes to the fueldraulic system could be made. Tragically, although nobody knew at the time, developments elsewhere meant that Flight No.24 would in fact be XR219's very last and as XR219 turned-off Warton's runway and jettisoned the brake parachute, few people could have imagined that 31 March was the day on which all TSR2 flying had just ended for good.

CHAPTER EIGHT

Engineered for Success

EVEN though Vickers had been awarded overall control of the TSR2 project, English Electric's team had a major influence upon the aircraft's continuing design and in many respects, the TSR2 (which was still defiantly referred to as the Type 571 on all manufacturing drawings until completion of the project) was in effect English Electric's P.17A, incorporating the weapons systems of the Type 571. The final P.17A design remained virtually unchanged during the subsequent BAC design process which combined the talents of the Preston and Weybridge teams. English Electric's considerable experience in supersonic design was an asset which BAC naturally exploited and when combined with Vickers expertise in electronic systems and other airborne equipment (not least its established interest in terrain-following radar), the resulting design process was based around what was almost a simple division of the aircraft into two halves; the wings, tail and rear fuselage being the responsibility of English Electric, and the forward fuselage (including all the necessary systems) assigned to Vickers.

Technicians loading an Olympus engine into XR219 at Weybridge. The aircraft's fuselage structure was barely wide enough to accommodate each engine and clearances of only a fraction of an inch would have been common to production aircraft (it had been reduced to just 0.3in by 1964) . Each aircraft was to have its own set of gauges in order to ensure that any particular engine would actually fit. Changes to the engine accessories bay (which was considered to be a flight safety risk in its existing configuration) were likely to reduce space still further, decreasing fuel capacity and affecting the air brake configuration. These changes had yet to be addressed by the time that the project was cancelled. It seems likely that the proposed "easy" engine change for field operations would have been impossible to attain. *BAC*

The same division of responsibility was carried through to the manufacturing process where a fifty-fifty work-share was created and it was proposed that the Vickers-built forward fuselage (and other sub-assemblies) would be completed at Weybridge before being mated with the main aircraft structure (rear fuselage, wings and tail) which would be constructed by English Electric at Samlesbury and then transported south by road. It seems certain that the process would in fact have been reversed for a full production contract so that the completed aircraft could have been flown out of the Samlesbury factory and test-flown from nearby Warton.

During 1958 English Electric had produced a report ('The Economics of GOR.339') which reviewed the research and development costs of the airframe, engines and all other equipment. Vickers had quoted fairly definitive cost estimates in its Type 571 submission (which undoubtedly helped it in securing eventual control of the contract when it was issued), but English Electric had adopted a more cautious approach, being prepared only to offer quotes against a specific and firm specification. The report reached some interesting conclusions, not least that the final design should ideally be set at the overall dimensions of the P.17 project. A larger aircraft would increase costs without any immediate major gains in performance, whereas a smaller aircraft would increase costs and prohibit further development potential. The report emphasised that wherever possible, use should be made of existing equipment and material and that the greatest economy would come from the use of an existing engine and reheat system – something which English Electric still firmly believed in when BAC was eventually obliged to adopt the new and untested Bristol Olympus.

Likewise, English Electric also questioned whether even terrain-following radar or the proposed linescan reconnaissance/navigation system was essential and that a refined inertial navigation system might be sufficient. Other engineering issues were also addressed including the preference for the use of simplified structures whenever possible, including constant or right-angle structural joints, the employment of straight lines (such as the wing contours and spars), flat skins (particularly the flap surfaces) and parallel fuselage surfaces. The report also stated that a simplified landing gear without joints or complex structure would also save money but this was one aspiration which eventually became a victim of Vickers' enthusiasm for a much more complex system which eventually became a major hindrance to flight-testing progress. The large, ungainly and seemingly over-engineered landing gear assemblies were a direct result of the Air Ministry's insistence upon a short-field performance which it believed would be essential if the aircraft was to operate within a 'battlefield' scenario where conventional airfields would probably be destroyed. The ability to operate in and out of a small, unprepared strip which was no better than that necessary for a C-47 was not, in itself, a difficult proposition, but designing such a capability (the term 'Mach Two from a Cabbage Patch' became popular at Weybridge) for a supersonic bomber was far from easy.

The need for STOL (Short Take-Off and Landing) ability had been written into the OR.339 requirement and had been addressed by English Electric right from the start. As part of its original submission, a derivative of the P.17A (the P.17D) was

Graphic image of the Olympus test bed Vulcan XA894, pictured at Filton shortly after the installed trials engine broke-up during a ground run, engulfing the aircraft in flames. The crew successfully evacuated the aircraft in a matter of seconds but the aircraft was completely destroyed. The loss of the aircraft and delays to the engine development programme (no replacement aircraft being attainable within the time scale required) were a significant factor in the project's troubled history. *Rolls-Royce*

also offered, which would at least, in theory, have given the Air Staff a VTOL (Vertical Take-Off and Landing) tactical strike aircraft, without any risk of complicated and time-consuming design problems within the actual aircraft. Produced in collaboration with Shorts in Belfast (a company which already had a close working arrangement with English Electric), the P.17D concept took advantage of Shorts experience in short and vertical take-off technology, and instead of incorporating this capability into the P.17A aircraft itself, the proposal outlined a means of creating a separate VTOL 'lifting body' which was, in effect, a flying platform on which the P.17A could be carried into the air vertically, launched in forward flight, and then recovered through a reversal of the process. The advantage of this design was that it enabled the P.17A to be designed without any compromises that would be necessary in order to incorporate STOL capability (such as cumbersome landing gear, vectored thrust or aerodynamic changes), and it would also allow English Electric to concentrate exclusively on the P.17's design while Shorts addressed the VTOL/STOL issue as a separate project. The disadvantage of the P.17D proposal was that it was wildly ambitious and ultimately unrealistic. The lifting body was to be powered by no fewer than 56 Rolls-Royce RB.108 engines and the concept of relying on so many engines to function perfectly, especially in field conditions, seemed optimistic as best and naïve at worst. Not surprisingly, the idea never proceeded beyond a basic concept stage.

As a more practical alternative the P.17B (also proposed as part of English Electric's submission) incorporated three RB.108 lift engines which would give the actual aircraft a respectable short-field capability, but this inevitably reduced the aircraft's range and/or increased its weight, and ran the risk of prolonged developmental problems. Shorts also proposed its own P.17 derivative, having first created a design submission for OR.339 which, after having agreed with English Electric

Impressive image of XR219 captured at the start of another ground-shaking take-off run at Boscombe Down. The immensely powerful engines were appropriate for the aircraft's supersonic performance and their thrust was vital for the short-field take-off requirement stipulated by the Air Staff. But reliance upon engine thrust for short take-off (including wing blowing for additional lift) would have been a risky business. Although the aircraft incorporated a "thrust meter" (which measured nine parameters), the aircraft could not be held at full thrust on the brakes, therefore the pilot would not know how much thrust was available for take-off until the aircraft had started rolling – hardly an ideal situation when the available take-off distance was already severely limited. *BAC*

that it shared many of the P.17's features, was modified to incorporate some of the advances which English Electric had made as part of its own project. The joint proposal (the P.17C) was a true VTOL aircraft which showed great promise, but it was quickly established that had it been selected, it too would suffer inevitably from cost increases and delivery delays which would result from the complicated jet lift design, and in order to ensure that a practical design was delivered within a realistic timescale, a more conventional aircraft would have to be adopted. Ultimately, all of these imaginative proposals were abandoned when the P.17A became part of the combined English Electric Vickers (BAC) design, and Shorts' input (much to its great disappointment) was consigned to history. Ultimately, it was the influence of the Vickers design (or more precisely the influence of Supermarine) with its wing-blowing devices which resulted in a conventional aircraft layout, but one which relied upon a bulky and complex undercarriage.

The initial design of the Type 571 had been heavily influenced by the Supermarine team's recent experience (notably with the Scimitar) and its belief that the new design might

eventually have a useful naval application (and as mentioned previously, this notion was encouraged by Ministry officials). Consequently, a supremely strong undercarriage assembly combined with a high-lift wing employing 'blowing' (as had been employed in the Scimitar) was its preference, and this was developed into a twin-wheel bogie design when the Supermarine concept was combined with input from Vickers, where the huge twin-wheel assembly created for the Valiant was undoubtedly influential. But like English Electric, Vickers also considered at least one distinctly unorthodox means of giving the Type 571 a vertical (or at least very short) take-off capability through the use of a system which had first been explored in Australia during 1952, and later tested by the US Navy.

The basic concept was a reversed piston design with a pair of rollers attached to the aircraft which gripped a 'hose' device. When the hose was inflated at high pressure (with compressed air) the rollers (and attached aircraft) would be propelled forwards. A reverse principle could be used to arrest an aircraft within a short distance. The idea seems even more absurd than the P.17D launch platform, but it was given serious consideration until the ever-increasing weight of the proposed aircraft became far too high to enable such a launch concept to work. Thus, attention shifted back to a more conventional system comprising a high-lift wing, high engine thrust and wing 'blowing' devices, combined with a conventional undercarriage which could support a heavy aircraft on rough terrain. With hindsight, the wing-blowing system was fundamental to the aircraft's success, but the landing gear which was finally adopted was undoubtedly far too complex and the endless malfunctions which dogged the prototype's early test flight serve to confirm that a simpler design would have saved a great deal of time and money. Vickers clearly believed that it was important to meet the Air Ministry's requirement for short-field performance, but English Electric appear to have been far more inclined to question whether it was a requirement which really would be needed – at least to such a high specification.

Although the belief that, inevitably, all airfields of significant size would be destroyed during any conflict seemed reasonable, the notion that an aircraft with TSR2's performance and complexity would be operated from a 'cabbage patch' seems almost ludicrous. Yet few people (at least beyond the walls of English Electric's Preston office) seem to have ever questioned the validity of the concept at the time. It seems far more likely that had TSR2 ever been used in a conflict, it would have relied upon existing paved roads for dispersal away from airfields, and would probably have operated from motorways and other similar stretches of prepared surface, where extreme STOL capability would no longer be necessary, and a complicated undercarriage capable of absorbing very high rates of descent, would not be required. But as with other aspects of the TSR2 programme, the aircraft short-field performance was designed to a standard which was so good that it was arguably far better than what was really required. The emphasis continued to be placed on ambitious performance almost for its own sake, with little consideration of the true nature of any likely future conflicts.

But in overall terms, it is clear that English Electric's emphasis on simplified engineering was carried through the design and construction process, until the design was finally frozen in 1962, enabling attention to shift from continual modifications to the aircraft's layout and structure, and on to the task of physically cutting metal. The overall proportions of the fuselage remained virtually unchanged throughout the design process and the finalised layout was remarkably similar to the original P.17 which, itself, was similar to the Type 571, albeit somewhat larger. It was the wing design which went through a number of subtle changes and although the finished result was still very similar to the P.17A's, it was very different to the design which had been envisaged for the swept-wing Type 571. The 'saw tooth' leading edge which had first been proposed was eventually abandoned after wind tunnel tests confirmed that the modification was unnecessary and in effect, the finalised wing design was a simple delta which offered the best performance in terms of crew comfort at high speed and low level. With high wing loading and a low aspect ratio design, any increase in incidence caused by vertical gust response gave a correspondingly small lift increase and therefore maintained a surprisingly smooth ride which was

(and probably still would be) better than anything which could be achieved by virtually any other aircraft type.

The distinctive down-turned wing tips were a later modification which was introduced after it was established that the wings would provide greater lateral stability if they incorporated a small degree of anhedral (downwards) deflection. However, this would encourage the airflow from the wings to interfere with the smooth flow over the tailplanes, particularly at lower speeds, and so in order to avoid this potential problem, the wings were maintained at their original level position, but with the outer portions deflected sharply downwards by some thirty degrees, creating the same aerodynamic effect as a smaller deflection across the entire wing.

The main torque box which also served as an integral fuel tank, had a total of seven spars, each of which was joined on each side of the aircraft to the top of a fuselage frame, the joints being two-pin swinging links which could move longitudinally or transversely or slide up to a distance of 6mm, enabling the entire wing structure to flex. This ensured that none of these joints was likely to suffer from fatigue stress and also contributed greatly to the reduction of vertical and lateral accelerations which would otherwise be transmitted to the cockpits. In effect, this design allowed the wing to absorb a great deal of turbulence without transmitting it to the fuselage and with the cockpits positioned at a nodal point of flexture, the ride for the crew was exceptionally smooth.

The wing design was a remarkable piece of engineering and fundamental to TSR2's outstanding performance, and it is testament to English Electric's design skills that the basic proportions of the wing remained virtually unchanged from the P.17 right through to the production-standard aircraft, the only late change being a shift of some three inches along the fuselage which was made in 1960 before the overall design was finally fixed. Although simple in design, the wing's supersonic profile was, of course, completely at odds with the short-field take-off and landing capability which the Air Ministry also wanted, but with supremely powerful engines (giving an excellent thrust-to-weight ratio), and full-span blown flaps, the aircraft would still be capable of rapid acceleration and a brisk take-off performance. This was further enhanced by an unusual nose wheel landing gear assembly which was designed to extend by an additional 42 inches, giving the aircraft a pronounced nose-up attitude. The extension could be selected either before take-off or during the take-off run (almost all forward vision was lost once the nose was raised) to provide a positive rotational force which would be much greater than that provided only by the tailplanes. The concept seemed plausible although it was obviously fraught with potential problems, and the TSR2 test pilots were certainly less than convinced that the system would work safely. However, when flight-testing began it was quickly established that the tailplanes provided much greater control authority than had been expected which rendered the nose gear extension unnecessary, and it is likely that the system would have been omitted from production aircraft, enabling the nose gear to be simpler and lighter.

The aircraft's tail surfaces were, if anything, more innovative than the main wing, in that they were designed to be all-moving

Moving map display unit pictured whilst powered-up, illustrating a typical image which would have been available to both pilot and navigator.

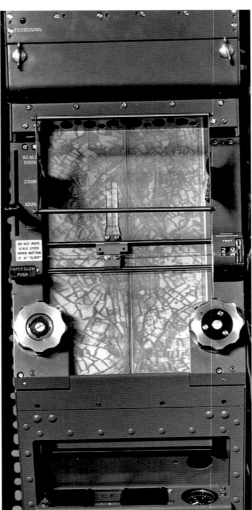

The sideways-looking radar unit produced an image which was translated onto photographic paper (as illustrated). Although crude by modern standards, the system was certainly effective, but the time required to process the image meant that the navigator would have been obliged to rely on "retrospective navigation" in order to fix the aircraft's position.

structures. In much the same way that an air-to-air missile relies upon fins which provide free control in each axis, the TSR2 had no fixed control surfaces. The tailplanes were one-piece designs which operated together to provide pitch control, and in opposition to create a rolling motion, there being no conventional ailerons on the wing with which to achieve this (the entire wing trailing edge being made available for flaps, in order to improve the aircraft's low-speed capability). In high speed or supersonic flight, very little surface movement was necessary but at lower speeds the tailplanes (what would now be referred to as 'tailerons') could be deflected quite significantly to produce tremendous authority which was enhanced still further by the operation of additional geared elevators which came into operation when the wing flaps were deployed.

The fin was also a one-piece structure which had originally included two additional ventral surfaces (on the P.17 design) but these were subsequently dropped. Likewise, consideration was also given to slightly smaller twin fins mounted obliquely (in a similar fashion to the modern F-22), but English Electric's pursuance of simplicity again triumphed and the resulting fin design was surprisingly uncomplicated with only a small leading edge intake and an even smaller trailing edge navigation light breaking the clean lines. The overall size of the fin (including thickness) was kept down to reduce both drag and weight, and predicted flutter problems were avoided by the inclusion of a large mass at the apex of the fin, thereby avoiding clumsy horn balances. Above Mach 1.7 the aircraft was directionally unstable without the control of an artificial stability system. It is interesting to note that during the design process, a Warton factory memo mentions that "...this may well be the time to abandon ideas of a stable airframe." Of course the concept of directionally unstable combat aircraft was to become common within combat aircraft designs some decades later.

The brilliance of the TSR2's aerodynamic properties was only part of the aircraft's capabilities and as a 'Weapons System' a great deal of the aircraft's performance relied upon sophisticated avionics, and the equipment housed inside the aircraft was just as important as the airframe itself. While the aircraft's design was based largely upon English Electric's P.17A, the avionics were very much part of Vickers' expertise and Weybridge took responsibility for most of the system design. Fundamental to the whole TSR2 concept was the aircraft's ability to fly at high speed and low level in order to press home an attack and although the concept was not new, the TSR2 embraced the technique like no other aircraft had ever done before. Indeed it is true to say that during the early 1960s no other aircraft was even nearly capable of flying an operational mission at speeds of around Mach 0.9, flying just

200ft above the ground for sustained periods. The fact that TSR2 was actually capable of performing this feat at Mach 1.2 is therefore all the more astonishing and even 50 years later it represents a capability which few other aircraft (if any) could match. At the very heart of this system was the Ferranti Terrain Following Radar (TFR) which was developed in co-operation with Vickers specifically for the TSR2 programme.

The use of forward-looking radar to provide terrain clearance was not a completely new concept at the time of TSR2's development, and some experimental work had been progressing in the USA since 1955 when Cornell University embarked on a research study which was funded by the US Department of Defense. Surprisingly, the concept's potential was largely ignored by the DoD and it was the intervention of Vickers that kept it alive. They took over the existing development contract and work on TFR continued as a joint project between Vickers, Cornell University and Ferranti – a company with plenty of expertise in the field of radar design and manufacture.

Most of the research and development relied on conventional existing technology but the combined team embarked upon investigations into how the concept of terrain avoidance could be developed still further. Traditionally, Terrain Avoidance consisted of a radar system which identified ground obstructions, or rising terrain, and issued a 'nose up' demand which would enable a pilot to climb out of danger. This provided an obvious ability to fly low with a good degree of safety, but in tactical terms the system was flawed, because once a radar obstruction had been avoided, the aircraft would emerge over the crest of a hill and become instantly vulnerable to visual or radar detection. A truly effective system would be one which enabled the pilot to hug the ground and not only climb to avoid rising terrain, but to immediately pull back downwards to follow the terrain as it

fell away again. Cornell's work was said to be some two years ahead of any comparable work being done elsewhere, and with the input of Ferranti and Vickers experts, they eventually expanded their existing 'Autoflite' avoidance system to work as an efficient TFR. This was achieved by the creation of what is referred-to as a 'ski toe locus' which comprised a forward-looking radar beam which acted upon a set of references which matched the shape of a ski toe, slowly curving upwards ahead of the aircraft. When the locus came into contact with any terrain, a pull-up command signal was issued and once the aircraft began to manoeuvre, the radar's references immediately reverted to a pull-down command until the locus again made contact with the ground, continuing this process in a flowing series of commands which matched the terrain as it presented itself in front of the aircraft. The result was a system which enabled the aircraft to safely hug the contours of any terrain ahead of the aircraft, at altitudes as low as just 200ft, with no limitation on speed.

The TFR was sufficiently reliable to enable the input commands to be fed directly into TSR2's internal autopilot system so that the pilot would not have to follow slavishly the radar's commands, and could allow the aircraft to fly automatically, monitoring the TFR's commands through his Head Up Display. The TFR was capable of sustaining itself through turning flight of up to 40 degrees and in order to accommodate level ground and over-water flight, the system was combined with a conventional radar altimeter signal. In order to provide a good degree of safety, the TFR also relied on a duplicated two-signal system and if the radar should fail for any reason, it was designed to immediately issue an automatic pull-up command so that the aircraft would be positioned away from any obstacles, enabling the pilot to immediately resume manual control.

A rare illustration of the extended nose gear facility, the access ladder emphasising the pronounced nose-up attitude created by the system. Although the short take-off system seemed practical in theory, the TSR2 test pilots remained sceptical as to whether it would have been of use for operational missions. With the nose gear extended, forward vision was lost and with a critically small area available for take-off, the risk of losing forward vision seemed at best a risky idea. Thankfully the aircraft's tailerons were more than capable of providing the aircraft with good rotation authority. On this photograph the nose-mounted pitot tube probe appears to have been temporarily removed. *BAC*

Ferranti assumed responsibility for the TSR2's definitive TFR system and although the development process was far from smooth (with many delays which almost resulted in the system being abandoned in favour of an inferior American option) it showed great promise. The TFR system was never actively flown in a TSR2 as the entire project was cancelled before flight trials could begin, but there is every reason to suppose that it would have worked well, not least because extensive flight trials were performed by Ferranti, using its own Canberra and Buccaneer aircraft, and the desolate Scottish Highlands regularly reverberated to the sound of Ferranti's low-flying white-painted Buccaneer, thundering across the hills, lochs and forests almost at treetop height. TFR is of course almost a standard piece of equipment in many modern attack aircraft, but for an aircraft of the 1960s it was a revolutionary concept.

The primary navigation system for TSR2 was a Ferranti inertial platform (comprising of three single-axis gyros) which was designed in association with the Royal Aircraft Establishment (RAE) at Farnborough. Originally planned to have a margin of error which equated to around 2 miles after an hour's supersonic flight, it proved to be rather less reliable and generally fluctuated around a 6-miles error after a distance of 700-800 miles. However the INS (Inertial Navigation System) was linked to a Doppler radar developed by Decca. The INS calculated heading and velocity whilst Doppler calculated ground speed and drift and together they were fed into the aircraft's central computer system, resulting in a much better accuracy which matched or exceeded the original 2-mile error requirement. The on-board computer (in fact there were two) was a development of the American Autonetics Verdan system which had first been created for ballistic missile use and was subsequently fitted in the North American Vigilante. An equivalent British system known as DEXAN (Digital Experimental Airborne Navigator) was also pursued by GEC as part of a government-funded programme designed to

investigate the potential of digital computing, but this was largely abandoned following the 1957 Defence Review when it was assumed, rather foolishly, that with no further plans for manned combat aircraft, such developments would be unnecessary. Ultimately, it was accepted that only the Verdan computer would be suitable for TSR2 and this was heavily modified by Elliott Automation until it was sufficiently capable, although it is interesting to note that the computer's memory was only a meagre 2k which was stored on hard disk – ridiculously small by modern standards, but sufficient with which to handle TSR2's systems – only just.

The combined information was presented to the aircraft's navigator as a distance-to-go and track input, as calculated against a series of pre-set fix points which would be pre-set by the navigator. However, even with a combined Doppler and INS input, the speed and distances covered required even more navigational precision and this was achieved by the use of SLAR – Sideways Looking Airborne Radar. Developed by EMI, the SLAR system consisted of two 90-inch antennae which were accommodated in the nose section under the cockpits. With one antenna on each side of the aircraft, a radar picture of the surrounding landscape could be captured which could then be matched with the other navigational data to provide extremely accurate positional information. However, the system was not nearly as sophisticated as this description might seem and the resulting SLAR picture was recorded onto what was effectively simple photographic film which was chemically processed before being presented to the navigator as a read-out strip. Consequently there was a significant time lapse between the actual position of the aircraft and the SLAR image by the time that the navigator received it, and some considerable skill would have been required to correlate the SLAR image with real-time data.

But even with this deficiency, the SLAR could be used to update the aircraft's position every 100 miles or so, and the combination of all three systems and the navigator's skills would have ensured that the aircraft maintained a position which had an error of only yards even after many hundreds of miles had been flown. The navigator also had other systems at his disposal, not least of which was the moving map display which was first developed by the RAE at Farnborough and subsequently produced by Ferranti. A wide catalogue of aeronautical maps (covering all of the TSR2's likely operating areas) were recorded onto microfilm and these could be magnified onto a ground glass screen for both pilot and navigator. Linked to the aircraft's computer, the map image would shift in relation to the computer's inputs with a central cursor identifying the aircraft's position. The moving map was another innovative system which was successfully employed on many later aircraft programmes including the Jaguar, therefore it seems certain that it would have performed well in the TSR2. The navigator could also employ radar ground mapping, using the FLR to present a picture of the path ahead of the aircraft out to a maximum distance of 100 miles. Similarly, air-to-surface ranging would

Julian Amery, George Edwards and Beamont, three of the key individuals involved in the TSR2 programme, engaged in a post-flight conversation at Boscombe Down. *BAC*

Vulcan test bed XA894, displaying the 22R engine test pod and bifurcated intakes, attached to the aircraft's bomb bay. The loss of this aircraft dealt a severe blow to the engine development programme. By the time that another Vulcan could be converted into a test bed, the TSR2 flight test programme would have been well underway, therefore Bristol-Siddeley's only practical option was to subsequently rely exclusively on ground bench-testing of the engine. *Rolls-Royce*

present the navigator with a radar picture of the aircraft's projected path up to a distance of around 7 miles, and this could be linked-in to the radar's TFR mode so that a target site could be locked-in onto the radar after the final pre-attack navigational fixed point had been passed.

Other facilities included standard radio communications and it was also possible to operate a Beacon Mode in which the aircraft could interrogate a suitable beacon (either on the ground or in another aircraft such as a refuelling tanker), and the on-board computer would present steering instructions to the target beacon as required. This combination of systems would have given the TSR2 a formidable array of navigational and attack options which at the time were far in advance of anything available to comparable aircraft. Many of the systems were autonomous and 'discrete' which would have ensured that the aircraft was not vulnerable to radar and communications jamming, and that it also remained less visible to enemy sensor equipment, emphasising the TSR2's excellent ability to 'get through' to its targets.

But as development of the weapons system got underway, it soon became clear that, like most aspects of the programme,

significant delays would be incurred as various systems required modifications and improvements. For example, the aircraft's computing capacity was already small even from the outset (pitifully small when compared to modern systems). By 1964 it was established that additional computing capacity would be needed, and as an example it was necessary to reduce the number of automated nuclear weapons delivery modes from ten to just six, simply because insufficient memory capacity was available. A note from the DCAS issued early in 1965 stated that "…at the present stage of development it would be possible to programme only one mode of weapon delivery (e.g. lay-down or dive but not both) and ten pre-set fix points for any given sortie."

It was estimated that at least an additional ten per cent computing capacity would be required before the aircraft was issued to operational units but even with this additional power it would have been difficult to complete an operational sortie even without the pre-set fix points. The solution would have been a more powerful version of the verdant computer but this would have meant another development programme, more delays and more cost.

Perhaps the most complex and important TSR2 system was of course the engine and this was one of the primary elements which contributed to a series of developmental delays and cost increases. In many respects it is hardly surprising that the engine programme proved to be so difficult as the selected power plant – the Bristol Olympus – was in effect a completely new and untested design even though it was based on the hugely successful engine (of the same name) which already powered the Vulcan bomber.

At the beginning of the OR.339 project it seemed clear that English Electric would have preferred (for the P.17A) to adopt a new, but comparable, Rolls-Royce design which had first been designed to power the HS681, the jet transport which was to have replaced the Beverley and Hastings (until, like many other programmes, it was cancelled).

The Rolls-Royce RB141 Medway was expected to offer a dry thrust of 17,000lb which increased to 23,000lb with reheat. However unlike the Olympus, the Medway was a by-pass turbofan design which was consequently somewhat lighter (and cooler) than the Olympus and was likely to be more economic in terms of fuel consumption (which would directly translate into available range). There was some doubt as to whether a practical reheat design could be applied to a turbofan engine because of the increased oxygen flow and temperatures it would create, together with the more complicated exhaust flows. But trials with a Conway engine (a by-pass design) had already shown that reheat could be made to work and, of course, such systems became almost standard on modern combat aircraft.

In the USA a Medway was successfully modified by the Allison company to run with a reheat system, but with no such trials in Britain, there was little enthusiasm for the engine within official circles. English Electric and Vickers both eventually expressed their preference for the engine (George Edwards stated that it clearly had a much greater growth potential than the Olympus), but the Ministry of Supply concluded that as the Medway was likely to require further development (and would therefore delay the first flight of the TSR2 prototype) and because the Olympus offered a higher thrust, it would be selected in preference to the Medway. Of course, the Ministry failed to grasp that the Olympus engine for TSR2 would not be a simple development of the existing power plant. The need for sustained supersonic speed meant that the engine would have to be re-designed and tested, and the necessary research and development would be almost as much as that required for the creation of a completely new engine. Had the MoS understood this point, its decision might have been different, but on the basis of what it did know at the time, it seems that the Ministry did – for once – make what was clearly the right decision at the time, in order to expedite the TSR2's progress. Likewise, the merger of Bristol with Armstrong-Siddeley, de Havilland and Blackburn (to form Bristol-Siddeley Engines) also had an important part to play in the story, as the Government was ever-keen to support the concept of company amalgamation which had been forced upon English Electric and Vickers.

Rear view of the Olympus 320-22R engine, showing to advantage the long jet pipe and reheat unit which was developed by Bristol-Siddeley on co-operation with Solar. Also visible is the 36-piece variable-diameter nozzle which was operated pneumatically. Infinitely-variable reheat nozzles are now common to most combat aircraft, but at the time of TSR2's inception the concept was new and required a significant amount of design work, which would have been subject to a separate development programme. As part of the TSR2 programme, it became another source of delay and expense. *Tim McLelland*

The choice of the Olympus was therefore both a practical and political decision – at least as far as the Ministry was concerned. In comparison to the Olympus 301 which was fitted to late-production Mk.2 Vulcans, the new Olympus 320-22R was radically different, chiefly because the engine would have significantly greater demands placed upon it. The engine would be expected to successfully power TSR2 at speeds in excess of Mach 2.0 where temperatures are far beyond those which could ever be experienced by a high-flying Vulcan. It was estimated that when TSR2 accelerated to twice the speed of sound, the intake temperatures would be at least 160 degrees Celsius. This compares with a more typical temperature of maybe ten degrees or less for an aircraft flying at 2-300 knots. Consequently, the much-modified engine incorporated not only changes to the basic structure and composition of the internal components, but also required the use of various specialised metals (such as titanium and other even more exotic alloys) which were capable of sustaining prolonged periods of high temperature, and as expected this led to a huge amount of development work which naturally took time and raised costs quite considerably. Much could have been done to keep costs and delays to a minimum by accepting less ambitious performance figures and in the same way that English Electric often questioned the need for the seemingly excessive specifications, Bristol's Chief Engineer (Sir Stanley Hooker) also maintained that a much less complex and more affordable power plant could have been developed if the Ministries had not insisted upon such extremes.

The quest for speeds in excess of Mach Two placed design requirements on the engine which were out of all proportion to the costs incurred. In one exchange with the Vice Chief of Air Staffs, Hooker commented that the notion of attaining a range of 1,000 miles was one which had seemingly been "plucked out of the sky" and that the costs of attaining this figure probably equated to a £1 million per mile for the last 100 miles. But the Ministries stayed firm and TSR2's performance figures stayed as they were – or increased still further.

Even the design of the reheat (afterburner) unit for the Olympus presented Bristol with many problems. Back in 1956 a relatively unsophisticated reheat assembly (manufactured by the American company Solar) was successfully run on an Olympus, but the Solar reheat was intended only for relatively short periods of use (mostly during take-off) whereas the TSR2's engine would be expected to operate in reheat for sustained lengths of time. Eventually, Bristol, in co-operation with Solar, produced a new reheat unit which incorporated a 36-flap convergent-divergent variable-diameter nozzle which used a series of concentric ring burner manifolds to create an even gas flow and also maintain the reheat jet within the centre of the jet pipe, thereby keeping the pipe's walls cooler. The burner manifolds were ignited in sequence in direct relation to the pilot's engine throttle position and this, in effect, created a three-stage facility which – thanks to its electronic control – was not susceptible to misuse due to clumsy throttle use. When completed and tested, the reheat system proved to be surprisingly reliable and was markedly superior to may other reheat units employed in other aircraft which had often failed to ignite during ground and flight trials.

The Olympus 22R was subjected to its first test run in March 1961 and although the initial tests were largely successful, power output was unsatisfactory and development continued. It was not until the following year that the first setback occurred when a turbine blade broke during testing, leading to the disintegration of an entire turbine stage. After having concluded that the cast metal blade was too brittle, they were subsequently forged and as a fortunate by-product of this process, fuel efficiency was improved. After some 1,900 hours of bench-testing both at Bristol's Patchway works and the national Gas Turbine Establishment at Pyestock, flight-testing began from Filton using Vulcan XA894 which was modified to carry an Olympus 22R in an external fairing under the aircraft's bomb bay, fed by its own bifurcated air intake. Fuel for the engine was housed in the bomb bay and beyond the reheat exhaust an acoustic shield was fitted under the Vulcan's belly and a 35mm camera was installed to film the engine when in use (in fact the camera was never used successfully). The test flights commenced on 23 February 1962 and proceeded smoothly, eventually culminating in the first selection of full third-stage reheat on 12 November. Months later, however, the programme came to an abrupt halt when the Vulcan was destroyed during a ground run at Filton, and many months of remedial work were required to bring the engine up to an acceptably reliable standard. By the time of the TSR2's cancellation in 1965, the Olympus 22R was still somewhat short of achieving this goal. Ultimately the engine was refined into an outstanding piece of engineering which went on to power industrial power stations, warships and, of course, the Concorde airliner, which suggests that once the developmental problems had been finally resolved, it would have been the perfect engine for operational use in the TSR2. Yet because the design, development and testing of the engine was conducted directly in support of TSR2 (rather than as a separate programme), the development of the Olympus simply served to add to TSR2's problems as the delays and cost estimates grew ever larger.

CHAPTER NINE

Cost Concerns

BY 1961 it was already becoming clear that the TSR2 project was emerging as a victim of continual delays and seemingly endless cost increases, all of which appeared to be in danger of spiralling out of control. By June of that year BAC had revised its cost estimates from £41.7 million to £48.5 million and less than a year later the project's endlessly inflating price was enough to make the company embark on a serious re-appraisal of the whole programme, in an effort to find ways in which it might be brought back under control through the introduction of economies. The Air Ministry (describing costs as "expensive by any reckoning") informed the Chief of the Air Staff that the Treasury had "…experienced great difficulty in getting any up-to-date estimates out of the MoA" and that their "main anxiety" had been generated by various reports that the aircraft would be "very late into service." On 27 March 1962 the Minister of Aviation (Peter Thorneycroft) advised the Minister for Defence that the estimated costs of development for the airframe plus engines and equipment had now reached £137 million, some of this figure being attributable to a "wide variety of equipments" for which design studies had not been completed and for which the projected costs were "necessarily in some degree uncertain." He also added that there had been a "serious increase in the engine cost."

Thorneycroft now estimated that TSR2 would enter RAF service in the third quarter of 1966 in what would effectively be a strategic strike role, with the original tactical operations being assigned later. This was providing that the aircraft's forward-looking radar development was concluded satisfactorily with no decision having been made as to whether proceeding with the preferred Ferranti system would continue, or if American Texas Instruments equipment would be bought as a substitute. Thorneycroft had already established that much of the aircraft's electronic equipment was "lagging behind the aircraft programme." The Minister of Defence responded by declaring that the project would have to be re-submitted to the Defence Committee as it had originally approved it "on the basis of much lower estimates of cost." In May a decision was finally made to proceed with the Ferranti FLR although the Minister for Defence also agreed that some sort of contractual agreement on performance and delivery dates should be obtained. He also added that despite the rising costs of the overall programme, the Government was "fully committed to the TSR2" and that it was "an essential element in our plans for the RAF." The Defence Committee concurred and requested that the Minister should make a final decision on the aircraft's development and production "before the summer recess."

A rare colour image of XR219 landing at Boscombe Down. The brake parachute door is visible in the open position, hinged upwards. Initial use of the brake parachute demonstrated that it was very effective, although there was some debate as to whether it was, in fact, too effective and that it might have a detrimental effect upon the airframe structure under certain conditions. *BAC*

By June 1962 it was disclosed that the first flight of the prototype would now be set for August 1963, delays having been caused by a failure to produce the correct amount of detailed design drawings which had left some aircraft components awaiting manufacture. Efforts were made to address this problem but by the end of that month, BAC reported that its costs for airframe development had again increased from £48.5m to £59.7m. However, further governmental approval was still given in August when it was also decided to cancel BAC's Blue Water missile project and despite an attempt made by the Chief of the Defence Staff to embark upon another full re-appraisal of the whole TSR2 programme. Just four months later the cost estimates had risen again to an estimated £137m for the whole programme and an atmosphere of insecurity slowly descended upon Weybridge and Warton. BAC's Management Board recommended changes to the management system and these changes were endorsed by the Ministry of Aviation who also expressed a similar dissatisfaction at the way in which the project was being handled – a rather ironic viewpoint when one considers that many of the fundamental management difficulties had been created by the Government in the first place.

In January 1963 the Research and Development Board approved continued development at an overall cost of up to £200m. The Minister of Aviation reported to the Minister of Defence (now Peter Thorneycroft) that as of April 1962 the cost of developing the whole TSR2 weapons system had been estimated at £137m with an initial CA release in the third quarter of 1966 and full Release late in the following year. After setbacks in both airframe and engine progress it was now envisaged that these Release dates had slipped by a whole year and that the airframe costs might be likely to rise to as much as £80m. The loss of the Vulcan test bed and other difficulties would probably increase the estimated engine development costs from £34m to as much as £45m and that total costs from the whole programme might now be "not less than £175 million." Such astronomical figures – bearing in mind that this was 1963 – seem almost incredible, but even they did not provide a complete picture of just how much money had been invested in the project. Research and development costs might now reach £200m whilst a projected total production run of 138 aircraft might cost a further £340m – a total of £540 million. As one ministerial minute recorded, "…the cost increases in this project continue to break all records." During February, Thorneycroft suggested that the envisaged production run of 138 aircraft might be reduced to just 50 or 60, the remainder of the total comprising Mk.2 variants of the Buccaneer as a cheaper alternative. The Secretary of State for Air and the Minister of Aviation rejected the idea, although the Admiralty (not surprisingly) continued to pursue the concept with some vigour, but despite the increasing costs and increasingly vocal misgivings, the DRPC endorsed continuation of the project. However, late in March the Chiefs of Staff approved a report on the military implications of replacing a proportion of the TSR2 production batch with Buccaneers and as a result, the Chief Scientific Advisor to the Minister of Defence (Sir Solly Zuckerman) was asked to investigate how the Buccaneer's capabilities might be "maximised".

In effect, the proposal was to consider whether the Buccaneer (in an improved Mk.2 version) could successfully fulfil TSR2's tactical strike role while a smaller batch of TSR2's could be produced to fulfil the strategic bomber role which was now seen as vital to create a stopgap capability pending the introduction of Polaris. It was at this stage that the situation was confused still further when Lieutenant-General Sir John Hackett remarked that he had "serious misgivings about the extent to which it might be possible to meet the Army's needs from manned aircraft resources." Given that the Army was to rely upon TSR2 for tactical support and reconnaissance, his comments suggested that even it might no longer be quite so convinced that TSR2 was a system that it needed – at least not at the expense of other projects which it had also hoped for. It seems certain that the cancellation of Blue Water destroyed much Army support for TSR2 (its assumption, rightly or wrongly, being that it was probably abandoned in order to find more money for TSR2), and now that considerable support for the concept of replacing TSR2 with the Buccaneer in the tactical role was emerging, the Chiefs of the Defence Staff were hard-pressed to defend TSR2. The best that they could offer was a conclusion that "our ability to meet certain essential commitment in our strategy, for which TSR2 is designed, would be seriously prejudiced by TSR2's being replaced by the Buccaneer even with the contemplated improvements."

This rather vague defence of TSR2 probably serves to emphasise that by 1963 the Defence Chiefs viewed TSR2 more in terms of strategic bomber capability, rather than the key tactical role for which it had first been designed and were already beginning to envisage a situation in which they might never get the tactical strike aircraft which they had sought for so long. In a letter dated 3 April Thorneycroft stated that "…the cost of the present planned programme of 138 TSR2's is of the same broad order of magnitude as the aircraft carrier programme or the strategic nuclear deterrent programme", adding that this was "a remarkable figure for a light bomber replacement." He recorded that he had "…from time to time upon professional advice" described TSR2's role as "anything from a substitute for Blue Water to a substitute for a V-Bomber." Thorneycroft felt that while some parts of TSR2's proposed roles could not be efficiently undertaken by other aircraft, some roles could undoubtedly be performed by aircraft which possessed capabilities "far short" of those afforded to TSR2. Even the Prime Minister (Harold Macmillan) was uneasy. In a minute to the Minister of Aviation dated 24 April he asked "Can you give me the latest position about the TSR2? What will it cost? Will it ever fly?" Of course the Minister (Julian Amery) could say very little with any degree of confidence.

Uncertainty continued to surround the programme and while optimism was being expressed, the misgivings of both industry and government figures intensified. A proposed time-scale was being pursued on an official level while another was seemingly being implemented from an industrial viewpoint. Treasury approval for continued development was given in October at a cost of £175m, on the understanding that this might rise to £200m, but by this stage the DRPC had already agreed to inform the Minister of Defence that the overall cost of the programme was now likely to reach £222m. The target

Magnificent view of XR219 at low speed, the intake auxiliary doors open, flaps down and landing gear extended. The landing gear was undoubtedly one of the aircraft's most troublesome features. Designed for field operations, the aircraft would almost certainly have never been deployed into the field conditions which had been stipulated by the Air Staff – and which led to the aircraft's over-engineered landing gear. TSR2 was a complex aircraft relying on many systems, all of which would require technical and logistical support. Operating the aircraft from small clearings and rough fields was simply unrealistic. *BAC*

date of October 1966 for Initial CA release had also slipped again by October and production of the development batch aircraft was estimated to be two months behind schedule. The Treasury authorised production of 11 pre-production aircraft in June and agreed to the announcement being made on production aircraft, but carefully declined to specify how many (the Air Ministry asked for 30). Eventually the Chancellor agreed to a statement which outlined "a development batch order for nine and a pre-production order for 11 aircraft", but when the announcement was made by the Ministry of Aviation it was less specific: "In addition to the orders already placed for TSR2... for development and introductory flying by the RAF, British Aircraft Corporation have now been authorised to acquire long-dated materials to enable production of TSR2's for squadron service to begin."

On 28 October the Air Ministry briefed the media in order to "dispel some current misconceptions in the press about the role and operational uses of TSR2", although the briefing was inevitably dominated by discussion of the cost figures which were being associated with the programme. Just a few weeks later The Times newspaper ran a long article which examined the TSR2 and a Commons debate which had discussed the project some days previously. The article claimed that for some time "…the air had been thick with inflated estimates of cost on one side and exaggerated claims of performance on the other."

Of course the performance claims were not exaggerated at all, but when set against the ever-increasing cost estimates, an atmosphere of 'political spin' was clearly being sensed. The Times continued, with references to "dark rumours of cancellation" which had been met with official denials that were "…strenuous enough to spread panic through an arms industry still groping fearfully about in the ruins of Blue Streak and Blue Water."

Surprisingly (as this still was not acknowledged official policy), the report also claimed that TSR2 "was to carry the main weight of the strategic nuclear strike task between the decline of the V-Bomber and the introduction of the Polaris missile" and that the Air Staff had therefore "contrived an extension of the airborne deterrent by the simple expedient of calling it something else." With the benefit of hindsight it is clear that this accusation was technically correct, but it prompted the Air Minister to make an official statement to the effect that the use of TSR2 in a strategic role was "a bonus – nothing more, nothing less" (although it was of course a vital bonus which had been anticipated for some time) and that the aircraft's design had been frozen "…long before there was any question of cancelling Skybolt." This too was technically true, but it failed to explain that no significant design changes (apart from modifications to the weapons bay doors) had actually been necessary.

As the project progressed into 1964 the cost estimates and delays showed little signs of improvement and by the middle of the year, the prospect of actually getting a prototype aircraft into the air was being overshadowed by the gloomy news of a continual postponement of a first flight date which was first estimated to be likely at the end of July, only to be delayed again until August. Development costs had climbed still further and were now pegged at £260m and the production price of each aircraft was now expected to be £2.8m. Early in the year at a meeting between the Minister of Aviation and the heads of BAC and BSE, it was concluded (by the Secretary of State for Air) that the costs were "uncontrollable." The projected first flight in August led to some hope that the aircraft might make a public appearance at the 1964 SBAC Farnborough show, where the public, media and official spectators could finally see a tangible result of this long and hideously expensive programme. The engine failure (and destruction of the Vulcan test bed) in July effectively dashed any such plans and although the aircraft was still expected to be undertaking taxi trials by September and therefore be ready to fly, the chances of appearing at Farnborough were said to be "poor." On 3 September the Minister of Aviation advised the Controller of Aircraft that despite the obvious pressures and the "strong reasons of industrial national prestige involved", the Government would not wish him or his department to agree to such a flight in any circumstances where the "safety of the aircraft, the crew or the public night be jeopardised." Sadly, the sight of the first TSR2 over Farnborough remained only as a dream, and it was not until a fortnight after the show that the prototype finally made its first flight from Boscombe Down. This hugely significant event was considered to be a turning point in the troubled TSR2 programme and an active flight test programme was expected to provide a useful tool for dispelling any further notion that the aircraft was destined to forever remain a monstrously expensive paper project. But just one month after the TSR2 had finally embarked upon the most encouraging and useful stage of its development, another far more pivotal event took place. The Conservatives were defeated and a Labour Government moved into Downing Street.

Almost since its inception, the TSR2 programme had certainly been controversial, but few people originally anticipated that this factor would result in the project's complete cancellation, not least because patently the RAF needed a Canberra replacement. Inevitably there was a great deal of uncertainty as to precisely how TSR2 would be employed, in what roles and in what quantities, but when construction of the first pre-production batch began, it seemed clear that the RAF would get TSR2 – even if it sometimes seemed unclear as to precisely how many and what would be done with it when it was delivered. But as the programme slowly fell victim to endless delays, and as the costs began to climb higher and higher, an atmosphere of doubt settled over the aircraft. The Conservative Government had undoubtedly supported TSR2 and had continued to do so even at the stage when any intelligent observer would have concluded that its costs were unacceptably high. Having already cancelled 26 significant defence projects (including Blue Streak and Blue Water) in order to save £300 million, it would not have been such a surprise if TSR2 had been added to the list. But the aircraft's potential had been understood, and when a stopgap strategic aircraft had suddenly become an urgent requirement (after Skybolt was cancelled), the prospect of abandoning what seemed to be the only available solution must have seemed unthinkable. Yet as the development and projected production costs slowly spiralled out of control and it became clearer that the likelihood that TSR2 would come into service only two years before Polaris, the Conservatives appetite for the project started to wane.

For the Labour Party, the whole issue seemed much clearer. Long before the election, Opposition politicians had used every opportunity to criticise the TSR2 programme, often implying (and sometimes unequivocally stating) that if Labour were voted into power, the project would be scrapped. Of course their knee-jerk reactions were politically driven and when Harold Wilson arrived at Downing Street, a more serious appraisal of Britain's defence requirements proved to be a complicated and troublesome issue, chiefly because the Government was faced with a set of conflicting issues. The Labour Party was not an enthusiastic supporter of nuclear armament and many of its most vociferous members were adamant that Britain should rid itself of its stockpile of nuclear weapons, together with the machinery with which to deliver them. Although some of the more influential members of the party could at least tolerate the concept of a strategic nuclear deterrent, the very idea of producing a nuclear-capable tactical aircraft was rather more difficult to accept, and with Polaris firmly on the horizon, the prospect of introducing a new strategic bomber almost by proxy was unacceptable. The country was also very nearly bankrupt. With a serious sterling crisis affecting the economy, Wilson's primary objective was to save money wherever possible, and defence expenditure already drained a huge amount of money from the Treasury. Therefore it was inevitable that it would face the most intense scrutiny. But Wilson, and his Cabinet, also wanted to maintain Britain's international position, both within NATO and on a more global basis. In order to maintain the all-important place at the proverbial 'top table', it was vital that Britain maintained a strong influence, and effectively this meant maintaining a strong defensive (and therefore offensive) posture which would be heard and understood by America in particular. It was also essential that from a purely introspective point of view, the country needed to be adequately defended, particularly when East-West tensions were still high and the political situation in the Soviet Union was far from stable. It was with these conflicting interests in mind that Wilson gathered his ministers at Chequers, his country residence, during November.

Denis Healey was the new Minister of Defence. Countless accounts of TSR2's history have portrayed him not only as the person who was ultimately responsible for the cancellation of the aircraft, but often dismissively regard him as an anti-military socialist who was determined to destroy the project almost at any cost. In fact, it is fairer to say that Healey was very much a pro-military man and he quickly earned himself a reputation as a serious, wise and practical presence in the corridors of Whitehall; indeed some later claimed that he was one of the best Defence Ministers Britain has ever had. It was of course Healey who made the final recommendation to abandon TSR2, but to suggest that he was set against the very idea of the RAF having a tactical strike aircraft would be entirely wrong. At Chequers, the first issue to be raised was the broad question of whether Britain should retain a nuclear capability. Although many rank and file members of the Labour Party were increasingly set against nuclear weapons, the case for unilateral disarmament was not taken particularly seriously within the Cabinet, and little more than lip-service was paid to the notion at Chequers, now that Polaris was just a few years away and (at least in terms of proportional costs) was seen to be favourably inexpensive. Some ministers were still unenthusiastic, but with 'heavyweights' such as Healey, James Callaghan and Roy Jenkins set firmly in favour of Polaris and the retention of tactical nuclear weapons too, the whole issue was hardly in any doubt even before it was discussed.

The Labour Party remained unilateralist by nature, but the Cabinet took a more realistic view. However, the acceptance of a nuclear deterrent did not necessarily imply that TSR2 would be needed in order to deliver it, even as a short-term measure. In fact the new Government appears to have regarded TSR2 as a purely tactical aircraft – and a conventional non-nuclear one at that, and both Healey and Wilson made specific public references to the TSR2 as being an aircraft which the Government might still purchase, but primarily (if not exclusively) as a carrier of conventional weapons. Whether this was their honest viewpoint or one which was intended primarily for public consumption is unclear, but almost overnight, the perceived urgent need for a stopgap strategic bomber which had influenced TSR2's progress was dropped and the aircraft was once again regarded as the straightforward Canberra replacement which had first been proposed many years previously.

Healey subsequently stated in Parliament that "…when we decide the size and pattern of our defences, we must watch with extreme vigilance their impact both on our balance of payments and, even more important, on our productive resources, particularly in scientists and skilled manpower. We must get value for money." He added that he "had looked at the books" and that he looked forward to "discussing some of the skeletons found in the cupboard." Of course, the biggest of these was TSR2 and with this project no doubt in mind, Healey commented: "Unless we are to allow our defence expenditure to rise continually, not only in absolute terms, but also as a percentage of our rising national wealth, we must be prepared to reduce the calls on our military resources." Most significantly, Healey was already keen to grasp some proverbial nettles which the Conservatives had carefully avoided, tackling projects which should have been examined and acted upon, but like Duncan Sandys, he was also willing to take on the fundamental issues of Britain's defence posture as a whole, stating the House of Commons: "One thing I have already learned from my first five weeks in office is that Britain is spending more on her defence forces than any other country of her size and wealth. We are still trying to sustain three major military roles – to maintain an independent strategic nuclear striking power, to make a major contribution towards the allied defence of Western Europe and to deploy a significant military capacity overseas, from British Guiana through the Mediterranean, Africa and the Middle East to Hong Kong. I put it seriously to the House – and I hope that Right Hon. and Hon.

Members will listen seriously because I do not think there is disagreement between those of us who know the facts – that unless we are to impose unacceptable strains on our own economy and to carry a handicap which none of our main competitors in world trade has to bear, Britain too must decide which of these three roles should have priority."

As Chancellor, Callaghan had expressed his view that overall Treasury expenditure should be capped at £200m. Given that a great deal of existing defence spending was allocated to essentials such as pay, accommodation, pensions and training, it was equipment which faced the closest scrutiny, and with a ten per cent defence budget reduction necessary, it followed that some 40 per cent would have to come from cuts in equipment. Aircraft projects were clearly the most expensive projects from where savings could be made. Healey was, according to colleague Lord Carver, "…appalled at the mess he discovered in the aircraft field."

The most expensive programmes still under development were the P.1154 supersonic replacement for the Hunter, the HS.681 jet transport and of course TSR2. Chief Projects Officer, Sir William Cook, was asked to prepare a report for Healey in anticipation of a Defence Review, and these three projects were identified as the most important, with spending on each programme continually rising and set to climb still further thanks to development and production delays which effectively allowed funding to correspondingly slip back, thereby ensuring that the greatest and most crippling spending was yet to come, in the year before full delivery. Healey immediately began to investigate ways in which these projects could be reduced in cost, and whether there was any alternative means of providing the RAF with the same capabilities for cheaply: "When I asked the Air Force if there was any alternative to the Conservative plans, they were only too glad to tell me. There was a cheaper American equivalent of all three major British Aircraft on order; in at least two cases they would be available much sooner, and of equal or superior performance. I decided to buy them instead, and met the Treasury's concern about their cost in Dollars by negotiating an offset agreement under which the United States would buy British goods to the same value."

So it was that Healey resolved to cancel the P.1154 (a project which, even if it had continued, may well have suffered from major development setbacks) and replace it with the F-4C Phantom, while the increasingly expensive (and increasingly complex) HS.681 would be replaced by the much more practical and significantly cheaper C-130 Hercules. As for TSR2, he was advised that America could provide a viable substitute in the shape of TFX – what was to become the F-111. Although it was slightly inferior to TSR2 in projected performance it was remarkably similar in most respects, and an improved 'Mk.2' version which was under development, would meet the RAF's needs even more closely. Most importantly, it would be available within a similar timescale and be much, much cheaper. Most importantly for Healey, while TSR2 would have to be paid for upon delivery, taking a massive chunk out of the defence budget (some £80m on top of his current projections), the TFX could be purchased over a much longer period (up to 1978) which would spread expenditure over a whole decade. The figures could not

XR219 looking particularly smart at the beginning of her test flight programme at Boscombe Down. Worthy of note are the typical 1960s-era vehicles in the background which contrast quite starkly with the futuristic lines of the aircraft. Almost fifty years on, TSR2 is still an impressively clean design, indicative of its supersonic capabilities. *BAC*

be disputed. According to Healey: "At the outset therefore it would seem that the continuance of TSR2 would automatically rule out any prospect of continuing defence expenditure within £2,000m (1964 prices) by 1969-70."

In December the first of a series of fact-finding visits to Washington began to look more closely at the possibility of purchasing TFX. In February 1965 the DCAS issued a paper which stated that while these visits were being made, the Ministry of Aviation had been tasked with a re-evaluation of TSR2's progress so that they might "negotiate a maximum price for it with the British Aircraft Corporation." In order to achieve this, it would be "necessary to have an up-to-date specification which took account of actual flight experience with the aircraft so far." At a subsequent meeting of the Standing Committee, some concern was expressed at an "apparent degradation in performance represented by the proposed revised specification" and this was also reflected in comments made during a meeting of the Air Force Board, where it was stated that if the specification represented "a realistic assessment of what the aircraft might now be capable of achieving" it could go forward to the MoA as a basis for obtaining a fixed-price quotation from BAC. Precisely how the revised specification suggested any degradation in performance remains unclear and it may well be that this was merely a clouded perception based on the problems which BAC had experienced with engine and undercarriage problems during the early flight trials. But with the F-111 now firmly established as a viable (and much cheaper) alternative, this may well have been the point at which the Air Staff almost imperceptibly shifted their preference away from TSR2 in favour of the American option, and late in January, Sam Elworthy, Chief of the Air Staff, advised Healey that the Air Staff did indeed prefer TFX to TSR2 on military grounds, rather than only on a politically-driven economic basis.

Elworthy had already concluded some months previously that TSR2 was a project which was now running a very real risk of ruining other fundamentally important parts of the RAF's expenditure, and it was no longer their proverbial 'sacred cow' which it had been for so long. It is difficult to pinpoint precisely why the Air Staff had finally relinquished support for what had been such a cherished project, but by this stage in the TSR2 programme the RAF had clearly accepted that they might never get the aircraft into service at all, and the prospect of a fixed-price and fixed-delivery alternative was undoubtedly a much more attractive proposition.

When Healey offered the Air Staff the opportunity to abandon what was perceived as a potentially unaffordable and possibly unattainable goal, they seized the chance to accept what the Minister assured them that they could have. BAC was still unable (or at least unwilling) to agree to a revised fixed-price contract for TSR2 production and in some ways it is perhaps understandable that it maintained this position. Bound by the complexities of the procurement and design process which had been laid down by the government, so much of the project had been beyond BAC's control that undoubtedly it would have been accepting a major financial risk had it committed themselves to a fixed price. But by refusing to limit the government's liability it effectively sealed the project's fate almost as securely as the Air Staff and Healey had done.

A brief on defence expenditure issued late in 1964 outlined the government's view of the situation with regard to TSR2: "The US F-111A – the TFX – appears likely to meet the United Kingdom requirement in all significant respects although it is the American custom to build separate versions for strike and reconnaissance. The United States has been very chary of releasing information about this aircraft. There is some reason to believe that there are difficulties about aerodynamics,

Pictured above a cloud layer which shrouds the countryside below, XR219 is seen during a low-speed handling test flight early in 1965. *BAC*

weight growth and rising cost. Research and development costs of the TSR2 are currently forecast as £272m and production costs for 158 aircraft as £469m. A total of £741m. About £160m has so far been spent or committed. The TFX will cost not less than £2m. 158 aircraft at £2m would, with spare engines, cost £332m. Cancelling the TSR2 and substituting the TFX would therefore save about £250m."

These figures could hardly be dismissed as insignificant. On this basis, the Government would save a huge amount of money and payment could be spread over many years, and the RAF would still get a full production order of tactical strike aircraft. Similar savings could be applied to other projects too, and Healey implemented the first of these as swiftly as he could. On 15 January the Defence and Overseas Policy Committee (DOPC) met and Healey proposed that the TSR2, P.1154 and HS.681 should be cancelled, to be replaced by the F-111, F-4, a developed version of the P.1127 (a less ambitious, more achievable and less expensive VTOL tactical aircraft which would eventually become the Harrier) and the C-130. The Chancellor accepted this recommendation but further work was requested to investigate "…measures which might be taken to deal with the difficulties which the aircraft industry might face in the event of a government decision to cancel certain of the current aircraft projects." In effect, the ministers were looking at how and when the projects should be cancelled, not whether they should be cancelled at all.

At another meeting on 29 January it was agreed that the P.1154 and HS.681 should finally be cancelled and replaced as had been discussed. The TSR2 however, was to continue for the time being, Harold Wilson in particular believing that the project should be allowed to progress while more information on its cost and performance was determined. It was agreed that development of the P.1127 (Harrier) should go ahead (Healey had pressed vigorously for this particular project) and that 40 Phantoms should be ordered with an option for a further 110, together with 24 C-130s and an option on a further 58. It was also agreed that the Shackleton Anti-Submarine Warfare aircraft should be replaced by a development of the Comet airliner and this eventually became Nimrod.

All of these decisions were confirmed by Cabinet on 1 February and TSR2 survived, but not with Healey's full blessing. In reality it was only Cabinet disagreement (and Wilson's viewpoint) which kept the project alive, prompted by uneasiness over possible industry job losses, lack of confidence in the F-111's capabilities, and a general sense that cancelling three projects simultaneously would be a difficult task to defend both within Parliament and across the country. Disposing of the projects which were defended less-fiercely seemed like a preferable option. Healey commented that he "…had to keep development going purely for political reasons at a cost of £4 million a week until April 6th. I was deeply conscious of what could have been done with the £40m for more useful purposes."

The deadline of 6 April was when Callaghan would introduce his first Budget, and he had made it very clear to Wilson and Healey that he would prefer to incorporate the TSR2's cancellation into his Budget speech. Roy Jenkins later commented that he believed Callaghan had "…evolved a tactic of announcing the cancellation in April in order to provide a boost for sterling at what was bound to be a difficult time." In other words, Callaghan thought there would be some advantage in presenting the cancellation as an example of financial prudence rather than military policy.

Meanwhile, the Ministry of Aviation looked at ways in which TSR2's costs might be brought down by reducing the aircraft's capabilities and/or the roles it would undertake. The exercise was largely fruitless as the aircraft was designed, undergoing flight-testing, and could not be altered unless even more money was spent on it. TSR2 was a near-complete package which could only be accepted as it now was… or abandoned.

By this time BAC was only too aware that a final decision would come in April 1965, and it was under no illusions as to what the outcome would probably be, although Roy Jenkins continued to assure BAC that the project was not yet completely dead. Jenkins also firmly believed that although Healey had been given assurances (by his US counterpart Robert McNamara) that Britain could exercise an option on purchasing F-111, he would have the right to subsequently cancel it if it was decided that the aircraft was no longer required. It was also important to maintain a strong bargaining position with America, and prematurely cancelling TSR2 would leave Britain with no other option than to buy F-111 – or have nothing – which was hardly a strong position from which to strike a favourable deal. It was not the most encouraging basis on which to keep TSR2 alive, but it was better than nothing. Indeed he had proposed to Healey that purchasing a smaller batch of TSR2s (probably no more than 50) might be acceptable, and although Healey saw no logic in this idea, he did look at the possibility of reducing the number of F-111s which might be ordered. Healey suggested that 80 might be sufficient, but Elworthy, the Chief of the Air Staff, insisted that the RAF could not fulfil its tasks with anything less than 110 aircraft (be they F-111s or TSR2s) and that substituting the Phantom or Buccaneer for some roles just was not acceptable in his opinion.

Of course the two aircraft did eventually assume some of TSR2's planned roles and Elworthy had undoubtedly been dismissive of the Buccaneer and Phantom in order to justify a substantial F-111 order. Having abandoned interest in TSR2, the RAF was desperate not to allow F-111 to slip away too, and

Healey assured Elworthy that it would get what it wanted. When Jenkins was briefed in March, he was advised (almost as if history was repeating itself) that TSR2 should be replaced by the Buccaneer, but after having given his assurances to the RAF, Healey's response was that he found it "difficult to conceive of any future military role for this country which would enable us to do without any aircraft of the TSR-2/F-111A class." The idea of opting for the Buccaneer was finally dropped almost for good – or so it seemed at the time. Of course, the whole issue re-emerged some years later following the cancellation of F-111 and the Buccaneer did eventually enter RAF service.

The notion that the RAF could not successfully function without a TSR2/F-111 aircraft was almost entirely based on the premise that Britain was to maintain a significant presence East of Suez and this was by no means a certainty now that the Labour Party was governing the country. Healey was unashamedly in favour of Britain's military commitments far beyond Europe and so was Wilson, but many others within the Government were set firmly against what they regarded as an outdated (and unaffordable) relic of imperialism. Healey's support for Britain's East of Suez roles was undoubtedly fostered by his relationship with America, and in particular

This imposing view of XR219 shows the tread pattern of the nose wheel tyres which differed to the type employed on the next aircraft, XR220. Dunlop tyres were expected to be standard to production aircraft with Goodyear equivalents being available as an alternative. Successive pre-production aircraft were expected to be fitted alternately with each type. *BAC*

XR219 pictured at Warton shortly after having arrived from Boscombe Down. Engines still running, the weapons bay doors have been opened and chocks placed under the wheels prior to shutdown. Today, the same location plays host to Hawks and Typhoons, both of which are part of BAE's current military production programmes. Weybridge failed to survive the cancellation of TSR2, the combination of this project's loss and the firm's equally-troublesome airliner projects being sufficient to eventually force the factory's closure. Conversely, Warton flourished and is now the home of BAE System's hugely successful military aircraft programme. *BAC*

Robert McNamara, who made no secret of the fact that he wanted Britain to maintain its overseas commitments, not only in order to avoid the responsibilities being handed to America, but in order to ensure that Britain was seen to be effectively endorsing America's international position. With the East of Suez commitments came the requirement for a long-range tactical bomber. Without these roles, the F-111 or TSR2 were unnecessarily over-specified and therefore hugely over-priced, given that the prospect of also using either aircraft as a stopgap strategic bomber was not a priority for the Labour Government, which was never entirely comfortable with the prospect of an overtly over-abundance of nuclear capability. Polaris was on the way and this was grudgingly accepted, but there was no appetite to create an additional strategic capability even as a short-term fix. Despite advocates such as Wilson and Healey, there was a growing appetite to abandon Britain's global presence and everyone knew this only too well. This fact (together with the aircraft's diminishing pseudo-strategic role) was one of the key reasons why TSR2 had slowly become less and less important to both the Government and the RAF. It was being pursued at huge cost, in order to fulfil a role which no longer existed. Finally, the Cabinet met on 1 April to make a binding decision ahead of the Chancellor's Budget speech. In such situations it was, according to Jenkins, "Wilson's practice to let everyone talk themselves out" and in his typical style the Prime Minister allowed discussion to flow, avoiding expressing any firm view on TSR2 himself. It was the other members of the Cabinet who argued long and hard through a long meeting which began at 1000 hrs, and began again at 2200 hrs after Healey had insisted on a second meeting to reach a firm conclusion on this divisive matter, which was in effect the Government's first 'Cabinet crisis'.

Whilst Healey was convinced that TSR2 was no longer sustainable, he remained resolutely in favour of giving the RAF what it wanted – a fleet of F-111s in the shape of an initial order of ten F-111As, to be followed by a later, more advanced F-111K version. He bombarded his colleagues with figures which indicated that purchasing F-111 would save £280m over 13 years and that orders for the Mk.2 F-111 would not have to be placed until 1967, by which time the Government would have had more than enough time to establish precisely what,

if any, role Britain was to maintain East of Suez. Some Cabinet ministers were reluctant to formally abandon TSR2 immediately, preferring to wait until a full Defence Review could be completed. Others, including Roy Jenkins, were still unconvinced that purchasing F-111 would be a wise move, Jenkins commenting that by purchasing an initial batch of ten Mk.1 aircraft, it would be difficult not to justify purchasing the larger batch of Mk.2 aircraft. Given the choice, he would probably have preferred to buy Buccaneers.

Callaghan, driven by financial considerations, was happy to cancel both TSR2 and F-111 too, and Healey's position was shared by only a few, most notably the Foreign Secretary, Michael Stewart, who naturally advocated a continuing East of Suez presence. Ironically, despite having often being branded as a 'butcher' responsible for TSR2's demise, Healey was, in fact, firmly on the RAF's side, and he fought long and hard against a Cabinet which was largely in favour of simply abandoning both aircraft. When the second (evening) meeting began, Healey had again spoken to McNamara (largely upon the insistence of Jenkins) and he reported that provided a firm order for F-111As was placed in 1966 and provided that Britain ordered at least 70 Mk.2s in 1967, the US would not only keep the current favourable terms on the table, but would also fix the price of the Mk.2 at the level of the F-111A. McNamara could hardly have done any more, short of almost giving the F-111s to Britain for free. But the same arguments bounced back and forth: how would cancelling TSR2 affect BAC and its work force? Would the Buccaneer be suitable if Britain was to remain East of Suez? What effect would an F-111 purchase have on foreign exchange? Would Britain's aircraft industry survive? As midnight passed, Wilson concluded that the Cabinet effectively had three options: Postpone a decision on TSR-2 even longer; cancel the aircraft without an F-111 option, or cancel it and take the American offer, presenting the ministers with a situation which Wilson later described as a "difficult – indeed, I think, in all our time, a unique situation."

Ten of the 24 ministers remained convinced that TSR2 should be retained, if only because its abandonment would leave Britain with no other option than to buy American, should a tactical strike aircraft still be needed. But with a small majority of ministers now in favour of accepting Healey's proposal to take-up a non-committal option on the F-111, and no appetite for allowing the Government to be seen as indecisive on this issue any longer, it was finally accepted that Healey's solution was the only politically acceptable route which made sense (only six ministers finally opposed him). Thus, at around 1230 hrs on the morning of 2 April 1965, the cabinet agreed to formally cancel TSR2.

CHAPTER TEN

The Axe Falls

THE public announcement of TSR2's cancellation was made, as Callaghan had proposed, in his Budget speech on 6 April 1965, although leaks began to emerge almost immediately after the Cabinet meeting. BAC's Directors were informed of the decision on the morning of the 6th but they were immediately instructed to keep the news within the managerial team (it being accepted practice to keep all details of a Budget Speech secret until announced in Parliament), which meant that the hapless workforces at Warton and Weybridge were destined to learn of the decision at the same time as the rest of the country, when Callaghan spoke in the House of Commons. But by 6 April the workforce was under no illusions as to how perilous the project's future really was, and few believed that the project would survive; the Chancellor's announcement was little more than a confirmation of what everybody had anticipated. Buried in a long and detailed Budget Speech, TSR2 appeared as part of Callaghan's outline of future public expenditure. After highlighting the cost of Britain's overseas commitments and the need to drastically reduce their cost, he immediately turned to TSR2 – signifying how the aircraft was inextricably linked with Britain's East of Suez role: "It is against this background that the Government have had to consider the future of the TSR2 project. My Right

Hon. friend, the Secretary of State for Defence hopes to catch your eye later in the debate, Horace King (the Deputy Speaker), in order to make a full statement about the Government's policy and its decision to cancel the project. The effect of this decision is to save £35 million of Government expenditure in 1965-66 after taking account of the terminal costs which may become due to be paid this year. We all admire the technical skill that has been put into this advanced aircraft. Members opposite may speak for themselves but, so far, the aircraft has cost £125 million and the cost is mounting every week. It has, and would have, diverted hundreds of factories employing thousands of skilled and semi-skilled men from other work of national importance, including export orders in particular. This is not a sensible use of our overstrained resources. The Government's decision will, in the next five years, release £350 million of resources of an advanced kind for more productive work."

Amid a torrent of derisive comments from the Conservative benches, Callaghan swiftly moved on to other subjects. Although there was an obvious atmosphere of satisfaction on the Labour benches, the Conservatives were furious, not least because Callaghan's announcement – being part of the Budget Speech – could not be directly challenged fully by the Opposition. Parliamentary rules dictated that questions could only be presented if they referred directly to financial issues, which meant that any wider discussion of the TSR2's fate would not be permitted. During his response to the Budget Speech, the Shadow Chancellor, Sir Alec Douglas-Home, was understandably keen to address the

A sad image of Weybridge taken shortly after the project's cancellation. Two partially-completed aircraft await destruction while the remnants of a third machine are just visible on the other side of Brooklands airfield. These were all removed as scrap to RJ Coley's yard in Hounslow, although some sections were subsequently moved to BA Taylor's yard at West Bromwich. *BAC*

Possibly the last picture ever taken of XR219, showing the rotting hulk of the fuselage during the late 1970's, at the P&EE, Shoeburyness. It was removed as scrap shortly thereafter, together with the remaining components from sister aircraft XR221. *BAE Heritage*

subject: "I turn to the Right Hon. Gentleman's conclusion about the cancellation of the TSR2. I rose as he was speaking in order to complain that while he told us of the savings that he expected to be made from the cancellation of this aircraft, he did not tell us whether it was intended to buy the TFX from America or what would take its place… I have never seen a more scurvy trick played on Parliament than the one that has been played today. The Chancellor has taken credit for the savings on TSR2, but he has not told us whether we are to buy an American aircraft, or have no substitute at all. His figures are worthless until we have those facts. What I complain of in the Right Hon. Gentleman and his colleagues is that they have included in the statement of the national accounts that the Chancellor makes annually in the Budget, a decision that alters all the strategic concept of our defence planning and the industrial organisation which services our armed forces."

XR220 pictured at Boscombe Down being winched onto air bags, during recovery attempts following the catastrophic unloading incident which had occurred a couple of days previously. Note the BAC technician overseeing activities with the aid of a megaphone! Had the accident not occurred, XR220 would have begun flight testing towards the end of 1964 and two aircraft would have been actively flying during the vital six-month "reprieve" which Harold Wilson and his Cabinet gave to the project. Whether the two aircraft would have been sufficient to convince the Government to allow the programme to continue still further is a question which can never be answered, but it seems likely that even the input of XR220 would not have been enough to enable the project to survive. *BAC*

XR220 slowly returning to upright position with the aid of a crane and air bags, on 9th September 1964, following her unfortunate accident upon arrival at Boscombe Down. After a thorough inspection, it was established that damage to the aircraft was surprisingly superficial, most of the impact having been borne by the taileron spigot. However, various unexplained items of debris were found inside the airframe and although the aircraft was restored and cleared for flight testing, there is of course a possibility that further defects may have manifested themselves at a later stage, and XR220's flight test programme might have been troublesome. *BAC*

Indeed, Callaghan's insistence that the TSR2 announcement should be wrapped up within his Budget statement was a political mistake. His eagerness to portray the cancellation as an act of skilful monetary control was undoubtedly his motivation, knowing that Healey would explain the decision in detail immediately after his speech. But to the Opposition (and the media) it appeared to be nothing more than a shabby attempt to avoid a proper debate on the subject. Douglas-Home continued: "What use is it for the Prime Minister to say to General de Gaulle that we shall go into partnership in aircraft production… when in advance of a really worthwhile project being worked out with French or European allies, he has taken a decision which is bound to send all design teams scurrying to seek employment and security elsewhere, and when he gets rid of our greatest asset of this kind – this great aeroplane, probably the best of its kind in the world. I do not think this is the best way to enter into future projects with Europeans for future projects of this kind. There is only one explanation for the procedure that the Right Hon. Gentleman has adopted and it is funk. The Government are ashamed of what they are doing and they want to cover it up by hiding it amongst the rest of the things which the Chancellor of the Exchequer normally says on Budget Day".

Healey was in no mood to shy away from the issue. After duly catching the Speaker's attention, he rose to his feet after Douglas-Home sat down, and proceeded to explain at great length his reasons for cancelling the project, amid constant interjections from the Conservative benches and continual interruptions from the Speaker, who had a difficult time keeping the House under control. Healey subsequently recorded in his diary that he "…had a very difficult House of continuous interruptions over TSR2 – ten minute speech." This spectacularly plays down the fact that because of the constant interruptions the speech took more than an hour to deliver. "The Government have been wrestling continuously with this problem ever since they took office six months ago. It has always been obvious that the cost of continuing the TSR2 programme was likely to impose an intolerable burden on the national economy in general, and the defence budget in particular. But we have had to consider also the operational needs of our defence forces and the needs of the sort of aircraft industry which Britain is likely to require in the 1970s for both military, technological and commercial reasons. We discovered when we came into office that the programme for the TSR2 planned by the previous Government would have cost about

XR220 after successful repair and assembly at Boscombe Down in 1965, with the BAC flight test team gathered for a photo-call.

£750 million for research, development and production. An order for 150 aircraft would have meant that each one would have cost over £6 million of which nearly £5 million would still remain to be spent. These were the figures that the previous Government accepted as the basis of their policy. I submit that a programme of this order was not one which, in any circumstances, could be held to represent value for money. It was not only too costly in terms of defence expenditure. It was also making far too great a demand on our country's scarce resources of skilled manpower. Nevertheless I do not believe that the Government would have been justified in taking a decision to cancel TSR2 at the time when they decided on the other changes in our military aircraft programme two months ago. We needed better information than we then possessed on the probable cost of TSR2 and on the cost and performance of possible alternative aircraft. As the Prime Minister explained on 2 February it was the mounting cost of the TSR2 programme on which the previous administration had embarked which was the essential reason for the review which has been undertaken. We now have further information to take a decision, and it is clear that no more significant information is likely to be obtained for some months. The House of Commons was informed earlier that we should seek a fixed price for TSR2. In view of all the complexities of the programme, the manufacturers have not been able to offer such a price. The best arrangements that they have felt able to offer would have given no assurance that Her Majesty's Government's ultimate financial liability would have been limited. The likely course of completing the development of TSR2 would have been as high as, or even higher than previous estimates. Meanwhile, every week that the programme continues, it its costing the taxpayer something in the order of £1 million. In the circumstances, we do not feel that we can justify any further delay. With deep reluctance, Her Majesty's

Government have decided that they must now cancel the TSR2 programme. I hope that no one believes that this has been an easy or welcome decision, particularly at a moment when the aircraft was making good progress in its development programme. We are fully conscious of the disappointment that our decision must cause to those thousands of people who have worked so long and hard on a project which has been cancelled through no fault of theirs. The fundamental reason for cancellation – I ask the Committee to accept this – is the stark fact that the economic implications of modern military technology rule out British development and production of this type of aircraft for a purely national market. Her Majesty's Government have no intention of requiring our forces to forgo the aircraft at present planned to replace the Canberra towards the end of this decade without making certain that they can carry out their operational tasks by other means. It will not be possible to define these tasks precisely until the Defence Review is completed later this year. The review may show that the number of aircraft required with TSR2 performance characteristics may be substantially below the existing TSR2 programme. On certain hypotheses about long-term commitments it might even be possible to re-shape our defences in such a way that as to dispense with this type of aircraft altogether."

This last comment was the first clear indication that the Government was indeed seriously considering the future of Britain's overseas commitments East of Suez. It prompted Julian Ridsdale, the Parliamentary Under-Secretary of State for Air, to intervene: "The Right Hon. Gentleman has said that under certain hypotheses he envisages the RAF without a strike aircraft. Surely, the only circumstance in which he can envisage the RAF without a strike aircraft would be the complete withdrawal of our forces from the Far East, Middle East and Cyprus. Is that the Government's policy?"

In response, Healey appeared to contradict himself somewhat and said that he thought it "…most unlikely that these hypotheses would be fulfilled. They would indeed require such a radical change in our commitments as to imply tremendous changes not only in the RAF weapons programme, but the weapons programme of the whole of our forces. In order to make certain that, whatever happens, our Services will have appropriate aircraft in sufficient numbers, Her Majesty's Government have secured from the United States Government an option on the F-111A aircraft at a price per aircraft which, even on a full-scale programme, would represent less than half the estimated total TSR2 research, development and production cost."

After explaining that any substantial order for the F-111 would actually be for the later "Mk.2" variant (which would become the F-111K in RAF service), he returned to his statement: "On a smaller order than a full-scale order, the advantage over TSR2 would be even greater. But even on the full order, on the basis of money yet to be spent, the F-111A Mk.2 is still well over one-third cheaper. After taking account of all future charges and payments on both aircraft, including cancellation charges on TSR2, it is now estimated that a full programme based on the F-111A would cost £300 million less than the corresponding TSR2 programme. The nature of the option on the F-111A is such that Her Majesty's Government will have until the end of this year to decide whether to take it up. Any initial order would be a very small number for training purposes. It would not be necessary for Her Majesty's Government to place a follow-up order until as late as April 1967 – that is, two years from now. This arrangement will enable us to complete our defence review before deciding whether to place any orders at all, and it gives us two years from now before we need to take a final decision on the total numbers that we require."

Healey continued to battle through his speech despite continual interruptions and challenges from across the floor of the House. It was clear that TSR2 was not going to be abandoned easily, and as promised, Douglas-Home demanded a Censure debate on the subject, and this was quickly arranged for 13 April. Although primarily an opportunity to discuss TSR2's cancellation at length, the debate was seized upon by the Conservatives as an opportunity to criticise the Government for the way in which the announcement of its cancellation had been made. But during the debate, Healey once again outlined the Government's position: "It is true, of course, that the cost of the F-111A, if we buy it, will have to be paid in dollars. But the terms of the credit facilities which the United States Government have agreed should be made available to us will greatly reduce their impact on the balance of payments. Over the next five years the cancellation of the TSR2 will free for redeployment resources at least £350m. During this time we have to pay out only about £20m in dollars. Incidentally, this is almost exactly the dollar cost of the American components in the TSR2. The bulk of our dollar payments would be spread fairly evenly over the following eight years… Our export industries are crying out for the sort of skilled manpower which will be released by the decision to cancel the TSR2. As far as we have been able to judge, the TSR2 was supporting up to 20,000 jobs. Not all the people who filled them will now have to find new jobs. But, in any case, at the moment there are 25,000 vacancies nationally for skilled engineers, or three and a quarter vacancies for every engineer unemployed. For draftsmen, who will be released in very large numbers by this decision, there are five vacancies to every draftsman unemployed. We deeply sympathize with those who have worked so hard and so long on a project on which such hopes were based, and we shall do our level best to help them. For too many years we have been spending far too much money on too few aircraft. This has not been in the interest of the Services, the aviation industry or the nation. The day of national self-sufficiency in aviation is past. We must co-operate with other countries to share research and development costs and to provide a sufficiently large market for production. The British aviation industry cannot hope to prosper, as Right Hon. gentlemen opposite seem to think, by producing smaller and smaller batches of military aircraft for this country alone at higher and higher costs. It just is not on. Man for man, our aviation industry is the equal of any in the world. The basic cause of its difficulties is that until now the Government have consistently chosen the wrong sort of military projects for the size of the potential market. I know that the American aircraft companies often employ unscrupulous methods in making sales, but the fact is that, so long as the American domestic market for military aircraft is ten times the size of ours, we can hope to retain a capacity in this field at a time when the cost and complexity of aircraft is continually rising on one condition only: that is, if we decide from the start to co-operate with our allies. That is why my Right Hon. friend the Minister of Aviation and I went over to Paris a month ago to discuss collaboration with the French on the development and production of a strike/trainer and a joint programme for a variable geometry aircraft in the second half of the 1970s. That is why I spent half of my time with the German Defence Minister last week discussing the possibility of co-operation in meeting our common needs for vertical take-off aircraft. That is why we are continuously in touch with the United States on collaboration in the development and production of aircraft engines. The future of our aircraft industry – and this, I think, is common ground on both sides of the House – is likely to lie essentially with Europe rather than with the United States, and above all with France, because the French aircraft industry is of the same order of size as our own and faces similar problems. My experience in recent weeks in discussing the situation with representatives of various European countries is that all the European aircraft industries are beginning to recognize that they must hang together or they may hang separately. It is quite clear that the sort of co-operation that we are now able to discuss with the French and German Governments would have been totally impracticable had we kept the TSR2 in our programme. I ask Right Hon. and Hon. Members to remember the costs of aircraft production of the previous Government's programme: £1,200m in the four years from 1969 to 1972; £740m on the TSR2 alone. If we kept these aircraft in the programme, the resources for development of other aircraft during those years simply would not have been available. The country would not have been able to afford it. So that by the time the TSR2 programme was finally completed in the middle 1970s, we would probably have found that there was no European industry left with which we could co-operate, and for that reason we would have come to the end

An unusual photograph and possibly the only picture which shows the first two aircraft together. XR220 (foreground) and XR219 are pictured at Boscombe Down in the hangar assigned to BAC by the A&AEE for the duration of the initial test programme. XR220 is partially re-assembled following delivery from Weybridge, extensive repairs having been made to the aircraft after it suffered a major accident upon arrival. Had the programme continued, more aircraft would have appeared in this hangar, assigned to the test programme and issued to A&AEE for evaluation. *BAC*

of the line ourselves as well. It is this fact that no country of our size can any longer afford to produce the more sophisticated modern weapons for itself alone which makes so much nonsense of all the talk by Right Hon. Members opposite that, by co-operating with our allies or buying foreign equipment, we are somehow giving up our independence. The TSR2 is a symbol not of British independence but of interdependence with the United States. It would have depended entirely on American computers made or assembled in Britain under licence. We are living in a world which is technologically one today. If we accept that fact and act upon it, we can draw benefit for ourselves and others. If we sink into daydreams of total national independence in defence or in technology, or in foreign policy, we shall sink inexorably into national decline."

Amongst the many responses, Christopher Soames (the Opposition's defence spokesman) made the strongest and most considered contribution: "This House deplores the action of Her Majesty's Government in cancelling the TSR2 project, believing that this decision, following on the cancellation already announced of the HS.681 and the P.1154, will have grave effects on the future of the British aircraft industry and on the

development of science-based industries, while denying to the Royal Air Force these advanced weapon systems; and strongly deprecates the method which Her Majesty's Government chose for announcing their decision to this House."

Soames went on to say that in his view the Government had placed too much emphasis on in-service dates and not enough on V/STOL ability. The P.1154, HS.681 and TSR2 were interdependent ("...each an integral part of the V/STOL family of aircraft needed in the 1970s for strike, defence and supply with a high survival capacity"), and just as the Phantom and Hercules fell short in many respects as replacements for the P.1154 and the HS.681, so also did the F-111 when compared with the TSR2. In the reconnaissance role, in particular, the F-111 was deficient: "Whatever else it may have, the Mk.2 will not have the capability for all weather reconnaissance."

As for the Buccaneer, Soames stated that "...a jazzed-up Buccaneer would be way behind any single feature of the operational requirement for the TSR2. If it flew high it would be shot to pieces by fighters, and if it stayed on the deck it would be bounced to pieces. Supposing we were involved in a local war in the Far East in the early 1970s, how would (Mr Healey) like

Tragic scene at Samlesbury as a TSR2 wooden mock-up is dismantled and burned. Conspiracy theorists have insisted for over 40 years that the decision to destroy all traces of the TSR2 programme was a political exercise. In fact, both Jenkins and Healey had offered BAC the opportunity to continue flying XR219 and XR222 (at their expense) therefore the notion that they had any interest in destroying TSR2 hardware is patently wrong. Official (detailed) Government instructions for the wind-down of aircraft programmes were already stipulated and they were simply applied to TSR2 as soon as the programme ended. *BAC*

Above: XR220 pictured after repairs and re-assembly, embarking on engine and system ground runs in front of the trials hangar at Boscombe Down. The cancellation of the TSR2 programme just a few days later ensured that XR220 never got airborne and was destined to remain grounded at Boscombe Down, spending many subsequent months as a trials aircraft for noise investigation and engine development work – a monumental waste of an expensive and very capable machine. *BAC*

Right: Pictured at the usual operating base on the eastern perimeter of Boscombe Down's airfield, XR219 is surrounded by the usual array of support equipment and collection drums, attached to various vents. Colour photographs of XR219 are somewhat unusual, very few having been taken thanks to the relative unavailability (and cost) of colour film and processing, back in 1964-5. Almost all photographs taken during the flight test programme were taken by BAC's photographers and many images have gradually disappeared over the past 40 years, many having been lost, some having been damaged. But considering the relatively short nature of XR219's test programme, it is perhaps surprising that any images have survived. *BAC*

to explain to our soldiers that the reason that they were under constant air attack was because their protective air umbrella, Phantom-based, had been put out of action, and he had cancelled the P.1154? Or that our battlefield strike air power was spasmodic because the C-130 lumbering propellered transports had been denied the use of the supply airfield which was targeted by the enemy, and he had cancelled the HS.681? Or that the enemy supplies and reinforcements were unimpeded because it was raining and we had no all-weather reconnaissance ability, and he had cancelled the TSR2? Or, worst of all, that we were in danger of having to escalate into nuclear war because our conventional deficiencies had proved so serious, and he had cancelled all three aircraft? It seems that the Government is committing the country to a dollar expenditure amounting to £600m over a period of years. At the same time the cancellations will have a serious effect on the future of the aircraft industry's exports. The House had totally inadequate information on the extent to which the Government had entered into commitments with the USA; would the Minister please publish a White Paper on this?"

Soames claimed that the Opposition feared that the Government was mortgaging the future, trying to "…get their defence on the never-never and leaving the next Government to be saddled with the dollar bill. The effect of the cancellation of the three big military projects was to pull the carpet from under the British aircraft industry's feet. The industry was already having a hard enough struggle to sell the BAC-111 Eleven and the VC10 in the face of American competition, but things would be much harder for the industry now. Orders for the VC10, BAC One-Eleven, Trident and HS.125 would have run out by mid-1968, at which time orders for the P.1127 (Harrier) and the Coastal Command Comet will be through to all intents and purposes. Apart from the Concorde, therefore, the airframe industry cannot see production orders for one rivet to be put into one metal sheet after 1968." Soames concluded by observing that the previous (Conservative) government had "…always considered that the family of aircraft comprising the P.1154, HS.681 and TSR2 would be the last generation to be built purely by the British industry to a purely national requirement. After this we would catch the tide with Europe and proceed with general European requirements. But the present Government have withdrawn projects from the industry before it has caught the European tide."

After further questions and statements from many others – most of which offered nothing but criticism for the Government's decision – it was the turn of the Minister of Aviation, Roy Jenkins, to offer his views. He began by stating his belief that TSR2 was a fine technical achievement: "It was an advanced aircraft. It handled well in flight, and it was a tribute to many of those who worked on it. There is nothing technically wrong with this or any other British aircraft. But, to be a success, aircraft projects must be more than this. They must have controllable costs; they must fulfil the country's needs at a price that the country can afford; they must be broadly price competitive with comparable aircraft produced in other countries, and they must have the prospect of an overseas market commensurate with the resources tied up in their development. On all these four counts I regret to say that the TSR2 was not a prize project, but a prize albatross."

The Government, Jenkins said, was faced with a development cost well over three times the original and an estimated production cost which had more than doubled. With one aircraft flying and another nearly completed it seemed that the Government might be past the worst dangers of further escalation but, on the other hand, it was only 40 per cent of the way through the development programme. It had asked the firms for a fixed or maximum price. They could not give one, and Jenkins admitted he did not blame them for this: "They offered a target price. At this target price there would have been no profit, and for a limited stage beyond it they would have shared losses, up to a maximum of £9m for BAC and £2m for Bristol-Siddeley Engines. After that the Government's liability remained complete and open-ended. Furthermore, the target price was £30m more than the worst estimates on which we were working in January and February, and which we were then told were ludicrously high."

The overseas market for the TSR2 was non-existent, Jenkins continued, and even the home market was narrowly circumscribed. Among export customers the Australians looked the most likely, but they had opted for the F-111 for "hard-headed reasons" including price support arrangements, longer ferry range, and lower maintenance costs. It had been suggested that the Government had made a bad bargain with the Americans. This was not the case; there were no penalties if no firm order was placed, and no higher price if the numbers were substantially reduced. The fixed maximum price of the F-111A was 20 per cent less than "…the price at which we did all our comparative calculations with the TSR2." The F-111 Mk.2 was more uncertain, but the difference between the two versions was simply one of avionics, the cost of which was likely to be about 15 per cent of the total. Even if the estimated price for the cost of the Mk.2 avionics were exceeded by 150 per cent, Jenkins believed that "…we would still be within the total cost figures on which we did our comparison. Secondly, in our discussions with the British contractors, we have to leave a roughly equal proportion for components and electronic equipment – 15 per cent – completely open-ended, without even a target price. Thirdly, escalation is less likely with the American plane. That is because the run is so much longer and because, if research and development costs on the avionics did escalate, we should have to pay only less than 10 per cent of the total, and not the whole amount, as is the case with the TSR2."

On a full purchase, Jenkins said the Government should save at least £300m after making allowances for the TSR2 cancellation charges and the lower running costs of the F-111: "Such uncertainty as there is in the comparison means that, because of our failure to get a maximum price for the TSR2, the saving would be more likely to turn out greater than less. If we were making a straightforward switch from TSR2's to F-111's, the change would be overwhelmingly justified on budgetary grounds. Admittedly the dollar costs would be substantial, although we should have a number of years in which to prepare for them. If we had kept the TSR2 going, this would have meant the equivalent of a tariff of 135 per cent (not allowing for money already spent) or 90 per cent (allowing for money already spent). We were in fact not doing a straight switch; we were giving ourselves more time for thought on the minimum defence requirements and the possibilities of

XR220, fully assembled at Boscombe Down, pictured at the start of her engine test and ground run programme. After the programme was terminated, XR220 remained at Boscombe Down and became a familiar sight and sound on the airfield, performing many (reheated) engine runs in pursuance of a noise disturbance research programme – a useful but rather unchallenging task for such a capable and sophisticated aircraft. *BAC*

meeting them by developing existing aircraft. So long as we kept the TSR2 going we had to pay for this room for manoeuvre at the rate of £1m a week, £4m a month, £50m a year. We felt justified in paying for time at this rate so long as there were important facts about the two planes which we did not know. However, once we saw that we could not get a fixed price for the TSR2, and knew how high was the target price, we could justify no further postponement. We knew that the TSR2 had become a plane we could not afford. If we can do without a plane of this sort altogether, or manage with only a very few, the savings will be immense. If we need a substantial number of F-111s the savings will still be big. By the option we have taken we can keep these different possibilities open without paying for them at the rate of £1m a week. But in defence matters the objective should always be to discharge a role as economically as possible. This objective should be a particularly compelling one for a British Government today and in the next few years. The purpose of many of our current roles is not to defend this island, but to give us influence in the world, to make our foreign policy more effective. But nothing is more crucial to the effectiveness of our foreign policy than our national solvency here at home. If we sacrifice that we shall achieve nothing by worldwide commitments. While we were prisoners on the TSR2 escalator the pressures were against such an economical approach. With the F-111 they will operate the

other way. The fewer we can buy the bigger the budgetary saving, the smaller the dollar expenditure, the same the unit cost. We are now at a crucial planning stage for Anglo-French co-operation, we are very near to a firm agreement on the fixed-wing trainer, we are making good progress with our discussions on a joint versatile light variable-geometry aircraft and we are hopeful of an arrangement on helicopters and on an airborne early-warning plane. Had the TSR2 continued in the programme it would have been quite impossible, with any sense of financial responsibility, to have made funds available for all these projects."

Jenkins added that he did not underestimate the danger of American competition, "…but it seems to me to be the most extraordinary proposition that the correct way to deal with American competition is to keep a vast quantity of men, money and skill tied up in a project which the country cannot afford and for which the export prospects are nil." It had been suggested that the effect of the cancellation on the allocation of BAC overheads on the VC10, BAC-111 and Concorde would damage the price competitiveness of these aircraft; Jenkins refuted this. "That is not so. In negotiating compensation payments we will take into account the overhead problem for the next three years or so, by which date the firm will have had plenty of time to make its own adjustments. If we had not cancelled, everything in the industry would have gone on very much as before. It would have remained very much the same size and the same shape, and it would have continued to nestle equally comfortably on the cushion of easy government spending. And that pattern would have remained fairly fixed up to 1970. Confronted with this very big industry, with its voracious appetite for skill and money, with its export difficulties, with its output per man – which is only four-sevenths that of the French industry, although its labour force is three times as big – I did not believe it right to maintain that frozen pattern."

Away from Parliament, after the Budget Speech on 6 April, the TSR2 project had been cancelled immediately and BAC embarked upon the sad business of company re-appraisal, looking at what work was available for the current and future timescales, and the even more unpleasant business of deciding which jobs would survive. The immediate future of the TSR2 'prototype' aircraft XR219 was also the subject of some debate. Having been laid up for modification work at Warton, it was still technically airworthy, but with no project to support, the aircraft no longer had any valid purpose. Meanwhile over at Boscombe Down, another TSR2 was also complete, airworthy, and suddenly redundant. XR220 had been completed at Weybridge during August 1964 and with the future of the programme already in serious jeopardy by that stage, there was great eagerness to get the aircraft into the flight-test programme as swiftly as possible so that even more tangible progress could be demonstrated. Once dismantled for transportation, the aircraft's journey to Boscombe Down had begun on 9 September after a brief delay which was caused by BAC's Chief Works Foreman who had expressed some doubt as to the suitability of the trailer unit on which XR220 was to be carried. The standard Queen Mary trailer on which XR219 had been carried some months previously was still at Boscombe Down,

but Weybridge's management team decided that despite the Foreman's reservations, the substitute trailer would be adequate, and XR220 finally set off towards Wiltshire, arriving safely at Boscombe Down shortly before 1700 hrs.

Rather than work into the night, it was agreed that the trailers would be stored in hangar B3 (borrowed by BAC for the TSR2 trials) overnight, and unloaded the next day, and it was at this stage that catastrophe occurred. BAC's Lightning T4 chase aircraft was parked immediately outside the hangar, and the driver of the trailer carrying XR220's fuselage was obliged to manoeuvre around it in order to get the bulky load into the hangar. It was at this point that the choice of a non-standard transporter proved disastrous; whilst attempting to perform a tight turn, the entire trailer unit suddenly lifted and toppled over, depositing the fuselage of XR220 onto the concrete with a stomach-churning crash.

In a matter of seconds the future of the second prototype's test programme appeared to be over. XR220 laid on her port side for two days until a means of safely lifting the aircraft had been devised, and although the trailer was a write-off, the TSR2 fuselage had survived the fall surprisingly well, most of the impact having been absorbed by the port taileron spigot. Much of the external damage was confined to panels and cowlings. Subsequent checks, based on the location of known jigging holes, revealed that the fuselage structure did not appear to have been distorted, and work began on replacement of various parts (the most significant being an inner jacking beam), in an effort to return the aircraft to a flyable condition. Most of this work was relatively simple but to BAC's distress it ensured that XR220 remained firmly grounded in the hangar at Boscombe Down for a long time.

XR219 returning to the test flight base on Boscombe's runway, after completing a sortie during 1964. With the nose gear in the standard (compressed) configuration, the aircraft had a slight nose-down attitude which gave the pilot an excellent forward view.

It was March of the following year when the aircraft was finally fit to fly again, and ground runs of the fuel and hydraulic systems finally began. With most of the pre-flight testing having been done by Beamont in XR219, Jimmy Dell (and navigator/observer Peter Moneypenny) confined XR220's activities to a short series of fast runs along Boscombe's runway, and with these successfully completed the aircraft was – at long last – ready to fly on 6 April 1965 – the infamous day of Callaghan's Budget speech. Sadly, XR220 was unable to fly during the morning as a fuel pump leak was discovered during engine tests, and the crew retired to a nearby pub for lunch while the ground crew fixed the problem. Whilst waiting for the aircraft to be repaired the crew watched the news of Callaghan's speech on television and when he confirmed that TSR2 was cancelled, they immediately drove back to Boscombe Down in the hope that they could fly XR220 and achieve some sort of 'political' victory on this, the blackest of days for the project. But when they arrived at Boscombe they were informed that although XR220 was indeed now ready to fly, an order had already been issued to prohibit any further flying. It was too late.

So it was that XR220 remained in hangar B3 at Boscombe Down awaiting a decision on her future while XR219 remained at Warton, virtually complete and ready to fly. BAC concluded that it would be foolish to simply destroy two very capable and expensive aircraft at a time when they were able to deliver very useful research data which, even if no longer applicable to TSR2, would be extremely useful for future developmental work on other projects, not least Concorde which, like TSR2, was expected to operate for sustained periods at supersonic speeds. Shortly after TSR2 was cancelled, BAC proposed that the two completed aircraft should be maintained in flying condition and used for a limited research programme, effectively completing much of the flight-testing for which they had been built. It was estimated that a useful programme could be conducted for £2-3m and that this relatively small amount (at least when compared to the whole TSR2 project) would yield more than enough research data to make the project worthwhile. Roy Jenkins gave the idea some careful thought and Denis Healey agreed that it certainly had some merit. But by June, Roy Jenkins had clearly decided that the Government had no desire to spend so much as another penny on TSR2 unless absolutely necessary. He informed BAC that Treasury funding would not be appropriate but that he had no objection to BAC flying both aircraft, providing that the costs were met by them, and deducted from the agreed cancellation costs which were being arranged.

BAC concluded that although it could see substantial benefits from the use of the aircraft, it was not prepared to finance the project itself and so any plans to continue flying the aircraft were finally abandoned forever. XR219 was therefore allocated to the Proof & Experimental Establishment and dismantled at Warton, eventually being transported to Shoeburyness by road, together with XR221 which had been completed and moved to Wisley. XR221 had, in fact, already assumed an important part of the test programme, having been fitted with early pre-production versions of much of the avionics fit, including the forward-looking radar. Some testing of the aircraft's systems had been conducted on the aircraft by the time of the project's cancellation and a fully representative sortie had been run through with great success, much to everybody's surprise and encouragement; nobody realistically expected this stage of the systems development testing to proceed smoothly.

But XR221 was not yet in a flyable condition and after being removed from Wisley together with XR219 from Warton, it remained dismantled at Shoeburyness for some time, various components being used for destructive testing. After XR221 had languished in the fields of Essex for some years, personnel at the P&EE conspired to restore the aircraft to a representation of her former glory, and the main sections of XR219 were again re-assembled (although it is possible that it was actually the wings of XR221 which were mated to the fuselage of XR219, creating a composite airframe), and a recognisable TSR2 was finally visible again, far out in the scrub land, many miles from public scrutiny, where the aircraft remained an iconic (but somewhat inaccessible) sight for many years until the remaining, deteriorating parts of both aircraft were finally reduced to scrap in the late 1970s.

Considering the amounts of money and effort which had been poured into the design and manufacture of XR219 and XR221, it was particularly tragic that no useful role for either aircraft was found. Testing components and metals to destruction was almost a case of testing for testing's sake, and allocating such valuable aircraft (and a batch of new Olympus engines) to such a distinctly low-tech project was certainly foolish and wasteful, when all of the completed TSR2 airframes could have undoubtedly contributed a great deal towards the development of future projects, even if only in terms of research data. A rather happier fate was bestowed upon XR220 which was not abandoned, and remained active at Boscombe Down until December 1966, conducting ground trials on behalf of Bristol-Siddeley.

A great deal of speculation over the noise generated by the aircraft's powerful Olympus engines had raised questions as to the acceptability of Concorde operations, bearing in mind that the new airliner would rely upon four examples of what would be effectively the same engine. Consequently, Bristol-Siddeley embarked upon a noise disturbance research programme, and XR220 was utilised to perform engine runs in a variety of configurations. These investigated the environmental effects of the Olympus, and also enabled Bristol-Siddeley to gather more research data on the engines, which were already being developed for eventual use by the Concorde programme at this stage. Although the aircraft never flew (and never had flown, thanks to its untimely accident), its presence at Boscombe Down was certainly in no doubt when the two mighty Olympus engines roared at full throttle with both reheats selected! The tests revealed that although the Olympus was undoubtedly noisy, it did not create any risk of structural damage, nor did it adversely affect residents in the local area. Ironically and once and for all, it also proved that the Olympus engines functioned almost perfectly. In 1967 the aircraft finally left Boscombe, arriving at RAF Henlow by road, where it was stored on behalf of the RAF Museum, eventually moving to Cosford in 1975 to what has now become its permanent home.

The only other virtually complete aircraft from the proposed flight test fleet was XR222 which was nearing the end of the assembly line at Weybridge by the time of the project's cancellation. This was donated to the Institute of Technology at Cranfield, and for many years the aircraft was used for engineering and systems instructional purposes in one of Cranfield's hangars before eventually being placed in external storage on the airfield. Never fully completed, the airframe was finally transferred to the Imperial War Museum at Duxford, and after undergoing a thorough restoration programme (during which various components were added to render the aircraft externally complete), it resumed its position inside the museum's display complex. These were the only TSR2 airframes which survived after the programme was cancelled, and virtually all of the other semi-complete fuselage, wings and nose structures which were undergoing construction both at Weybridge and Samlesbury, were simply dismantled on site and sold as scrap. Not surprisingly, BAC's management was keen to remove all of the TSR2 components from its factories as rapidly as possible, as there was no commercial benefit in allocating floor space to an abandoned programme. As ever, precise Government instructions had already been drawn up to cater for such contingencies and these were issued to BAC immediately after cancellation. The instructions embraced the destruction of all the surviving components, internal equipment, construction jigs, technical data, and any other material associated with the project, and with the worry of non-compliance penalties now being a distinct possibility, a surprising amount of effort was devoted to this process leading many of the BAC workers to conclude that the Government had embarked upon an unspecified political conspiracy to remove every trace of the project as quickly as they could. Some said that the attention given to the project's dismantlement seemed to be rather better than the efforts made to keep it alive and viable.

In fact, there is no evidence to suggest that there were any such dark motives behind the process, and the Government's only concern was probably the very real threat of espionage, something which was a major risk at that time. Many years later, Roy Jenkins did refer obliquely to a suggestion that BAC had proposed the retention of various jigs, components and documentation on the basis that the project might be worthy of reconsideration at a later date, but he claimed that he saw no industrial benefit in such an exercise and therefore it seems clear that although he did not encourage any aspects of the programme to survive, he certainly did not have any declared interest in destroying it either. Jenkins simply had no stomach to allocate any more Treasury money to a programme which had been so costly and controversial. Likewise, Healey insists that he most certainly never gave any direct order to destroy any of the programme's hardware and the very fact that both he and Jenkins were open to the idea of allowing BAC to continue flying XR219 and XR220 (albeit at BAC's expense) illustrates that there was no greater effort made to somehow eradicate any evidence of TSR2 beyond that which would have been applied to any other cancelled programme.

By the end of 1966 when XR220's ground trials ended, the TSR2 programme was consigned completely to history, although its legacy was still the subject of heated debate for some time to come, in the media, within the aviation industry, and within Parliament. Having promised the Air Staff that it would be given the F-111K, Healey pursued the purchase of the

aircraft with tenacity, even though the F-111's development programme proved to be even more troublesome than TSR2's had been. But with America's formidable technological and financial support behind it, the F-111 project forged ahead. However, the projected cost of Britain's purchase slowly increased and this factor was compounded by the relative exchange rates of British and American currencies which served to raise the project's cost by proxy. When Britain was eventually forced to devalue Sterling (in November 1967), it effectively increased the cost of F-111 still further, and so it was hardly surprising that the proposed purchase of F-111 eventually became as controversial as TSR2's proposed purchase had been.

By the end of 1967 the Labour Government had shifted its position on defence matters quite considerably. No longer hesitant over whether to maintain a presence East of Suez, its hand had been forced thanks to the country's dire financial state and on 16 January 1968, Harold Wilson presented a statement to the House of Commons which outlined the Government's future defence policy in some detail. In his speech, Wilson stated that the Government's decisions had been based on two main principles: first, it was in Britain's own interests, and those of her friends, for the country to strengthen her economic base quickly, as there was no military strength, whether for Britain or for her allies, except on the basis of economic strength. Secondly, reductions in capability must be based on a review of the commitments the Services were required to undertake; defence must be related to foreign policy, but it must not be asked in the name of that policy to undertake commitments beyond its capability. These comments were offered as an explanation for what was to follow. Britain was to withdraw from the Far East and Persian Gulf (including Malaysia and Singapore) by the end of 1971 so that "...apart from our remaining dependencies and certain other necessary exceptions, we shall by that date not be maintaining military bases outside Europe and the Mediterranean."

Britain's carrier fleet was to be phased out and, as expected, the order for the F-111K was cancelled: "We have decided to cancel the order for 50 F-111 aircraft. Further study is being given to the consequences of this decision on the future equipment of the Royal Air Force. Leaving out of account the results of this study, the cancellation of the F-111 is estimated to yield total savings on the Defence Budget of about £400 million between now and 1977-78. This figure allows for likely cancellation charges. The saving in dollar expenditure over the period, again allowing for likely cancellation charges, will be well over $700 million. Because of the credit arrangements, these savings will mature over a period of years."

In effect, the Government's decision to abandon its East of Suez role had instantly rendered OR.343 (and therefore TSR2 and F-111K) as redundant, and Britain's defence policy was now to be geared almost exclusively towards Europe and the NATO alliance. Arguably, this move should have been made many years previously.

Denis Healey was devastated by the loss of F-111 as he had worked hard to assure the Air Staff that, in the absence of TSR2, it would receive a suitable – some would say preferable – alternative. But despite his long and sometimes bitter fights within the Cabinet, the cost of F-111 (compounded by devaluation) was too great to bear, especially when the aircraft's primary purpose was to be removed at a stroke by the withdrawal from the Middle and Far East. Healey did try to emphasise that, like TSR2, the F-111 would have an important NATO role too, its deep strike and reconnaissance ability being unique amongst Britain's European allies. But having condoned (and eventually even encouraged) at least a partial withdrawal from commitments outside of Europe, he had unintentionally signed the F-111K's death warrant too. He considered resigning as a matter of principle, but eventually chose not to, even though the long battle for TSR2's cancellation and the purchase of F-111K had been a long, bitter and ultimately fruitless exercise both for him and the RAF. His frustration had been compounded by the cancellation of yet another project some months previously, when France pulled out of the AFVG, the Anglo-French Variable Geometry aircraft which Healey had agreed to develop in association with his French counterpart.

Keen to foster relations with France (and particularly keen to keep France within NATO), his negotiations led to the creation of both AFVG and ECAT, which would eventually become Jaguar, during 1965. The swing-wing AFVG was regarded as a design which would perform the same tactical strike and reconnaissance missions as TSR2 and once the design was complete, it was expected that the aircraft would enter RAF service in the mid-1970s to supplement TSR2 (or F-111) squadrons and ultimately replace the RAF's remaining Vulcans. Although AFVG's existence was certainly a factor during the final days of the TSR2 programme, it had no direct effect upon the pressure for TSR2's cancellation as it was inevitably regarded as a supplementary issue for the future, but when TSR2 was finally abandoned, it was anticipated that AFVG would supplement the proposed F-111K squadrons in the same way. But as is often the case with French co-operation, the AFVG project was driven primarily by politics, and as the concept entered the design stage, France's Dassault company embarked upon the creation of the 'Mirage G' which was, in effect, an indigenous version of the same design, encouraging the typically French notion of 'going it alone'.

By 1967 it was clear that France was becoming increasingly lukewarm towards AFVG and on 29 June, Defence Minister Pierre Messmer announced that the country was pulling out of the project due to "financial considerations" – although it seems clear that France's motivation was to simply withdraw from NATO and pursue her own combat aircraft design without the influence of British interference. This was a major blow to Healey, and the loss of F-111 made his continuation as Defence Minister seem (at least to him) almost untenable. Frustratingly, in a period of almost ten years, the efforts to create a replacement for the Canberra had resulted in TSR2, AFVG and F-111K, but despite the phenomenal amounts of manpower, technological expertise and money which had been poured into these programmes, the RAF still had no such direct replacement.

Left with only the preliminary AFVG studies as a basis, the termination of the joint programme encouraged the Ministry of Technology and BAC to continue work on their own variable geometry design and this eventually resulted in the emergence of the UKVG which was an all-British design created at

XR220 at Boscombe Down during ground testing. Just visible is the small plate aerial incorporated into the aircraft's tail fin. Similar aerials were also mated to the wing tips – the only discernable external difference from XR219 which did not have these aerials installed. *BAC*

Warton, similar in terms of projected performance to the now-defunct AFVG. With international collaboration in mind (and no appetite to sustain such an ambitious programme in isolation), the project was offered to Germany, but with its own designs for a similar combat aircraft underway, little enthusiasm was expressed by the Germans. Undeterred, Warton continued development of the design and expanded it to incorporate possible fighter applications (in response to a request from the Ministry of Technology) and eventually the UKVG grew into the Multi Role Combat Aircraft which became the basis for a collaborative programme between Britain, Germany and Italy, emerging as the Panavia Tornado – undoubtedly one of the most capable and successful combat aircraft ever created.

Tornado is in effect a direct descendant of TSR2, and despite being a multi-national product, it is very much a Warton design, with a tactical strike and reconnaissance capability (plus short-field take-off and landing ability), and systems which were directly developed from TSR2 experience. The aircraft's direct connections to TSR2 are obvious, and many of the RAF's Tornado pilots have examined TSR2's promised performance figures, remarking that Tornado is essentially the same aircraft, albeit with less range; a 'baby TSR2' in effect.

The RAF finally got its long-awaited Canberra replacement more than twenty years after the requirement had first emerged, when Tornado GR1 aircraft began to enter RAF operational service in 1982. Tornado was not capable of sustained supersonic flight at very low level, nor was it capable of long-range deep strike missions. However, by the 1980s Britain was a very different country than it was in the 1960s. Global projection was a thing of the past; Tornado was an all-European aircraft designed for an all-European environment and for this theatre of operations the aircraft was, and still is, unquestionably ideal. But excellent though Tornado undoubtedly is, nobody can derive much satisfaction from the knowledge that an even better and more capable aircraft could have been in RAF service more than ten years previously, had the country's industrial and political base been more competent at creating it.

CHAPTER ELEVEN

Victim of Circumstance

THE TSR2 programme occupied a significant part of Britain's defence strategy for almost a decade. An unprecedented amount of technological thinking and expertise was allocated to the project and the result was an aircraft which showed every sign of becoming a truly outstanding strike and reconnaissance platform which could have equipped the RAF's operational squadrons through the 1970s and onwards into the new millennium. The fact that it never progressed beyond the very earliest stages of a tentative flight-test programme is one which has inspired countless commentators, authors, historians and politicians to claim that it was perhaps the supreme example of political hooliganism. It has become almost accepted wisdom to cite the TSR2 programme as a classic illustration of the blinkered, short-sighted and sometimes malicious attitude of politicians who stand accused of putting party politics ahead of national defence needs. In some ways this accusation has solid foundation, in that it is undeniably true that TSR2 was, indeed, a tragic victim of politics. But it would be entirely wrong to claim that it was party politics which

destroyed TSR2. Ultimately, there was only one supremely important point which sealed TSR2's fate and that was its cost. Put simply, TSR2 was just too expensive. The key to understanding the reasons for TSR2's destruction is to establish precisely why TSR2 was so expensive and, more importantly, how Britain ever reached a situation whereby an aircraft was being developed for a customer that did not necessarily want it, on behalf of a Government that seemed to have no real understanding of its future defence requirements. Ultimately, the reasons for the project's failure are inevitably attributed to politics, but not those of the point-scoring party squabbles between the Labour and Conservative camps. It was the politics of bureaucracy, inter-service battles, foreign policy, industrial policy and international relations which conspired to create an atmosphere in which the TSR2 project was inevitably doomed to failure almost from the point at which it first began.

Wing vortices streaming, XR219 is pictured above the Wiltshire clouds during an early test flight, the landing gear still resolutely extended. Flaps are down and the auxiliary air intakes are open, indicating that this picture was captured during low-speed handling trials.

Everything down, XR219 is pictured on her first flight, turning west onto final approach back to Boscombe Down, high over Thruxton Airfield, over which Beamont had regularly flown during a series of practice sorties in Warton's Lightning T4. *BAC*

Fundamentally, there can be no doubt that TSR2 was a very sophisticated weapons platform. Unfortunately, it was too sophisticated, and the sheer effort of creating an aircraft which could meet such ambitious performance requirements was such that long delays and associated cost increases were inevitable. Many aspects of the programme were subsequently recognised as being so advanced that they were being attempted before the know-how with which to achieve them had been properly acquired. It was often a case of trying to run before one could even walk. The RAF clearly needed to replace its Canberra fleet, but the Air Staff did not give sufficient consideration to the precise nature of the aircraft which would be designed as its replacement. Instead, it indulged itself in what would now be described as 'blue sky thinking' and simply conjured-up an all-embracing requirement for an aircraft which could do pretty much everything that any combat aircraft might ever be called upon to do. It would have to fly at high altitude like the Canberra, but it would have to fly much faster – not just supersonic, but at twice the speed of sound or even more. But in view of the very obvious fact that Soviet defences would

A beautiful colour picture of XR219 in a gentle descent at high altitude, with the four air brake doors fully opened on 16th February 1965 during test flight No.13. TSR2 performed magnificently at high altitude as it did at low altitude – no mean achievement for a large, heavy and well-equipped bomber. Although the effectiveness of the aircraft's many systems had yet to be proved at the time of the project's cancellation, the aircraft's aerodynamic capabilities were explored quite thoroughly before the proverbial axe fell, and it was clear that the aircraft performed even better than had been expected. Whether the many complicated on-board systems would have performed quite so well remains unknown. *BAC*

soon be capable of destroying fast, high-flying bombers, the Canberra's replacement would have to fly low as well – not just very low, but as little as 200ft above the ground. Additionally, it would have to achieve this task in all weathers, day and night, and at supersonic speed.

Rather than opt for an aircraft which was ideally suited to this role, the Air Staff decided that it wanted both a low-level and a high-level supersonic bomber, endowing it with the luxury of being able to adopt whatever delivery tactics seemed likely to offer the best chance of success at any given time. Then to enhance the projected design a little further, it would also have to perform as a high-speed reconnaissance platform and also be capable of operating out of a grass field. In short, the Air Staff created the concept of a 'wonder plane' which would have all the capabilities normally attributed to a variety of different aircraft. Little wonder that English Electric even considered developing the design into an interceptor too – it was the only other additional capability which the Air Staff could have asked for.

It could be argued that in some respects the Air Staff's aspirations were admirable, or at least surprisingly honest. An aircraft which could operate to good effect in both high and low-level environments at supersonic speed would undoubtedly be an outstanding aircraft, and even if there was some doubt as to whether all of the demanding requirements could be met realistically (at least for a reasonable price), it was hardly a crime to ask for them. The difficulties began when the designer and manufacturer (Vickers) passively accepted all of the requirements and confidently agreed to achieve them all, almost encouraging the Air Staff to stretch its aspirations still further, all with complete disregard to the amount of time, effort and money which would be required in order to produce a viable result. English Electric (and Bristol-Siddeley) regularly

questioned the extreme nature of OR.343's demands and argued, quite reasonably, that a more affordable aircraft could be produced more rapidly, if the requirement was re-thought along less ambitious lines. In particular, there was no doubt that the specified maximum speed would add a disproportionately huge amount of development work and cost to the programme, and yet there seemed to be no logical reason for the way in which the Air Staff defiantly stuck to its proposed figures. But when Vickers seemingly made no effort to dispute the Air Staff's aspirations, it is hardly surprising that GOR.339 became more, rather than less, ambitious. Even Roly Beamont – possibly TSR2's fiercest defender, admitted that he had never understood why, ultimately, a top speed of Mach 2.25 had been called for. According to Beamont, it had been designed "…as a low-level transonic penetrator. The job could have been done by optimising the aircraft's low-level performance which would have resulted in a performance of Mach 1.7-1.8 at height. The aircraft would have been rather similar to the English Electric P.17!" It was this over-ambitious attitude, combined with other factors, which was the root cause of the aircraft's downfall.

The other, inescapable mistake was to discount the NA.39 (Buccaneer) as a suitable aircraft with which to meet the Air Staff's requirements. Despite protestations, it was abundantly clear that the Buccaneer could have been developed in line with the RAF's projected roles and would have provided the RAF with an aircraft which could have done everything that the RAF needed, much more affordably. The Air Staff successfully demonstrated that the Buccaneer did not meet the specifications of GOR.339 but, of course, it was obvious that GOR.339 was unrealistically ambitious and only one aircraft could ever hope to meet its stringent specifications – TSR2. But this was a self-fulfilling prophecy.

Returning from a test flight, XR219 is pictured with her huge brake parachute deployed. The parachute could be reefed in order to provide a less-harsh braking effect when crosswinds were a factor, and there was some concern that the considerable force exerted by the fully-deployed parachute might have had an effect of the aircraft's structure, suggesting that a smaller parachute might have been developed for production aircraft, or that the existing parachute might have been permanently reefed to a smaller diameter. Plans for a thrust reversal system never proceeded beyond the concept stage. *BAC*

In effect, GOR.339 had been specifically tailored to be beyond the capabilities of any other design, thereby ensuring that there would be only one possible solution with which to meet it. The reason why the Air Staff wilfully allowed this situation to prevail (and never entertained the possibility of re-writing the specification to enable other aircraft to be considered) was simply because the Air Staff had no intention of ever accepting the Buccaneer which had been created specifically for the Royal Navy and was, therefore, a naval aircraft – something which the RAF could not possibly accept. Lord Hill-Norton (Chief of the Defence Staff in 1971) commented that with regard to TSR2 and Buccaneer, the Navy "…was, for once, in a rather strong position versus our Light Blue allies… opponents? We had the Buccaneer which was a really first-rate aeroplane and we said to the RAF 'why don't you have the Buccaneer for Christ's sake?' 'Oh well, we couldn't have a Dark Blue aeroplane. The service would go raving mad.' It was as bad as that. Of course in the end they had to take it and it was five years too late. If they'd taken it and modernised it for land operations, they'd have been on the pig's back. Relations were so bad that they wouldn't take it for one reason, and that was because it was painted dark blue. If they had taken it, they would have been in a very strong position to have a new aeroplane about ten years later, the early 'seventies. At the time of course they were still smarting because they hadn't got Polaris. So they were damned if they were going to have it and the Navy could go to hell. I wasn't sympathetic."

Hill-Norton's view is characteristic of his typically forthright attitude, but the truth of his comments cannot be disputed. The tragedy was that no Government minister had the foresight – or guts – to force the Air Staff into overcoming their bitterness towards the Navy and accepting that the Buccaneer was the right aircraft. Of course, the irony of this story was that the RAF did finally have to grudgingly accept the Buccaneer (essentially in an unmodified naval configuration) in the early 1970s and it proved to be a truly brilliant aircraft which performed admirably both as a nuclear tactical strike aircraft and as a conventional tactical bomber, which the RAF was ultimately loath to part with when it eventually reached the end of its service life.

Healey also subsequently admitted that Buccaneer would have been the ideal solution: "I now think that my great mistake was not to have persuaded the RAF to adopt the Navy's Buccaneer. The Buccaneer could have done the job almost as well as F-111 or the TSR2 and infinitely cheaper, but one of the articles of faith observed by all three services was NIH – Not Invented Here; never accept any weapon sponsored by another service."

Another irony of the Buccaneer's part in TSR2's history is that Mountbatten – the avid supporter of the Buccaneer and strongest critic of TSR2 – was ultimately right to conclude that the RAF should have bought the Buccaneer. But the tactics he employed in order to try and influence this choice were undoubtedly suspect – some would say that they were often shameful. There is a well-known newspaper story (which, it should be said, is entirely unsubstantiated) that Mountbatten had a set of Buccaneer and TSR2 business cards printed, and during discussions with potential TSR2 export customers and any other supporters of the aircraft, he would slap one TSR2 card on a table, accompanied by five Buccaneer cards, exclaiming, "You could have all these for the price of one of these."

Interesting aerial view (taken from the A&AEE's rescue helicopter) of XR219 being prepared for a test flight at Boscombe Down. OR.343 stated that the aircraft and its ground equipment should be waterproof and capable of remaining serviceable with only a minimum of attention, for up to thirty days in open air conditions. Whether the aircraft would have been capable of sustaining this capability is doubtful. With an array of very complex systems, it seems unlikely that the aircraft would have remained serviceable without a significant amount of regular attention. *BAC*

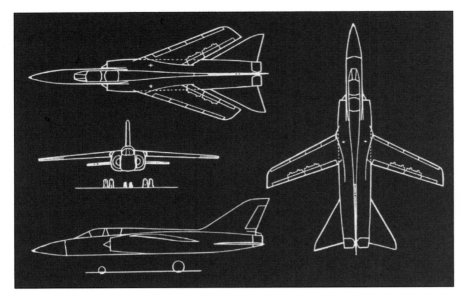

BAC general arrangement drawing of the Anglo French Variable Geometry Aircraft, which was to enter RAF service in the 1970's, joining TSR2 in the tactical strike and reconnaissance role. The concept of augmenting TSR2 with another design, possibly just five or six years after TSR2 had entered service, made little sense, and the project was undoubtedly driven by politics rather than military expedience. France quickly abandoned the project when the advantages of an all-French design became clear, much to the frustration of Denis Healey, who had been so keen to pursue the concept. However, AFVG eventually led to the creation of Tornado and the RAF finally received their Canberra Replacement – ten years after they could have had TSR2. *Courtesy BAE Heritage*

Lord Mountbatten – possibly the most vociferous critic of TSR2. His efforts to destroy the programme in order to secure an order for new aircraft carriers for the Navy were well-known both within the aviation industry and the corridors of Whitehall. Mountbatten shamelessly attempted to convince his Australian counterpart that the RAF would never receive TSR2 and that Australia should look elsewhere. Ultimately, his efforts to destroy TSR2 in order to ensure funding for new aircraft carriers was a futile exercise. TSR2 was abandoned but so were the carriers. Mountbatten's efforts also had little or no direct affect upon Australia's final decision to purchase F-111 which was actually based entirely on their desire to forge closer links with America. *A&AP*

Even if the story is more of a myth than a fact, it is certainly true that Mountbatten did all he could to push the RAF into accepting the Buccaneer, but to suggest that he was partly responsible for TSR2's cancellation is an over-estimation of his influence. For example, his efforts to dissuade Australia may have had some initial effect on that country's evaluation process, but its final strike aircraft purchase was very much a positive choice in favour of the F-111 rather than a more negative rejection of the TSR2; therefore Mountbatten's influence was ultimately of no consequence. Likewise, his efforts to persuade Defence Minister Watkinson to push for a Buccaneer purchase for the RAF eventually prompted Watkinson to ask Mountbatten to simply "… never mention the subject again", which suggests that his lobbying was regarded more as a nuisance rather than a serious influence. Mountbatten's opposition to TSR2 was clearly not based on any benevolent desire to give the Air Staff the most appropriate and affordable aircraft. He was concerned primarily with his desire to ensure that new aircraft carriers for the Navy would be ordered, and when Polaris was ordered for the Navy, it was obvious to him that there would be little appetite to allocate another huge sum to the Navy, when so much money would be required for the RAF's TSR2. He therefore concluded that by disposing of TSR2, the prospects of funding new carriers would be secure. Of course the events of the late 1960s conspired to ensure that both TSR2 and the carriers were abandoned and all of Mountbatten's manoeuvrings had achieved precisely nothing. But, ultimately, his impassioned view that the RAF should have bought the Buccaneer proved to be correct. It was sad though, that he reached this conclusion through the most suspect of motives.

Another issue which contributed to the TSR2's cancellation was the way in which the project was first set up. The original GOR.339 specification was issued to all of Britain's aircraft manufacturers and they all responded with good, viable proposals. Normal procedures would have then involved the examination of each design based on its relative technical merits and projected performance, combined with considerations of cost, production capacity, timescales and other relevant issues. By contrast, the GOR.339 submissions were patently not studied on this basis. Although all of the usual considerations were undoubtedly taken into account, the primary motive behind the final choice of designer and manufacturer was the Government's insistence that the project should only be awarded to a combination of two or more companies, thereby effectively forcing each of the individual companies into mergers. There was clearly some sound wisdom behind the concept of creating a more streamlined industry, but the notion of forcing the issue, almost by bribery, must surely have been seen as a potential source of trouble from the start, and yet the Government insisted upon implementing the policy which meant that almost all of the GOR.339 submissions had effectively been pointless exercises, as they never stood any plausible chance of being adopted. In reality, it was only the Hawker Siddeley, Vickers and English Electric designs which would ever be taken seriously. It was probably a simple case of good fortune that the most promising design was that proposed by English Electric, which happened to be part of the merger deal between itself and Vickers. Had a more convincing partnership between other companies looked likely, it is quite possible that an inferior design might have been adopted, simply to satisfy the Government's industrial criteria.

But even with the right design having been selected (either through sound judgement or luck, or a combination of both), all logic was again abandoned and instead of awarding a contract to English Electric with Vickers as sub-contractor, the obvious and practical approach was turned on its head and Vickers was given the contract, with English Electric acting as sub-contractor as part of the BAC combine. No satisfactory explanation for this absurd decision was ever given, other than that George Edward's management expertise was somehow deemed to be important, although nobody has ever ventured to suggest why Freddie Page's abilities were ever construed to be somehow inferior (because, of course, they were not). The very obvious fact that TSR2 was in effect the English Electric P.17A makes the notion of awarding control of the project to Vickers seem quite ludicrous, and there is absolutely no doubt that if a simple contract had been awarded to English Electric, without any of the complications of merging with Vickers, then TSR2 would have emerged far more rapidly and far more cheaply. Indeed, without the almost obligatory acceptance of the Air Staff's increasingly ambitious demands, English Electric would probably have developed a far more practical and affordable production version of the P.17A which could have reached squadron service by 1965.

However the Government's interference simply served to ensure that it stood little chance of getting what it wanted, even at the very point when it first set out to get it. Even if the choice of manufacturer was not a sure method of ensuring problems and ultimately failure, the Government then imposed its own management structure on BAC so that although Edwards was ostensibly in control of the programme, his actions were continually scrutinised to such an extent that his attempts to structure a logical and functional development process were continually frustrated. Consequently, TSR2 became a classic example of 'design by committee.'

At one now infamous progress meeting, the chairman insisted upon a head count and recorded that no fewer than 52 people were present, and that this absurdly high figure should be reduced for future meetings. At the next meeting the head count was 61! Chief Test Pilot Beamont later recalled that ridiculously long meetings would be devoted to the most insignificant of matters, such as group discussions on the placement of cockpit instruments which would finally result in a decision that, inevitably, would be revoked when the practicalities of actually flying the layout were exercised by the air crew (who should have made the decisions in the first place).

On a more serious level, the management structure was fatally flawed, not least in the way that so many sub-contractors

were either selected or approved by the Government, with little or no regard to Edward's advice and experience. The result was a guarantee of delays and cost increases which were compounded by the Government's failure to fix its requirements and place a production order, which encouraged sub-contractors to shift their attention to other projects. Quite understandably, no company would allocate priority to a project which showed no tangible signs of security or longevity.

But even though finally TSR2 fell victim to its own cost, there is also no doubt that part of the Government's decision to abandon the project was not attributable entirely to projected costs, or indeed any aspect of the aircraft's performance or technical standard. The contributory factor was the was a combination of two important emerging issues. First, there was the availability of the F-111. Contrary to most accounts of TSR2's history, the US Government did not embark upon a pseudo-covert mission to force the F-111 upon an unwilling or unenthusiastic British Government. Nor did the US try to somehow destroy TSR2 in order to pave the way for the F-111. In practical terms, the F-111 was designed for an American requirement and there was never any serious prospect of making substantial export sales, in much the same way as TSR2's export potential was undoubtedly poor. In essence, McNamara offered Britain the F-111 on the most reasonable terms that he could devise, clear in the knowledge that TSR2 was facing cancellation (thanks to its cost) and that unless Britain could afford to buy F-111, the country would be left without a long-range strike aircraft of any description. This was not a prospect that McNamara relished, as he (like his Government) was keen to encourage Britain to maintain its East of Suez role, with a significant presence that served to politically underpin America's overseas presence. Without F-111 Britain could not seriously maintain this role, and it was the very real prospect of losing TSR2 that encouraged McNamara to negotiate a favourable deal with Healey, so as to ensure that Britain could continue its international commitments. America's involvement in the story was never about destroying TSR2 in order to impose F-111 on Britain, even though many ill-informed writers have tried to imply that it was. On Healey's part, the F-111 offer was too good to resist. The F-111K was significantly cheaper than TSR2 and even with subsequent cost increases and currency values taken into account, F-111K was still a much better deal, especially when offset American purchases were added to the calculations. But most importantly for Healey, far beyond all the arguments which weighed the costs of the two aircraft types against each

Two partially-complete F-111K aircraft pictured whilst in storage late in 1968, awaiting a decision on their future. They were subsequently dismantled for spares recovery. Had Britain purchased F-111K, the RAF would have received an aircraft which was remarkably similar to TSR2 in almost every respect, apart from its overall cost which would have been considerably cheaper. It was only Britain's crippling financial situation which eventually rendered the aircraft unaffordable almost by proxy. But it is also true that had the aircraft been procured, it would have been somewhat over-specified for the exclusively European role to which it would have eventually been assigned. *General Dynamics*

Pictured in glorious colour towards the end of XR219's test programme, the aircraft is seen over northern England, the once-pristine paint finish looking decidedly worn after many months of activity. *BAC*

An unusual view of XR219 parked on its designated test area at the end of Boscombe Down's shortest (third) runway. Visible is the hinged cowling which houses the brake parachute, positioned between the jet pipes. While test flying progressed at Boscombe Down, the project's future was already looking grim, as illustrated by a briefing note prepared for the SoS for Defence, just weeks before this photograph was taken. It stated that "The whole project is characterised by deplorable technical delays, ineffective management and cost escalation (attributable largely to initial gross under-estimation of the technical problems involved and failure to ensure adequate cost control by the contractors), and by extreme tardiness in doing anything to remedy the Ministry of Aviation's own inadequate organisation." *BAC*

other, the F-111K was to be purchased on credit. The huge burden of TSR2's cost would have to be met by the Treasury over a short period, the bulk of the finance having to be allocated within a two years or so. By stark contrast, F-111K's payments would be spread over a whole decade which would enable the aircraft's proportion of each year's defence expenditure to be kept relatively low. It was a consideration which few commentators on TSR2's cancellation ever care to mention, and yet it was the key point which made the F-111 purchase so attractive to Healey and the Treasury.

The second of the final contributory issues facing TSR2 was of course Britain's overall defence posture. Although TSR2 had been designed with European NATO operations firmly in mind, the more advanced aspects of the aircraft's performance were developed in response to Britain's continuing East of Suez commitments. Without the RAF's presence in the Middle and Far East, TSR2 would probably have been a rather less ambitious design (the Tornado in effect), tailored exclusively to the needs of the European Theatre. But the Government wanted much more than this, even though there was an increasing acceptance that Britain probably could not afford to maintain the kind of commitments for which TSR2 was being created. Of course, it was only two years after TSR2 was cancelled that the Government finally accepted that Britain should withdraw from East of Suez, which clearly illustrates that even if TSR2's development had continued, it would have been a technically redundant design by the time that it was due to enter service, produced at huge expense for a role that simply no longer existed. If successive Governments had possessed the foresight (or at least the courage) to address the issue of overseas commitments sooner, the TSR2 programme could have been terminated long before so much effort and money was spent on it. Indeed it is clear that with a more honest and far-reaching appraisal of Britain's defence posture, TSR2 might never have even been started.

Yet if TSR2 had survived, it would undoubtedly have become a rather different aircraft to the one which was outlined by GOR.339 and although it would still have entered service as a conventional and nuclear strike/reconnaissance platform, its deep strike ability, tailored to operations in the Middle and Far East, would have already been rendered unnecessary. In essence, TSR2 would have been somewhat over-specified for the roles in which it operated. Not a bad prospect by any means and rarely has the RAF had a weapons system which is technically superior to the one which it might actually need, but in view of the country's circumstances it would hardly have been an achievement to be proud of. A near bankrupt country would have poured resources into a brilliantly advanced strike aircraft which, ultimately, was not even needed and could barely be afforded. As Healey later commented, there would have existed a situation whereby "…the loss of a single aircraft could have been seen as a national disaster."

But the luxury of an over-specified aircraft was not one which the RAF was destined to enjoy. The RAF did finally – and reluctantly – accept the Buccaneer, and subsequently realised (or accepted) that it was, in fact, an excellent aircraft. Not that the Air Staff would ever have admitted this in the 1960s. Conversely, F-111K turned out to be an aircraft that Britain could indeed just about afford, but ultimately one which, like TSR2, it did not actually need. The abortive AFVG project was also perhaps another aircraft which the RAF did not necessarily need, but it was one which would probably have been just as effective as the Buccaneer – maybe even more so – and as a joint project it would undoubtedly have been much more affordable than TSR2 could ever have been. But France's obsession with nationalistic self-interest put paid to AFVG before it even left the drawing board.

Some would say that it was a pity that TSR2 had not suffered the same fate, long before any metal was cut, but TSR2 and AFVG did at least lay the foundations for what was to eventually become Tornado, and nobody could deny that in this project the RAF finally received a brilliant aircraft which was, for once, right for the job for which it had been procured. It also embraced a design lineage which can be traced right back to TSR2, and indeed the Tornado (like other aircraft such as Jaguar, Nimrod and Harrier) incorporated systems which had first been developed as part of the TSR2 programme. Thus, it is fair to say that not all of the effort which was put into TSR2 was entirely wasted and today's Tornado is a direct result of work which was first assigned to the TSR2 programme.

Likewise, a great deal of knowledge gleaned from TSR2 went on to become part of the civil Concorde programme and of course the TSR2's mighty Olympus engines finally reached their ultimate developmental potential in this, the most iconic of all airliners. But no matter how much one might look for positive outcomes, the story of TSR2 is not one from which any pleasure or satisfaction can be gleaned, and despite the undeniable fact that TSR2 (or the Supermarine Type 571 to be technically precise) was an inspiring example of British aeronautical engineering and systems technology, it was an aircraft which Britain simply could not afford and one which should have been cancelled long before it reached the flight test stage, like so many other projects which preceded and succeeded it. The fact that it did reach test-flight status was no more than a symptom of the Conservative Government's failure to address an issue which should have been resolved long before the Labour Government took power, and finally did what any Government (Labour or Conservative) would ultimately have been forced to do, given the country's position at that time.

Allowing TSR2 to progress so far, and to eventually emerge from the Weybridge production line into the air, certainly demonstrated the exciting potential of this truly great aircraft, but it also enabled everyone – the public, media, manufacturers, designers, RAF and Government – to see precisely what might have been achieved, given a limitless amount of money with which to pay for it. Thus, it was all the more painful and frustrating to then see it consigned, quite literally, to the scrap heap. But if any blame is to be attributed for TSR2's failure, it cannot be fairly directed at any one person. There are no individual culprits in this story who can assume true responsibility for the cancellation of TSR2, as so many factors contributed to the project's eventual demise. Certainly Denis Healey, who was forced to finally propose the project's termination and who is often portrayed as the story's 'criminal', was by no means opposed to the aircraft in principle; in fact, he was a staunch supporter of his friends within the Air Staff and clearly wanted the RAF to have the best aircraft possible for the roles assigned to it. Unfortunately, by the time that he inherited responsibility for defence policy, TSR2 had already become unsustainable, and the opportunity to dispose of it in favour of a much more affordable F-111 was a choice which any sensible politician would have made, given the same circumstances. Even Roy Jenkins was essentially ambivalent towards the issue, but he could immediately see the attractiveness of F-111. His only real difference with Healey was that he could see the folly of maintaining a significant East of Suez presence, which obviously reflected upon the perceived importance of both TSR2 and F-111 as far as he was concerned.

Mountbatten was undeniably set against TSR2 from the start, and it was he more than anyone else who worked hard to dispose of it. But Mountbatten's influence was by no means as strong as he either imagined or wished, and ultimately he had no tangible effect upon the project's status. Criticism can only be directed at collective decision makers, all of whom presumably acted with the best of motives, but all of whom conspired to destroy the very project they were striving to create and perfect. For example, Vickers-Armstrong must share some responsibility for when its design influences and procedures often conflicted with English Electric, which had significant supersonic experience and ought to have been afforded a greater influence over the programme, particularly when it came to questioning the validity of some of the Air Staff's over-ambitious requirements. Vickers could and should have done more to prevent the aircraft from becoming unnecessarily over-complex. But Vickers was also a victim of the Government's stifling management control, and it was this aspect of the programme which provided the framework through which development costs and time delays were allowed to run unchecked.

One of the last photographs ever taken of XR219, an elevated view of the slowly-deteriorating airframe, out on the range at Shoeburyness, where it was being used infrequently for destructive firing tests. After having been re-assembled at P&EE, the wing tips are known to have been procured from another aircraft (possibly XR221) and it is therefore possible that the main wing section may also have been from another aircraft. *BAC*

Criticism could also be directed at the Air Staff; the customer who is supposedly always right but who clearly was not in the case of TSR2. Aspirations are to be admired, but over-specifying a requirement almost for its own sake is hardly an indication of sound defence thinking. It is even less admirable if the requirement is deliberately over-specified in order to ensure that only one design can possibly meet it.

With these issues in mind it is impossible to attribute the cause of TSR2's demise to just one issue or one person. There are many factors to consider, all of which conspired to assure ultimate failure. TSR2 was simply a victim of circumstances. It came along at precisely the time when Britain could least afford it, and at precisely the time when the Government was not even sure what it wanted. It had the misfortune to emerge just as a competing American design appeared which promised to be significantly less expensive, and it was used as a political lever to rationalise the industry which would create it. TSR2 had the odds stacked against it from the moment that GOR.339 was drawn-up and like so many other abandoned British aircraft projects, it should have been terminated before any significant money was spent on it. But TSR2 did survive for quite some time, and although its eventual demise made the whole story appear even more tragic and wasteful, it did at least demonstrate what a magnificent aircraft TSR2 was – or would have been.

Many commentators have lamented the way in which Britain's aircraft industry contracted so rapidly and significantly after TSR2. But although TSR2 was undoubtedly the catalyst for this change, it was not the fundamental cause. Britain's aircraft industry was already destined to follow the path which it inevitably followed, and TSR2's successful production would have ultimately had no effect on this process, even though many romantically-inclined commentators often like to imagine that things would have somehow been different had TSR2 survived. Britain's defence industry and policy makers had reached a definitive moment in history where Britain's position was to change forever. TSR2 just happened to be the conduit through which much of this change started to happen. TSR2's creation and subsequent cancellation was not the cause of the aircraft industry's wholesale contraction, it merely happened to be the most significant programme being pursued at this – the most critical – time. Yet it was not all bad news. Although Weybridge never truly recovered from the loss of TSR2, Warton, by comparison, eventually flourished, and today BAE Systems is a hugely successful aerospace design and manufacturing name which is recognised around the globe.

Where XR219 once thundered into the air, Hawks, Typhoons and Nimrods soar skywards, illustrating that Britain's aircraft industry might well be a very different creature from that of the 1960s, but it is certainly still very much alive – and doing remarkably well too.

TSR2 is now nothing more than an evocative museum exhibit, which serves to remind some of us of what might have been, had circumstances been different. The sheer size and beauty of the surviving TSR2 airframes still makes every museum visitor pause to admire a unique design which is now half a century old, and yet still looks truly formidable. But away from the stuffy atmosphere of the museums, out amongst the mountains of Wales and Scotland, the hills and valleys still regularly reverberate to the sound of TSR2's little cousin, the magnificent Tornado, which has provided the RAF with a first-class tactical strike platform for some three decades. Few of the hardy aircraft enthusiasts who climb the hillsides to photograph these noisy grey-painted war veterans as they thunder past almost every day, stop to consider the curious history behind the Tornado, and the complicated – if not confused – history of Britain's defence policies which ultimately created it. Even fewer pause to realise that, in some respects, a little bit of TSR2 has just flown right past them too.

CHAPTER TWELVE

TSR2 Described

Aircraft structure, systems, performance and production details

TSR2 is designed to operate at 200ft above ground level with automatic terrain following at speeds up to Mach 1.1. It is capable of Mach 2 plus at medium altitudes. Without external fuel tanks a radius of 1,000nm is obtained of which 100nm are flown supersonically at altitude and 200nm into and out of the target area are flown at Mach 0.9 at sea level. The corresponding take-off ground roll is approximately 3,000ft. With under-wing tanks an economical sortie radius of over 1,500nm is obtained. For worldwide deployment a ferry range of 2,870nm can be flown with internal fuel.

The automatic navigation system provides an accuracy of 0.3% of distance gone, and with a fix 30nm from the target, leads to a blind nuclear lay-down accuracy of better than 600ft. 50% CEP. At present the aiming of high explosive weapons is visual, with assistance in target acquisition from the navigation system and head up display. High resolution radar, active linescan and photographic reconnaissance are provided.

The complete TSR2 weapons system is designed for mobility and flexibility in operation, reversing previous trends towards reliance on major base facilities. It can be deployed rapidly throughout the world with nominal support and is then ready for immediate operational use to an extent depending on the level of support, In-built test facilities, pre-checked packages for armament, etc., and an auxiliary power plant for operating aircraft electrics, cooling and other systems are used during turn round, thereby avoiding reliance upon complex support equipment. All support equipment is air transportable.

The development of a high performance weapons system capable of operating with a minimum of support equipment requires that even greater emphasis than usual be placed on reliability. The required levels have been specified and development to those targets is proceeding.

Without much of the aircraft's internal fit, and minus her Olympus engines, XR222 stands tall on her undercarriage, looking almost like a huge bird of prey. Indeed, some commentators have suggested that the aircraft should have been named "Eagle" but there is no evidence to suggest that the idea was ever considered at an official level. In actual fact, no name for the aircraft was ever given serious consideration although English Electric had proposed to name their P.17 design "Thunder". *BAE Heritage*

With a weapons system of this type, emphasis is placed on reducing losses due to accidents arising from defects, particularly during training and peacetime operations. This is being achieved by duplication to a level more usually found in civil rather than military aircraft. In most airframe and electronic systems the full specified performance is obtained from either of two systems: after failure of one system the operation may usually be continued, and a return to base is only necessary after a second failure.

The emphasis has been placed on high component reliability with additional integrity obtained by duplication in critical areas.

The TSR2's overall design configuration is dictated by three main factors: Firstly, the performance specifications as laid down by the original requirement for low-level and high-speed flight as outlined in OR.339 and subsequently OR.343. Secondly, a Short Take-off and Landing capability necessary for operations in and out of small unprepared strips (and including a cross wind operational ability), and thirdly the performance specifications as laid down for operational and ferry range, including the carriage of internal and external stores. The thin, delta wing was adopted as the optimum compromise with small surface area and low gust response which is essential for low-level flight at supersonic speed, combined with an aspect ratio which is appropriate for STOL capability, and the structure of the airframe was kept to a minimum at the rear of the aircraft in order to facilitate maximum ground incidence (useful for STOL operations). In order to achieve adequate control response from the tailplane surfaces, these are positioned well below the wing so that satisfactory trimming-out high lift at low speeds. The wing tips are down-turned in order to avoid the need for anhedral across the entire wing surface (countering the wing's inherent dihedral effect), which would have affected air flow across the tailplanes. This configuration avoids the risk of pitch-up and both tailplane surfaces can pivot in opposition (acting as 'tailerons') in order to achieve roll control and lateral trim. Both tailerons are operated by a tandem piston jack which could be controlled via a mechanical linkage to the pilot's controls, or via the duplicated automatic flight control system actuator. The actuator system has built-in redundancy so that if one system fails, the taileron can be operated by a back-up system, albeit at a slower rate. The taileron's maximum deflection angles are 10 degrees nose up and 20 degrees nose down, with 6 degrees nose-down established for level flight. The entire wing trailing edge is consequently left free for the incorporation of full-span 'blown' flaps which take high-pressure air that was bled from the two engines. The full-span flaps are each operated by three screw jacks, driven by screw shafts incorporated into the wing trailing edge, and powered by individual hydraulic motors. Flap settings are 0, 20, 35 and 50 degrees. Boundary Layer Control blowing comes into operation at 15 degrees and continued through to full deflection at 50 degrees. A cross-over system ensures that the blowing system will continue to operate if one engine fails, and the system is entirely automatic, the pilot being able to override the system if required. The tail fin is a one-piece all-moving surface which provides authoritative directional stability and control. Powered by a twin piston jack, it is connected via a mechanical linkage to the pilot's rudder pedals and linked to triple automatic flying control actuators. Control deflection is relatively modest, the huge fin surface requiring very little movement to achieve effect and the maximum deflection of 12.5 degrees in either direction is fixed. At lower speeds the fin is under the direct control of the pilot but at supersonic speeds an automatic stiffening and control system will take over. Artificial feel is incorporated into the control system which ensures that stick forces remain similar at all speeds and altitudes. The hugely effective blown flaps combined with the aircraft's high thrust/weight ratio provide excellent STOL performance and with the flaps lowered the centre of lift is well aft of the centre of gravity. In order to provide trim at low speeds without excessive tailplane deflection or overall area, a tailplane flap is incorporated and the combination of high lift, high thrust and good tailplane authority renders the extendable nose gear leg unnecessary for most STOL operations. The landing gear was specifically designed for rough field operations and enables the aircraft to successfully take-off from grass (or other unprepared) surfaces with an overall length of no more than 3,000ft. For short landings a large braking parachute (manufactured by Irving) is fitted and as this would have an adverse effect on cross-wind landings, a reefing facility is incorporated – the first time that such a facility was fitted to an aircraft. Four petal-type air brakes are incorporated into the fuselage ahead of the fin, all being operated by screw jacks powered by an actuator motor. In order to ensure that the brake doors are not over-stressed, an automatic blow-back system ensures that the doors retract to a safe angle when under extreme pressure.

The choices of structural materials for the airframe was largely dictated by the high temperature environment in which the aircraft is intended to operate, combined by the problems associated with low-level flight which would include severe vibration due to gusts and rapid (and severe) reversals. This requires the use of fatigue-resistant materials which can also withstand bird or insect impact damage. High temperature operations (caused by supersonic flight) create additional demands upon the structure and required detailed investigation into the ways in which temperature would vary with speeds, altitudes, starting temperatures and heat sink (affected by the amount of fuel being carried), all these considerations being additional to the usual requirements of overall strength and fatigue resistance. At speeds of Mach 2 the aircraft operates at the very limits of most light alloys and some established alloys were developed to higher levels of tolerance. Some which were applicable to the hotter portions of the airframe are aluminium/lithium alloys which are lighter and stiffer with better high-temperature properties than more conventional aluminium/copper alloys, and these were imported from the United States through ICI Metals Ltd. Most of the airframe structure surrounding the engine bays comprises of high-strength heat-treated aluminium with a strength/weight ratio of almost twice that of heat-resistant steel and this was developed specifically for the aircraft by ICI Metals. Non-metallic components created even bigger developmental problems and BAC embarked upon detailed research into the properties of various materials in hot environments, and the behaviour of small elements of selected materials. Transparencies for the windscreen were specifically developed with new types of

Pilot's instrument layout diagram

Key:-

1   Incidence Meter
2   Flap Pressure Indicator
3   Flap Position Indicator
4   Roll/Yaw Indicator
5   Flap Indicator
6   Fuselage Tanks Fuel Gauge
7   Wing Tanks Fuel Gauge
8   Air Brake Pressure Indicator
9   Standby Artificial Horizon
10 Air Speed Indicator
11 Combined Speed Indicator
12 Standby Altimeter
13 Brake Pressure Indicators
14 Hydraulic Accumulator Gauges
15 Rate of Climb Indicator

16 Attitude Display (Artificial Horizon)
17 Navigation (Compass)/ILS Display
18 Moving Map Display
19 Turbine Temperature (Port Engine)
20 Thrust RPM (Port Engine)
21 Altimeter
22 Radio Altimeter
23 Aircraft Skin Temperature
24 Local Altimeter
25 Thrust RPM (Starboard Engine)
26 Intake Cone/Nozzle Position
27 Turbine Temperature (Starboard Engine)
28 Rudder Pedal Adjustment
29 HUD Brightness
30 Accelerometer
31 Oxygen Contents
32 AFC Selector Switch (Altitude)
33 AFC Selector Switch (Speed)

34 AFC Selector Switch (Direction)
35 HUD Rotation Speed Selector Switch
36 Starboard Reheat Warnings & LP Cock
37 Starboard Engine Fire Warnings
38 Central Warning Panel
39 Central Warning panel
40 Port Engine Fire Warnings
41 Port Reheat Warnings & LP Cock
42 Brake Parachute Reefing Switch
43 Brake Parachute Door Selector
44 Brake Parachute Jettison Switch
45 Nose wheel Extension Switch and Manual
    Flap Blow Switch
46 Parking Brake Handle
47 Nose wheel Normal/Extended Indicator
48 Air Brake Standby Switch
49 Undercarriage selection Level
50 Flap Position lever
51 Undercarriage Indicator
52 Emergency Engine Throttle Change-over Switch
53 Fuel balance Indicator
54 Fuel Transfer Switches
55 Engine Throttle Levers
56 Air Intake Control Switches
57 Trim Control
58 Fin Trim Switches
59 Canopy Jettison Handle
60 Left Rudder Pedal
61 Moving Map Display Lamp Switch
62 Moving Map Display Brilliance Control
63 ILS Controls
64 Radio Channel Selector
65 VHF/UHF Selection Switches
66 Starboard Selector Switch Panel A
67 Starboard Selector Switch Panel B
68 Starboard Selector Switch Panel C
69 No.2 generator Switch
70 Windscreen Washer switches

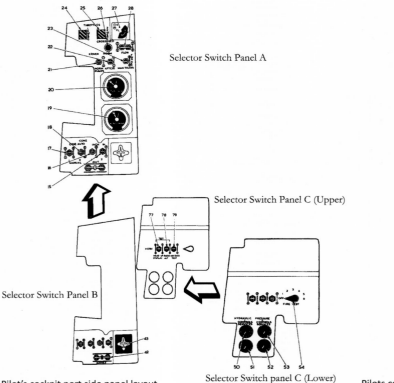

Selector Switch Panel A

Selector Switch Panel A

Selector Switch Panel B

Selector Switch Panel C (Upper)

Selector Switch Panel C

Selector Switch Panel B

Selector Switch panel C (Lower)

Pilot's cockpit port side panel layout

Pilots cockpit starboard side panel layout

STARBOARD SELECTOR SWITCH PANEL A
71 Attitude Gyro Switch
72 AFCS Control Channel 1
73 AFCS Control Channel 2
74 Standby Artificial Horizon Switch
75 AFCS Control Channel 3
76 HUD Master Switch

STARBOARD SELECTOR SWITCH PANEL B
44 Nose Wheel Steering Gearing Switch
45 Auto Engage Selector
46 Bank Control
47 Track Lock Mode Selector
48 Heading Lock Mode Selector
49 ILS Localiser Mode Selector
50 Take-off Director Mode Selector
51 Bombing Mode Selector
52 Ride Control
53 Ground Mapping Mode Selector
54 Beacon Homing Mode Selector
55 Terrain Following Height Set Selector
56 Terrain Following Height Selector
57 Terrain Following Mode Selector
58 Auto Trim Cut-Out Switch
59 Fin Control Master Switch
60 ILS Glide Path Mode Selector
61 Turn Co-ordination Cut-out Switch
62 Taileron Control Master switch
63 Height Lock Mode Selector
64 Acquire Height Mode selector
65 Datum Height Adjustment switch
66 Acquire Height Setting Control
67 Indicated Air Speed Lock Mode Selector
68 Acquire Height Indicator
69 Mach Number Lock Mode Selector
70 Datum Speed Adjustment Switch

STARBOARD SELECTOR SWITCH PANEL C
27 TRU Test Switch
28 Navigation Lights & Beacons Switch
29 No.2 Engine & Windscreen Anti-Ice Switch
30 No.1 Engine & Windscreen Anti-Ice Switch
31 Air Conditioning No.1 & 2 Engine Isolating valve Switch
32 Lighting Control Switch – general
33 Lighting Control Switch – Instruments
34 Lighting Control Switch – Panels
35 High Intensity Lighting switch
36 Forward-Looking Camera Film remaining Indicator
37 No.2 Sideways-Looking Camera Film Remaining Indicator
38 No.1 Sideways-Looking Camera Film remaining Indicator
39 No.1 Generator Switch

PORT SELECTOR PANEL A
15 No.2 Engine Air Intake Cone Inching Control Switch
16 No.1 Engine Air Intake Cone Inching Control Switch
17 No.1 Engine Air Intake Cone Auto/Manual Switch
18 No.2 Engine Air Intake Cone Auto/Manual Switch
19 Wing tanks Fuel Gauge
20 Fuselage Fuel Tanks Gauge
21 Fueldraulic Cross-Over Switch
22 Fuel Balance Normal/Aft CG Change-Over Switch
23 Fuel Balance Forward/Aft Manual Transfer Switch
24 No.1 Engine Throttle Emergency Change-Over Switch

25 No.2 Engine Throttle Emergency Change-Over Switch
26 Fuel Cross-Feed Magnetic Indicator
27 Fuel Balance Indicator
28 Fuel Balance Gauge/Flow Change-Over & Cross-Feed Switches

PORT SELECTOR PANEL B
42 Fin trim Switches
43 Emergency Trim Control

PORT SELECTOR PANEL C (UPPER)
77 HUD Test Switch
78 Radio Altimeter Test Switch
79 Air Data Test Switch

PORT SELECTOR PANEL C (LOWER)
50 Hydraulic Pressure Gauge No.1 Controls
51 Hydraulic Pressure Gauge No.1 Services
52 Hydraulic Pressure Gauge No.2 Services
53 Hydraulic Pressure Gauge No.2 Controls
54 Fire Detection Test Switch

Navigator's position as seen from an oblique angle. Most of the switches and dials relate to the aircraft's weapons and navigation systems, although the pilot's primary flight instruments are also repeated in the rear cockpit. The sideways-looking radar read-out unit has been temporarily removed.

Contemporary Internal layout drawing, illustrating the location of the aircraft's main equipment. Please note that this drawing is missing the main centre-section.

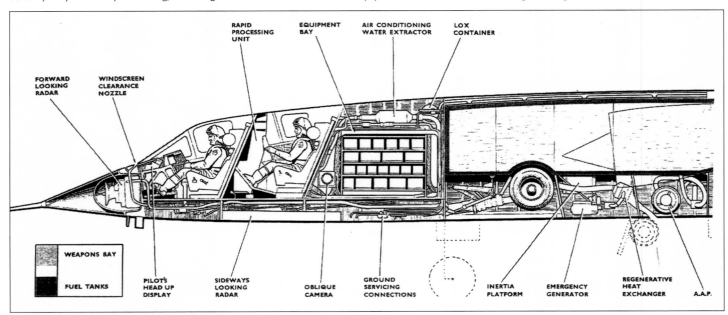

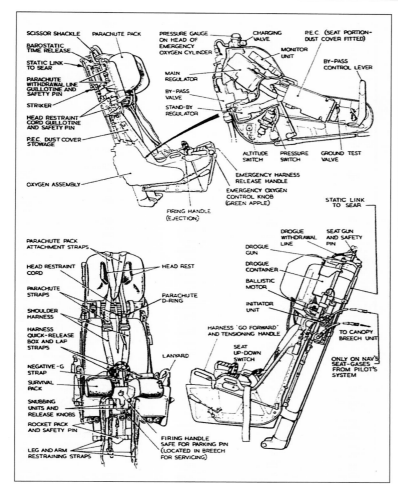

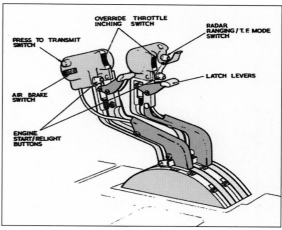

Above: Throttle levers detail. The throttle unit proved to be troublesome during the initial stages of the flight test programme. Harsh braking (and the ensuing rapid deceleration) caused the throttle levers to slip, which could lead to inadvertent application of engine power at a critical stage during the landing run. Modification of the unit would have been required before the aircraft was acceptable for service use.

Left: The Martin Baker Mk.8A ejection seat, designed and manufactured specifically for TSR2. A rocket-powered zero-zero seat (capable of operating with zero forward speed at ground level), it incorporated both leg and arm restraints – an innovative design for the early 1960s. *Drawings courtesy Martin Baker*

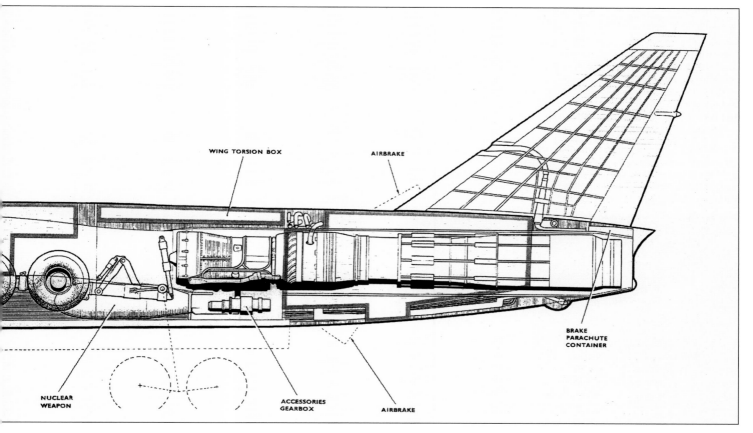

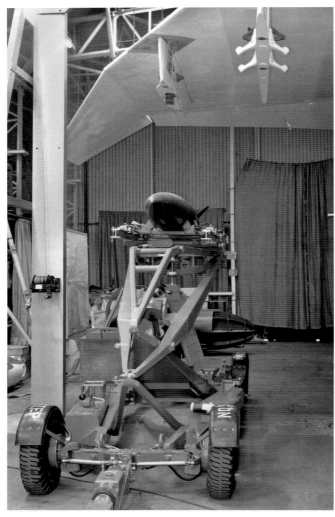

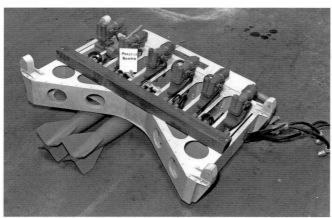

Mock-up of a 1,000lb Type N.1 bomb being presented to the aircraft's outer wing plyon, on its loading trolley. This streamlined weapon was designed for supersonic flight, whilst more conventional 1,000lb HE bombs could be carried in the weapons bay. Other conventional weapons available to TSR2 would have included Martel (in TV-guided or anti-radar versions), and the Matra 155 68mm rocket, carried in a 36-round launching pod. Napalm and chemical weapons were also likely to have been designed for carriage by the aircraft. *BAC*

Practice bombs (Smoke and Flash Mk.1 and the Retarded Mk.1) could be carried within a specifically-designed carrier, attached to the forward portion of the weapons bay. Four retarded or six standard bombs could be carried. These would have been used for live drops over weapon ranges, as part of day-to-day training sorties. *BAC*

interlayers, and similar materials were created for the canopies and radome. High temperature resins (imported from the USA) are employed in the small areas of honeycomb structure featured in the aircraft's structure. The hydraulic system utilises Silicodyne H (DP47) high temperature fluid produced by ICI and most of the aircraft's fluid-tight seals are manufactured from silicone rubber. Fuel tank sealing at high temperatures created more difficulties for the designers. The tanks are of integral construction with holes and cut-outs kept to a minimum but there was still the problem of sealing the points where two stiff members met, and specially-developed sealants had to be utilised for the task, these being imported from Products Research Inc. in the US, but with supplies from Bostik being developed for subsequent use. Effective sealing requires close-fitting parts which rely upon close machining tolerances and very accurate jigging. The wings and fuselage are largely of integral construction with stiffened skins machined from stretched billet. The Weybridge-inspired technique of machining integral skin and stringer construction from solid slabs with shot-peen-forming to curvature, which was previously applied to the comparatively thick skins of Vanguards, VC10s and BAC-111 airliners, was developed to produce much thinner skins and sections, stiffness being achieved by machining-out to form deep flanged stringers. This skin-milling technique, which was new to BAC's Preston Division, was taken up in a big way by their subcontractor, the English Electric Co facility at Accrington. Here, numerous Marwin skin millers were installed specially for the production of TSR2 wing and fuselage planks. Ferranti tape-control was eventually applied to these machines. Also at these works, an automatic-scanning ultrasonic testing machine was installed for inspecting all incoming billets. This machine could identify flaws on an oscilloscope, and also pin-point on the metal the approximate zone of the flaw. The aircraft's fins, tailerons and airbrakes were also manufactured at Accrington, to a very high standard of interchange ability which was necessary in order to ensure that each component would mate perfectly with those produced at Weybridge. The forming of the milled planks to the required curvature was carried out by the main contractor

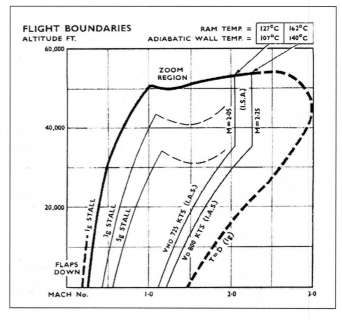

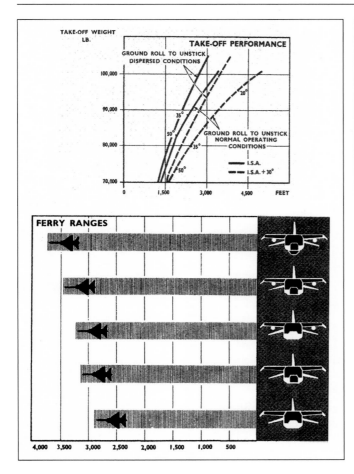

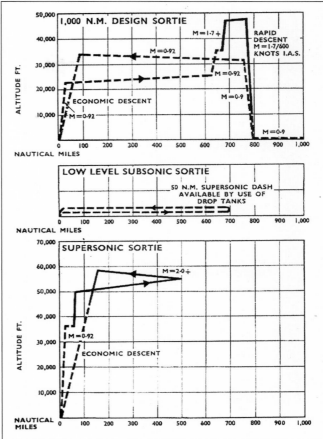

at their Samlesbury works, which was fully equipped for shot-peen-forming and presswork. The all-moving taileron surfaces were designed to be supported on plain bearings, since ball or even needle-roller bearings would have occupied too much bulk inside these extremely thin structures. For these bearings, Ampep produced (under licence) new materials which minimised friction and breakout forces. Production of TSR2 accelerated the introduction of digitally-controlled machine tools and in addition to those introduced at Accrington, the BAC Preston Division acquired Ferranti-tape-controlled Kearney & Trecker milling machines. At one stage the machining of hard titanium alloy presented problems, and in order to get satisfactory results it was important that the cutting tools had a very uniform speed. The new tape-controlled machine provided the best way of achieving this improved control of cutter movement, resulting in longer cutter life, closer tolerances, a better finish on the component and also reduced tooling costs.

Aircraft Performance

TSR2 has been designed to combine flexibility of flight plan with the ability to operate from small, rudimentary airfields. It is capable of penetrating to target at high subsonic speed and very low altitude or, alternatively, it can fly at Mach numbers in excess of 2 at high altitude.

The thin, low aspect ratio wing gives low drag at supersonic speeds and minimises longitudinal stability problems in the transonic range. The plan form and relatively small wing area are also of fundamental importance in keeping gust response low, thus ensuring the comfort of the crew when flying at high speed through the turbulent conditions likely to be encountered at low level.

The power plants are Bristol-Siddeley Olympus 22R twin-spool engines with reheat and ejector nozzles. The high compression ratio of the basic engines gives good economy for the important subsonic cruise while variable intakes assist matching at the various flight conditions. Reheat is used to provide the high thrust necessary to achieve short take-off distances and supersonic flight. Air tapped from the engine is blown over the trailing-edge flaps to provide additional lift for take-off and landing.

Speed

Shows the permissible height and speed boundaries. The present capability at altitude is Mach 2 plus cruise, increasing to Mach 2.5 with development. The excess thrust in flight is used for rapid acceleration to high supersonic speeds and high climb rates. The climb rate is in excess of 50,000ft/min at sea level.

Take-off

The specification calls for a ground roll of not more than 1,800ft at sea level under dispersed conditions. Full flap and water injection are used to meet these conditions. For maximum range operation the take-off ground roll is approximately 3,000ft. For normal operations from standard runways partial flap settings are used so that a safe accelerate stop or climb away can be achieved with engine failure at any time.

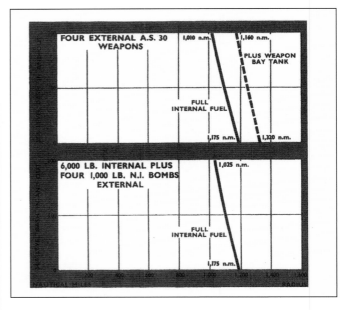

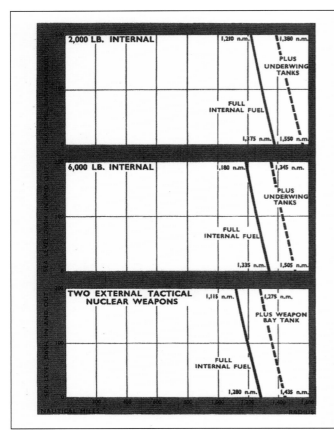

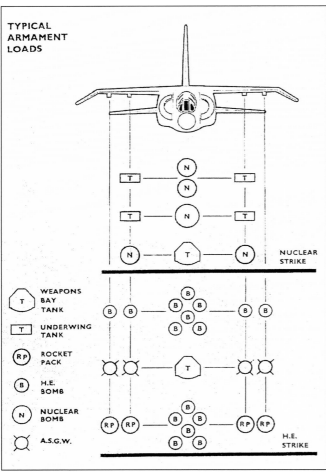

TYPICAL
ARMAMENT
LOADS

NUCLEAR
STRIKE

T — WEAPONS BAY TANK

T — UNDERWING TANK

RP — ROCKET PACK

B — H.E. BOMB

N — NUCLEAR BOMB

— A.S.G.W.

H.E.
STRIKE

Landing

The landing ground roll at sea level is 1,500ft at a landing weight of 57,200lb when using the brake parachute.

Ferry Range

Ferry ranges in still air are illustrated for a combination of internal fuel and jettison able fuel tanks, with full allowance for take-off, climb, acceleration, descent, hold and 5% internal fuel reserve. With internal fuel the ferry range is 2,870nm. Using jettisonable fuel tanks this can be extended to 3,700nm. Flight refuelling may be used to extend the ferry range as required.

Mission Radii

The specification requires a standard 1,000nm mission to be flown when carrying one 2,000lb bomb internally throughout and with a fuel reserve of 5% of take-off fuel plus 8 minutes loiter. Of this radius 100nm are flown at Mach 1.7 at altitude and the last 200nm into and out of the target area are flown at Mach 0.9 at 200ft. The remainder is flown economically at Mach 0.92 at altitude. This requirement is met at the normal take-off weight of 95,000lb using less than the full internal fuel capability available.

With the same bomb and fuel load TSR2 has a radius of 500nm at Mach 2 at medium altitude and a radius of 700nm at Mach 0.9 at 200ft. Similar performances are obtained when carrying the reconnaissance pack in place of the weapons.

A shorter tactical sortie has a 450nm radius of action. A high/low approach to the target with supersonic cruise or a low altitude sortie all the way to and from the target may be flown. The take-off weight for this sortie is 78,800lb. The fuel load includes reserves for permit 8 minutes loiter at 1,000ft above ground level plus 5% of the starting fuel.

The take-off weight for TSR2 is readily increased with only minor restrictions on manoeuvring capability. A jettisonable external tank of 450gal (540 US gal) may be carried in place of bombs in the weapons bay; and a jettisonable ventral 1,000gal (1,201 US gal) may be carried under the fuselage. Mission radius may be increased by the use of these tanks as required.

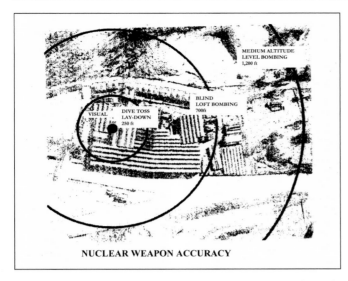

NUCLEAR WEAPON ACCURACY

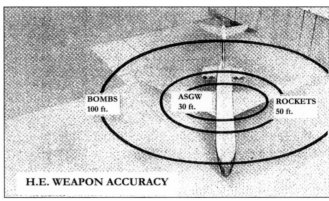

H.E. WEAPON ACCURACY

Attack System Nuclear Role

Delivery	Conditions	Height	Speed	50% CEP
MED. ALTITUDE LEVEL BOMBING	BLIND	25,000ft	1.7M	1,200ft
DIVE TOSS	VISUAL	15,000ft	1.7M	250ft
LOW ALTITUDE LOFT	BLIND	200ft	0.9-1.1M	700ft
LOW ALTITUDE LAY DOWN	VISUAL	200ft	0.9-1.1M	250ft
LOW ALTITUDE LAY DOWN	BLIND	200ft	0.9-1.1M	600ft

Mission radius with the alternative weapon loads shown is given. The sortie pattern assumed is that the final penetration to the target and the escape from the target area are flown at Mach 0.9 and at 200ft and the remainder of the flight at economic speed and altitude. The total mission radius with 0-400nm at sea level is shown for the following weapon loads:

2,000lb internal

6,000lb internal

2 nuclear external

4 air-to-surface guided weapons external

6,000lb internal plus 4 x 1,000lb bombs external with, where appropriate, additional fuel as indicated.

Attack Systems – Nuclear Role

Nuclear strike missions may be carried out by TSR2 using free fall or lay-down nuclear bombs, or guided nuclear weapons of the types under development. This flexibility is enhanced by the wide range of delivery manoeuvres available to the pilot, each fully automatic if required, and which may be selected to give optimum weapon performance bearing in mind such factors as weapon yield, aircraft vulnerability and target hardness. More than one nuclear weapon can be carried if desired. The performance obtained from the nuclear weapon aiming system in a number of representative roles is shown in the accompanying table. Although provision is made for medium altitude bombing, in attacking a defended target it is desirable to remain at low altitude in the target area. Nuclear deliveries from terrain following height may be made by using a lay-down technique or a loft manoeuvre. Lay-down deliveries may be made without an increase in altitude above terrain following height, and this is especially useful when the target is heavily defended. The lay-down bomb is a parachute-retarded device which gives a ground burst. Very high accuracy is readily achieved. In the loft manoeuvre the aircraft starts to climb when it is a few miles short of the target at a constant pitch rate corresponding to about 4g. At a predetermined pitch angle the bomb is released and travels on to the target while the aircraft makes its escape using a wing-over manoeuvre. Flight to the release point may be completely automatic from the time of the last navigational fix or the pilot may choose to follow the directions presented to him on the Head Up Display. The aircraft computing system corrects the instant of release to allow for the required speed and flight path. A number of pre-set angles are available for the pilot to use according to the knowledge available of the target characteristics. The exposure of the aircraft to ground fire which occurs when release angles of more than 90 degrees are used, can be avoided by using a 'button hook' manoeuvre. In this attack the pilot flies over the target and returns to complete a shallow loft attack from another direction. Vulnerability studies indicate that this is preferable to the use of 'over the shoulder' loft attacks. Medium altitude delivery of nuclear weapons may be made in level flight or in a dive toss manoeuvre. Full computer capabilities are again available. The accuracy of delivery of nuclear weapons is illustrated in relation to a typical target. Each circle represents the 50% CEP obtainable for the various delivery manoeuvres with a final navigational fix 30 nautical miles before the target. Provision is made for the carriage of the guided and stand-off nuclear weapons under development. Use of these weapons will improve the accuracy of delivery, decrease the likelihood of the aircraft being damaged by defensive fire, and will provide air burst of the weapons without any increase in aircraft altitude above terrain following height. Reversionary nuclear bombing modes are provided to cater for most equipment failures. These modes enable the weapon to be delivered with slightly degraded accuracy.

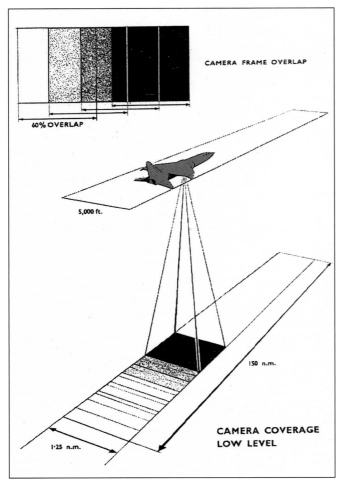

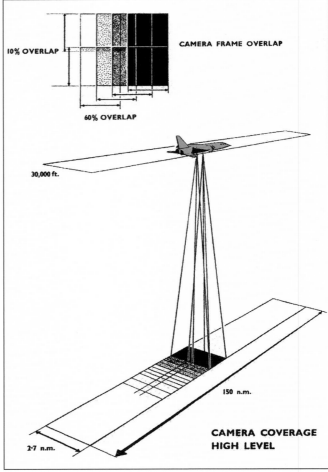

Attack System – H.E. Role

The weapons bay and the under wing pylons of TSR2 allow great flexibility in the carriage of High Explosive weapons. Three types are carried: free fall bombs, 2-inch calibre rocket projectiles, and air-to-surface guided weapons (ASGW) of the AS.30 type. Provision is made to carry advanced ASGW at present being developed. Up to six 1,000lb HE bombs of various types can be carried internally; rocket pods, ASGW or bombs are carried under the wings. Attack with HE bombs under blind conditions can be performed from medium altitude in level flight using the forward looking radar for target sighting. From low altitude the 'depressed sight line' technique can be used to deliver HE bombs under visual conditions with automatic flight control of the aircraft if desired. A depressed sight line attack is carried out by approaching the target at terrain following altitude. A few miles before the predicted position of the target, pull-up is initiated followed by a bunt manoeuvre which brings the aircraft into a diving attitude about 3-4 miles short of the target with a dive angle between 6 and 25 degrees. During the whole of this process the computed target position is indicated to the pilot on his Head Up Display; at the diving stage the target should be acquired visually, and final corrections can be made to the flight path of the aircraft. The forward looking radar measures target range, and at the correct instant the HE weapon aiming computer initiates automatic bomb release. After release the aircraft escapes and returns to the terrain following mode.

Blind delivery is possible using the technique described. The lead-in to the target provided by the Head Up Display aiming mark will ensure target acquisition by the pilot visually unless conditions are exceptionally unfavourable. This feature, allied to the precision of the TSR2 navigation system, gives the highest probability of making a successful attack. Targets of opportunity will be attacked under visual conditions with rockets, bombs or ASGW using a wing-over manoeuvre as illustrated. The automatic control capability and the steadiness of TSR2 as an aiming platform are particularly valuable in the use of ASGW. Should one of the components of the HE weapon aiming system fail, reversion is made to the use of a fixed windscreen aiming mark in association with a predetermined speed and approach manoeuvre. The accompanying illustration shows, to scale, performance of TSR2 when striking with HE weapons against a typical target. The inner circle shows the 30ft 50% CEP which is a conservative estimate of the system when ASGW are used. For rocket attack a 50ft, 50% CEP is achieved, while in visual dive bombing the 50% CEP is 100ft.

Reconnaissance System (see diagrams above)

The reconnaissance role of TSR2 is alternative to the strike role and of equal importance. The reconnaissance capability conferred upon the aircraft by means of the pack carried in the weapons bay is not matched by any other single aircraft system. Although there is no requirement for a combined strike and reconnaissance sortie, the sideways looking navigation radar and the three cameras permanently fitted to the airframe do provide a useful limited reconnaissance capability when the aircraft is operating on a strike mission. The special reconnaissance pack contains a high resolution Q-band sideways looking radar, active optical linescan equipment and a comprehensive camera installation. By these means high grade target intelligence may be obtained by day and by night regardless of weather conditions. The pack also contains the recorders needed to store the data, and the microwave transmitter used to transmit the linescan picture information during flight.

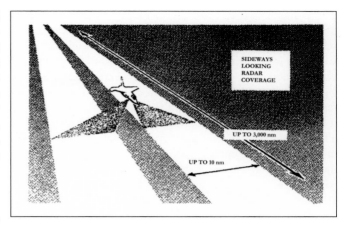

Photographic Reconnaissance

The weapons bay pack contains three FX126 cameras in the rear compartment; two of these cameras are for medium altitude use and the third for low level. The former can be fitted with 24in or 36in lenses which give a photographic scale of 1:10,000 from 20,000ft or 30,000ft respectively. The low altitude camera has a 6in lens which gives a scale of 1:10,000 from a height of 5,000ft. All of the FX126 cameras are temperature controlled, have image movement compensation (IMC) and automatic exposure adjustment. Each contains 250ft of film in easily changed cassettes. The IMC and exposure intervals are controlled from the navigation system of the aircraft; an along-track overlap of 60% is provided and for the two long focus cameras the across-track overlap is 10%. The film magazines are sufficiently large to allow a 150nm strip to be covered, 1.25nm wide from low level and 2.7nm wide from medium altitude. The latitude and longitude of the aircraft are marked on the edge of each camera exposure in binary decimal form for automatic or visual read-out. When both the sideways looking reconnaissance radar and cameras are in use then the position of the camera shots is indicated on the radar data. Reconnaissance information may also be obtained from the one forward and two sideways looking F95 cameras with 3in lenses permanently fitted in the nose of the aircraft.

Survey Facility (see diagram bottom right)

The TSR2 high grade reconnaissance is allied to very accurate navigation and this suggests the application of the aircraft to survey duties. In many areas the navigation accuracy of better than 0.3% of distance travelled is a significant improvement on the geologic accuracy of existing maps. This degree of precision enables new maps to be made or old ones to be corrected with a minimum of accurately surveyed reference points.

Sideways Looking Reconnaissance Radar

Wide angular cover and all weather operation are characteristic of the TSR2's reconnaissance radar. High definition is provided by the use of Q-band in association with a 15ft aerial aperture. If required, Moving Target Indication (MTI) may be obtained when operating at low altitude. To improve the performance at low altitude the aerial aperture is reduced. The radar aerials look out either side of the aircraft track, scanning two strips, each strip up to 10nm wide according to altitude. The depression angle of the aerials may be adjusted to obtain optimum performance at all flight altitudes. The radar outputs and navigation information are stored in a special recorder using photographic film. The recorder capacity is sufficient for a total scanned strip length of 1,500nm at a scale of 5nm per inch or 3,000nm at a scale of 10nm per inch. After a sortie the exposed material can be fed immediately into a rapid processing unit and the recorder may be quickly reloaded with fresh film. A strip 20nm long at 400nm from the aircraft base can be reconnoitred and data be in the hands of the field commander less than 2 hours after his original request for information. The developed film record presents the reconnaissance data in three parallel strips. On one side is the basic radar data and on the other the MTI information; a narrow central strip contains the navigation and flight parameters in digital form. When the MTI facility is not in use the whole of the film except for the central strip may be used to display the radar map to an enlarged scale.

Linescan

The optical linescan equipment provides photographic pictures of a quality and definition approaching that of conventional cameras. The system has two outstanding advantages – it may be used by day or by night, and the reconnaissance information obtained may be immediately transmitted over a radio link to a ground station where the picture is printed. Alternatively, the lines cane input may be stored in a video tape recorder for processing when the aircraft returns. Signals from the aircraft navigation system are also recorded so that the interpreter of the final picture is able to fix the position and flight parameters of the aircraft at the time when the linescan exposures were made. The remote transmission facility has a range of up to 110nm. The system has been designed to operate at altitudes below 1,500ft; at an altitude of 1,000ft a strip one nautical mile wide is covered immediately beneath the aircraft. The recording capacity covers

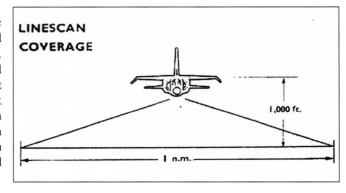

a strip length of over 100nm in the daylight mode, and about 350nm in the night mode. In the linescan system a rotating mirror scans successive strips of ground beneath the aircraft. The variations in intensity of the light reflected from the ground for each position of the mirror scanner are converted to an electrical signal by means of a photoelectric cell. This signal may be recorded or transmitted back to a forward ground station where it is used to control special printing equipment which produces a final picture similar to (a photographic print). At night there is insufficient light to operate the system; a high intensity source is therefore arranged to sweep the ground in synchronism with the receiving mirror, illuminating each element as it is scanned. Because of the high speed of rotation of the mirror and the light source, the linear velocity of the spot on the ground is too great to be seen by the human eye, so that it is not possible to detect or track the aircraft optically.

Airfield Operation

The ground support required by TSR2 has been reduced to such a level that full operations for long periods are possible with airfield equipment which is entirely air-transportable in the AW.660 or similar aircraft. Emergency reinforcement of overseas theatres, subsequent operation from primitive airstrips, or dispersion from main base under nuclear threat, will be feasible for limited periods with little or no airfield equipment. The requirements for TSR2 have reversed the previous trend towards reliance upon extensive main base facilities, and these requirements have defined important aspects of the aircraft systems and the ground support equipment. Firstly, an auxiliary power plant is provided in the aircraft to run the main gearboxes. After declutching the gearboxes from the engines, the complete cooling, hydraulic, fuel and electrical systems can be run at full power. With main systems 'live' all the components of the system can be checked without the usual large hydraulic and other power rigs. This facility will be used during dispersed operations but main bases will still carry the normal power rigs, although in smaller numbers than usual. Secondly, monitoring or test equipment is built into the aircraft to provide a 'go/no-go' checks of those systems which must be operating if a safe all weather take-off and re-land is to be made. This is sometimes called 'intuitive' testing equipment since, given power supplies and an operator, the weapons system can check itself. The remaining systems, required for completion of the operational task, can be checked in the air, and normally this will be undertaken shortly after take off. Airborne setting-up facilities are provided; for example the inertial navigation system can be aligned in the air; this process takes less that quarter of an hour. The Doppler/Compass reversionary mode is used for navigation during the setting-up operation. Finally, all equipment and operational loads are designed in the form of quickly replaceable packages. Thus, self-contained facilities can be used for normal operations and both turn round and fault rectification are possible with a minimum of airfield facilities. These features make possible unsupported ferrying via the existing Transport Command routes, local deployment on standby for periods up to 3 days without support, and dispersion followed by 30 days standby. Under the latter conditions very little support is needed to provide instant readiness.

Rapid Reaction Standby

The aircraft is provided with roll-away disconnect couplings enabling wheels-rolling within 60 seconds of the signal to go. Although operations are possible without support, at some stage a build-up of airfield equipment may be required. Since this must be air transportable in an Argosy AW.660 with a load limit of 20,000lb, for full range, considerable emphasis has been placed on simplifying and commoning the ground equipment. When the periods of readiness required, or the extent of servicing is such that the airborne auxiliary power plant cannot be used, then the electric, hydraulic and air supplies must be produced on the ground. This is achieved by the General Servicing vehicle whose use is illustrated. This vehicle will tow the aircraft to the refuelling point, refuel it from fuel bags, assist with any fault diagnosis and rearming, or hold the aircraft at readiness for rapid reaction. The components of this vehicle are designed on a package principle so that a single failure does not result in a complete loss of facility. The other major equipment required, under circumstances where the in-built equipment is not suitable, is the Automatic Test Equipment (ATE) for the electronic systems. After pre-flight checks with built-in equipment, or during routine checks or in flight, the faults will sometimes remain undiagnosed. The ATE, which is self-checking and diagnostic, is then employed. An adequate level of duplication or parallel functioning is employed to prevent single failures causing loss of test facility. Package replacement is employed. The TSR will carry its ground equipment when necessary:-

A ladder for access to cockpits, equipment bays and brake parachute stowage.

Covers for canopies, windscreen and wheels.

Covers, blanks and bungs for all openings and certain detectors.

Locks for undercarriage, control surfaces, canopies and weapons bay doors.

Winches and extension equipment for equipment and weapon loading.

Refuelling adaptor.

A brake parachute spare.

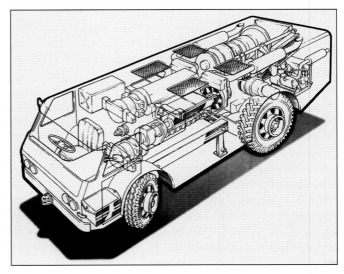

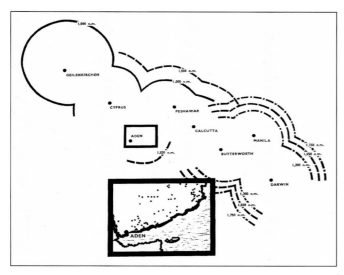

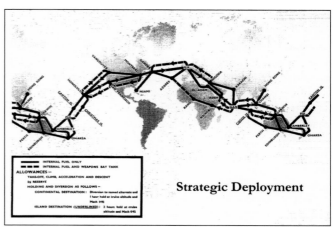

Strategic Deployment

Radii of Action

Some typical radii of action are shown to illustrate the capability of TSR2.

The 1,750nm sortie is an all high-level sortie carrying a 2,000lb weapon together with overload fuel in the under wing and ventral tanks, which are jettisoned when empty.

The 1,550nm sortie is calculated on similar assumptions but includes 200nm into the target area and 100nm out, flown at sea level.

The 1,300nm sortie is based on the carriage of 10 x 1,000lb HE bombs and a ventral tank, with a high-low profile as before.

The 1,000nm sortie is the standard sortie as described previously.

Although the radii of action are shown centred on main bases, TSR2 can disperse to rudimentary airstrips. The high availability of such airstrips is exemplified by an area around Aden as illustrated.

Navigation System (see diagrams below)

The navigation system is independent of ground aids and contains all sensing and computing elements required to control and direct a planned sortie from take off to return to base. Before take off a flight plan defining the sortie is fed into the Verdan digital computer. This plan is in the form of a punched tape prepared with the aid of tape punching equipment. The flight plan is initially defined in terms of fixing landmarks and the latitude and longitude of all turning points

and objectives so that specific tracks are flown. Navigation is based on dead reckoning using Doppler, inertia platform and Air data Computer information sources. The digital computer continuously calculates instantaneous position using ground speed and drift from the Doppler, and heading and velocity from the inertia platform. This is displayed to the navigator continuously as latitude and longitude and as the distance to go along and across track to the next defined point of the sortie. The digital computer also drives a moving map display for monitoring purposes. The position of the aircraft calculated in this way is compared with the desired position defined on the punched tape. Any differences in position are used to provide error signals to the Automatic Flight Control System and the pilot's display so that he may monitor the performance of the aircraft when it is being flown automatically and take any necessary action. The Doppler and inertia platform are of high accuracy, but in view of the long sortie range and the small error allowable at the target, both position and azimuth corrections are required. These corrections are made by referring to external fix points. Fixing consists of comparing the computed position of the fix point with the actual position of the point as shown by radar. Both these positions are shown on the navigator's radar display and his action in comparing these produces a signal proportional to the displacement between them. This signal is fed into the inertia platform if necessary. Alternatively a visual fix may be taken to correct the system. The radar display used in the fix-taking process is a high fidelity image of the ground produced by photographic integration of the returns from the sideways looking radar (SLR). Due to natural terrain masking and to the limitations

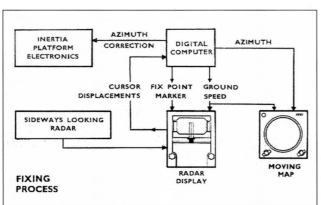

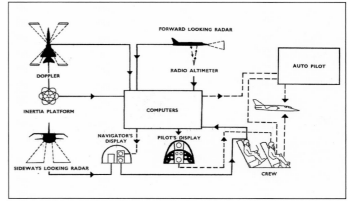

imposed by low glancing angles, the effective range of the radar is between one and two miles at low altitude, and both port and starboard radar returns are therefore displayed. As altitude increases, the effective radar horizon is extended and the display is switched to present only that side on which the next fix is expected. The navigator may select the display scale and aerial depression angle to allow for aircraft altitude changes. On a typical sortie over well mapped territory, the navigator fixes the position of the aircraft about every 100nm. To do this he sets up his SLR display and checks his fix data. When approaching the fix a warning light alerts him and he will see the computed fix on his radar display together with the actual fix painted by the radar. The fix process is completed by his moving the map display cursors first onto the computed fix position and pressing the 'Computed Fix' button, and then moving the cursors onto the radar-displayed fix point and pressing the 'Actual Fix' button. This process is facilitated by the collimation of the SLR display to infinity, which minimises the effect of aircraft movement due to turbulence, and the 'cursor lock' which ensures that the cursors, once set, remain on the same point on the display and move with it. To cater for the cases when, for some unforeseen reason, pre-planned fixes cannot be used, it is possible for the navigator to select his own fix points en route, reverting to the planned programme when this is possible. In addition, further reversionary modes cater for data source failures. For example, the forward looking radar can be used for fixing.

Terrain Following

Survival in the surface-to-air guided weapon environment which TSR2 is designed to penetrate requires that the enemy weapon control systems be deprived of the opportunity to see the TSR2 for a period long enough to set up and activate their weapons. Studies based on existing and projected weapons have indicated that terrain following at a nominal height of

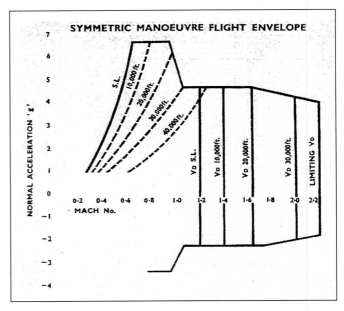

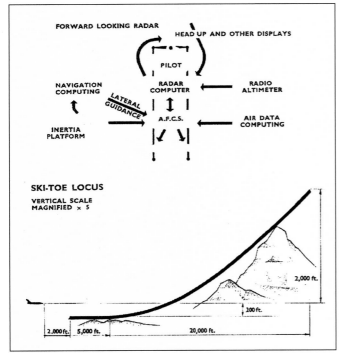

200ft reduces the effective range of the weapon control radars to so low a value that coverage of an area containing tactical targets becomes prohibitively expensive. The terrain following system depends for its basic data on a forward looking radar (FLR). This monopulse radar has a double bar scan of U-form and the returns provide the terrain following computer with continuous information on the shape of the terrain ahead in terms of range and angle. From these data the computer can determine the angle by which the aircraft flight vector must be raised or lowered to follow the ground profile. As a simple analogy, the terrain following system can be likened to a stiff spring extended forward from the aircraft and slightly convex on the side touching the ground. The spring riding over the undulations in the terrain raises or lowers the flight vector as required. The shape of this spring is defined within the radar and is termed the ski-toe locus. The nominal flight altitude may be selected by the pilot. An adjustment to the stiffness of the 'spring' is also provided so that the system may be tuned for optimum performance according to the type of terrain being traversed and roughness of ride that is tolerable. Signals from the terrain following system are fed into the Automatic Flight Control System (AFCS) and to the pilot's Head Up Display. He choice of either automatic or manual flight in this mode is at the pilot's discretion. The radio altimeter is used to monitor the clearance height of the aircraft when flying over water or in other situations when FLR signals are not available. The FLR scanning system is roll stabilised and can be offset to either side to allow for turns. Thus, the pilot can choose to fly round rather than over an obstacle, and turns demanded by the navigation system can be accepted while terrain following. Great care has been taken to ensure that under failure conditions or in other unfavourable circumstances, only 'Up' signals are passed to the pilot or AFCS.

Communications

In TSR2 the internal and external communications facilities are completely integrated. Two control units provide for inter-communication between the crew and for control or the radio equipment installed. Communication with ground servicing personnel can be maintained up to the moment of wheels-rolling. For long distance communication a single sideband radio telephony high frequency set is provided which has a peak envelope power output of 1kW. The range of this equipment will depend on propagation and flight conditions. and will be greater than 1,000nm. The navigator may select in night any one of the 23,000 channels provided. Short range communication over line-of-sight paths of up to 200nm is provided by the VHF/UHF equipment. This has 3,600 channels available in the UHF band of 225 to 400 Mc/s and 600 channels between 1 10 and 140 Mc/s. Any channel may be selected by the navigator, while the pilot has a choice from 20 reselected channels. The standby UHF covers failure or the normal UHF by providing duplicate facilities powered directly from the aircraft battery supplies with automatic change-over in the event or failure of the normal UHF system. For identification purposes the Special Identification Facility (SIF) is fitted. The equipment is derived from IFF Mk.10 and operates in the 1,000 Mc/s band, and provides identification codes, any or which can be pre-selected so that on interrogation the correct reply is given. Facilities are also provided for operation in conjunction with the civil air traffic control network. To assist the crew in avoiding defended areas and to increase further the effectiveness of the terrain following system, the aircraft is fitted with a radar illumination warning receiver. This covers the radar spectrum from 2,500 to 18,000 Mc/s and gives a lamp indication to the pilot when the aircraft is illuminated with signals in this frequency band which exceed a preset power level and duration.

Aircraft Structure

The structural form of TSR2 has been dictated by the requirement for manoeuvres at high speed and low altitude and high Mach number operations at the tropopause. The former gives rise to the most severe loadings on the aircraft in association with moderate structural temperatures; the latter results in the maximum airframe temperatures, in combination with less severe loadings. Fatigue aspects are more critical in the low level mode of operation. The above considerations have led to the use of aluminium alloys of high structural efficiency over a wide temperature range together with good fatigue characteristics. Aluminium alloys which satisfy these requirements are rich in copper and the following materials are used generally throughout the airframe:-

DTD5020 (L65) – for the thick plate used in integrally machined frames and panels.

X2020 – for general formed sheet work.

RR58 – for the thick plate used in integrally machined panels in the hotter regions, such as those near the power plant.

It is estimated that 100 hours of the overall airframe life will be spent at elevated temperature. The adiabatic wall temperature corresponding to the maximum Mach number of 2.05 under ISA conditions is 107 degrees C; that corresponding to the design limit Mach number of 2.25 is 140 degrees C. Advantage has also been taken – particularly where space is at a premium, such as in the case of the landing gear – of the ultra-high strength, vacuum-melted steels now

available. Limited use has also been made of titanium alloys, largely for heat shields, hot ducts, etc. The airframe is designed to withstand a thermal dose of 50 Calories per Square cm. Methods of construction follow well established techniques already in use on existing aircraft.

Crew Stations

The crew of two are carried in tandem ejector seats in a pressurised air conditioned cockpit. The pilot has an unrestricted forward view over the nose at all times and unimpaired visibility ensured by a hot air blast rain dispersal and anti-icing system, and heated windscreen panels. A water based solution can be flushed over the windscreen to clear insect accumulations. Considerable research has been carried out into the problems of crew comfort and efficiency, with reference to flight at very high speed close to the ground, and the results have been incorporated the configuration of the TSR2 cockpits. Particular attention has been paid to achieving the best possible standard of seating, adequate and comfortable personal equipment, a logical and easily-operated control and instrument layout with collimated main displays, an effective failure warning system, and satisfactory cockpit lighting. The results of vibration and other rig tests on human subjects showed that with the aerodynamic design of TSR2 for minimum gust response, no special seating provisions are required provided that the crew are firmly strapped into their seats. To achieve this tight strapping without discomfort, a new harness assembly has been designed.

When a sortie requires it, pressure jerkins will be worn as provision is made for the use of full pressure suits and helmets for special sorties. The pilot is provided with a conventional instrument presentation including an OR946 type flight director navigation display and moving map position indicator. In addition, a head up display (HUD) collimated to infinity is projected onto his windscreen. This display provides the information to operate and monitor the aircraft in its various modes, at the same time giving him freedom to view the outside world. The information presented on the HUD includes a flight director and speed director; in the attack mode an event marker is also displayed, while on take-off and landing, height and speed are also shown.

Engineering – Fuselage

The fuselage houses the two crew members, packaged electronic equipment in readily accessible bays, the landing gear, the engines and the weapons bay. Approximately 80% of the total fuel load is carried in integral tanks in the fuselage; the structure has therefore been designed from the outset as an integral tank. Careful disposition of the major internal items has resulted in low frontal area and a controlled area distribution along the length, so ensuring low supersonic wave drag and a high subsonic cruise Mach number. At the same time, easy access for servicing has been achieved. The structure consists mainly of skin stringer panels supported by transverse bulkhead frames. Extensive use of machined panels, particularly in the region of the integral tanks, has reduced the sealing problems. In these areas panels may be machined from billets of 2in thickness down to as little as 40 thousandths of

an inch. Chemically etched skins with separate stringers are used where significant forming of the skin is required. The crew compartments are structurally conventional, with allowance for heat insulation requirements. Windscreen and canopy are based on high temperature aluminium-silicate and stretched acrylic laminate respectively. The forward screen provides for head up display projection and withstands the hot air blast used for windscreen clearance, in addition to having adequate strength to withstand impact of a 1lb bird at transonic speeds. Systems and installations are routed through the lower portion of the fuselage where natural access is provided by the main and nose undercarriage doors, the weapons and accessories bays, and readily detachable access doors in the lower skin. The Olympus

engines are housed side-by-side in the rear fuselage. The air intakes and the engine and jet pipe tunnels form an integral part of the fuselage structure. Secondary cooling air is bled from the main intake and passed around the engine and through the tunnels to maintain temperature levels acceptable for light alloy structure. The integral fuel tanks are located in two areas; the forward tanks extend aft from the equipment bay to a point between the air intakes; the rear tanks are built around the engine tunnels. Heat shields are fitted to the interior of the tunnel structure to minimise fire hazards and provide a second wall to the fuel tank in the area. Engine injection water is carried in a tank shaped to fit between the engine tunnels.

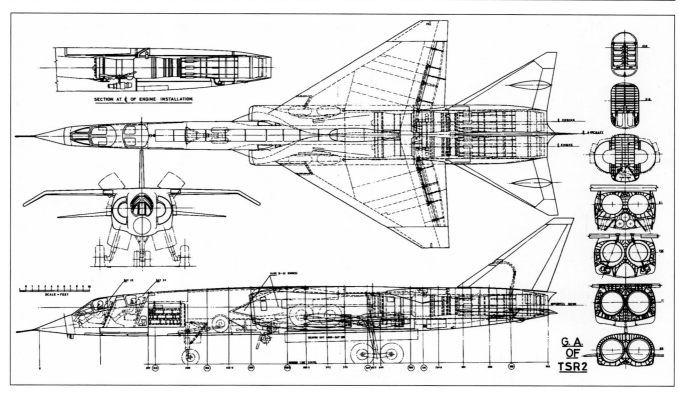

SECTION AT ℄ OF ENGINE INSTALLATION.

G. A.
OF
TSR2

Wing

The wing is of an approximately delta plan form, flush with the top of the fuselage. The basic chord plane of the majority of the wing is normal to the vertical centre line, but the tip chord plane is inclined downward at 30 degrees anhedral, to provide correct lateral stability characteristics while at the same time maintaining vertical separation between the wing and tailplane. The wing is constructed as a single box and is a scaled integral fuel tank. No lateral control surfaces are fitted, but blown trailing edge flaps occupy almost the full span. Multi-web construction is used for the primary box, which consists of six integrally-machined panels per side, top and bottom, and an internal structure of machined webs and post-stabilised stringers. This ensures a fail-safe design and, together with special features such as tapered interference fit bolts, provides the required long fatigue life.

Empennage

Two horizontal and single vertical tail surfaces are each of the all-moving type. The horizontal surfaces move either together to provide longitudinal control, or differentially to provide lateral control; they are fitted with flaps for additional power. Structurally the tail surfaces also follow the multi-web form and employ tapered skin machined from X2020 supported by full depth webs and ribs with intermediate stiffeners.

Landing Gear

The Landing gear comprises a twin-wheel, steerable nose undercarriage and port and starboard two-wheels-in-tandem main undercarriages. Each undercarriage retracts into an unpressurised compartment in the fuselage. The landing gear will support an emergency landing at maximum take-off weight and is suitable

for use on poorly prepared surfaces. For short take-off, provision has been made to raise the nose of the aircraft by hydraulic extension of the nose undercarriage shock-absorber strut. The main wheels are fitted with hydraulically operated disc-type brakes; a fractional horse-power motor, housed in the axle, draws air through the wheel to create forced ventilation which lowers the temperature of the wheel and brakes for safe accelerate-stop after a short turn round period. Axle-mounted anti-skid control devices are incorporated in the brake system. The nose gear incorporates not only hydraulic (forward) retraction and steering (normal maximum angle of 10 degrees which can be switched to a coarse angle of up to 68 degrees), but also a hydraulic extension, shortening and locking capability which enables TSR2 to sit on the ground at two markedly different angles. In the nose-high attitude (raised by 30 inches) both lift and drag (countered by high engine thrust) are increased, to reduce the field take-off length required. Each main gear unit has a single leg attached to one of the main fuselage/wing frames, carrying two wheels in tandem. The unit retracted forwards into a compartment close beside the armament bay and intake duct. Supersonic wave-drag considerations demanded minimum cross-section in this region, and this posed installation problems accentuated by the need to splay the legs outwards, in order to create adequate track. In order to achieve adequate strength for operating this very heavy aircraft from rough unprepared surfaces, without exceeding these severe restrictions on available cross-section, all major leg members were forged and machined in a very high quality ultra-high-tensile steel to an English Steel Corporation specification. This was the first time that steel of such strength was used in a major production application in Britain. It was clearly no easy task to work in steels of this kind, and the manufacture of the complete units was subcontracted to Electro-Hydraulics Ltd in Warrington, a company which had undertaken considerable development work

Above: Starboard main undercarriage unit as fitted to XR220, showing the additional strut which was to be fitted to production aircraft, to solve the persistent landing vibration problems. XR219 was in the process of having similarly-modified landing gear fitted at Warton when the project was cancelled, and never flew in this configuration. *Tim McLelland*

Left: Close-up view of XR220's nose undercarriage unit. *Tim McLelland*

in this field during the preceding few years, and had also installed a number of advanced machine tools necessitated by the high-grade materials. Heat-treatment methods were developed in co-operation with BAC and the English Steel Corp. BAC designed the legs to have a very long stroke, in order to accommodate the undulations of the long wavelength met within semi-prepared surfaces. The oleo has a soft characteristic over most of its travel, but it stiffens towards the limit of its stroke. To meet the requirement of withstanding high impact and single-wheel loads at high speeds while operating from soft dispersed areas, TSR2 has relatively large wheels with low-pressure tyres. These were the subject of development at the Goodyear Tyre & Rubber Co (Great Britain) Ltd and the Dunlop Rubber Co Ltd since the original GOR.339 specification was first considered. From the outset it was realized that the tyre designers would be faced with new and formidable problems. The required type of tyre became known as the 'high-speed puff bag.' It was necessary to devise a shape and type of construction which would operate at low inflation pressure without the formation of potentially destructive traction waves in the tyre during high-speed and high-load conditions experienced during take-off and landing. The take-off conditions are the most difficult to meet; Traction waves give rise to excessive shear, tensile and compressive stresses in the tyre carcase, and accelerations of a very high order are experienced on portions of the tread. All this generates considerable heat, and ply and tread start to separate. In these conditions tyres can disintegrate extremely quickly. These potential problems were eventually surmounted, and Goodyear claimed to have been the first to meet the TSR2 specification during realistic and exhaustive dynamometer testing. Goodyear and Dunlop tyres were to be used alternately on the first batch of pre-production aircraft. The Dunlop contribution also includes wheels and brakes (incorporating axle-mounted Maxaret anti-skid units), brake-operating equipment and brake cooling. Each of the two split-type

main wheels, for use with tubeless tyres, accommodates a plate brake and an air-cooling installation. The wheel rims incorporate fusible plugs which ensure controlled deflation of the tyre in the event of excessive heat build-up resulting from emergency braking. The air-cooling dissipates heat normally generated by the brake before it can soak into the rim and tyre beads. It consists of a fractional-horsepower electric motor driving a shrouded impeller, and the complete assembly is housed within the axle adjacent to the anti-skid unit. Each Maxaret anti-skid unit is driven through a flexible coupling from the wheel hub, thus ensuring immunity to the effects of weather and any damaging material flung up by the wheels. Maxaret allows the use of maximum braking power in all conditions of weather and runway without resulting in wheel lock and consequent skidding. Multi-piston brakes are employed, incorporating jigsaw-type segmented rotor assemblies, and stator assemblies carrying inorganic pads. Automatic adjusters ensure that, as the pads wear down, the working clearance remains the same, so that the displacement of the operating fluid is maintained at a constant figure throughout the service life of the unit. The principal brake structure is of either steel or titanium. Problems arising from the high operating temperatures necessitated special test rigs at Dunlop's Aviation Division factories in Coventry, so that components could be tested under all conditions likely to be encountered in service.

In order to enable the aircraft to land safely on short runways or unprepared strips, a large 28-foot braking parachute is provided, which can be deployed on touch-down. Fitted into a pack between the engine exhausts, the system can be operated automatically, and as the aircraft lands a small 6-foot drogue chute is deployed from the hinged fairing in which the system is housed, immediately pulling-out the main parachute. For short-field landings the system can be over-ridden and operated manually to ensure the swiftest sequence. The main parachute can not be jettisoned once deployed and if the pilot requires to make a rolling take-off once the parachute is deployed, the specified procedure is to apply full afterburner power which will burn-off the chute. For normal landings the main parachute canopy can be reefed to a smaller 16-foot diameter enabling the aircraft to land in crosswinds up to 35 knots (the normal limit for the full canopy is 20 knots). Some consideration was given to the design of a reverse thrust system for the aircraft which comprised a deployable bucket arrangement fitted to the exhausts, but no plans were made to introduce this into production aircraft.

Engineering

Power Plant

The TSR2 is powered by two Bristol-Siddeley Olympus 22R twin-spool jet turbine engines, with water injection and variable reheat. At sea level the static thrust of each engine is 19,600lb dry and 30,610lb with full reheat. The main features of the engine are two compounded axial flow compressors, two axial flow single stage turbines each driving one compressor, straight flow flame tube combustion chambers, and a fully variable reheat system with a fixed shroud aerodynamic nozzle. The engines are installed side-by-side in separate tunnels in the rear fuselage, with their vertical design datum rotated through 21 degrees. Each engine has three mounting attachments; a main thrust trunnion located at the top of the delivery casing, a locating spigot and spherical bush at the front of the engine and a transverse strut for torsional restraint. Alternative port and starboard mounting attachment positions make the engines non-handed. The engine change unit complete with jet pipe is installed from the rear of the airframe after removing the rear fairing. Engine-mounted rollers run on rails in the tunnels to guide each engine and maintain clearance between engine and tunnel. Air is fed to the engines from semi-circular intakes mounted on the fuselage sides forward of the wing leading edge. Each intake is of variable area controlled by movement of a conical centre body and is provided with independent automatic and manual (pilot) control. Auxiliary intake doors, at the rear of the intake lip, provide additional intake area at low speeds. Each engine has an automatic electrical control, the normal system being AC with a standby DC system. The system provides a linear relationship between the pilot's throttle lever angle and engine thrust, from flight idling up to maximum reheat. Each engine drives an accessories gearbox which can be de-clutched from the engine. The gearbox drives a constant speed drive starter (CSDS), an alternator, two fueldraulic motors, and two hydraulic pumps. THE CSDS acts as an air starter, and maintains a constant speed drive to the generator. It provides an air motor powered drive for ground checking accessories and systems when supplied with air from the airborne auxiliary power plant or a ground source; the generator is driven at normal speed and the gearbox at reduced speed. In flight, with the engine inoperative and gearbox declutched, it can drive the gearbox through its air motor supplied with air from the other engine.

Fire Protection

Two fireproof zones with fire protection and suppression equipment protect the area surrounding each engine. Triple firewire detection systems are used to initiate audible and visual warning of fire. Methyl bromide extinguishers and distribution spray rings provide fire suppression. These are push button operated or, in the crash case, automatically discharged by inertia switch operation.

Cooling and Ventilation

A straight through cooling and ventilation air flow system is provided for the engine and jet pipe tunnels. This is effected by ram air bled from the engine air intakes. In low speed flight conditions and ground running, cooling is provided by auxiliary intake doors in the side of the engine tunnels.

Auxiliary Power

The airborne auxiliary power plans (AAPP) is stowed ventrally inside the fuselage forward of the weapons bay. On the ground the AAPP is lowered by hydraulic jacks; a lock is provided to prevent inadvertent lowering during flight. The AAPP is started by a hydraulic motor fed from an accumulator in the aircraft; it can only be started when in the fully down position. The AAPP provides low pressure air for:-

Engine starting and AC electrical power for fuel pumps, throttles and the inertia platform.

Ground running of the main engine gearboxes to provide electrical and hydraulic power for general aircraft purposes.

Air conditioning of the crew compartments and equipment bay.

The navigator's instruments, displays and controls are grouped according to their function; the sideways and forward looking radar displays are also collimated to infinity. A panel containing all essential switches to be operated before take-off is fitted in each cockpit. These are switched 'on' by one movement of a spring-loaded gang bar, but are individually switched 'off'. Emergency crew escape is effected by operation of the seat ejection handle to operate a sequenced and programmed system linking the two canopies and two ejector seats. Operation of the pilot's handle jettisons both canopies, operates the navigator's seat ejection and, after a short delay, the pilot's own seat ejection. Operation of the navigator's seat handle operates the navigator's canopy jettison and seat ejection only, leaving the pilot to take his own action.

Principal among Category One subcontractors for the programme are Bristol-Siddeley Engines Ltd, responsible directly to the MoA for the supply of the Olympus 22R turbojet. This power plant is equipped with a reheat unit providing a thrust of 30,000-35,000lb, and two engines are installed in tight-fitting tunnels within the rear fuselage of the aircraft structure. The company's Patchway division worked long and hard on the development of this power plant, which was developed directly from the earlier two-spool Olympus engines that served the RAF so well in Vulcan bombers, and earned a reputation for exceptional reliability. The technical specification for the 22R, calling for a high maximum thrust and a very low specific fuel consumption, was a tough one, but it was successfully achieved, with ample potential for further development. Problems that had to be overcome in the development included, on the one hand, those associated with operation at Mach numbers greater than Two, high-temperature lubrication and increased severity of vibration stresses. Likewise there were problems of very-low-altitude operation such as increased engine structural loads resulting from higher air density, and greater likelihood of damage from foreign-body ingestion. Bristol-Siddeley's experience of low-altitude operation of the Orpheus turbojet in the Fiat G.91 gave them a good understanding of these difficulties, and damage by birds and other foreign bodies is minimized by the inherently robust design of the Olympus. Basic strength requirements for a supersonic turbojet demanded the use of guide vanes and compressor blading of steel. The use of specialized materials in some areas also demanded the evolution of new manufacturing techniques. The Concorde's Olympus 593 engines were eventually derived from the 22R in the same way that the 22R was directly developed from the less-sophisticated two-spool Olympus which powered the Vulcan. In TSR2 the Olympus 22R has a fully variable intake and variable-area nozzle, and a reheat system fully controllable over the entire range by a single lever. It is possible for both power plants to operate under well-matched conditions in every phase of flight, and at low altitude the aircraft can cruise without reheat. The intake cone is moved by a Lucas jack with manual or automatic controls, and the intake lip incorporates Dunlop anti-icing heater elements. Bristol Aero-Engines had previously entered a licensing agreement for developing and manufacturing the American Solar reheat system, although the system now in use on the Olympus 22R differs widely, both thermodynamically and mechanically, from the original Solar system, with materials, layout, construction and fuel-injection system all being very different. A Rotax 12-joule high-energy ignition unit is fitted to each engine, and the engine fuel system is manufactured by Lucas Gas Turbine Equipment. Except for the flow distributor and nozzles, all fuel-system components are mounted on a single chassis, with consequent reduction in pipework and simplified installation and removal.

The system incorporates two pumps, venturi meters and appropriate nozzles. Flight trials of the Olympus 22R engine, installed in a Vulcan test-bed aircraft, began in February 1962. When the aircraft was subsequently destroyed by a fire on the ground at Filton, development of the engine was carried out both at Bristol-Siddeley's own facilities at Patchway, and by a Bristol Siddeley team in the high-altitude, high-speed test chamber at the National Gas Turbine Establishment at Pyestock. The Patchway test-bed was provided with an air intake heater for simulating conditions at speeds greater than Mach 2. As well as the propulsive engines, Bristol-Siddeley also provide TSR2's on-board auxiliary power unit. This consists of a Cumulus turbo-compressor with power take-off. It is capable of providing pneumatic power for main-engine starting and cockpit and electronic air-conditioning, as well as shaft power for electrical and hydraulic services on the ground. The Cumulus is a 50 hp single shaft gas turbine, with a single-stage oversize centrifugal compressor driven by a two-stage axial turbine. Compressed air bled from the outer casing of the annular combustion chamber provides a maximum flow of 2.6 lb/sec for aircraft services.

Fuel System

The aircraft's fuel system will operate on Avtag, Avtur or Avcat without adjustment to engines or controls. The maximum refuelling rate is 450 gal per minute (540 US gal/min) and a duel refuelling connection enables two refuelling vehicles to deliver simultaneously. Refuelling to a partial fuel load condition can be selected to meet a short-range sortie requirement. At dispersed airstrips where permanent fuel storage facilities are not available, the aircraft can be refuelled from temporary bulk storage provided by collapsible bag tanks. A hydraulically operated fuel pump may be powered by the General Servicing Vehicle. A fuselage nose probe is fitted for in-flight refuelling at a maximum rate of 400 gal per minute (480 US gal/min). The low pressure system incorporates fueldraulic booster pumps powered by engine gearbox driven supply pumps. This type of installation, besides being lighter and more efficient than an electrical booster pump system, allows booster pump output to be easily varied, a feature which has permitted the installation of a cavitation sensing and correcting system. The failure of any single pump does not reduce the fuel flow to the engines. A water injection system is fitted to increase engine thrust for short field take-off particularly in hot conditions. A tank of 80 gal (96 US gal) capacity is fitted between the jet pipes; this is sufficient for nearly one minute of operation of both engines.

Fuel Capacities (Imp gal/US gal)

Internal Fuel Wing tanks	Forward fuselage tanks	Aft fuselage tanks	Collector boxes
Port – 737/885	No.1 – 1,132/1,360	No.3 – 991/1,191	Forward – 30.5/37
Starboard – 737/885	No.2 – 1,023/1,228	No.4 – 909/1,091	Aft – 28.5/34
Total usable internal fuel – 5,588/6,711			

External fuel
Jettisonable wing tanks

Port – 450/540
Starboard – 450/540
Non-jettison able weapons bay tank – 570/685
Jettisonable ventral tank – 1,000/1,201

Hydraulic System

Four self-contained hydraulic systems operate the flying controls and general services – two for flying controls and two for general services. High temperature, low-flammability, silicon-based Silicodyne-H (DP.47) fluid is used. Power is supplied by four engine-driven pumps; two pumps are mounted on each accessories gearbox, one for a services system, the other for a controls system. This arrangement ensures that all flying controls and essential services are capable of single system operation. He duplication of supplies and services ensures that a sortie does not need to be abandoned in the event of failure of any one hydraulic system. Each pump draws fluid from its own reservoir, and by-pass fluid is returned to the reservoir via a fuel-cooled heat exchanger, a non-return valve and a by-pass filter. The by-pass filters and those in the pressure lines have elements of stainless steel mesh providing 10-micron (absolute) filtration. The nominal delivery pressure is 4,000psi but in the event of failure of the pressure control, a relief valve in each pump pressure line connects to the system return to limit the pressure to 4,800psi. The pumps are off-loaded during engine starting. The four reservoirs housed in the rear fuselage are similar in construction, comprising a metal body and a rubber bladder which contains the hydraulic fluid. Fluid from the relief valves is collected in overflow tanks. Excess fluid is vented overboard. The reservoirs are pressurised with air fed from the flap-blowing air systems, or from a ground charging connection. Seven accumulators are provided. One in each control system augments the control pump delivery during maximum rate manoeuvres and provides an emergency supply for a limited period with both engines stopped. Two in the services system supply pressure for the feel units and the roll/yaw gearbox. Three more supply pressure for the emergency nose wheel steering selector, wheel brake reducing valves and AAPP lowering and starting. Two hand pumps are provided for emergency charging of the three aft accumulators. For ground operation of the services supplied by these accumulators, manually operated isolating valves blank off the pressure lines from the remainder of the services systems. A pressure switch is provided in each system, so that indication of failure of either both services systems, or both controls systems, is given by a red warning light on the pilot's centralised alert warning panel. Single system failure is indicated by illumination of an amber lamp on the same panel.

Services System

Pressure supplies for normal landing gear operation are taken from No.1 system for the port undercarriage and from No.2 system for the starboard and nose undercarriages. If one system fails the remaining system will operate its own circuits and, through an emergency system, those of the failed system. Pressure supplies for nose wheel steering and nose strut extension are taken from No.2 system and emergency supplies from one AAPP accumulator and No.1 system respectively. Petal-type forward hinged air brakes are operated by screw jacks through a gearbox driven by two hydraulic motors, one supplied from each system. Wheel brakes are applied by operation of foot motors attached to the rudder pedals,

permitting differential braking. One accumulator in each system supplies the pressure to the brake control valve via pressure-reducing valves which reduce the system pressure to 1,500psi. Anti-skid units are fitted. The weapons bay doors are operated by double-acting tandem-piston jacks supplied by No.1 and No.2 systems. Wing trailing edge flaps are operated through a gearbox driven by two hydraulic motors supplied by both No.1 and No.2 systems. The standby generator is driven by a hydraulic motor supplied by either of the systems through a double shuttle valve, biased towards No.2 system. Air intake cones and auxiliary intake doors are automatically operated by hydraulic jacks, the port supplied by No.1 system and the starboard by No.2 system. A manual over-ride system is provided. A hydraulic simulated feel system provides artificial feel on the pitching and yawing controls. One simulator in each circuit is fed from an accumulator in No.1 system and one from an accumulator in No.2 system via a change-over valve which automatically ensures a supply from No.1 system should No.2 fail. Hydraulic pressure for lowering and raising the AAPP is supplied by one of two accumulators in No.2 system. First start pressure is supplied by one accumulator in No.1 system, and second start pressure by two accumulators in No.2 system. Wing fuel transfer pumps are driven by a single hydraulic motor fed from No.2 system. Hydraulic pressure for the operation of the refuelling probe is taken from No.2 system, and emergency supplies from No.1 system.

Controls System

The two halves of the tailplane are operated by two separate powered flying control units connected into the pitch and roll control circuits. The units are basically tandem-piston hydraulic jacks supplied with pressure (through accumulators) by both systems; each system feeds one of two independent, mechanically coupled control valves on each unit. The fin is operated in the same manner by a single control unit powered by both systems. The tailplane flaps are mechanically geared to the tailplanes so that when the wing flaps are selected 'down' the angular position of the tailplane flaps is related to tailplane angle. When the wing flaps are selected 'up' the tailplane flaps gearing is moved to a neutral position by tandem-piston hydraulic jacks; one in each tailplane supplied with pressure from both No.1 and No.2 systems. Restrictors are fitted to control the rate of operation. The brake parachute door is opened by a hydraulic jack fed from both systems, but is shut manually.

Pressurization and Air Conditioning

Air tapped from the final stage of the engine compressors, and cooled by an air-cycle cooling system, pressurizes and conditions the crew compartments and equipment bay. It is passed through three heat exchangers, two ram-air cooled and one aircraft fuel-cooled, and a duplicated cold air unit system provided with automatic change-over to allow for failure. The air supplied to the crew is automatically controlled and distributed to provide maximum comfort. The high temperature ducting is double-walled for protection, and the crew compartments are lagged to minimise heat input and inner wall temperature fluctuations. Air inlet temperature is controlled by reference to cabin mean temperature, and flow is controlled on the basis of a crew compartment temperature difference; thus a constant mean temperature is maintained under all conditions. A manual selector is provided to adjust the control level. Pressurization commences on the ground and is automatically controlled to reach a maximum differential pressure of 5psi at an altitude of approximately 28,000ft. The rate of change of the crew compartment pressure does not exceed 5psi per minute under any conditions up to those of a tactical descent on the Mach 1.7/725kt IAS boundary. A switch in the pilot's cockpit over-rides the main and emergency pressure controllers for quick depressurisation of the compartments, or for use after landing at airfields above sea level. Air discharged from the crew compartments pressurizes and conditions the equipment bays; it then passes through a regenerative heat exchanger before being exhausted overboard. Combined safety and inward-relief valves safeguard the crew and equipment should either discharge valve fail or the pressure differential rise above safe limits. When a canopy is opened, thus cutting off the supply of air to the equipment bays, or if cooling is insufficient, an automatically operated by-pass valve passes additional air to the bay to maintain the equipment at the required temperature. The inertia platform, forward looking radar and sideways looking cameras, attitude gyros, accelerometers and ventilated suits are all conditioned from the main air supply. The ventilated suit is optional equipment, since the requirement for a fully-conditioned crew compartment has been met. Partially cooled air is supplied for crew compartment heating, rain dispersal and anti-icing, seal inflation, radome pressurization and anti-g suit operation. Additional cold air units are fitted when the reconnaissance pack is used, but the capacity of the main heat exchangers is adequate for both the aircraft and the additional units. On the ground with the engines stopped, air supplies can be provided by the AAPP, or a ground source. Ground supply couplings are made with lanyard release connectors to allow rapid take-off.

Anti-icing

Icing condition are indicated by a light on the alert warning panel, operated by an ice detector. The anti-icing system will handle all icing conditions that will be met by TSR2. Both hot air and electrical heating systems are provided for anti-icing. The hot air system feeds the engine intake guide blades, the nose bullet, and the pilot's centre windscreen. An electrical heating cable is brazed to each intake lip; this is provided with an overheat cut-out switch. All transparent surfaces are demisted by electrically heated gold film controlled by temperature sensing devices. Gold film is also used to anti-ice the pilot's side screens.

Oxygen System

Converted liquid oxygen supplies crew demands at a comfortable breathing temperature. The storage capacity of 10 litres is sufficient to provide 100% oxygen to both crew members for a standard sortie following a one hour flight and a three day standby. Personal equipment connections (PEC) and seat mounted regulators are separately provided for pilot and navigator. Each has two demand regulators with the facility to change from one to the other. The main regulator controls either air and oxygen mixed, or 100 oxygen; the secondary system supplies oxygen only. An emergency cylinder is fitted to each seat so that oxygen is automatically fed to the face mask in the event of seat ejection. This supply can be manually controlled during any other emergency. Ejecting the seat breaks the quick-disconnect coupling; the regulator in use at the time of ejection will remain operative during this period.

Electrical Power

Electrical power is provided by two engine-driven generators supplemented by a small emergency unit. DC supplies are provided by two 150 amp rating transformer rectifier units (TRU) and one 50 amp TRU for emergency use. A battery power source is used for the UHF emergency radio. Fully automatic generator overload protection is incorporated. The constant speed drives used to couple the generators to the engines are arranged to allow for each generator to be driven from its respective engine or, in case of failure, for both generators to be driven from one engine. In an emergency, all essential services may be powered by the emergency generator driven by hydraulic power. A wind milling engine will supply sufficient power above 250 knots IAS to maintain full output from the emergency generator. An auxiliary generator for ground use is mounted on the airborne auxiliary power plant. It is used for maintaining supplies to the inertia platform and other critical units during standby. A roll-away disconnect coupling for an external ground power supply can be used.

Lighting

Conventional lighting is used for the servicing bays and all external lighting. The cockpit lighting is based on red neon integrally-lit instruments with red electro-luminescent illumination of panel legends. Red flood light of adjustable intensity is also available. High intensity white lighting is used for conditions where atomic flash may be expected.

The following outputs are provided:-

Main supply – 200 volt +2% 3 phase AC at 400cps +3%

Main generator output – 30 kVA each, 55 kVA in overload conditions.

Emergency generator output – 3.5 kVA, 6.5 kVA in overload conditions.

Looking at TSR2's avionics: the Systems Division E (Electrics and Electronics), responsible for the whole of British Aircraft Corporation's activities in the fields of communications, radar, electric power generation, cockpit instrumentation, automatic flight control and flight instrumentation engineering, had the prime task of integrating the entire weapon system. The Division commanded elaborate laboratories for carrying out rig tests, and comprehensive computing facilities. It includes a microwave division specializing in the design of suppressed aerials and the cutting of waveguides, for outside customers as well as for BAC's own needs. The nav-attack system specified for TSR2 posed new problems for the Corporation, and new solutions had to be found. The high degree of accuracy necessary demanded great complexity of equipment. This was accentuated in the case of TSR2 by the versatility of the aeroplane and its exceptionally wide range of altitude and speed. When the specification was issued no existing electronic equipment was capable of meeting the expected range of performance and environment. When terrain-following at exceptionally low altitudes it is important that the pilot should be completely happy, and confident in the reliability of the indications presented to him. The aircraft itself must respond immediately to pilot demand. Obviously, the forward-looking nose radar must be of the highest possible standard; and here, it was claimed, Ferranti set a level surpassing anything achieved on the other side of the Atlantic. In fact the TSR.2 concept involves a thorough review of the design of radar, airframe structure, handling characteristics, automatic guidance and auto-stabilisation. An intricate chain of equipment has to be co-ordinated to work reliably under exceedingly stringent conditions, and every phase of flight and variation of mission has to be taken into account. British Aircraft Corporation have approached this problem of co-ordination in what was a completely new way. In the United States, hitherto pre-eminent in the weapon system concept, it had usually been the practice for the airframe contractor to subcontract out to an electronics manufacturer the responsibility of integrating the various electronic systems. But because this is only one stage in integration it had been necessary to have an airframe team working in parallel with the electronics contractor, and this created unnecessary duplication. BAC tackled the problem as a whole, and by this means, they claimed they cut development costs by more than half as compared with American philosophy. They outlined the system, agreed the specification with the subcontractors, and ensured that the elements of the system worked in accordance with requirements. This was done by carrying out detailed functioning tests in their laboratories on rigs representative of the aircraft. By this means problems of interference and cross-talk could be ironed out, and reliability of the system components ensured under every possible variation of working conditions. The rig tests also helped tremendously in assessing the scale of the servicing problems, and in evolving checkout equipment suitable for RAF use. As a result of the complexity of the electronic subsystems, and the vast number of inputs and outputs that required checking, BAC introduced 'integrated systems testing' in order to make servicing a practical and efficient possibility. In other words, they specified one piece of test equipment which used the working system as a stimulus, and by running a test routine it was possible to discriminate any faulty element in each system – which can then be withdrawn, replaced, and rechecked. All the major elements in the various subsystems were therefore fitted with pick-off points for automatic checkout. It is believed that this was the most comprehensive automatic checkout system yet developed, the integrated weapon system involving over 1,000 types of measurement. Design of the automatic test equipment was entrusted to Hawker Siddeley Dynamics Ltd, as a development of TRACE (Tape-controlled Recording Automatic Checkout Equipment), versions of which had

already been supplied to the British and French Governments. The test routines were automatically switched through a taped programmed sequence to every subsystem element in turn. Any faulty element would cause a warning signal to operate, and would stop the test sequence. TRACE for TSR2 was to be mounted in a waterproof trailer designed for high-speed towing over unprepared surfaces. Complete environmental testing was to be carried out on the equipment to ensure that it could not be penetrated by dust or water, and that it would operate efficiently in all climates. Altogether the demands of TSR2 for field support promises to be remarkably light. Manual testing was also a requirement, and was catered for by using the same test pick-off points as were required for the automatic test equipment. These manual test sets were manufactured by the subcontractors responsible for the systems themselves.

Flying Controls

Manual Control

The main control surfaces, consisting of two all-moving tailplanes and an all-moving fin, are each driven by duplicated hydraulic power controls signalled by conventional mechanical rod drives from conventional pilot's controls. The two tailplanes are moved together for pitch control and in opposite directions for roll control. The stick to 'elevator' gearing is non-linear. The stick to 'aileron' gearing is automatically modified in relation to speed and altitude; the aileron angular range is increased progressively as the flaps are lowered. The rudder pedals operate the fin via a hydraulic buffer which is controlled by a mechanical signal from the roll control to neutralise aerodynamic coupling. Artificial feel in each circuit is provided by duplicated actuators and feel units. Conventional trimming is by electrical actuators. The change of trim due to operation of the wing flaps and the air brakes has been designed to be a minimum.

Autostabilisation

On the manual system alone the aircraft will have at least adequate, and under many conditions good handling qualities except at the highest supersonic speeds. Full auto stabilisation is provided by an Automatic Flight Control System (AFCS); this operates through two electro-hydraulic actuators incorporated in each tailplane power control and three electro-hydraulic actuators in the fin power control. The actuators are operated in response to signals from rate gyros and accelerometers to provide ideal handling qualities under all conditions. Manoeuvre boost is provided which, when selected, increases the magnitude of the pitch signals from the pilot in subsonic flight. This facility is particularly valuable for manoeuvring close to the ground during terrain following or ground attack work. At high supersonic speeds, reliance is placed on synthetic yawing stiffness and the complete system is therefore triplicated. After a single failure the flight Mach number would normally be reduced slightly.

Automatic Control

The AFCS has been developed to satisfy the specific operational requirements and aerodynamic characteristics of the aircraft. In

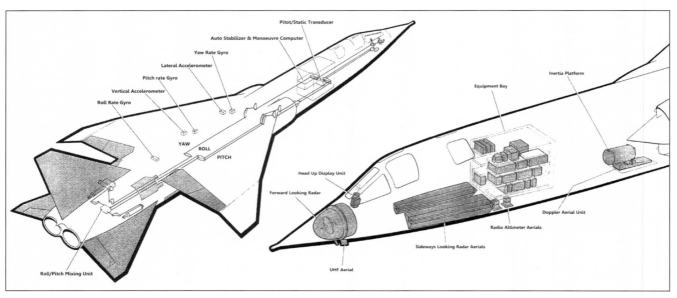

Contemporary diagram showing main Flying controls.   Contemporary diagram showing main navigation and Attack installations.

addition to the usual modes of operation, e.g. height and heading locks, the manoeuvre computer will accept inputs from the normal computer system to enable the aircraft to be flown on a track lock, through standard climb and descent patterns or by the automatic navigation and attack system. The latter provides automatic navigation from point to point, terrain following, the lead-in to visual acquisition of targets for high explosive delivery, and the various automatic nuclear weapons approach and delivery manoeuvres. Command signals produced by the AFCS manoeuvre computer are also presented to the pilot on his flight director displays in order that he may monitor the AFCS or fly the aircraft manually. In the terrain following mode the pilot's response to commands are themselves monitored by the AFCS. The safety of the aircraft is ensured by the provision of response monitoring, the duplication of pitch manoeuvre computing, and automatic cut-out in the event of excessive manoeuvres. Auto trim follow-up is employed to maintain approximately zero out-of-balance, and no violent change of trim therefore occurs upon AFCS disengagement.

Integration of Flying Control and Instrument Systems

The instrument system comprising the head-up and head-down displays is fully integrated with the AFCS in that if the pilot selects a particular mode of flight, e.g. a height lock, this is selected throughout the system.

Navigation and Attack Installation

With the exception of the inertia platform, the Doppler, the sideways looking radar (SLR) aerial and the forward looking radar (FLR), all navigation and attack system equipment is installed in a special air conditioned bay immediately behind the navigator's cockpit. The inertia platform and the Doppler are in a bay just aft of the nose wheel; the SLR aerials are situated low on the fuselage forward of the equipment bay; the FLR, including the terrain following and HE weapon delivery computers, occupies a pressurised compartment in the nose. The installation in the equipment bay utilizes the modular racking principle. All modules are of a standard length and have rear-

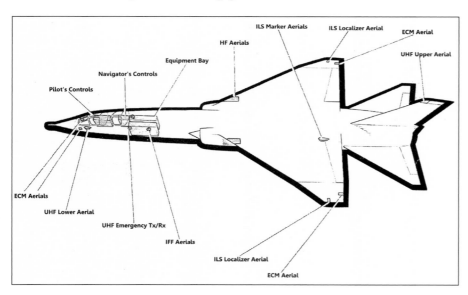

Contemporary diagram showing main
Communication installations.

mounted electrical connections. Coded locating pins are provided to prevent accidental transposition of modules. The shelves of the bay are individually shock mounted and of shallow box construction; they act as plenum chambers for the cooling air, which is metered to each module through ports in the shelf and in the module which mate and seal when the module is locked home. Locking and unlocking are simply accomplished by lowering or raising the carrying handle, which has a cam action to assist in making and breaking the electrical multi-pin connections. Face-mounted test sockets on each module allow in-situ testing. The inertia platform and Doppler aerial are jig mounted since extreme accuracy of mutual alignment is required. The inertia platform has a direct cooling air supply and the exhaust air is spilled over the Doppler aerial. The SLR aerials are two X-band slotted arrays, each approximately 7ft 6in long, mounted in horizontal recesses one on each side of the fuselage immediately below the level of the navigator's station floor beam. Each aerial access is covered by a plastic dielectric panel. The tilt angle of the aerial assembly can be varied so that optimum performance is achieved at any altitude; the navigator operates the aerial tilt selector switch. The FLR is also jig-mounted to give accurate alignment with the airframe. The associated electronic equipment and terrain following and conventional weapon aiming computers are contained in a pressurised canister behind the scanner. This canister has its own cooling system with a heat exchanger fed with cold air from the main aircraft system.

Displays

The navigator's compartment contains all the displays necessary for aircraft navigation:-

Central computer display and controls.

Rapid processing unit for the SLR picture.

FLR cathode ray tube display for use when the SLR is in the ground mapping or beacon modes.

Moving map.

Optical sight giving a downward view.

Displays of Doppler ground speed, heading and other data obtained from the navigation system.

The fuel system displays are also repeated to the navigator so that he may monitor them, although fuel management is the pilot's responsibility. The navigator also has several standby flight instruments. The pilot's compartment contains certain navigation displays including a duplicate moving map, as well as the flight instruments.

Communications Installation

The communications installation comprises multi-channel HF, VHF/UHF and standby UHF transmitter-receivers, SIF and ECM equipment. The main units of each system are housed in the equipment bay, and are packaged and mounted in the same way as the navigation and strike equipment. All the communications equipment installations incorporate duplicate aerials to provide good all-round cover. Notch aerials fitted in the root of each wing leading edge are used for the HF system. A pressurised aerial tuner is housed in each notch; tuning is instantaneous and controlled by the navigator. The main VHF/UHF suppressed aerial is mounted below a glass-fibre cover in the fin tip, whilst the gap-filler aerial is positioned below the forward fuselage. This aerial also serves as the aerial for the standby system. Selection of alternative aerials is performed by the pilot. All the ECM aerials are of wide band design covering the full radar frequency spectrum. The EM and SIF transponder systems are controlled from panels at the navigator's station. The pilot's and navigator's stations are both equipped with integrated control panels permitting either crew member to use any of the communication facilities. Standby equipment and duplication of intercommunication channels assures reliable operation of these key features. In order to avoid visual distraction, the pilot's VHF/UHF channel selector is fitted with an annunciator, whereby he is verbally informed of the channel selected by means of pre-recorded tape.

The electrical power system, for which Rotax were the principal subcontractors, is tailored to the requirements of the electronics systems. The environmental temperature in which the generators have to operate – imposed by supersonic flight plus local engine temperatures – is well above the limits of previous designs. With the conventional salient-pole type of generator, mechanical difficulties were encountered under conditions of high temperature and vibration. Accordingly, solid-rotor air-cooled alternators, with no rotating windings, were specified for TSR2. This is believed to be the first time that solid-rotor alternators have been used in a major power-generating system. Another unusual feature of the electrical system is the adoption of solid-state voltage regulators for high-speed response; these were subcontracted by Rotax to Mullard Ltd. Each main solid-rotor alternator is driven by a Plessey constant speed drive, and supplied 30-55kVA output for the two main ac generating channels. A solid-rotor alternator, with its associated regulator, is driven by a Lucas hydraulic motor and provides what is a constant-frequency supply for a third emergency channel. Rotax, who have vast testing facilities, were responsible for the co-ordination of the generating systems, and over 2,500 hours development time was spent in determining the various characteristics. In addition, the alternator and associated equipment were subjected to environmental tests, including altitude and temperature. In TSR2, the central digital computing system is supplied by Elliott Flight Automation. The sensor group, consisting of inertial platform (Ferranti), forward-looking radar (Ferranti), sideways-looking radar (EMI), Doppler (Decca) and air-data system (Smiths) provide raw signals to the computer. The computer processes these signals to provide outputs for the display of position and steering information (Smiths, Rank-Cintel head-up display) and also for the direct control of the aircraft through the autopilot (Elliott Flight Automation) and for the preparation and release of weapons. The computer selected for the aircraft is a much-modified version of the Verdan system created by Autonetics in the US, but subsequently developed under licence in the UK by Elliott. Two computers are installed to ensure redundancy, should one system fail, although the computers are entirely independent and cannot communicate with each other. While the computing system can be programmed by means of previously-prepared tapes for a very wide range of military missions, the crew are not, in fact, immutably tied down to a pre-programmed flight. Should local or tactical considerations demand a change of in-flight plan, the crew can feed in the necessary information and the pilot can at any time take charge manually. Outputs provided by the Smiths air-data computer include true airspeed, Mach number, rate of climb, altitude, indicated airspeed, dynamic pressure, static pressure, stagnation temperature and rate of change of height. Corrections for pressure error and Mach number are also incorporated. Ferranti's forward-looking radar provides terrain-following signals to allow the aircraft to approach its target at very low level, safe from detection by enemy ground radars. Ferranti also provide the stable platform used in the Doppler/inertial navigation system, a three-gyro and four-gimbal system, fully manoeuvrable. The Doppler radar, supplied by Decca Radar Ltd, measures ground speed and drift angle to a very high degree of accuracy throughout the complete flight envelope, and under extremely severe environmental conditions. As with all TSR2 subsystems, maximum reliability is a prime consideration, and a high degree of fail-safe operation is included. Outputs are available in both analogue and digital form. Two sideways-looking radars are installed in TSR2, both supplied by EMI Electronics Ltd. One is for navigational purposes, for correcting Doppler/inertial fixes. The other is a new electronic aid to aerial reconnaissance: this radar looks sideways and downwards from the aircraft, with the radar beam fixed nominally at right angles to the fore-and-aft axis. As the aerial does not rotate and lays parallel to the axis of the aircraft, it is made comparatively long, so giving a narrow beam width and better resolution. The time-base trace, which 'paints' the picture on a radar screen, is kept stationary on a small display tube, and a long strip of film is moved past this display at a rate proportional to the ground speed. The film thus forms a complete record of what the radar has seen. Such a radar can 'see' through cloud and operates equally effectively in the dark. The mapping picture can reveal geographical features such as rivers, lakes and hills, and can also define man-made features such as roads, canals and buildings. Moving-target indication can also be provided, to make moving targets show up on the radar map in a distinctive fashion. Objects such as bridges and high buildings will screen the area behind them from the radar beam and will cause the formation of shadows on the film record. The films can be developed and processed rapidly on return to base, and skilled interpreters are therefore able to give the Command detailed information within a few minutes about the area which has been reconnoitred. Line-scan is another form of reconnaissance device supplied for TSR2 by EMI Electronics. This is an optical scanning system which can be likened to an 'electronic eye' scanning the ground beneath the aircraft. It is possible to have both a passive and an active form. In the passive role the electronic eye scans without any illumination. In the active mode, a spot of light scans at the same time as the electronic eye, so illuminating the portion of the ground at which the eye is looking. The system can be used at night to give a performance comparable with that obtained during daylight, with little chance of detection. The output can be recorded in the aircraft or transmitted back to base by TV link. TR unit for the reconnaissance radar is made by Mullard Ltd, and the IFF system is provided by Cossor. The Marconi Company's contributions to TSR2 include high power HF communications equipment (which provides both single and double-sideband transmission at high

output power) and the instrument landing system from the Marconi Sixty Series. The latter, fully transistorized and incorporating new constructional techniques for maximum reliability in service, included localiser, glide-slope and marker beacon reception (other aircraft using this series of equipment include the VC10, Trident and BAC-111 airliners). Other electronic equipment includes communications radio by The Plessey Co (UK) Ltd, and a radio altimeter by Standard Telephones and Cables. Moving-map displays, provided for both pilot and navigator, were developed for TSR2 by Ferranti Ltd. The displays use standard topographical charts photographed on 35mm colour film which is projected optically on to a ground-glass screen. As the aircraft moves over the ground, the projected map moves under a fixed marker which indicates the instantaneous position of the aircraft, and a pointer indicates aircraft track. The two displays are driven under command from a computer which accepts navigational inputs from the aircraft's central digital computer. A large number of maps can be stored on the film. This Ferranti system was developed from an invention by RAE Farnborough, who themselves did a great deal of work on the project. The film strip is driven along its length for change of East headings, and across its width for change of North headings, by means of M-type repeater servos driven by a suitable ground-position computer. The display map can be either North-stabilized or Track-stabilized. With North-stabilized, North is at the top of the display and the rotating compass bezel, calibrated in degrees, will be stationary. The track input drives the track line which rotates about the present position indicator to show the track across the map. When track stabilized, the track line is fixed on the vertical diameter, and the track input used to rotate the map and the degrees scale together. In the Ferranti system, track stabilization is carried out optically by means of a servo-driven prism in the optical projection system, and the track input is in the form of a synchro transmission. An electro mechanical computer accepts ground-speed information and contains an electro mechanical memory system for storing resolved ground mileage information during a map-change sequence. A control panel on one display unit provides for selecting and accurately positioning the required map. North/South map changes can be made semi-automatically; East/West changes are made manually. TSR2's head-up display subsystem is provided by the Rank-Cintel division of the Rank Organization. It presents attitude information in relation to the outside world, throughout the flight, by reflection on to the windscreen. Developed from earlier systems produced for the Buccaneer, it consists of two units: the pilot's display unit and display computer. The data input signals are provided by the aircraft nav-attack subsystems, and are processed by the display computer to provide bright-up and deflection voltages for the pilot's display unit. This unit contains a 3in high-intensity cathode-ray tube, on the face of which are written the symbols or combination of symbols that are utilised for a given flight mode. The display generated on the CRT is collimated by a 6in Fl lens and reflected directly on to the windscreen, so that the pilot is able to view the display, at infinity focus, from the normal head position. This was the first head-up display installation designed to reflect the display directly on to the windscreen. In previous installations an intermediate 50/50 reflector had been necessary. The Head Up Display was to have been projected directly onto the inner face of the windscreen, and the foremost inner surface was manufactured from high-quality optical glass in order to provide a sharp visual presentation, but early experience with the two completed prototype aircraft suggested that wave distortion would have made HUD resolution unreliable and the production version of the HUD system would probably have incorporated a separate internal reflective screen, similar to that employed in modern combat aircraft. One of the largest periscopes built by Smiths, the TSR2 navigator's downward sight, is servo-driven both in elevation and in azimuth. With ability to rotate through 360° in azimuth, the instrument provides a very wide field of vision. The navigator's combined instrument display supplied by Smiths presents on a single panel three indications: vertical speed, altitude (by counter/pointer display) and airspeed information. The airspeed indicator is servo-driven from the air-data computer. The servo-altimeter supplies information in digital form, so that data can be fed to other systems should this be necessary. The digital encoder can be set manually. Three indications are displayed on the ASI: Doppler ground-speed transmitted by torque synchro link from the Doppler equipment; computed ground-speed fed by torque synchro from the navigational computer; and true airspeed fed by servo from the air-data computer. Also supplied by Smiths, the pilot's altimeter was similar to that included in the navigator's display. The digital encoder, however, is replaced by a precision potentiometer, and feeds altitude information to the head-up display, hence there is no manual setting facility. A stand-by altimeter is also supplied. The pilot's head-down display, developed from a flight-data system designed by Smiths specifically for high-performance military aircraft, presents two instruments which combine the function of a normal set of flight and radio-navigation instruments. ILS, attitude, slip, localizer, compass and heading information is shown. The windscreen (designed and manufactured by the Triplex Safety Glass Company) is designed to withstand a 3lb bird strike and incorporates a hot air rain-dispersal system which utilises air bled from the engine to keep the pilot's forward view clear of rain or insect debris. The main canopy components are manufactured from Plexiglas 55 and all of the transparent surfaces include a layer of gold film which facilitates rapid demisting as required.

Since the powered flying controls were highly integrated with the aerodynamics of TSR2, BAC (Preston) set up a special joint management system with the system subcontractor, H. M. Hobson Ltd. So that if any urgent changes in the agreed specification were required, under the joint management system these could be carried out with the minimum of delay. Each powered flying control unit comprises hydraulic jacks responding to pilot control movements or autopilot demand via electronic signals. In developing the primary and ancillary flying controls – namely, fin, taileron, airbrakes, wing flaps, taileron flaps and pilot feel – H.M. Hobson were faced with a design requirement surpassing anything previously attempted in Europe. Control specifications were based upon the need to satisfy a high-speed, terrain-following capability within the environments evoked by supersonic all-weather conditions. The terrain-following mode dictates that positional accuracy of every surface, in response to a signalled input, should be of an unusually high order. The

considerable inherent structural elasticity and control-surface inertia necessitated the development of powered controls with unique stabilizing concepts. Special approaches were evolved to assess stiffness and mass effects. Manufacturing methods were refined to produce a new class of controls giving accuracies better than 0.1 per cent, and yet with parts having a useful service life. Extremes of environment pioneered the use of new materials, techniques and processes. Much of the development programme carried out was to prove the capability under simulated flight conditions of special fluids, seal arrangements and treated materials. An extensive test laboratory was commissioned specifically for this purpose. The performance requirements supplied by the contractor were progressive, and left little or no margin for change. Only by insisting on such requirements could the necessary breakthrough in control engineering, compatible with the demand of the aircraft, be achieved.

As already mentioned, the aircraft hydraulic systems operate on DP.47 Silicodyne H fluid. For weight-saving, an operating pressure of 4,000Ib/sq in was adopted. This involved a development problem in itself, accentuated by exacting response requirements coupled with the inevitable contamination encountered in service and the high-temperature environment. Pumps and various valves for the hydraulic system were supplied by Lucas; other valves and selectors were supplied by Dowty-Rotol Ltd, who also contributed the two accessory gearboxes. One installation problem encountered with the hydraulics was to achieve satisfactory pipe couplings. The traditional bell-mouthed pipe and screwed coupling proved inadequate to stand up to service conditions, and it was found necessary to develop a method of brazing in situ on the aircraft. This process, developed at Warton, demanded precise dimensioning of the pipes to be joined. The two ends were closely mated, and the joint effected by brazing on a sleeve in an argon atmosphere both inside and outside the pipe. An expendable induction coil was used to raise the temperature to 1,000°C, the heating equipment being by Radyne Ltd. The process was used on stainless-steel pipes from 0.5in to 2.5in diameter. Electro-Hydraulics Ltd was also involved with the manufacture and development testing of many items of hydraulic equipment for the TSR2. The main features in which these components differed from those generally in use were in the wide temperature range to be met and in the use of titanium. Titanium presents no difficulty in manufacture but an appreciable development programme had to be undertaken to find materials which could be used in bearing contact with it. It was also necessary to develop suitable seals for the extreme temperatures, and to ensure that all components worked satisfactorily with DP.47 fluid. Internal fuel capacity is spread between tanks spread along the fuselage. The forward group (tanks 1 and 2) contain 9,060lb and 8,182lb respectively, whilst the rear group (3 and 4) have respective capacities of 7,391lb and 7,270lb. Additionally, the main wing box also acts as a fuel tank and holds a further 11,792lb. External fuel capacity is confined to a pair of drop tanks which can be carried on the wing inner weapons pylon, each with a capacity of 3,600lb. Further development may have included alternative drop tank derivatives and a large ventral tank. In-flight refuelling capacity is also incorporated into the fuel system, the necessary extendible probe being housed in a bolt-on fairing positioned on the port forward fuselage.

The low-pressure fuel boost system, supplied by Lucas Gas Turbine Equipment Ltd, includes a centrifugal fuel booster pump, tank balancing valve and low-pressure warning switch. A number of other specialist companies also contributed; notably, valves were supplied by the Saunders Valve Co Ltd, Normalair Ltd and Flight Refuelling Ltd. Fuel-gauging was developed by Smiths, the design being based on well-proven equipment which used the capacitance principle. The system incorporates reference units which compensate for variations in fuel permittivity over a given range. Control and distribution of fuel to maintain a predetermined centre of gravity, and automatic control of refuel/defuel operations, are examples of fuel management which are performed by the system. The whole fuel system was worked out at Warton on a full-scale rig to ensure proper sequencing of all the valves under every feed combination and in every flight configuration. Sir George Godfrey & Partners were the principal subcontractors for the TSR2 air conditioning system, which serves the crew compartments, and also for cooling the equipment in the electronics bay. Subcontractors to Godfrey were Marston Excelsior (heat exchangers), Teddington Aircraft Controls Ltd (temperature control) and Normalair Ltd (pressure control). Two air-cycle bootstrap cold-air units are used, of which one is a standby automatically brought into operation should the working unit fail. The system is unusual in that mass airflow to the crew can be varied, as well as temperature. Another unusual feature of the air-conditioning system is the use of fuel-cooled heat exchangers. The system was designed to maintain the crew in comfort, at a mean cabin temperature of 15°C, without the use of special clothing. Nevertheless provision is made for fitting ventilated suits. The escape system, including canopy jettison arrangements and mechanisms, together with two advanced rocket ejection seats (Mk.8VA models), was designed, developed and manufactured by the Martin-Baker Aircraft Co, in close association with BAC. Since the operational role of this aircraft involves protracted high-speed flying at low altitudes, very exacting demands are placed on the emergency escape system. Among many new features of the seats and canopy jettison arrangements are the facilities for rapid exit, the power to obtain a high trajectory peak, and maximum structural strength to endure ejection at high indicated airspeeds near the ground. Furthermore, extensive detail-design improvements were made to the structures and mechanisms to ensure reliability, efficiency and to afford maximum protection against damage during ejection. Both seats are designed to operate at all speeds and height from a minimum of zero feet and zero forward speed, up to an altitude of 56,000ft and a speed of 650kt/Mach 2.0. Ease of servicing is obtained by providing for the quick removal of the seat pan, parachute and headrest assemblies, as well as time-delay mechanisms, whilst the structure remains in the aircraft. An exceptionally high degree of comfort for the crew is achieved, and the harness restraint is particularly effective. A hand operated ratchet control positioned on the left side of the seat enables the pilot and navigator to obtain any desired degree of harness tightness instantly, as well as to slacken off for comfort; pre-tensioning of the harness is ballistically accomplished immediately before ejection. The navigator can jettison his canopy and eject at any time; if the pilot should operate his seat firing with the navigator still in the aircraft, then the navigator

would be ejected first, followed automatically by the pilot. This arrangement eliminates the need for an abandonment command by the pilot and subsequent action by the navigator, thus reducing abandonment time – a vital requirement in emergency escapes near the ground. Automatic harness pre-tensioning and effective head restraint brings both the pilot and navigator into a favourable posture before ejection at all times, and this facility ensures a satisfactory posture for the navigator if he is fired out by the pilot. Propulsion is provided by an ejection gun of proven efficiency and reliability, and the thrust thus obtained is augmented by the thrust developed by the Martin patented rocket motor fitted underneath the seat pan. Peak acceleration and onset of g are held at a much lower level than in earlier types of seat. This propulsion system was developed and verified by a most extensive test programme, including a number of live ejections. Unusually for aircraft of this era, the crew are equipped with arm restraint connections which automatically pull back the crew's arms into the seat when it is fired, in much the same way as more typical leg restraints function on other contemporary seats.

Armament Installation

The TSR2 weapons bay occupies the lower part of the fuselage. It is 20ft long, has a cross section of approximately 36in by 18in and is equipped with hydraulically operated doors. Two external pylons on each wing may be used for weapons; underwing fuel tanks may be carried at the inboard stations. An indication of the wide variety of loads which may be carried is illustrated. To load the weapons bay the selected bombs are fitted into the appropriate carrier which is equipped with the store ejectors. This carrier is then raised into the bay either by the portable hoists carried by the aircraft or by using the Universal Lifting Trolley. The complete package of bombs and carrier is retained in the bay by a clip-in system which allows quick installation and removal. Swinging suspension links isolate structural deflections from the weapons package. To release the stores, the weapons bay doors are opened, the store ejectors fired, and the doors closed. The complete store release sequence takes five seconds, minimising the aerodynamic disturbance to the aircraft. The store ejectors are operated by electrically initiated explosive cartridges which give the stores an ejection velocity of about 25fps. A similar arrangement is used for the wing pylon store positions. Full jettison facilities are provided for emergency use. The various access panels and windows in the stores which may require late inspection can all be reached without difficulty through the open weapons bay doors or via the undercarriage bay walls. Armament control panels are fitted at the navigator's station enabling him to select the weapons to be released, and the appropriate fusing. Bombs can be released separately or together.

Reconnaissance Installation

The reconnaissance pack is mounted in the weapons bay after removal of the doors. It is designed for rapid clip-in installation using standard ground equipment only. Installation of the complete reconnaissance pack can be effected by the Universal Lifting Trolley or by 'Minilift' hoists and a standard bomb trolley. The pack is divided into a forward equipment

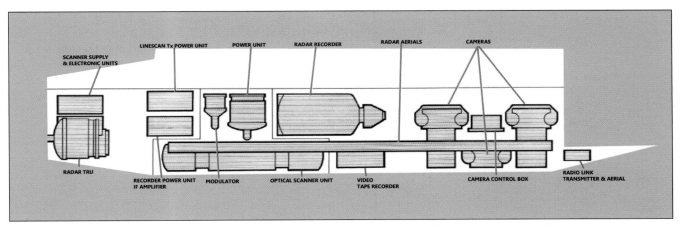

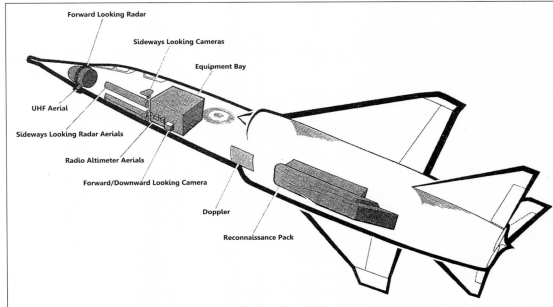

Above: Contemporary diagram showing main Radar and Reconnaissance systems.

Right: Camera and equipment stowage in the Reconnaissance role.

compartment and a rear camera compartment. The cameras are mounted in the rear and the linescan unit towards the forward end, with the sideways looking radar aerials occupying almost the full length of the pack along each side. Various electronic units are carried in the forward bay of the pack and this equipment can be rapidly serviced through doors and access panels in the base. Full air conditioning of the pack is maintained during flight and connectors are provided for external ground conditioning. The linescan data link transmitter and its steerable aerial are installed in the reconnaissance pack. The direction in which the aerial points is computed from navigation information and the known position of the ground receiving station. The camera windows in the pack are protected by electrically operated shutters and hot air demisting prevents optical distortion. Provision is made for the use of hoists within the pack to facilitate the removal of heavy components. The cameras are mounted on a frame so that the complete installation can be lowered through the servicing door for rapid magazine changing. Similar arrangements are made to allow quick replacement of the linescan recorder spools. Control of all the reconnaissance equipment is the responsibility of the navigator who has two control panels which replace the weapon controls fitted in the strike role. In addition to the reconnaissance pack

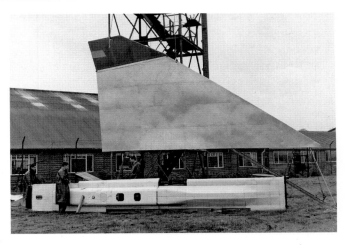

Rare photograph of the reconnaissance pod designed for TSR2. In this picture a trials pod is being positioned next to a TSR2 wing mock-up for a polar diagram test. *Brooklands Museum*

the aircraft carries three fixed cameras in the nose. These, together with the sideways looking navigation radar, enable a limited amount of reconnaissance information to be obtained when the aircraft is operating in the strike role.

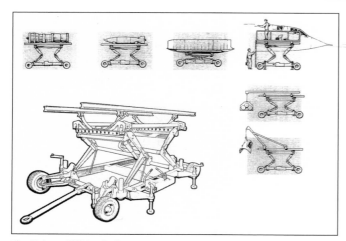

The Universal Lifting Trolley.

Ground Equipment

Special attention has been given to the ground equipment for TSR2 to reduce weight and size to facilitate air transportability.

Ground Servicing Vehicle

This vehicle provides the numerous services normally drawn from a large number of separate trucks and trailers and thus reduces very considerably the logistic effort involved in air lifting ground support equipment. The services provided are:-

Air for engine starting – at 4lb per second at 60psi.

Air conditioning – two independent temperature controlled air supplies within the temperature range of 0-40 degrees Centigrade.

Electrical supplies – Up to 20 kVA at 200V 3-phase AC

Hydraulic replenishing – Delivers hydraulic fluid against a back pressure of up to 80 psi.

Hydraulic power – Two independent supplies each provide up to 32 gallons per minute at 4,000 psi.

Hydraulic power off-take – A supply of 87 gallons per minute at 4,000 psi to drive a hydraulic motor to provide power for auxiliary services such as refuelling or water replenishing pumps, fuel pump test rig, etc.

Towing or pushing – A tractive effort of 10,000lb

The vehicle is therefore capable of towing the aircraft to a refuelling area, powering the refuelling and water replenishing units, producing electrical and air conditioning facilities, and replenishing and function testing the hydraulic systems as required. The vehicle can then tow the aircraft to its standby position and maintain it at instant readiness for periods up to 30 days. Although the airborne auxiliary power plant installation is capable of maintaining the aircraft at readiness and providing a one minute start, the General Servicing vehicle provides these services without consuming fuel from the aircraft or using up the life of aircraft components, and also enables the aircraft to react with full fuel load in 30 seconds. If desired, two aircraft can be held at readiness by one vehicle and started consecutively in a total time of approximately one minute. The vehicle has sufficient clearance to negotiate a 20 degree ramp angle and has been designed for transportation in

an AW.660 Argosy freighter or similar type of aircraft. Slinging discs are provided on all four wheels for lifting. The multi-fuel engine drives the electrical and hydraulic outputs. The hydraulic power available is also used to drive the vehicle; a hydraulic transmission obviates the need for clutches, gearbox and differentials. The driver's cabin, apart from the normal controls, also contains the instruments and controls for the various services to the aircraft. The cabin is air conditioned to enable the operator to work efficiently under any conditions.

Universal Lifting Trolley

The universal lifting trolley and its associated equipment provide a quick and safe method of removal, transfer and installation of heavy aircraft components such as the engine, radar, mainplane and weapons. The trolley can also be used as a servicing platform. The lifting rails are capable of movement laterally and vertically. The trolley has four wheels and is hydraulically operated by an electrically operated power pack with provision for manual operation. The trolley has been designed for air transportability.

Hydraulic Test equipment

This is a diesel-driven pump unit delivering 30 gallons per minute at 4,000 psi. It may be used at base when the general Servicing Vehicle is not available. This pump will replace any one of the four pumps carried in the aircraft; a four-pump rig is not used as this would be unwieldy. The Hydraulic Fluid Dispenser replenishes the hydraulic fluid in the aircraft; a special connector is fitted to ensure that the correct hydraulic fluid is used. The equipment includes filtration facilities so that the hydraulic fluid in the aircraft may be cleaned. It is able to operate against a back pressure of 80 psi.

System Test Equipment

The navigator of TSR2 is provided with limited go/no go test facilities for the navigation and attack system. These test may be conducted on the ground before take-off or in the air. For more comprehensive testing and fault diagnosis, automatic and manual test equipment is available. The Automatic Test equipment (ATE) is contained in a four-wheel trailer. It is connected to the aircraft through a number of cables plugged into the equipment bay. By means of a tape programmed test sequence, the ATE feeds signals into the aircraft sensing elements and checks that the corresponding outputs appear in the correct places. If a fault is indicated, further programmes are initiated by the ATE until the tests show which removable package is unserviceable. This can then be replaced and the defective unit returned for base servicing. A self-checking tape programme is also provided in the ATE. The equipment is rack-mounted in a four-wheeled, weather-proofed trailer containing the central control and evaluation equipment. The top of this trailer has a non-slip surface which is usable as a work platform for access to the aircraft equipment bay. The ATE trailer is able to negotiate a 20-degree ramp angle and is designed for transportation in the AW.660 Argosy freighter or similar aircraft. For use at base and in equipment servicing centres, special-to-type annual test equipment of conventional design is also available.

Leading particulars

TSR2 (Supermarine Type 571)

WEIGHTS	DIMENSIONS
Take-off weight (normal) for 1,000 nm sortie – 95,000lb	Length overall – 89 ft
Take-off weight for 450 nm sortie – 78,000 lb	Height overall – 24 ft
Landing weight – 57,200lb	Wing span – 37 ft
	Wing area – 700 sq ft
	Aspect ratio – 2

POWER PLANT	UNDERCARRIAGE
Two Bristol-Siddeley Olympus 22R engines	Airfield load classification number
Total thrust (dry) – 39,200 lb	At 95,900 lb (rigid runway) – 29
Total thrust (with reheat) – 61,220 lb	At 95,900 lb (flexible runway) – 26
Internal fuel capacity – 5,588 gal (6,711 US gal)	At 78,800 lb (rigid runway) – 23
	At 78,800 lb (flexible runway) – 19
	Minimum turning circle – 58 ft
	Tyre pressure
	At 95,900 lb – 105 psi
	At 78,800 lb – 86 psi

PERFORMANCE

Maximum Speed at sea level – 840mph (Mach 1.1)
Maximum speed at 30,000ft – 1,350mph plus (up to Mach 2.25)
Climb Rate – 50,000ft/min at sea level
Tactical radius – 1,500 miles (varying, depending on external loads)
Ferry range – 3,300 miles or 4,250 miles with external tanks
Weapons load – 6,000lb internal, 8,000lb external

For the flight test programme, Airborne recorders were ordered from Royston Instruments Ltd, designers and makers of the MIDAS range of flight-data recorders and data-processing systems, for installation in TSR2 development aircraft. The equipment was ejectable complete with recovery aids: parachute, flotation bag, UHF homing beacon and marker dye. It could record 270 channels of information every 0.6sec. Production aircraft would have been equipped with similar crash recorder equipment manufactured by Redifon Ltd.

Aircraft Production

The Pre-Production Batch

Contract KD/2L/02CB42a was placed on 6 October 1960, covering the production of nine aircraft, XR219 to XR227:

XR219 (K0.1)

Although referred to as the prototype, the production line method of construction for the first batch of development aircraft meant that there was no true prototype as such. However XR219 was the first aircraft to be completed and was, of course, the only aircraft to fly, and conducted all of the initial flight-test programme up until the project's cancellation. Retained at Warton until August 1965, the aircraft was dismantled and transported by road to the P&EE at Shoeburyness where it was subsequently re-assembled and used for destructive testing. It was virtually destroyed by the mid-1970s. The remains of the airframe were eventually removed as scrap during the early 1980s.

XR220 (K0.2)

The second TSR2, XR220 was scheduled to join the flight-test

programme in 1964 but after suffering major damage during transportation to Boscombe Down, the aircraft was not ready for flight until the day of the project's cancellation in April 1965. After initial shake-down flights, the aircraft was to have been allocated to flutter and stability investigations and engine development, together with research into airframe structural temperatures. During 1966 the aircraft was to be assigned to vibration measurement trials followed by low-speed handling trials, buffet and stall investigations. In 1967 the aircraft would be assigned to the A&AEE for initial assessment before being returned to BAC, after which the aircraft was to have been mostly assigned to the carriage of external stores, and the aircraft was fitted with cameras (housed in fairings attached to the sides of the engine intakes) to record these trials. Following cancellation of the programme, the aircraft was retained at Boscombe Down for ground trials associated with engine development and noise investigations, which continued until the end of 1966. The aircraft was subsequently transported to Henlow by road and placed in storage, before being moved to Cosford, where the aircraft was placed on permanent public display.

XR221 (K0.3)

The third aircraft on the production line, XR221 was assigned to avionics development and pre-production examples of the various systems were installed in the aircraft during 1964 with ground trials beginning at Wisley early in 1965. A fully representative sortie was successfully performed on the ground and revealed that, contrary to expectations, the systems all functioned very well. BAC anticipated few significant problems to develop once the aircraft's flight trials began. The

Test Flights

Sortie No.	Date	Duration	Pilot	Navigator/Observer	
1	24/09/64	00:14	Beamont	Bowen	Boscombe Down
2	31/12/64	00:14	Beamont	Bowen	Boscombe Down
3	02/01/65	00:08	Beamont	Bowen	Boscombe Down
4	08/01/65	00:20	Beamont	Bowen	Boscombe Down
5	14/01/65	00:22	Beamont	Bowen	Boscombe Down
6	15/01/65	00:24	Dell	Bowen	Boscombe Down
7	22/01/65	00:28	Beamont	Moneypenny	Boscombe Down
8	23/01/65	00:27	Dell	Moneypenny	Boscombe Down
9	27/01/65	00:22	Beamont	Bowen	Boscombe Down
10	06/02/65	00:29	Beamont	Bowen	Boscombe Down
11	08/02/65	00:38	Dell	Moneypenny	Boscombe Down
12	10/02/65	00:36	Knight	Moneypenny	Boscombe Down
13	16/02/65	00:45	Dell	Bowen	Boscombe Down
14	22/02/65	00:41	Beamont	Moneypenny	To Warton (including supersonic run)
15	25/02/65	01:12	Dell	Moneypenny	Warton
16	26/02/65	00:47	Beamont	Moneypenny	Warton
17	08/03/65	00:52	Dell	McCann	Warton
18	08/03/65	00:35	Dell	Moneypenny	Warton
19	11/03/65	00:33	Dell	McCann	Warton
20	12/03/65	00:46	Dell	Moneypenny	Warton
21	26/03/65	00:33	Dell	McCann	Warton
22	26/03/65	00:35	Dell	McCann	Warton
23	27/03/65	00:34	Knight	Moneypenny	Warton
24	31/03/65	00:32	Dell	McCann	Warton

aircraft was scheduled to go to Boscombe Down late in 1965 for assessment of the navigation and attack system and after further modifications by BAC, the aircraft was scheduled to return to the A&AEE in 1966. From late 1966 onwards XR221 was to conduct terrain-following radar trials, after which BAC would operate the aircraft for auto-navigation and auto-attack development until the end of 1968. When the programme was cancelled, the airframe was dismantled at Wisley and transported to the P&EE at Shoeburyness. There is no evidence to suggest that it was re-assembled and the various components were removed from the site as scrap by the early 1980s.

XR222 (K0.4)

Initially assigned to auto-stabilisation and longitudinal handling research, XR222 was then expected to explore height, heading and speed lock capabilities and mode integration within the supersonic envelope, after which A&AEE would acquire the aircraft for systems assessment. Subsequently, the aircraft was to have been allocated to auto-ILS trials, followed by an investigation of manual terrain following, leading to auto-terrain-following trials in 1968. Finally, it was expected that the aircraft would conduct auto-terrain-following whilst carrying external loads. After the project's cancellation, the airframe was dismantled at Weybridge and removed by road to Cranfield where it was assigned to the Institute of Technology for ground-training purposes, although it is believed that some of the components came from other airframes, therefore the surviving aircraft may well be a composite assembly. It was then placed in external storage on the airfield at Cranfield and finally transferred to the Imperial War Museum at Duxford,

where it was fully restored to exhibition standard and placed on permanent public display.

XR223 (K0.5)

The first of the remaining pre-production batch which was not completed at the time of cancellation, XR223 was expected to begin flight trials towards the end of 1965 and initially would have been assigned to aerodynamic trials with both canopies removed, together with preliminary investigations of the aircraft's weapon delivery systems. In 1966 the aircraft was expected to undertake air system trials and structural temperature investigations and would then be prepared for tropical trials which were to begin early in 1967. At the point of cancellation, the airframe components were removed from Weybridge as scrap.

XR224 (K0.6)

Scheduled to first fly in October 1966, this aircraft was allocated to engine and airframe performance trails which would include periodic assignments to Boscombe Down for assessment by A&AEE crews. By the end of 1967 it was to have been assigned to external stores carriage trials. Incomplete at the time of cancellation, the airframe components were removed from Weybridge as scrap.

XR225 (K0.7)

Expected to join the test programme in 1966, XR225 would have first been assigned to fuel, hydraulic and electrical system trials, and it is believed that this aircraft would have been fitted with an in-flight refuelling probe system to undertake

preliminary air-to-air refuelling trials. It was then expected to
be fitted with a development-standard reconnaissance pack in
the weapons bay for initial investigations which would
continue into the summer of 1967, followed by more advanced
reconnaissance trials in 1968. The airframe components were
removed as scrap when the project was cancelled.

XR226 (K0.8)

This aircraft was expected to perform a significant amount of
the navigation and attack trials, based on earlier preliminary
assessment, together with the first trials of the radio systems.
These trials would lead to fully representative sorties (including
attack manoeuvres) at subsonic speeds, eventually leading to
further trials at supersonic speeds, at altitude. Once these trials
were complete, XR226 was expected to conduct a number of
proving flights. After cancellation, the aircraft's components
were removed from Weybridge as scrap.

XR227 (K0.9)

The final aircraft in the pre-production batch, XR227 was
expected to begin flight trials early in 1966 and would have
been assigned to development of internal and external weapons
carriage, with stores ranging from 950lb up to 2,100lb in
weight, and including assessment periods with the A&AEE.
The first trials would cover stores carried in the weapons bay,
but later trials would extend to cover various stores options
which could be carried on the wing hard points, including
rocket packs, with all of these trials expected to be concluded
by the end of 1968. As the last aircraft of the batch, the aircraft
had not progressed far into the assembly line at Weybridge by
the time of cancellation, and the various components were
removed as scrap together with all other surviving parts from
the first full production batch order.

Contract No. KD/2L/13/CB42a placed on 28 June 1963
covered a batch of 11 aircraft, serials XS660 to XS670. The
first five of these aircraft were provisionally allocated to trials
and evaluation work (and would probably have been assigned
to the A&AEE at Boscombe Down), the remainder of the
batch being delivered directly to the RAF at Coningsby.

Contract No. KD/2L/16/CB42a placed on 20 March 1954
completed the initial production order with a further 19 aircraft,
serials XS944 to XS954 and XS977 to XS995. These were to
have been operational aircraft and would probably have been
assigned to No. 40 Squadron and/or No. 237 OCU at Coningsby.

At the time of cancellation, no further serial allocations had
been made in anticipation of any further orders, although the
subsequent allocation of serials for the proposed purchase of
F-111K's suggests that the remainder of TSR2's production
run would have been allocated serials from the ranges XV884
to XV887 and XV902 to XV947.

Proposals for Operational Service

Very few plans for TSR2's anticipated operational debut had been
completed at the time when the project was cancelled. With the
prospect of squadron service still at least four years away, planning
was at a very early stage in 1965 and although some evidence of
the RAF's intentions did survive, there is very little which can be

relied upon as a definitive guide to how and where the aircraft
would have been operated. The most useful guide to the RAF's
plans was a costing report issued in March 1964 (often referred-to
as 'Plan P') which suggested that the RAF was anticipating an
eventual delivery of 193 aircraft which would be distributed
between two bomber squadrons and one reconnaissance squadron
in the UK, two bomber squadrons and two reconnaissance
squadrons based in Germany, two bomber squadrons and one
reconnaissance squadron with the Near East Air Force, and one
combined bomber and reconnaissance squadron with the Far East
Air Force. The projected front line strength of TSR2 aircraft was
expected to be 106 aircraft, with a further 18 machines assigned
to an Operational Conversion Unit, and other aircraft held in
reserve or assigned to trials and evaluation work.

Of course, this report can only be regarded as a guide to what
might have happened, and ultimately may have been very
different from reality, not least in terms of the overall number
of aircraft purchased – a figure which always looked likely to
be reduced to a minimum. An additional report was issued later
in March 1964 (the 'Spotswood Report') which offered a
slightly different account of how TSR2 might be deployed,
suggesting that 123 aircraft could be distributed between the UK
(63 aircraft assigned to NATO, replacing Valiants and
Canberras), 20 aircraft assigned to NEAF, 20 aircraft assigned
to FEAF (provided on rotation from the UK) and a further 20
aircraft held as a strategic reserve, eight of which would be
assigned to NATO. Significantly, this report also suggested that
there was no reason why any of the TSR2 squadrons should be
deployed in Germany and – thanks to the aircraft's excellent
range capability – these aircraft could be based in the UK where
they would be less vulnerable to surprise attack. However, both
reports were no more than proposals which would undoubtedly
have been succeeded by more concrete plans at a later date, and
the precise nature of TSR2's operational disposal will now never
be known. Perhaps the most reliable indication of how the
aircraft might have been deployed, is an appraisal of how the
RAF's forces were assigned in the early 1970s. The Buccaneer
strike squadrons (effectively TSR2's direct replacements) were
eventually based at Laarbruch, therefore it seems reasonable to
assume that TSR2 would also have been based there, divided
between two squadrons, with either a secondary reconnaissance
capability, or with a third squadron assigned specifically to the
role (probably depending upon how many aircraft were finally
ordered). It is known that Laarbruch was identified as a potential
base for the aircraft, as was Bruggen, although some documents
suggest that Geilenkirchen was also considered at some stage.

In the UK, plans were made for the aircraft to enter RAF
service at Coningsby, where an Operational Development
Squadron was to be formed, once the first aircraft were ready
for delivery. The ODS (which was to have been No. 40
Squadron) would have been tasked with the training of the first
OCU instructors and to evaluate the aircraft in the context of
operational usage, equipped with first six aircraft from the
initial production batch. These would later be joined by an
additional six aircraft and the squadron would have then
become an operational unit, moving to Honington in the
process. Back at Coningsby, the Operational Conversion Unit
(designated as No. 237 OCU) would have then assumed all

XR222 undergoing restoration at Duxford, illustrating the (empty) sideways-looking radar bay, the starboard camera bay (also empty), and the all-white fibreglass nose cone. As with other contemporary RAF aircraft, it seems certain that when the aircraft was painted in camouflage colours for operational use, the radome would eventually have been painted black. *BAE Haeritage*

XR222 posing for media photographers after completion of a thorough restoration programme at Duxford. Only two TSR2 airframes survice, the other being with the Royal Air Force Museum at Cosford. Both are hugely popular attractions for visitors. *BAE Heritage*

Pictured enjoying some post-restoration sunshine, the freshly-painted XR222 illustrates her clean lines. The damaged windscreen shows evidence of age-related de-lamination but in all other respects the aircraft looks as if she has just emerged from the Weybridge production line. *BAE Heritage*

training requirements for the aircraft, equipped with up to 18 aircraft, together with a fleet of up to 12 twin-seat Hunters which would have been used for familiarisation, lead-in training and weapons training. Only one such Hunter was actually built, this being Mk.12 XE531 which was converted from a single-seat Mk.6 airframe, and equipped with a Head Up Display and other related equipment, to serve as a prototype for the new variant and as a trials aircraft for equipment which would be necessary for the aircraft's new role. It was proposed that in addition to the OCU's fleet of Hunters, a pair of these aircraft would also be assigned to each operational squadron for continuation training and other familiarisation tasks. Undoubtedly, the RAF would have preferred to have had a dedicated dual-control variant of TSR2 for conversion training and some effort was directed towards this possibility. Initially, the Air Staff expressed a preference for a trainer variant with side-by-side seating for student and instructor, but the cost and complexity of re-engineering the aircraft for this configuration was quickly accepted as being impractical. As a more affordable solution it was proposed that the existing tandem seating arrangement be retained, but with a new one-piece canopy which would provide better vision for the instructor. The Air Staff were in favour of a design which would enable the aircraft to be converted to and from the trainer or operational role as required, but even though the idea was pursued (and a mock-up constructed), it was hardly an ideal solution, with forward visibility for the instructor being almost nil. Precisely how the issue of trainer variants would have been resolved cannot now be established, as the concept was still being considered at the time of the project's cancellation. However, given that a fleet of Hunters was to have been purchased to act as relatively unsophisticated basic conversion trainers for TSR2, it seems quite likely that no trainer derivative of TSR2 would ever have been built, and that all conversion requirements would have been handled by the Hunter, in much the same way as the Hunter was eventually used as a lead-in trainer for the RAF's Buccaneer OCU and squadrons.

Coningsby's choice as the first TSR2 base was probably a result of two factors – the first being that the station had been an established base for Vulcan operations for many years, and the local community had endured the noisy presence of the huge bombers without complaint. It followed therefore, that the even noisier TSR2 would be welcomed into the local area without any undue fuss. The other consideration was that the base had storage facilities for American nuclear bombs (which had previously been assigned to Canberra squadrons), and with the prospect of operational units eventually forming at the base, the storage facility may well have been judged to be a useful asset (US-supplied bombs would probably have been made available for TSR2 operations). However, the home of the RAF's first operational TSR2 squadrons would almost certainly have been Honington, even though both Wyton and Bassingbourn were identified as potential bases for reconnaissance squadrons, and Marham was also considered as a potential TSR2 bomber base. However the prospect of noise disturbance eventually ruled out Wyton, Bassingbourn's relatively small size eventually became a factor against the use of this station, and Marham was eventually selected as a base for the RAF's fleet of Victor tankers, therefore Honington appears to have become the preferred base almost by proxy. Far overseas, the NEAF TSR2 squadrons would have been stationed at Akrotiri, and for FEAF operations, the squadrons would have been based at Tengah, in Singapore. But TSR2 would undoubtedly have become a familiar site at other airfields too, not least on the island of Malta, where Hal Far was

to have been a base for TSR2 units conducting low flying and weapons training over ranges in Libya, and nearby Luqa was identified as a potential base for reconnaissance operations if required. The only other indication as to where TSR2 might have been deployed, comes from proposals for the fitment of runway arrestor gear at airfields where TSR2 was likely to be operated on a temporary basis, and in addition to the planned list of potentially permanent bases, these proposals covered Gan, Butterworth, Sharjah, Khormaksar and El Adem.

At the time of TSR2's cancellation, virtually no consideration had been afforded to the question of which squadrons would be assigned to TSR2 operations. No. 40 Squadron was identified as the ODS at Coningsby, and No. 237 OCU was chosen as the TSR2 training unit. The only other surviving reference is to No.13 Squadron which appears to have been identified as one of the proposed reconnaissance squadrons. Other than these units, the question of squadron allocations remains entirely speculative, and would have depended of the final number of aircraft actually purchased, and of course the Government's overseas commitments which would have changed considerably by the time that TSR2 entered service. Different conclusions can be derived from different scenarios, and so the only helpful guidance comes from a look at what really did happen in the 1970s. It seems logical to assume that the RAF's Buccaneer and Vulcan squadrons would have become TSR2 units had the project survived, but beyond this basic extrapolation, it is impossible to speculate any further. But whatever the outcome of the RAF's plans might have been, it seems likely that the aircraft would have remained in service through the 1970s and 1980s, and possibly even into the beginning of the new millennium.

Ultimately, only one TSR2 unit was actually formed prior to the termination of the project, and this was the TSR2 Ground School which was established on 1 October 1964. The unit was based at RAF Hemswell in Lincolnshire, a former Canberra strike base which had been part of the RAF's Thor ICBM force until 1963. It is assumed that Hemswell would have continued to operate as a non-flying station, although the airfield remained intact and could have been re-assigned to flight operations, although there is no evidence to suggest that TSR2 aircraft would ever have been based there, other than a couple of instructional airframes which would presumably have been withdrawn from the pre-production fleet at the end of their test flight programme. It seems likely that they would have flown directly to Hemswell but would have then been grounded.

XR222 at Duxford after having being restored to exhibition standard. Just visible under the aircraft's nose is the familiar shape of a Panavia Tornado – the aircraft which eventually entered service as the direct descendant of the TSR2 concept, and which took advantage of TSR2's systems development programme. Tornado was in affect a "baby TSR2" designed to perform the same tactical strike role but within a European theatre – the only role which was still required by the 1970s. In effect, Tornado was the "Canberra Replacement" which the RAF had been waiting for since the 1960s.
BAE Heritage

General Dynamics F-111K for the RAF

By Tony Buttler AMRAeS

Note: The General Dynamics F-111 proved to be a direct rival to the TSR2 and was built in numbers for the US Air Force. Some of what follows may duplicate what Tim has written earlier, but almost all of it comes directly from original documents.

FOLLOWING the cancellation of TSR2 in April 1965 the British Government signed a Memorandum of Understanding with the US Government to take an option on the General Dynamics F-111A, since the American type was seen to be a timely and cheaper Canberra replacement. However, although this appeared to be a sensible and straightforward move in 1965, as the programme moved forward problems with the American versions of this strike aircraft coupled with increases in its price, and a very difficult economic situation in the UK as well, saw the British F-111K subsequently cancelled.

Well known artwork showing the F-111K in RAF service. *Joe Cherrie*

Assessments

The BAC TSR2 had been developed against Air Staff Requirement ASR.343 (Issue 2) as a long-range strike and reconnaissance replacement for the hugely successful English Electric Canberra. Because of cost escalation and technical problems with TSR2, this Staff Requirement had been reviewed on many occasions and at the highest ministerial level, but the document had passed closest scrutiny without any reduction in operational capability being requested. After TSR2 had gone ASR.343 was taken as the baseline for the reconfiguration of the F-111 to British requirements and the decision was made to re-write it (though at this stage the selection of the F-111 as the TSR2 replacement had not been confirmed). This became ASR.343 (Issue 3) and it was prepared during May 1965. It was pointed out that now that TSR2 had been cancelled the ASR could no longer be expected to influence the basic design of the aircraft to meet it, so Issue 3 merely stated the performance, capabilities and facilities required (in many respects it was written around the F-111). The main elements of the document read as follows:

> "The Air Staff requires as soon as possible a new aircraft for tactical strike and reconnaissance operations using conventional and nuclear weapons. Such an aircraft will enable the Royal Air Force to continue to provide tactical support for the Army, to make an effective contribution to the strength of our Regional Pact forces and to the strength of SACEUR's (Supreme Allied Commander Europe) shield." The aircraft would "exploit to the full a combination of high speed with low altitude and thus gain all possible advantage from the difficulties which an enemy will face in producing an effective defence in these conditions. The aircraft's operational flexibility will, however, be greatly enhanced by a Mach 2 capability at medium altitudes."

The strike aircraft would be produced as a weapon system that would permit effective delivery of high explosive or nuclear weapons from low altitudes in poor visibility and at night. Low altitude operations were to be possible down to 200ft above ground level, and even lower where the terrain permitted. An alternative delivery capability from medium altitudes was also required and of equal importance was the provision of a comprehensive system for all-weather reconnaissance, thus giving the aircraft a major alternative role. It was also considered desirable to retain some strike capability in the reconnaissance role and at least a day photographic capability in the strike role. And this flexibility of role and tactics was to be dependent upon an ability to use small airfields with rudimentary surfaces and restricted maintenance facilities.

The penetration speed to target at sea level was to be not less than Mach 0.9, there must also be the ability to make a short burst at supersonic speed at low level and to attain Mach 2.0 at the tropopause. Continuous operation in level flight was to be possible at altitudes up to 56,000ft. Without resort to in-flight refuelling or overload fuel tanks the aircraft had to be capable of attacking targets at a radius of action of at least 1,000nm, a ferry range of at least 2,500nm in still air without overload fuel or in-flight refuelling was required, and it was to be possible to further increase the ferry range by the use of jettisonable overload tanks. Normally the aircraft would operate from airfields with paved runways of about 2,000 yards in length, but under the threat of an attack it would be necessary to disperse to semi-prepared airstrips or other existing airfields, the length of which might be less than 1,500 yards and which may have deteriorated or rudimentary surfaces.

The navigation/strike radar was to provide the following:-

a. Blind fixing with an error not exceeding 700ft on a point radar discrete target.

b. A means of blind bombing

c. Radar ranging information for use in the visual aiming of rockets and bombs.

The attack radar and terrain following radars were initially listed as for the American F-111A, except for the interface of the terrain-following radar with the UK type radio altimeter. The navigation system was to include TACAN (tactical air navigation) equipment and the aircraft was to be capable of carrying the weapons listed below. With the exception of AJ168 there was no requirement for any conventional weapons to be carried simultaneously with nuclear weapons.

General Dynamics F-111A #4 comes into land with its swing wings in the forward position and various high-lift devices deployed. *General Dynamics*

Photo of a French Air Force Dassault Mirage IV bomber. As an alternative to the F-111K, BAC and Dassault offered a version of the Mirage IV fitted with Rolls-Royce Spey engines.
Wolfgang Muehlbauer

(1) 4 x AJ168 (TVM or ASM or in mixed loads), swivelling pylons only (a Martel AJ168 TV Pod would be carried on the ventral centerline).

(2) A minimum of 10 x ASR.1197 weapon clusters (500lb and 1,000lb), though carriage of a greater number was desired.

(3) A minimum of 10 x 1,000lb Mk 6 to 12 series medium capacity (MC) or high explosive (HE) bombs (free fall and retarded fan), and again carriage of greater numbers was desirable (the final number was 34).

(4) 4 x 68mm SNEB rocket launchers.

(5) Up to 4 Lepus night illumination flares on wing pylons only.

(6) 6 x 28lb practice bombs (free fall and retarded fan).

Later two WE.177 (A or B version) free-fall nuclear bombs were specified to be carried internally, and for weapon carriage British multiple ejector rack units were to be used with up to 6 stores per pylon up to a maximum of 5,000lb per pylon (the document quoted here stated "1,000lb bombs weigh well over 1,000lb").

AJ168 referred to the Martel air-to-ground missile system, while ASR.1197 detailed an air-to-ground weapon to replace the SNEB rocket and which became the BL.755 cluster bomb. The anti-radar (AR) version of the AJ168 Martel would enable the British F-111 to operate more safely at low level. Martel was being developed to counter the possible development and procurement of specialised low level surface-to-air missiles by potential enemies and it was considered essential for operations against targets with a strong local defence. Indeed, the targets that an enemy was most likely to defend with local point defences corresponded to those within the F-111 target list and it was against these which the Martel anti-radar (AR)

version could most profitably be used. Provision for the AR version could be made in all aircraft within the F-111 force, while the separate TV-guided version could only be carried by F-111s in the strike configuration. Subject to the order of 50 F-111s, it was recommended that both versions of Martel should be carried by the aircraft.

The powerplant was to be the Pratt & Whitney TF-30-P-3 or (assessed early on as an alternative) the Rolls-Royce Spey RB.168-36R. British substitute equipment would include three F95 Mk.7 cameras, a development of the Mk.2 camera in preparation for installation in the Hawker P.1127, the McDonnell F-4M Phantom and the F-111 (this camera was flown as a prototype at RAE Farnborough in 1966). The three cameras were to be fitted permanently under the fuselage nose.

The second draft of ASR.343 (Issue 3) was given full circulation throughout the Ministry on 25 August 1965. During September a joint Ministry of Aviation/Ministry of Defence (MoA/MoD) team visited the Dassault company in France to evaluate the Mirage IV supersonic bomber powered by the Rolls-Royce Spey which was being offered as an alternative to the F-111. In the meantime, more was learnt about the American F-111A version and it was realised that the Mk.1 avionics fitted in that aircraft were not up to British requirements. At the time of the signing of the Memorandum of Understanding, the alternatives open to the Air Force Department were the standard Mk.1 F-111A, and a possible development incorporating more advanced avionics (the Mk.2 avionics version). It was now recognised that the weapon aiming equipment on the Mk.1 was considerably inferior to that of TSR2, and this led to the decision to take an option to buy only ten Mk.1 aircraft (to be delivered between July and September 1968) and then to wait until July 1969 for follow-up deliveries, which it was hoped would have a better standard of equipment.

During July and August 1965 the Deputy Chief of the Air Staff (DCAS) visited the United States where he found that the Mk.2 avionics proposal was still in the project definition stage, and that the primary aim of the Mk.2 proposals was to improve the F-111's air-to-air capability (although not to the extent of giving it a first-class all-weather interceptor performance). For the strike role the accuracies of the weapon delivery were to be improved. Meanwhile, another variant intended for Strategic Air Command (SAC) use had come into the reckoning. Known formally as the B-111A (and later FB-111A), and informally as the SAC min/mod version, this offered a greater range and radius of action in the overload configuration due to the introduction of up to six 600gal(US) external fuel tanks in place of the six 450gal(US) tanks which the F-111A carried. The resulting increase in maximum overload weight had made necessary the use of the slightly longer span wing developed for the US Navy's F-111B fleet air defense fighter version (which was later abandoned), plus a stronger undercarriage.

So far as the equipment was concerned, the major changes in the B-111A were a new weapons computer which would provide a continuously computed solution to the weapon aiming problem, a combination of Doppler and astro-tracker to provide for airborne alignment of the inertial navigator, and a second radar offset bombing aim point. The second and third features were mainly required for the strategic deterrent role and were not essential for the RAF version, but the improved weapons computer was of prime importance because it eliminated the principal shortcoming of the standard F-111A, and provided an acceptable level of accuracy for weapons delivery.

At this point the Air Force Department view, therefore, was that a satisfactory substitute for the TSR2 could be provided by the following:-

a. F-111A (or B-111A) airframe arranged for pilot/navigator crew, with

b. B-111A continuous solution bombing computer,

c. AJ168 (TV) and (ARM),

d. An all-weather reconnaissance fitting (palletised) as an alternative to AJ168,

e. A dual trainer version.

Because the design of the F-111 incorporated a variable geometry wing, a feature which was not thought to be feasible way back when ASR.343 (Issue 1) was first written, the F-111 had in general a greater radius of action and ferry range than that conceived in the ASR. Moreover, if the configuration which included six 600gal(US) wing tanks was chosen, the maximum ferry range of the aircraft would be in the order of 4,500nm and that would reduce the aircraft's dependence on in-flight refuelling. The F-111 could also take off and land within the limitations of the ASR because its undercarriage and tyres had been designed especially for operations from rudimentary surfaces. The F-111 was also capable of speeds in excess of those required by the ASR both at low and high altitudes.

An Air Ministry review of the F-111A from 1965 summed up the following:

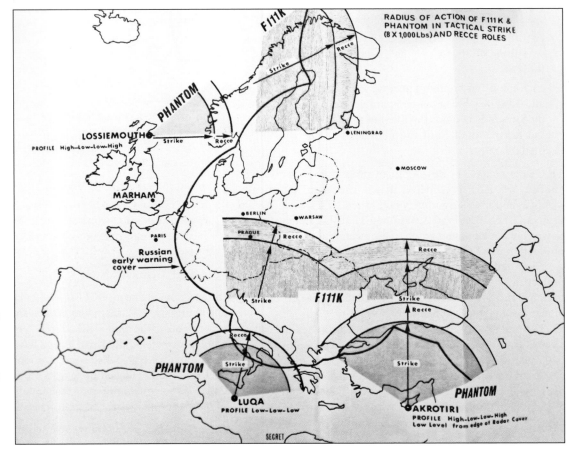

Though a poor quality reproduction, this unique map presents a comparison of the radius of action of the F-111K when carrying eight 1,000lb bombs and the McDonnell F-4 Phantom for both the tactical strike and reconnaissance roles.
National Archives Air 19/1146

"1. The F-111A is a two seat, twin engined, variable geometry aircraft. Its role is strike/ ground attack/air defence in order of priority. It has two pilots seated side by side and is designed for a fatigue life of 4,000 hours under representative flight conditions. No trainer version is contemplated and no reconnaissance version is funded. Flight refuelling is fitted and could easily be made compatible with British Victor tankers.

2. Variable geometry gives the aircraft an exceptional range of performance which is nowhere significantly worse than the TSR2, and in the fields of airfield requirements, economic cruise and slow speed manoeuvrability it is substantially better. The avionics have been deliberately kept simple in the interest of quick development, reliability and maintainability with the result that the full performance of the aircraft could not be exploited. Operationally this was by far the most controversial point of the system. The USAF was well aware that it needed to improve this and the intention was to replace the complete system at about the 200th aircraft.

3. The aircraft is optimised for economic cruise at Mach 0.75 at 30-40,000ft, and low cruise at Mach 0.55. Its top speed is Mach 1.2 at sea level rising to Mach 2.5 at 50,000ft."

This report continued by describing the main limitations of the nav/attack system, which were:

(i). the performance of the attack radar was roughly equivalent to that in the British V-bombers and experience indicated that this would be inadequate at speeds above 400 knots and heights at much below 500ft;

(ii). the bombing error in the lay down visual role was about 400ft, twice what had been expected from the TSR2;

(iii). the blind bombing accuracy was between 600ft and 1,000ft which was comparable with TSR2. Here the system was more flexible but the shortcomings of the radar would limit the choice of target and the method of attack.

The American F-111 development programme involved 18 aircraft, the RAF considered that it had been realistically planned, and it was rigorously controlled by a USAF System Project Office. The Pratt & Whitney TF30-P-1 engine was to power the development batch of 18 aircraft and also the first production machines. Subsequent production aircraft should then be fitted with the improved TF30-P-3 which should also replace the -1 engines fitted in the earlier airframes (the principal difference between the -1 and the -3 was the use of a higher turbine inlet temperature).

The report added that the "most noteworthy feature of this aircraft from the aerodynamics and structural points of view is the variable sweep. This had been fully recognised in the development programme. Extensive wind tunnel testing has been undertaken, a figure of 20,000 hours being quoted. An obvious outcome of the testing was the modified high-lift devices for use in the landing configuration. It was stated that, with the present design, wind tunnel tests indicated no particular problem during flight development." However, the Air Staff felt that the air intake was a potential source of development troubles, and noted also that the wing pivot was not in the optimum position from the point of view of wing flutter but the arrangement was satisfactory.

It was not easy for the reviewer to give an authoritative appreciation on the technical validity of the engine programme "as Pratt & Whitney manages to keep itself free of direct supervision by the Services to a remarkable degree. The engine appears to be running on or ahead of schedule and no mention of major problems has been heard. Pratt & Whitney is thought in the USA to be sufficiently conservative in its approach to be very likely to meet its guarantees on performance and reliability, and in this case the engine involves technology well within today's state of the art, the basic design having been laid down in 1959."

It was agreed in early 1966 that a British multiple ejector rack (MER) carrier would be developed but it proved difficult to establish at that time, and subsequently, the load criteria essential to the British design. Throughout the UK F-111 development period the objective was to obtain a satisfactory manoeuvre envelope for 4 x 1,000 stores on each swivelling pylon and an aircraft payload of 18 x 1,000lb stores in all. The Flat 4 carrier design was finally produced for this purpose, but a re-appraisal showed that it was subject to unacceptable penalties.

Order Numbers

Very early Air Ministry studies comparing the F-111 and TSR2 (and made before TSR2 was cancelled) suggested a possible requirement for 110 aircraft with 74 on front line strength, another 10 based at the type's Operational Conversion Unit (OCU), 5 considered to be under repair at any time and 21 classed as 'wastage'. The F-111 was described as being "less complex than the TSR2" but it was considered that a dual-control version would be essential for adequate training on aircraft of this performance and complexity. The F-111 in its operational form would already have dual controls, whereas a dual variant of the TSR2 had still to be developed. The 74 frontline machines were to be deployed as follows:

a. Based in the UK: 32 aircraft,

b. The Near East Air Force (NEAF – the Command organisation that controlled all RAF assets in the Eastern Mediterranean): 24 aircraft,

c. The Far East Air Force (FEAF): 16 aircraft,

d. RAF Germany: None.

It was assumed that an OCU of 10-12 aircraft would be needed and at this stage Marham was seen as the only base that could accommodate the entire strike force. No station could take the whole force including the OCU and RAF Coningsby and RAF Honington were also discussed as possible bases.

Once the F-111 had been selected, a further study broke down the potential order more accurately, stating that the tasks of the 74 aeroplanes in the front line would be as follows:-

a. UK. The force of (now) 36 aircraft would be required

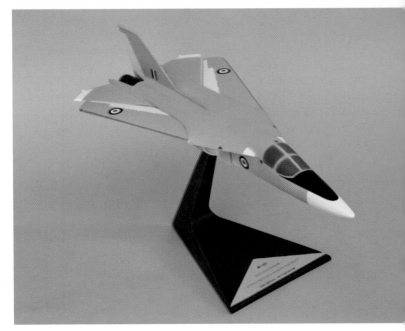

These views show an original General Dynamics model of the 'F-111 RAF Long Range Strike/Reconnaissance Aircraft'. It was made before the version had been designated F-111K. *All Sir George Cox*

Top left: Plan view photo with the wings in the near forward position and showing end fuselage and jetpipe detail.

Top right: The same flight configuration but here providing forward fuselage detail.

Middle left: Slightly more side-on angle with the air intakes now coming into view.

Middle Right: Three-quarter front view with the wings moved to the fully swept back position.

Left: The sleekness of the F-111 when its wings were swept to their full extent is seen in this nose-angle shot.

for worldwide reinforcement duties in the nuclear, conventional and reconnaissance roles, and the force would be earmarked (not assigned) to NATO. A total of 24 F-111 strike aircraft would be the sole strike force (except for 16 Handley Page Victor 2 aircraft if these were retained) based in the UK or Western Europe and these would, in effect, replace 24 Vickers Valiant V-Bombers and 48 strike Canberras based in RAF Germany. 24 was considered the minimum required for "roulement purposes" (continuous cover) and to provide an effective capability for reinforcement, particularly over the long distances to the Far East. Similarly the 12 reconnaissance F-111s would replace 8 PR version Canberras in UK service.

b. NEAF. The strike force (16 aircraft) would be declared to the Central Treaty Organization (CENTO) in the nuclear role. The full force of 24 aircraft would be required to meet all UK defence commitments in the Near and Middle East in the nuclear, conventional and reconnaissance roles.

c. FEAF. The force of (now) 14 F-111s would be committed to the defence of UK, Commonwealth and Malaysian interests in the conventional, nuclear and reconnaissance roles.

By late 1965, however, the decision had been made to concentrate the whole of the British F-111 Force in the United Kingdom. This would entail the deployment of 14 additional aircraft in this country with their associated equipment, facilities and personnel. Again, there was some consideration towards splitting the force at two different bases, at Honington but with a small specialist reconnaissance force at Wyton, but this idea was rejected. Concentration of the F-111 force on a single station would provide a simple Command structure for the control of the force at station level, whereas the location of a specialist element at a satellite airfield would complicate the chain of command and blur the division of responsibility between the two station commanders. Studies concluded therefore that the best form of deployment for the increased UK-based force was to locate all the aircraft at Honington in Suffolk and this airbase was earmarked for conversion to accommodate the new aircraft. Also by November 1965 reports had been prepared by General Dynamics and Rolls Royce which looked into the feasibility, costs and schedules for fitting the British Spey 36R engine into the F-111, and also during that month General Dynamics and Pratt & Whitney presented a progress report on the TF-30 engine to MoA and MoD representatives.

In the first week of December 1965 a limited Letter of Offer covering the purchase of 10 F-111 aircraft only was received from America and, as a result of consultations between the US Department of Defense, the MoA and MoD, a new statement of costs for 50, 80 and 110 aircraft was agreed. The UK studies had in addition looked at a British nav/attack system produced by Ferranti but this was eliminated in late December along with the alternative Spey engine. At the same time BAC and Dassault submitted new proposals for improving the nav/attack system of the Spey-powered Mirage, while Hawker Siddeley Aviation now proposed a supersonic

Buccaneer as a further alternative. The Letter of Offer for a 50 aircraft order was received in January 1966 and it was also during this month when it was finally agreed that both the AR and TV versions of Martel should be fitted. In addition the first flight in an F-111A by an RAF officer (Wg Cdr Fletcher from A&AEE Boscombe Down) took place at this time.

In February 1966 the UK's latest Defence White Paper established the need for 50 F-111s and also eliminated the Spey/Mirage and Buccaneer from consideration, and on 22 March the UK signed the Letter of Offer for the first ten aircraft. By now the Americans were intending to base their FB-111 on the new F-111A Mk.2 avionics rather than the original Mk.1 equipment. The UK F-111 configuration had consequently been amended and the British aircraft were now to have the new inertial navigation (IN) platform and the "digital computery" under development for the F-111A Mk.2.

Then, during a meeting held on 8 February, senior representatives from General Dynamics briefed MoA and MoD representatives on the present status of F-111 development, and here it was disclosed that flight tests had indicated that the base drag of the aircraft was some 20-25% higher than had been predicted. This appeared only to apply to the subsonic cruise condition with the wings swept forward and the afterburners out. There seemed little doubt that there would be delays in the US delivery programmes or at least an extensive retrofit programme. However, one reason for the UK choosing July 1968 as its first delivery date had been to provide eighteen months of 'breathing space' in case the development programme experienced delays. It appeared that this caution had been justified though GD gave assurances that they had sufficient industrial capacity to undertake a significant increase in US delivery rates in addition to the UK's proposed programme. The Ministry's Director General of Scientific Research (Air), (DGSR[A]), however, felt that the 25% shortfall would not be recovered in full, though GD expressed the opposite view.

A paper describing the US F-111A flight test programme, dated 11 February 1966, listed the problems which had arisen with 12 aircraft now flying:

(i) On drag, a problem has been revealed late in the day of a magnitude far greater than anyone had expected which would take many months of intricate flight measurement to analyse and diagnose, before cures could be designed and engineered.

(ii) On the engine, the US had a number of difficult problems (including matching the engine and airframe) which were being tackled but which were a long way from final resolution in terms of firm engineering design and production.

(iii) On handling, in the general stability and control picture there existed a gap in knowledge since it had not been possible to explore fully in flight the behaviour when manoeuvring; this was the result of an engine flame-out problem. Stability and control was always a delicate area and establishing the necessary corrective measures could mean increased drag.

Clearly the F-111A needed a lot more development before it would be ready for service. Nevertheless, a firm order had at last been placed for 10 F-111As and with options for another 40, covering the standard UK frontline model plus a number of dual-control trainers. The purchase price was approximately £2.1m ($5.95m) per unit in 1965 prices. In June 1966 RAF representatives visited Washington and General Dynamics at Fort Worth, Texas to review progress in the F-111 programme as a whole, while the Assistant Chief of the Air Staff (Operational Requirements), ACAS(OR), and another Ministry official visited Canberra in Australia to discuss with the Royal Australian Air Force's Air Staff items of mutual interest including the F-111 (which the RAAF had ordered having rejected the TSR2).

Following another MoD/MoA visit to Fort Worth in September, and after having been given a presentation by General Dynamics and avionics manufacturer Autonetics on the F-111 Mk.2 nav/attack system, the avionics installation for the British aircraft was finally agreed. Indeed all major areas of the British F-111 configuration were now fixed and the

other decisions which were taken during that month were:-

a. Money would not be spent on an air-to-air capability though, if possible, the fittings for a gun would be retained.

b. The requirement for loft bombing at 110° (over the shoulder) no longer existed.

c. The ability to retrofit SNEB rockets should be retained though no flight clearance trials were to be undertaken in the US.

However, the engine/airframe matching problems continued to be a major source of concern, though a proper assessment based on flight test data would not be possible before November at the earliest.

A memorandum dated 21 November 1966 reported that the US Air Force had now allocated model designations to the F-111 aircraft being purchased for the RAF. The Strike/Reconnaissance version would be known as the F-111K and the Trainer/Strike version the TF-111K, and from now on these titles were to be used

Drawing taken from a 1967 Air Staff brochure which shows in blue the items and modifications to be made or introduced on the F-111K from the original American F-111A – the items 'peculiar' to the F-111K. The shaded external fuel tanks in grey came from the FB-111A version. *Joe Cherrie via Chris Gibson*

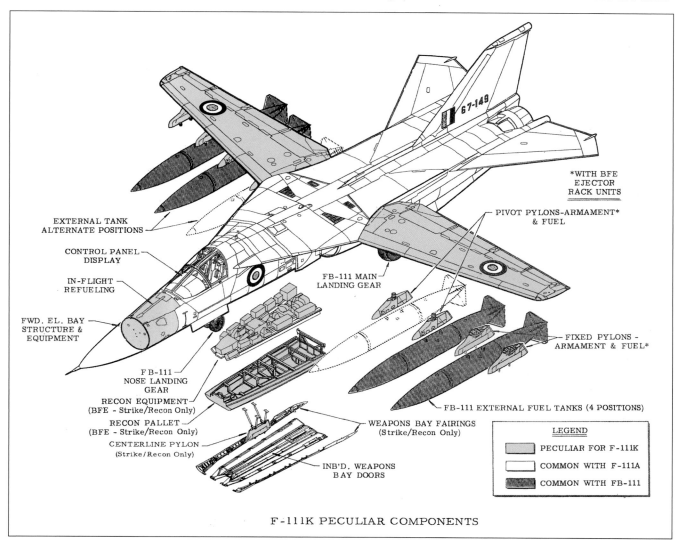

EXTERNAL TANK ALTERNATE POSITIONS

CONTROL PANEL DISPLAY

IN-FLIGHT REFUELING

FWD. EL. BAY STRUCTURE & EQUIPMENT

FB-111 NOSE LANDING GEAR

RECON EQUIPMENT (BFE - Strike/Recon Only)

RECON PALLET (BFE - Strike/Recon Only)

CENTERLINE PYLON (Strike/Recon Only)

FB-111 MAIN LANDING GEAR

*WITH BFE EJECTOR RACK UNITS

PIVOT PYLONS-ARMAMENT* & FUEL

FIXED PYLONS - ARMAMENT & FUEL*

FB-111 EXTERNAL FUEL TANKS (4 POSITIONS)

WEAPONS BAY FAIRINGS (Strike/Recon Only)

INB'D. WEAPONS BAY DOORS

LEGEND
PECULIAR FOR F-111K
COMMON WITH F-111A
COMMON WITH FB-111

F-111K PECULIAR COMPONENTS

in all correspondence. A Preliminary Design Review for the F-111K and TF-111K was held at Fort Worth between 6 and 12 November 1966 and attended by an MoD/MoA team. At this point the British version was basically a standard American F-111A airframe with a higher gross weight at take-off, some updated systems, some specific British systems and the capacity to carry British weapons. Structurally, it was similar to the F-111A but had the heavy duty undercarriage taken from the FB-111 strategic bomber, and from the structure point of view the two British versions would have near identical airframes. Each of the two prototypes would be configured to one form only with No.1 acting as the strike/reconnaissance prototype and 'wired' to carry and launch the Martel missile.

F-111K introduced a revised weapons bay with a new removable centreline weapons pylon. The original F-111 had just four weapon stations under each wing and only the inner pair were capable of pivoting to accommodate changes in wing sweep angle; this meant that when the wings were fully swept the outer pair could not be employed. Another feature specific to the F-111K was the provision for a pallet to go inside the weapons bay to house the British reconnaissance system with its three camera windows adjacent to the nosewheel. The Mk.2 inertial navigation and attack system avionics would comprise a Rockwell International AN/APQ-130 attack radar, IBM computer, Marconi AN/APN-189 Doppler navigation radar and Sperry AN/APQ-128 J-Band terrain-following radar. F-111K would also have an RAF-style "probe and drogue" in-flight refuelling system.

The serial numbers allocated to the 50 aircraft on order or planned were XV884-887 and XV902-947 and at September 1966 the data given for the F-111K was as follows:

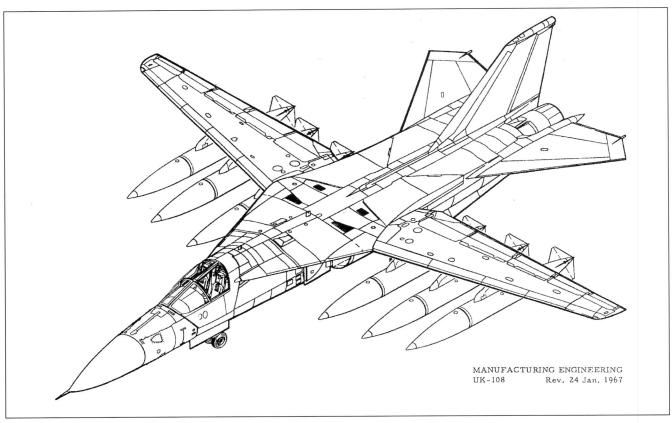

MANUFACTURING ENGINEERING
UK-108   Rev. 24 Jan. 1967

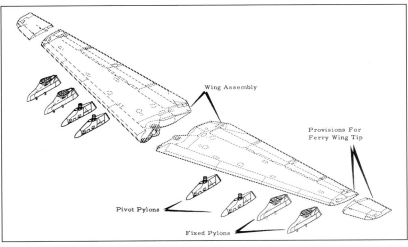

Wing Assembly

Provisions For
Ferry Wing Tip

Pivot Pylons

Fixed Pylons

Some publications have stated that the F-111Ks would have featured the larger wing used by the FB-111A, but archive sources indicate that they would have had the normal F-111A wing. However, these drawings from 1967, taken again from an F-111K brochure, show that the RAF machines would also have had wing tip extensions available for ferry flights. The brochure text states "the F-111K wing structure is common to the F-111A, including provisions for a ferry wing tip". *Joe Cherrie via Chris Gibson*

Crew: 2 (pilot and weapons system operator)

Length: 72ft 2in

Height: 17ft 2in

Wing span (16° wing sweep): 63ft 0in

Wing span (72° wing sweep): 32ft 0in

Wing area (16° wing sweep): 657.4sq.ft

Wing area (72° wing sweep): 525sq.ft

Take-off weight internal fuel only: 78,600lb

Internal fuel load: 31,500lb

Maximum overload weight: 119,070lb

Powerplant: 2 × Pratt & Whitney TF30-P-100 turbofans

Speeds:

Maximum at height: Mach 2.5 for 5 minutes

Maximum continuous at height: Mach 2.2

Maximum at low level: Mach 1.2 for 5 minutes

Combat cruise at low level: Mach 0.9

Ceiling: 60,000ft (by 28 October 1967 a ceiling of 60,250ft had been achieved by a clean US F-111A at combat weight and supersonic speed).

Reconnaissance ceiling: 57,000ft

Weapon hardpoints: 9 in all (8 under wings, 1 under fuselage in weapons bay)

Growing Problems

The publicity given to the F-111A's development problems meant that by now there was growing criticism of the aircraft in America. However, another Air Staff report summarised the situation, stating that the F-111 had been subject to criticism, for political reasons, ever since it had been selected by Robert McNamara (the US Secretary of State for Defense) in preference to its competitors, and imposed as a solution common to the Air Force and Navy (different versions of the same airframe were intended to fill quite different USAF and US Navy requirements). The report added that the F-111 "was more vulnerable to criticism than any previous US military aircraft project, because under the new systems introduced by McNamara details of its performance requirements had been made known from the outset, together with its expected price and programme schedule. Previous aircraft – the Boeing B-52 being a notable example – had encountered difficulties which had involved design changes at extremely high cost, but these had never been publicised in the way that much smaller difficulties with the F-111 had been."

General Dynamics had admitted that less thrust and increased drag had reduced the aircraft's capabilities to below those previously expected. They showed no prospect of restoring the position fully, though some reduction in drag might be achieved. The changes found necessary to overcome the engine/intake compatibility problems had as regards the airframe increased the drag and as regards the engine increased the specific fuel consumption, so reductions in range were inevitable. The USAF was known to be concerned about the loss of performance over what had originally been expected.

As regards some problems with compressor stall, GD claimed that the combination of the P-3 engine and the improved air intake had largely solved these, though stalls could still occur during certain manoeuvres. The manufacturer emphasised, however, that the stalling was not accompanied by any flame-out of the engine and that recovery was very rapid. The USAF appeared not to be unduly worried by the present situation here and considered it acceptable.

Some significant points did emerge from discussions between UK Air Staff officials and USAF officers who had flown the F-111 or at least been associated with it (though these pilots had only flown the early models with the P-1 engine). These were:

1. They were not impressed with the performance of the aircraft as a fighter and for this purpose they felt that it required considerably more thrust. It was said that the F-111A could out-turn the F-4 Phantom and had done so in mock engagements, but then it was slow to accelerate after the turn.

2. There was satisfaction amounting to enthusiasm concerning the Mk.1 avionics (which had produced navigational results considerably better than had been specified) and with the performance of the terrain following radar. The aircraft was judged to be "very suitable for the strike and recce roles" (though this statement made no reference to the question of range).

The Air Staff report concluded that in most respects the F-111 programme, containing as it did so many 'firsts', had been a remarkable success. Despite all the early predictions of disaster, according to GD and the USAF the swing wing philosophy had been entirely fault-free. The maintainability called for had also apparently been achieved and the F-111K programme remained on time. The RAF could be satisfied that the aircraft would meet the UK's requirements in all respects except that of its strike range in certain sorties.

On 1 February 1967 the Deputy Chief of the Air Staff (DCAS), P.G. Wykeham, completed a review of effectiveness of the F-111K against possible interception by Soviet aircraft. He noted that, on the assumption that the F-111K's top speed would not exceed Mach 2, it was seen for example that in the case of an 'F-4 Phantom' type defence with enemy radar cover of 250nm the F-111K, when standing off at a distance of 50nm, would be intercepted if the fighter scramble delay was less than six minutes. And the latest forecasts considered that such opposition would be re-equipped during this period with Mikoyan MiG-21 fighters possessing an AI radar as advanced as that of the Phantom, so it would therefore be prudent to judge the F-111K against a Phantom rather than a capability more akin to that of the current English Electric Lightning interceptor.

The option for the remaining 40 F-111Ks was exercised on 29 March 1967 and a Letter of Offer covering the total purchase of 50 F-111K aircraft was signed on the 31st. On 8 March the Air Staff had reported the following achievements by the F-111A:

a) A ferry range of 3,000nm had been flown. Based on this ferry performance, a radius of action of 1,400nm

In this retouched photo of an F-111 the aircraft has been given RAF roundels.

for the F-111K with normal loads was possible.

b) Stall free engine performance had generally been proved up to Mach 2.0 at high level.

c) Mach 1.2 at low level had now been flown.

During April McNamara and the British Minister of Defence Denis Healey agreed that their staffs should work towards a mutually acceptable slippage in the F-111K programme. However, on 20 April the aeronautical press reported increases in the overall cost of the F-111K programme, stating that "Mr Healey has confirmed that the cost of the 50 F-111Ks on order for the RAF (for delivery beginning in 1969) will rise as a result of increased costs of labour and materials in the United States. On 12 April Healey stated that the figure of £2.1 million was firm on 1965 prices. According to Whitehall, this means that the F-111K unit cost has risen by £100,000 in the two years April 1965 to April 1967." On 26 May 1967 RAF personnel were able to view and inspect an F-111A which had flown into the airbase at Wethersfield in Essex.

In June 1967 the Air Staff reported that in view of the costs involved in slipping the delivery programme, it had been decided to delay the introduction of the aircraft by some four months by postponing the first OCU course until 1 August 1969, and some changes in early aircraft deliveries were being negotiated. In July some modifications to the terrain-following radar (called ECP 826) were submitted for approval and in August the Treasury cleared the necessary expenditure to incorporate this into the F-111K (ECP 826 was designed to improve the aircraft's terrain-following, especially in bad weather). By October 1967 the 'Mk.IIK avionics', as they were now known, were running 11 weeks late and would not fly until August 1968, and the estimates for the aircraft's ultimate performance were now indicating a significant degradation in operational radius-of-action and in ceiling and altitude performance. Nevertheless, US flight testing had cleared full manoeuvring to Mach 2.0 but with some limitations to Mach 2.4.

The first F-111K entered final assembly on 18 September 1967 and (at 27 November) it was expected to be rolled out at Fort Worth on 28 March 1968 (another RAF Staff memo dated 16 November stated that roll-out would be during February 1968 and that the first flight would take place on 28 March). It was known that General Dynamics intended marking one or other of the occasions with a suitable ceremony and the quoted first flight date came very close of course to 1 April, the date when the RAF would celebrate its 50th Birthday. The Air Staff felt that it would be appropriate for the F-111K ceremony to reflect this, GD was aware of the 50th Anniversary and had expressed a willingness to present the first flight and handover ceremony accordingly.

Then on 25 November 1967, as a result of a devaluation of the British Pound, it was announced that the unit cost of the F-111K had risen again to £3.02 million. This very considerable increase was being considered by the Weapons Development Committee when UK Prime Minister Harold Wilson announced the cancellation of the F-111K programme in the House of Commons on 16 January 1968.

In 1967 the British Government, faced with a major economic crisis, had abandoned Britain's commitment 'East of Suez', and this move rendered one of the main roles envisaged for the F-111K (and TSR2 before it) as no longer necessary. In addition to the cost of the F-111K the production schedules were also slipping (it should be noted that while the Royal Australian Air Force did receive its first F-111C version in 1968, because of structural and other development problems the official acceptance of the type by the RAAF took until 1973, a further five years). However, the 50 F-111K aircraft order had been cancelled primarily as part of the economies to be made to the Defence Budget, and it was stressed later that the decision to cancel the contract was not in any way influenced by any technical shortcomings with the aircraft.

The F-111Ks were to have been bought under a credit arrangement with the United States Government under which the capital costs were to be repaid over a period of 12 years. The total cost of 50 F-111Ks, including running costs over this period, were estimated to be £450 million. Cancellation charges were expected

The first two part-built British F-111K airframes. *General Dynamics*

to be in the region of £60 million (though these would need to be negotiated). However, the dollar element of this programme had been offset by an arrangement under which the US Government was pledged to insure to the UK a roughly equivalent amount of foreign currency by offset purchases or collaborative sales of military equipment. Orders to the value of $180 million for direct sales had already been received in addition to some collaborative sales to Saudi Arabia. The US Government had agreed that offset orders already placed in this country would not be cancelled, which the UK Government described as "a generous gesture on their part since they were not under any legal obligation to do so". However, further offset orders related to the F-111K purchase would of course no longer be accepted.

Healey added later that "under the terms of the arrangement which I signed with Mr. McNamara last year, we secured the opportunity for a major breakthrough in the field of arms sales and the acceptance of the principle of ceiling price terms for the aircraft. In return, and in the light of the reductions in our total requirements from between 80 and 110 to 50 aircraft, we moved from an option basis to an undertaking to buy 50 aircraft in a two stage purchase of 10 and 40. The terms of the arrangements to buy 50 F-111s had been endorsed by the Cabinet on 14 February 1966."

In regard to the offset agreement, it had earlier been stated that "in less than two years British firms have been awarded contracts that are likely to lead to sales worth $178 million". The main contracts were for Rolls-Royce Spey engines and avionic equipment for the American A-7 Corsair aircraft worth over $120 million, auxiliary ships (three salvage tugs and two survey ships) for the US Navy worth $40 million, Elliotts head-up display equipment worth $40 million, and various items of equipment and machine tools.

Documents show that the response to the cancellation by the Air Staff was strong. For example the Chief of the Air Staff wrote "I am sure that my colleagues on the Chiefs Of Staff Committee must deplore the Cabinet decision on the F-111 no less than myself, coming as it does so soon after we had jointly affirmed our recognition that the highest quality long-range strike and reconnaissance was of transcending importance in our armoury. The decision leaves a void. I cannot stress too strongly that any F-111s would be vastly better than none at all. Even [just] sixteen aircraft would at least give a steel tip to our strike and reconnaissance forces for the 1970s. To plug as best we can for the [NATO] Alliance the hole left by the phasing out of the Canberra force within three years from now…boils down to the urgent need to address our resources of Buccaneers and V-bombers, with the object of finding the best way of prolonging and exploiting the ability of these aircraft to meet the above commitments as best they can."

The unanimous view of the Chiefs of Staff on the importance of the F-111 to all three services was summarised in the following statement: "The heart of the case for the quality of long-range strike and reconnaissance capability represented by the F-111 is that, broadly speaking, all other operations of war short of ultimate strategic nuclear attack take place either under cover of this capability or with the knowledge that we have it at our

The TSR.2 and F-111K were eventually replaced by the Blackburn/Hawker Siddeley Buccaneer and by the Panavia MRCA Tornado. To represent both types, this fascinating view shows Buccaneer S.Mk.2A serial XT272 at BAe Warton in January 1980 with a special nose fitting for Tornado radar trials, a role which it had performed through much of the 1970s. The picture is thought to have been taken on the day of XT272's last flight. *David Eagles*

disposal if necessary. If this capability is abandoned then our sea, land and air forces are not only deprived of the ability to find out by reconnaissance what an enemy or potential enemy is doing, or is planning to do, but are also thrown back on an essentially defensive strategy with all that this means in surrender of the initiative. The loss of the F-111 would, therefore, carry the gravest military implications for the United Kingdom's ability to participate in military operations in Europe and overseas, and remove an element of real significance in the process of control of escalation."

In fact these 50 aircraft, providing a frontline of 36, were to have been just one element in the replacement of the Canberra in RAF service. The second was to be the replacement of the remaining Canberra strike aircraft in 1969 by V-bombers, followed by their replacement in turn by the planned Anglo-French Variable Geometry strike aircraft (AFVG) in the middle 1970s. The AFVG was a joint BAC/Dassault swing wing aircraft programme introduced as another part replacement for the TSR2 and intended as a complimentary aircraft to F-111K, but it became a very political animal and was abandoned in June 1967 after the French had withdrawn from the project. In February 1968 ASR.343 was placed "in abeyance".

The first F-111K squadron was to have been formed in 1969. There was never any public announcement as to which specific RAF squadrons would operate the aircraft, but it is understood that some original papers indicate that Nos. 7, 12, 15 and 40 Squadrons may have been frontline F-111K units. No. 14 Maintenance Unit at Carlisle was earmarked as the centre for F-111K spares. The first two examples, XV884 and XV885, were intended to serve as development aeroplanes for airframe, avionics and weapons testing and would subsequently have been refurbished as operational aircraft. Serials XV886 and XV887 were to have been TF-111Ks and XV902 to XV947 further F-111Ks. The components which had already been manufactured for the F-111K production run, and which shared

commonality to the American FB-111A version, were subsequently diverted to the latter's production line. XV884 and XV885, both in an advanced stage of construction, were re-designated by the Americans as YF-111As with US serials 67-149 and 67-150. It is understood that the intention was to employ them as flight test aircraft in the F-111A programme, but in July 1968 the USAF opted not to take them on strength. Finally, in May 1969 GD was given the order to break them down for spares and component recovery, a process which had been completed by the end of September 1969.

In the 'short term' the F-111K was replaced by the Blackburn Buccaneer, 62 ex-Royal Navy examples being acquired from mid-1969 onwards followed by orders for 46 new airframes. The first unit to form was No. 12 Squadron at Honington and in RAF hands this 'short term' replacement would prove a great success, the last example not being retired until 1994. The main replacement, however, and also for the AFVG, was to be the Multi-Role Combat Aircraft or MRCA, a strike aircraft programme shared between West Germany, Italy and the UK and which eventually entered service as the Panavia Tornado. The RAF acquired both strike and interceptor versions of Tornado (an air-to-air version of F-111K was never considered seriously) and only now, at the time of writing in February 2018, is the UK Tornado force approaching the end of its lifetime.

APPENDIX TWO

TSR2 Detail Drawings

THE following selection of drawings and their captions
have been taken from original TSR2 Maintenance
Manuals and Crew Notes, all of which were prepared and
printed as a first issue in December 1963 and updated over the
following months until the aircraft programme was abandoned.
These Technical Manuals were produced specifically for early
TSR.2 serial numbers XR219 through XR227. Some
photographs have also been taken from an October 1961 Status
Report and June 1962 Progress Report.

A. Crew's Notes

Engine control and fuel systems.

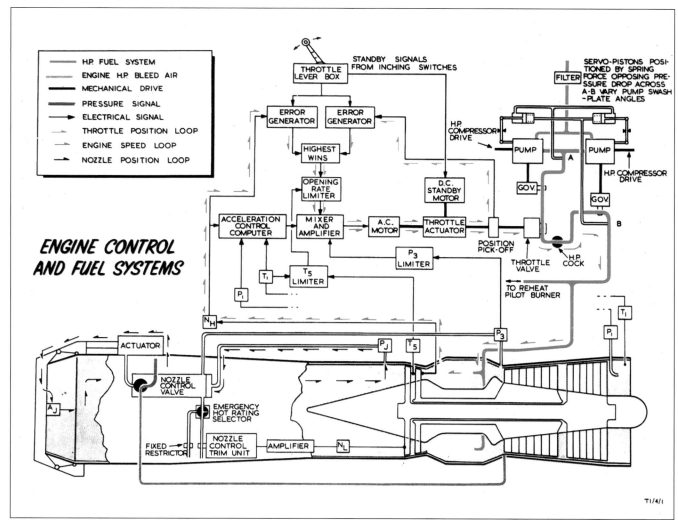

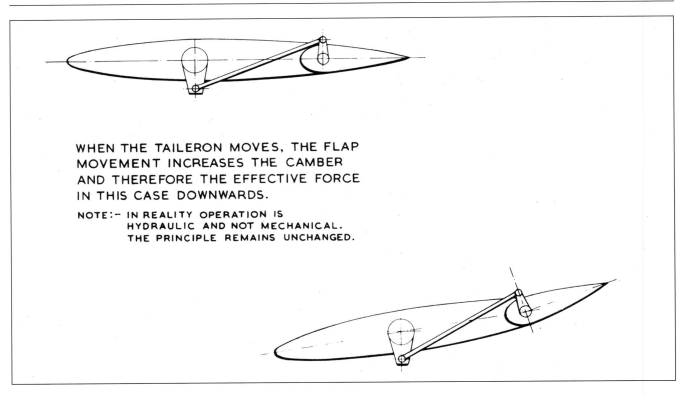

WHEN THE TAILERON MOVES, THE FLAP
MOVEMENT INCREASES THE CAMBER
AND THEREFORE THE EFFECTIVE FORCE
IN THIS CASE DOWNWARDS.

NOTE:- IN REALITY OPERATION IS
       HYDRAULIC AND NOT MECHANICAL.
       THE PRINCIPLE REMAINS UNCHANGED.

Principle of taileron flap operation.

B. Maintenance Manuals

General arrangement drawing of TSR2's propulsion unit installation.

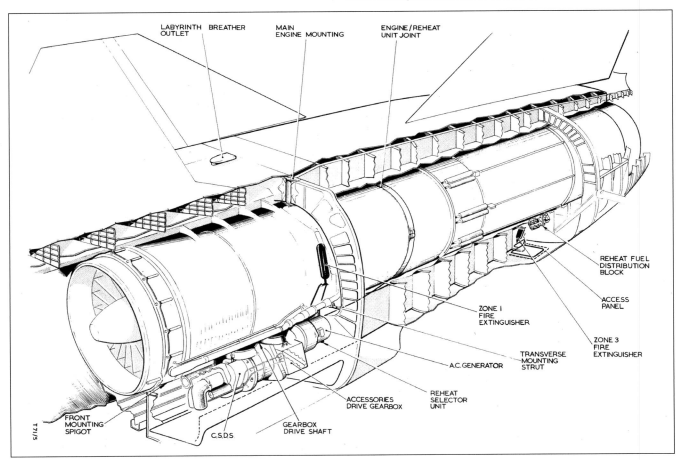

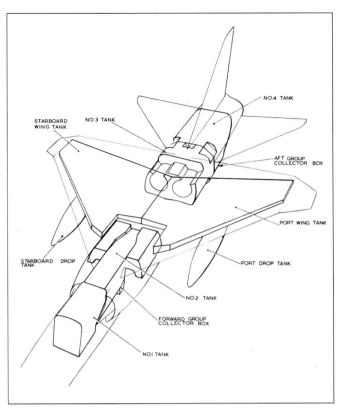

General arrangement drawing of TSR2's fuel tanks.

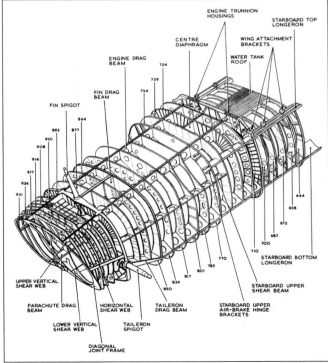

The aircraft's in-flight refuelling installation.

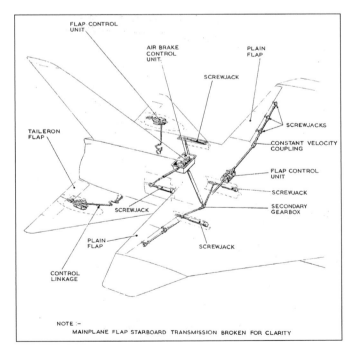

The arrangement of the aircraft airbrakes and flaps.

Rear fuselage structure.

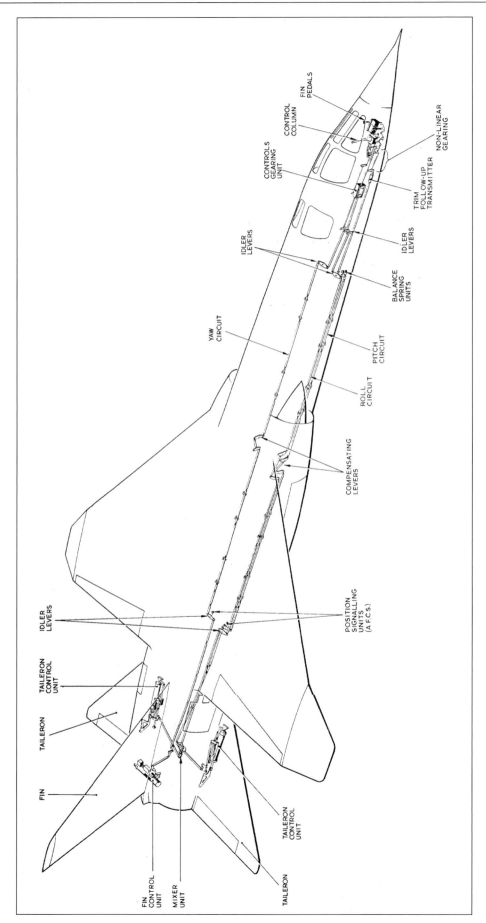

The arrangement and layout for TSR2's primary flight controls.

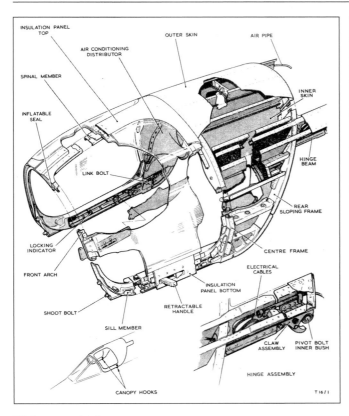

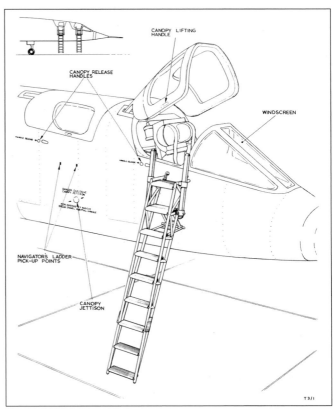

Navigator's canopy detail.

Pilot's canopy detail.

The pilot's control column handle.

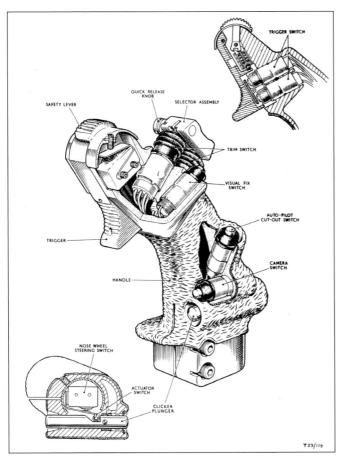

Cockpit access ladder.

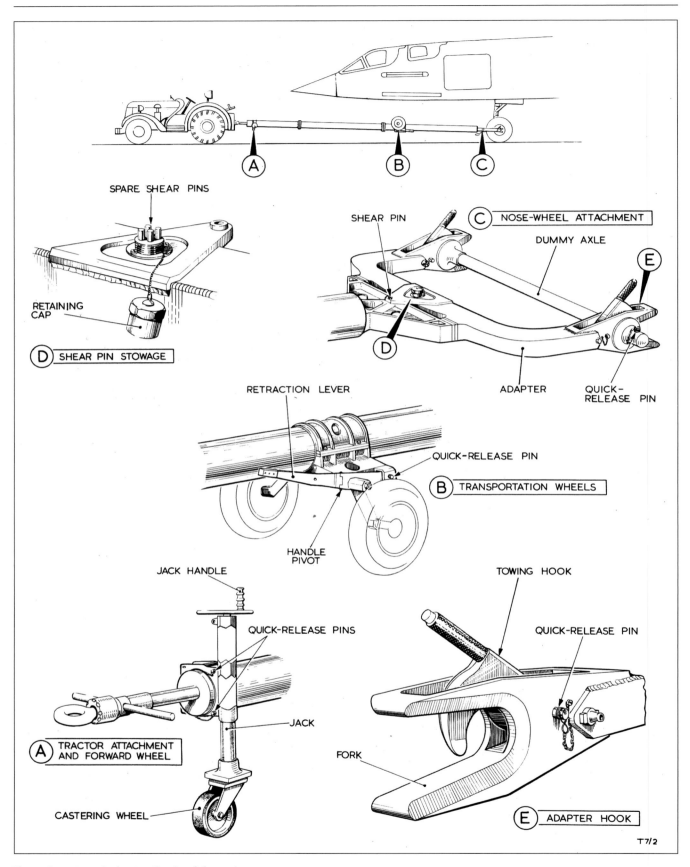

SPARE SHEAR PINS

SHEAR PIN

C | NOSE-WHEEL ATTACHMENT

DUMMY AXLE

E

RETAINING CAP

D | SHEAR PIN STOWAGE

ADAPTER

QUICK-RELEASE PIN

RETRACTION LEVER

QUICK-RELEASE PIN

B | TRANSPORTATION WHEELS

HANDLE PIVOT

JACK HANDLE

TOWING HOOK

QUICK-RELEASE PINS

QUICK-RELEASE PIN

JACK

A | TRACTOR ATTACHMENT AND FORWARD WHEEL

FORK

CASTERING WHEEL

E | ADAPTER HOOK

T7/2

The equipment required to tow the aircraft forward.

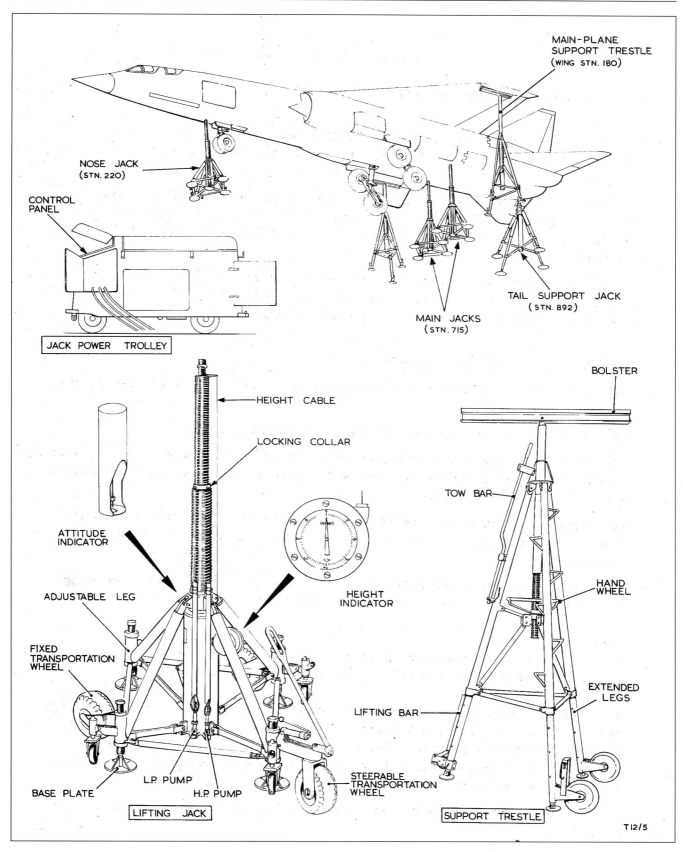

MAIN-PLANE
SUPPORT TRESTLE
(WING STN. 180)

NOSE JACK
(STN. 220)

CONTROL
PANEL

TAIL SUPPORT JACK
(STN. 892)

MAIN JACKS
(STN. 715)

JACK POWER TROLLEY

BOLSTER

HEIGHT CABLE

LOCKING COLLAR

TOW BAR

ATTITUDE
INDICATOR

HEIGHT
INDICATOR

HAND
WHEEL

ADJUSTABLE LEG

FIXED
TRANSPORTATION
WHEEL

EXTENDED
LEGS

LIFTING BAR

BASE PLATE

L.P. PUMP

H.P. PUMP

STEERABLE
TRANSPORTATION
WHEEL

LIFTING JACK

SUPPORT TRESTLE

T12/5

The equipment required for jacking and trestling a TSR2 for maintenance.

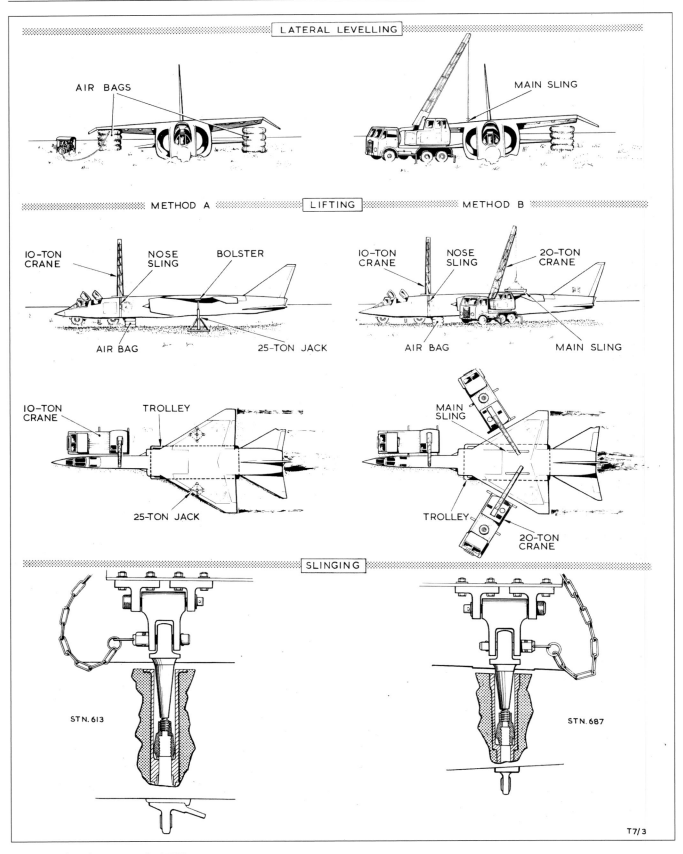

The process for salvaging a crashed TSR2.

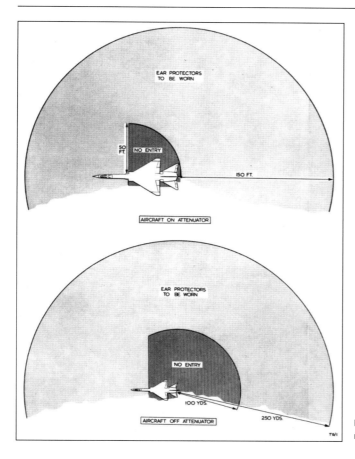

Drawing showing the noise hazard areas present when TSR2 engine ground running was underway.

C. Status Report – October 1961

The TSR2 Engineering Mock-Up at Weybridge in 1961.

Low speed wind tunnel model in the 9ft x 7ft tunnel at Warton in 1961. This was used to investigate the aircraft's high lift capabilities using boundary layer control at the flaps.

This TSR2 wing box structure test specimen combined bending, torsion, internal pressure and lateral loads. It eventually failed at the predicted levels.

Above: TSR2's mainplane fuel flow test specimen seen during its assembly in 1961.

Left: TSR2 Flight Simulation Cockpit. The instruments in the foreground were used to control the hydraulic feel to the pilot's controls. In addition the control circuit friction, backlash and inertia could all be adjusted. A cathode ray tube gave a simple representation of the perspective view outside, against which the aircraft's movements were interpreted.

D. Status Report – June 1962

Early model of the Ferranti Forward Looking Radar pictured during assembly. At the time when the June 1962 Status Report was produced an experimental model of this radar had been operating in terrain following mode at 1,000ft in a Canberra trials aircraft, and this was now moving on to trials at a lower altitude.

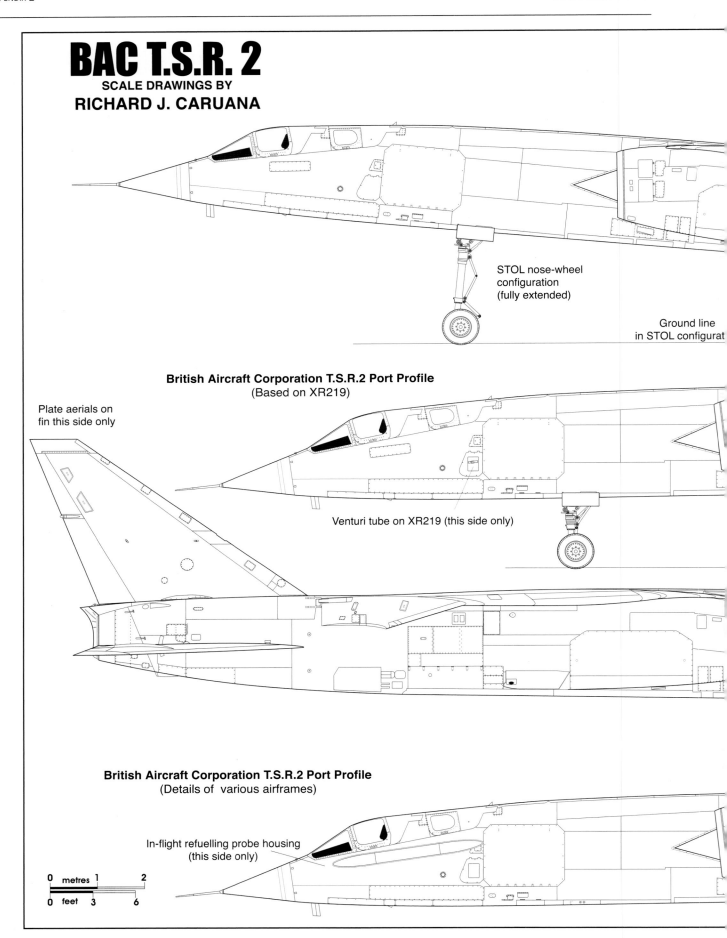

BAC T.S.R. 2
SCALE DRAWINGS BY
RICHARD J. CARUANA

STOL nose-wheel
configuration
(fully extended)

Ground line
in STOL configurat

British Aircraft Corporation T.S.R.2 Port Profile
(Based on XR219)

Plate aerials on
fin this side only

Venturi tube on XR219 (this side only)

British Aircraft Corporation T.S.R.2 Port Profile
(Details of various airframes)

In-flight refuelling probe housing
(this side only)

0 metres 1   2
0 feet 3   6

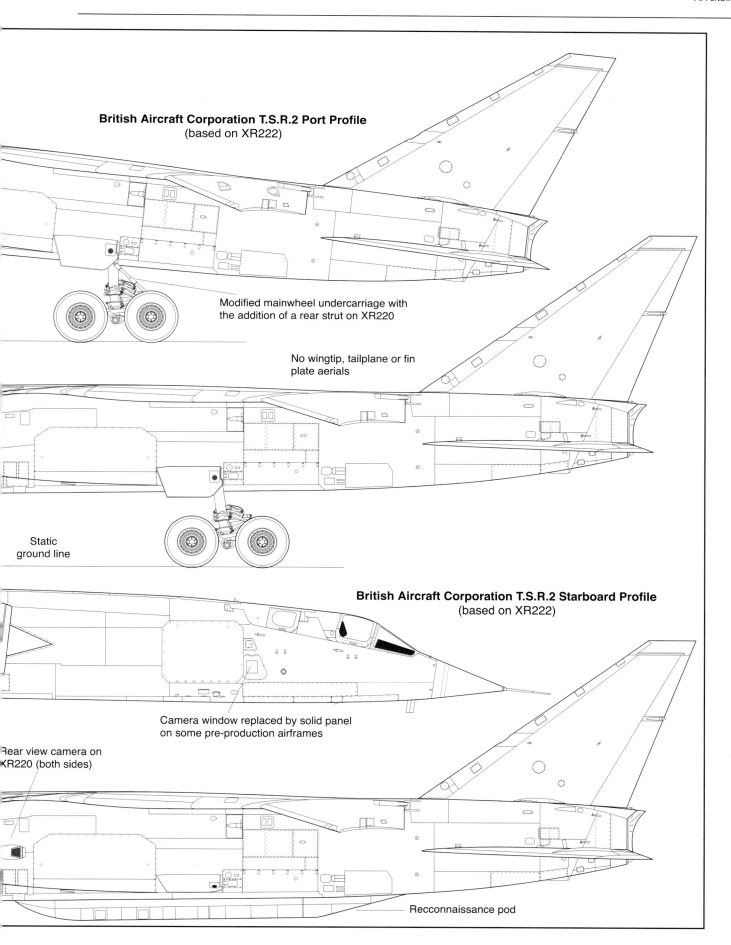

British Aircraft Corporation T.S.R.2 Port Profile
(based on XR222)

Modified mainwheel undercarriage with
the addition of a rear strut on XR220

No wingtip, tailplane or fin
plate aerials

Static
ground line

British Aircraft Corporation T.S.R.2 Starboard Profile
(based on XR222)

Camera window replaced by solid panel
on some pre-production airframes

Rear view camera on
XR220 (both sides)

Recconnaissance pod

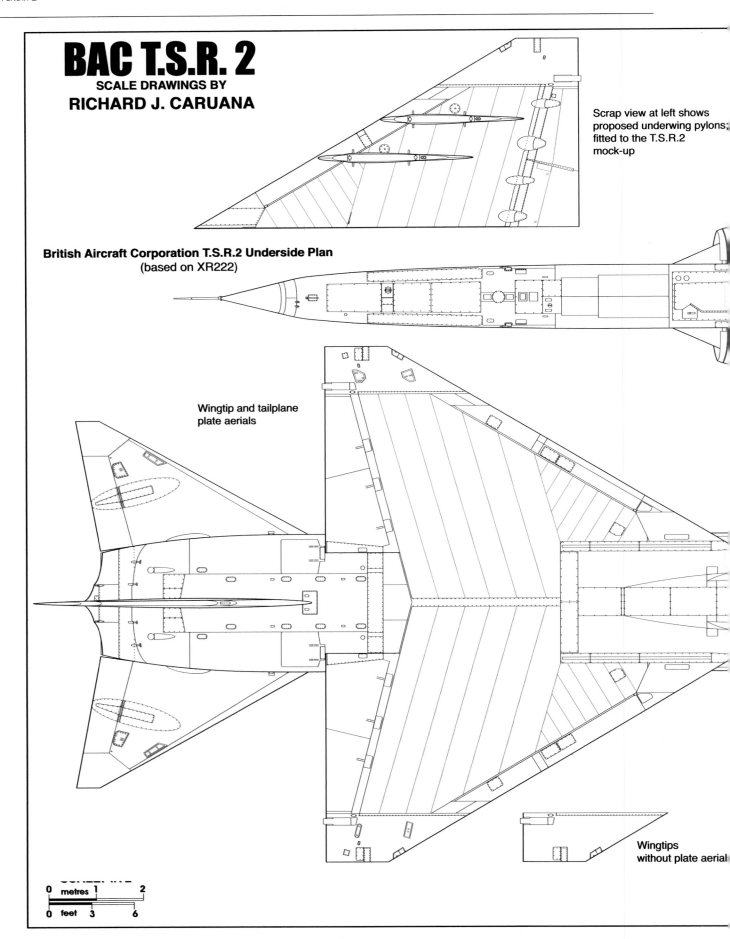

BAC T.S.R. 2
SCALE DRAWINGS BY
RICHARD J. CARUANA

Scrap view at left shows
proposed underwing pylons;
fitted to the T.S.R.2
mock-up

British Aircraft Corporation T.S.R.2 Underside Plan
(based on XR222)

Wingtip and tailplane
plate aerials

Wingtips
without plate aerial

metres

feet

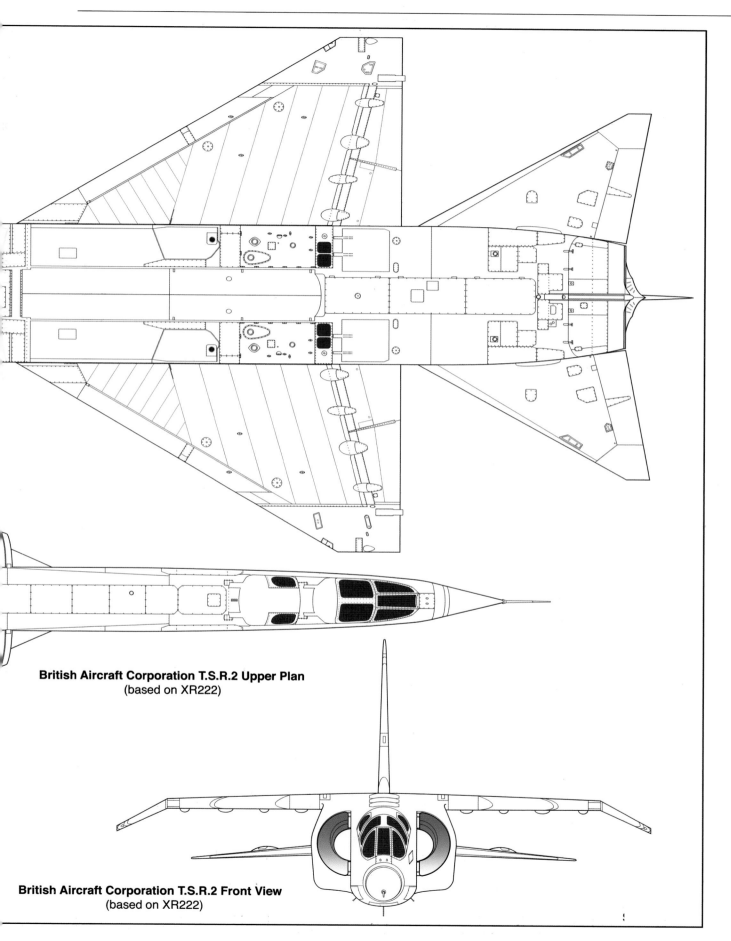

British Aircraft Corporation T.S.R.2 Upper Plan
(based on XR222)

British Aircraft Corporation T.S.R.2 Front View
(based on XR222)

BAC Type 571 (TSR2) XR222
A&AEE Boscombe Down 1965

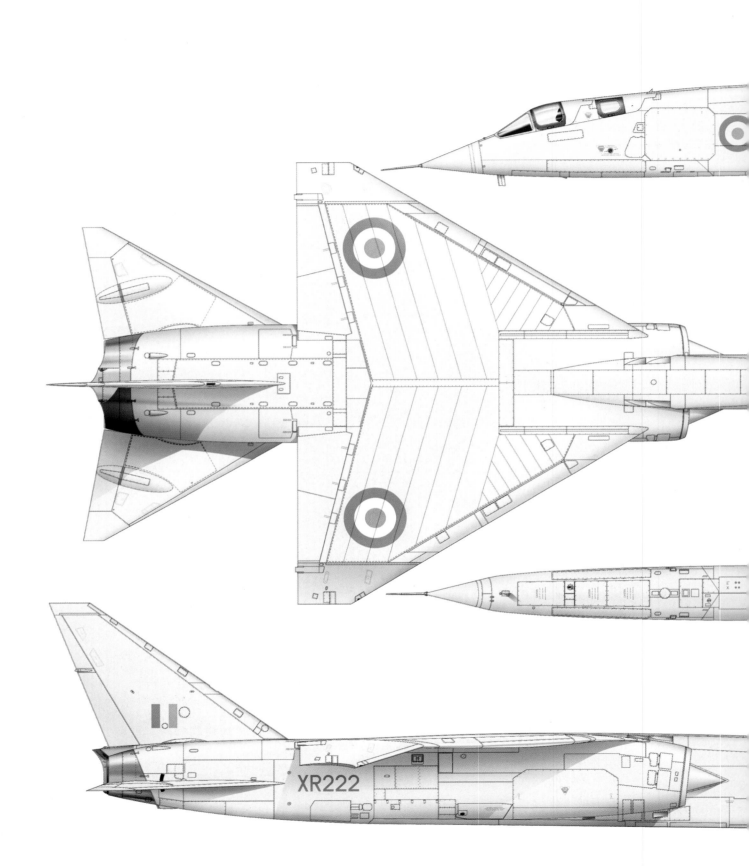

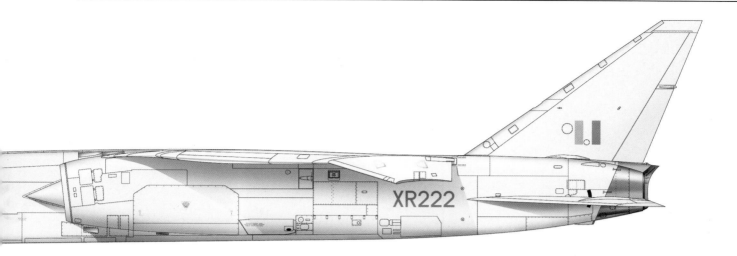

BAC T.S.R. 2
COLOUR DRAWINGS BY
RICHARD J. CARUANA

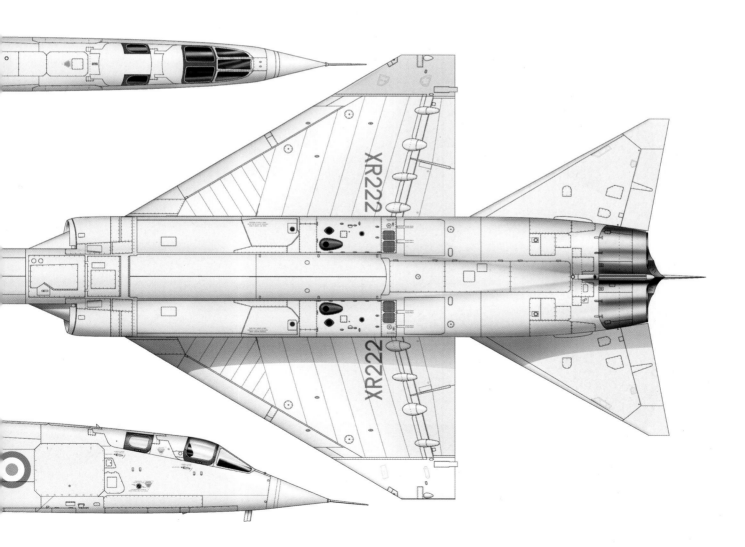

BAC Type 571 (TSR2) XS670
RAF Coningsby 1969
(Projected colour scheme based on official specifications)

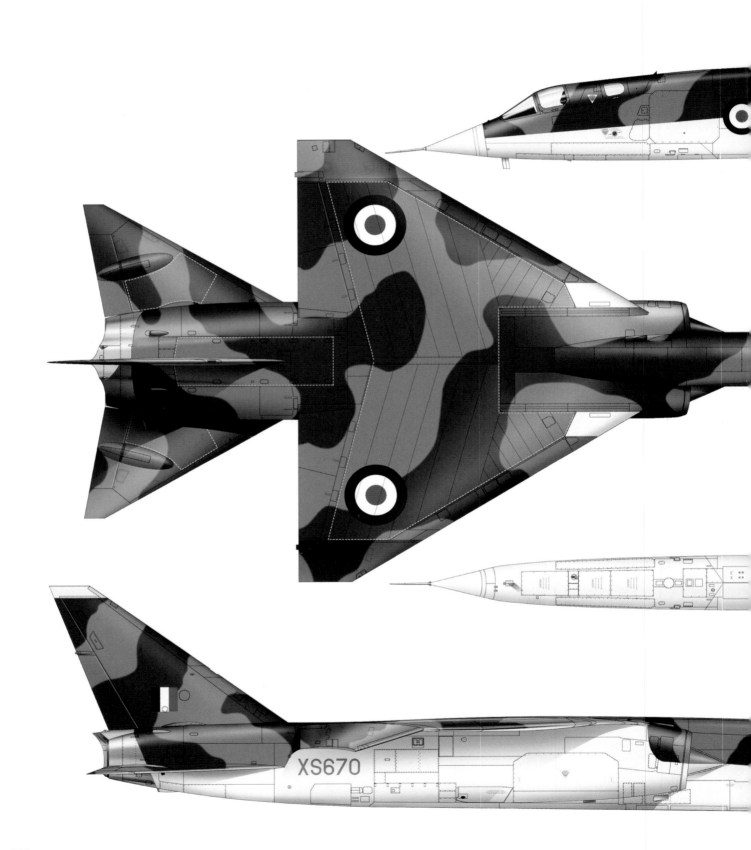

BAC T.S.R. 2
COLOUR DRAWINGS BY
RICHARD J. CARUANA

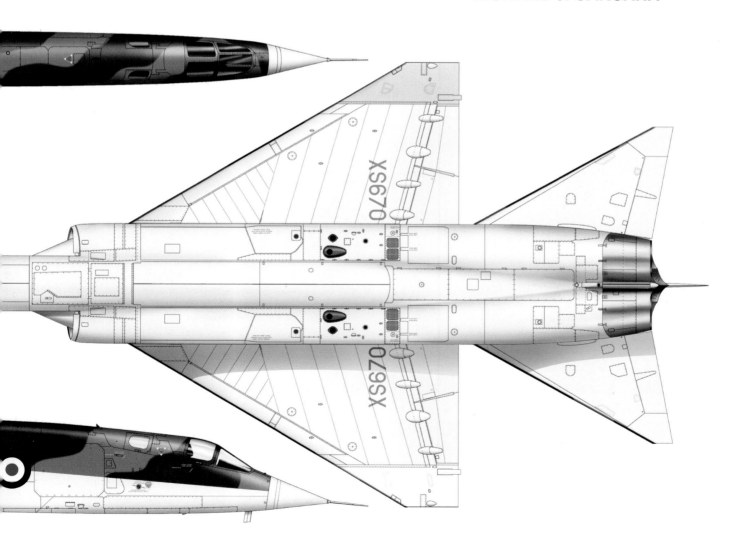

A classic British Aircraft Corporation advertisement from 1964.

A rare photograph of Buccaneer XK487 at Ferranti's Turnhouse facility near Edinburgh. Used to perform a series of trials, the aircraft was fitted with a representative Terrain Following Radar and was regularly seen zipping across the Scottish highlands at low level, using the TFR for guidance. There was a certainly irony in the sight of a Buccaneer equipped with this key TSR2 system – many believed that a Buccaneer suitably designed with a similar TFR would have been a much cheaper and much more suitable aircraft for the RAF's needs. *Ken Billingham collection*

The Hunter T.Mk.12 would have been assigned to the TSR2 OCU with at least one aircraft also being allocated to each operational squadron for familiarisation and training duties. Equipped with TSR2's instrumentation and Head Up Display, the Hunter would have provided a simple and inexpensive alternative to the concept of creating a dual-control version of TSR2 – a concept which proved to be far more complicated (and potentially expensive) than originally envisaged. Only one Hunter Mk.12 was actually constructed, this being XE531, converted from a single-seat Mk.6 airframe. *Tim McLelland*

References

ALTHOUGH the fascinating TSR2 project has featured in countless books and magazine features over nearly half a century, surprisingly few books have been published on the subject and until recently, the subject was undoubtedly somewhat neglected. TSR2 often appears as a significant part of many books which have explored aircraft projects of the 1960s, but very few authors and publishers have ventured to address the subject as a separate issue. It is also remarkable to note that even though TSR2 is evidently still a hugely popular subject with both enthusiasts and historians, surprisingly little information on the subject has been published via "new media" channels – at least not yet. The internet is littered with a wide variety of web sites which include sections (both large and small, and of varying quality) on TSR2 but they all inevitably present variations of the same limited information in different forms, sometimes accurately, and sometimes with a shameless degree of misinterpretation and inaccuracy. Consequently, although there is a very substantial amount of material devoted to TSR2 on the internet, there is nothing which offers any information (or even illustrative material) which has not already been published extensively in print form. Modelling enthusiasts will find plenty of information on TSR2 scattered across many different sites, many of which include close-up detail pictures of the surviving airframes and some web sites also include various imaginary colour scheme concepts of the aircraft. Indulgence in TSR2 fantasy is certainly a popular pastime but factual information is surprisingly scarce.

Thankfully, magazine features have continued to appear from time to time, some of which have included interesting snippets of information, but as with the internet, very little new information has ever appeared, and most magazine features have essentially been repetitions of previously-published material. The only notable exceptions were perhaps the first-hand accounts of test flights written by Roly Beamont, which have appeared in various magazines at various times, although these have also been explored in books too. From the very limited number of books which have been published on the subject, even fewer are still widely available, but the following titles are those which can be recommended as useful sources of information:-

Murder of the TSR2

By Stephen Hastings
Macdonald 1966

The first of only a small number of books devoted to the TSR2 project, this publication has long been out of print and is now almost impossible to obtain. It has earned a reputation as the most important TSR2 book, but this is probably a symptom of its relative obscurity, in that few people have actually obtained a copy to read. In actual fact, the book sheds very little light on the project beyond that which is available from many other sources, and simply traces the political and industrial story of TSR2, through to its cancellation. The greater part of the book is devoted to the Government's cancellation of TSR2, but although the story is undoubtedly interesting, the author provides little information which has not been published elsewhere. In fact, the book suffers from its age, in that the author completed it shortly after the TSR2 programme was terminated, many years before further information and facts emerged. Consequently, many of the author's views are based on suppositions which have subsequently been proved to be without foundation. In essence, the book is an expression of the author's viewpoint that the project's cancellation was a wasteful and expensive mistake, but even though he explains at great length his reasons for this conclusion (often attributing the cancellation to the cumulative actions of various people who didn't actually exercise as much influence on the programme as implied), he fails to acknowledge the simple fact that the project was ultimately unaffordable. Lamenting the destruction of Britain's aircraft industry makes good reading, but Hastings seems to be mistaken in suggesting that that this decline was a direct result of TSR2, which of course it was not. An interesting book nonetheless, but shamelessly biased towards the views of the author who, it should be mentioned, was a Conservative MP and Director of Handley Page – factors which seem to have coloured his opinion quite significantly.

TSR2 – Phoenix or Folly

By Frank Barnett-Jones
GMS Enterprises
ISBN 187038427X

Another book which is now only available through specialist stockists, this is probably the most comprehensive look at the whole TSR2 programme, providing plenty of information on all aspects of the aircraft's design and development, combined with a closer examination of some of the aircraft's systems. The author's style is somewhat clumsy in parts and there is a tendency to rely on the popular (but specious) notion that the project was a victim of political vandalism. But despite this, the book does contain some very interesting information which (despite some obvious errors and a great deal of irrelevant material) makes the publication well worth reading. Some illustrative material is also included, although photographic reproduction is poor. Overall, it is a book which presents the reader with a rather amateurish feel, but this shouldn't disguise the fact that it is undoubtedly a very thorough account of the TSR2 programme, and probably the best account to have been produced so far. It is therefore all the more surprising that it is currently out of print.

Phoenix into Ashes

By Roland Beamont
William Kimber
ISBN 718301218

Not strictly a book about the TSR2 as such, Beamont's recollections from his extensive flying career make fascinating reading, and naturally the book includes a very significant coverage of his flight test experience on TSR2. He provides the reader with some excellent insights into what it was like to actually fly the aircraft, and also includes some similarly interesting accounts of the wider industrial and political situation at the time of the project's cancellation. Beamont was one of TSR2's most fervent supporters and it is therefore understandable that he expresses his enthusiasm for the aircraft throughout his accounts. However, as English Electric's Chief Test Pilot, it is hardly surprising that he fails to address any of TSR2's deficiencies, not least the huge cost of the programme, and rarely mentions any of the project's wider considerations, preferring to concentrate on his admiration for the aircraft's excellent handling qualities, rather than the more troublesome aspects of the project. Undoubtedly an excellent book, but essentially one which provides a captivating examination of Beamont's first-hand experience with the aircraft, rather than any information on the project as a whole. Now out of print, the book can still be obtained through specialist suppliers.

TSR2 – Lost Tomorrows of an Eagle

By Paul Lucas
SAM Publications
ISBN 9780955185885

This relatively recent publication is aimed at modelling enthusiasts, but includes material which is of some interest to aviation enthusiasts too. The author looks at how TSR2 might have been operated, had the aircraft entered RAF service, relying on information drawn from documents which are now available through the Public Records Office and manufacturer's archives. The result is an interesting account of the many weapons fits, systems and deployment proposals which were created for TSR2, but which were abandoned when the project was finally cancelled. The author is obliged to make assumptions based on documents which were ostensibly little more than proposals, therefore the reader has to be careful to avoid the temptation to read the information as being factual, whereas it is of course merely speculative. Oddly, no photographs of TSR2 during the test flight era are included, and the book's photographic content seems both poorly thought-out and badly produced, but despite these disappointing aspects of the book, the author's exploration of what TSR2's service life might have been like is certainly worth reading.

British Aircraft Corporation TSR2

By Anthony Thornborough
Aeroguide Special
Ad Hoc Publications
ISBN 0946958475

This small but attractively-priced publication is ostensibly aimed at modellers but is of interest to all TSR2 enthusiasts. Designed as an illustrative exploration of the aircraft, the photographic content is comprehensive (mostly black and white but with some colour), and combines a selection of test flight pictures with more general images (showing the pre-production aircraft and the manufacturing process, etc.) and close-up illustrations of the aircraft's components, such as the undercarriage, weapons bay, cockpit and more. Text is kept to a minimum and provides the reader with a brief overview of the project. Also included is a set of well-produced 72nd scale plan drawings. Although now out of print, the book is available from many book stockists and can also be obtained through modelling suppliers.

BAC TSR2 – The White Ghost

By Chris Hughes
CMK Kits sro

Designed primarily with modellers in mind, this relatively recent publication is an interesting mix of material produced in an affordable soft-back format. A short but comprehensive account of TSR2's history is included, but the greater part of the booklet is devoted to all-colour images of the two surviving TSR2 airframes, with a huge selection of close-up detail pictures which illustrate every part of the aircraft's structure. All of the pictures are produced to a good size, some images being presented as full-page illustrations. Another section of the book is devoted to model building and describes the construction and detailing of an Airfix kit, based on the experience of a very talented modeller who has produced a stunning replica of the aircraft, using detail parts manufactured by CMK (the book's publisher). Also included are some interesting speculative colour scheme drawings and some good quality line drawings of the aircraft's weapons bay and cockpit interior. Undoubtedly an excellent reference guide for model-builders, and an interesting booklet for all TSR2 enthusiasts.

TSR2 – Precision Attack to Tornado

By John Forbat
Tempus Publishing
ISBN 9780752439198

The title of this publication is somewhat misleading in that the book is not devoted to either TSR2 or Tornado, in fact only half of the book explores TSR2-related subjects (and the Tornado is hardly mentioned at all). However, it must be said that the book is certainly of interest to anyone who wishes to learn more about the weapons systems which were being developed for use in TSR2. The author was part of the BAC development team for the programme and in this book he outlines the technical aspects of TSR2's navigation and weapon delivery equipment in extreme detail. It must be said that much of the information is of a rather technical nature and this does make some parts of the book fairly difficult reading, but for an authoritative account of the TSR2's systems, it is undoubtedly the best source of information that is ever likely to be produced. It is perhaps a pity that the entire book wasn't devoted to TSR2 and the author could perhaps have explained many of the technical systems in more basic terms for the less technically-minded, but for a very thorough appraisal of the equipment which would have enabled TSR2 to function as a supersonic tactical bomber, this book is undoubtedly a very useful and interesting publication.

Other books of interest which include some useful references to TSR2 include:-

Project Cancelled

by Derek Wood
Jane's Publishing
ISBN 0710604416

An interesting look at many British aircraft projects which were ultimately cancelled, including TSR2. Some proposed external stores fits which were being developed for TSR2 are illustrated, and the story of the project's development is described, although the book doesn't contain any particularly new or significant information on the subject. However the book does serve to place the TSR2 project into the wider context of Britain's aircraft development and procurement history, and provides a fascinating account of some of Britain's unusual and obscure design concepts.

British Secret Projects – Jet Bombers Since 1949

by Tony Buttler
Midland Publishing
ISBN 185780130X

A captivating look at a variety of British aircraft projects, some of which survived (in modified form) and many others which were cancelled. An excellent account of TSR2's design background is included together with some information on other development proposals for the aircraft which were subsequently abandoned.

Wings of Fame Volume 4

Includes an excellent sixteen-page illustrated account of the TSR2 project by leading author Bill Gunston.

Airfix 1/48th scale TSR2.

Modelling

Being an all-British subject, TSR2 was largely ignored by modelling manufacturers for many years, on the basis that international interest in the subject would restrict commercial possibilities. Only one kit of the aircraft was available, this being a vac-formed and white metal kit to 1/48th scale, which was produced by Dynavector. However, when Hornby bought the world-famous Airfix range, they quickly re-instated plans to produce an injection-moulded 72nd scale kit of the aircraft which was finally released as a limited-edition product. It was immediately snapped up by model-builders and collectors and is now very difficult to obtain, except through occasional one-off sales at surprisingly inflated prices. The Airfix kit's staggering success was sufficient to illustrate that modelling interest in the subject was actually very significant, and Airfix subsequently produced a larger 1/48th scale kit of the aircraft which, although also produced on a limited-edition basis, is still available from some stockists. Hornby plan to re-release the earlier 72nd scale kit towards the end of 2010 as a spin-off merchandise product in connection with a Japanese cartoon series (*Stratos 4*).

The Airfix kits encouraged a number of specialist manufacturers to produce a variety of improvement and detail sets with which to enhance the basics provided in the standard Airfix kits. These have also proved to be very popular, and new items are still appearing, together with specialised modelling reference publications and transfer sheets which provide speculative markings for "operational" aircraft. Die-cast model manufacturer Corgi also opted to take advantage of TSR2's popularity and a 72nd scale model of the was released in 2010 which also proved to be hugely popular, Corgi immediately selling their entire stock.

Accessory sets for TSR2 kits currently include a variety of items from leading manufacturers in this field, including the following:-

CMK Detail accessory sets

4220 (48 scale) Aircraft interior set
4221 (48 scale) Electronics bay
4222 Nose undercarriage bay
4223 (48 scale) Equipment (weapons bay) set
4224 (48 scale) Exhaust nozzles
4225 (48 scale) Airbrakes set
4226 (48 scale) Undercarriage bay
4227 (48 scale) Undercarriage legs (metal)

4228 (48 scale) Control surfaces
4229 (48 scale) Wheels set
4233 (48 scale) Canopy correction set
7131 (72 scale) Aircraft interior
7132 (72 scale) Aircraft exterior (engine exhaust)
7133 (72 scale) Control surfaces
7134 (72 scale) Undercarriage
7135 (72 scale) Armament set (weapons bay)

These excellent CMK kits can be purchased from modelling stockists or directly from the company's web site at:
   http://www.cmkkits.com

Resin detail sets for TSR2 are also available from Pavla Models:-

U48-30 (48 scale) Main wheel wells
U48-31 (48 scale) Nose wheel bay
C48016 (48 scale) Cockpit replacement set
S48031 (48 scale) Replacement seats

Available through modelling suppliers, these sets can also be obtained directly via the company's web site, which includes details of their entire accessory range:-
   http://www.pavlamodels.cz

Airwaves

AES48085 (48 scale) Ejection seats x 2
Available from http://www.hannants.co.uk

Eduard

ED48614 (48 scale) Etched metal undercarriage detail set
ED48616 (48 scale) Etched metal exterior detail set
ED49436 (48 scale) Etched metal interior detail set
EDCX151 (48 scale) Paint masks
EDEX267 (48 scale) Paint masks
EDSS257 (72 scale) Etched metal cockpit detail set

Model Alliance

ML48172 (48 scale) "What If" markings decal sheet
ML72172 (72 scale) "What If" markings decal sheet
Available directly from http://www.theaviationworkshop.co.uk

Xtradecal

X48068 (48 scale) "What If" markings decal sheet
X48069 (48 scale) "What If" markings decal sheet
X48070 (48 scale) "What If" markings decal sheet
X72059 (72 scale) "What If" markings decal sheet
X72060 (72 scale) "What If" markings decal sheet
Available directly from http://www.hannants.co.uk

Scale Aircraft Conversions

48026 (48 scale) Metal landing gear replacement set
Available directly from
http://www.scaleaircraftconversions.com

Cammett

CAMA48006 (48 scale) Blue Water missiles
CAMA48007 (48 scale) External fuel tanks
CAMA48008 (48 scale) Auxiliary air intake replacement parts
CAMA48009 (48 scale) Reconnaissance pack
CAMA48010 (48 scale) Martel anti-radar missiles
CAMA48011 (48 scale) Martel TV-guided missiles
      Available directly from http://www.cammett.co.uk

Index

INDEX OF PEOPLE